EATCS
Monographs on Theoretical Computer Science

Kurt Mehlhorn

Data Structures and Algorithms 2:

Graph Algorithms and NP-Completeness

With 54 Figures

Springer-Verlag
Berlin Heidelberg New York Tokyo 1984

Editors
Prof. Dr. Wilfried Brauer
FB Informatik der Universität
Rothenbaum-Chausee 67–69, 2000 Hamburg 13, Germany

Prof. Dr. Grzegorz Rozenberg
Institut of Applied Mathematics and Computer Science
University of Leiden, Wassenaarseweg 80, P. O. Box 9512
2300 RA Leiden, The Netherlands

Prof. Dr. Arto Salomaa
Department of Mathematics, University of Turku
20500 Turku 50, Finland

Author
Prof. Dr. Kurt Mehlhorn
FB 10, Angewandte Mathematik und Informatik
Universität des Saarlandes, 6600 Saarbrücken, Germany

With the permission of B. G. Teubner publishers, Stuttgart, arranged, solely authorized and revised English translation of the original German edition: Effiziente Allgorithmen (1977)

ISBN-13: 978-3-642-69899-6 e-ISBN-13: 978-3-642-69897-2
DOI: 10.1007/978-3-642-69897-2

Softcover reprint of the hardcover 1st edition 1984

2145/3140-543210

For Ena, Uli, Steffi, and Tim

Preface to Volume 2

The design and analysis of data structures and computer algorithms has gained considerable importance in recent years: The concept of "algorithm" is central in computer science and "efficiency" is central in the world of money.

This book treats graph algorithms and the theory of NP-completeness and comprises chapters IV to VI of the three volume series "Data Structures and Efficient Algorithms". The material covered in this book derives its importance from the universal role played by graphs in many areas of computer science. The other two volumes treat sorting and searching (chapters I to III) and multi-dimensional searching and computational geometry (chapters VII to VIII). All three volumes are organized according to problem areas. In addition, we have included a chapter (chapter IX) in all three volumes which gives a paradigm oriented view of the entire series and orders the material according to algorithmic methods.

In chapter IV we deal with algorithms on graphs. We start out with a discussion of various methods for representing a graph in a computer, and of simple algorithms for topological sorting and the transitive closure problem. The concept of a random graph is also introduced in these sections. We then turn to methods for graph exploration which we later refine to depth first and breadth first search. Depth first search is the basis for connectivity, biconnectivity and planarity algorithms for undirected graphs, and for an algorithm for strong connectivity of directed graphs. In the section on planar graphs we also present the planar separator theorem as well as a shortest path algorithm for planar graphs. Breadth first search is the basis for efficient least cost path algorithms and for network flow algorithms. Several algorithms for unweighted and weighted network flow and their application to matching and connectivity problems are discussed in detail. Finally, there is a section on minimum spanning trees.

Chapter V explores the algebraic interpretation of path problems on graphs. The concept of a path problem over a closed semi-ring is defined, a general solution is presented, and the connection with matrix multiplication is established. Then fast algorithms for matrix multiplication over rings are discussed, transformed to boolean matrix multiplication, and their implication for special path problems is investigated. Finally, a lower bound on the monotone complexity of boolean matrix multiplication is derived.

Chapter VI covers the theory of NP-completeness. Many efficient algorithms have been found in the past; nevertheless, a large number of problems have not yielded to the attack of algorithm designers. A particularly important class of such problems is the class of NP-complete problems. In the first half of the chapter this class is defined, and many well-known problems are shown to belong to the class. In the second half of the chapter we discuss methods for solving NP-complete problems. We first treat branch-and-bound and dynamic programming and then turn to approximation algorithms. The chapter closes with a short discussion of other complexity classes.

The book covers advanced material and leads the reader to very recent results and current research. It is intended for a reader who has some knowledge in algorithm design and analysis. The reader must be familiar with the fundamental data structures such as queues, stacks, and linked list structures. This material is covered in chapter I of volume 1 and also in many other books on computer science. Knowledge of the material allows the reader to appreciate most of the book. For some sections more advanced knowledge is required. Priority queues and balanced trees are used in sections IV.7, IV.8 and IV.9.1, algorithms for the union – find problem are used in IV.8, and bucket sort is employed at several places. Information about these problems can be found in volume 1 but also in many other books about algorithms and data structures.

The organization of the book is quite simple. There are three chapters which are numbered using roman numerals. Sections and subsections of chapters are numbered using arabic numerals. Within each section, theorems and lemmas are numbered consecutively. Cross references are made by giving the identifier of the section (or subsection) and the number of the theorem. The common prefix of the identifiers of origin and destination of a cross reference may be suppressed, i. e., a cross reference to section VII.1.2 in section VII.2 can be made by either referring to section VII.1.2 or to section 1.2.

Each chapter has an extensive list of exercises and a section on bibliographic remarks. The exercises are of varying degrees of difficulty. In many cases hints are given, or a reference is provided in the section on bibliographic remarks.

Most parts of this book were used as course notes either by myself or by my colleagues N. Blum, Th. Lengauer, and A. Tsakalidis. Their comments were a big help. I also want to thank H. Alt, O. Fries, St. Hertel, B. Schmidt, and K. Simon who collaborated with me on several sections and I want to thank the many students who helped to improve the presentation by their criticism. Discussions with many colleagues helped to shape my ideas: B. Becker, J. Berstel, B. Commentz-Walter, H. Edelsbrunner, B. Eisenbarth, Ph. Flajolet, M. Fontet, G. Gonnet, R. Güttler, G. Hotz, S. Huddleston, I. Munro, J. Nievergelt, Th. Ottmann, M. Overmars, M. Paterson, F. Preparata, A. Rozenberg, M. Stadel, R. E. Tarjan, J. van Leeuwen, D. Wood, and N. Ziviani.

The drawings and the proof reading were done by my student Hans Rohnert. He did a fantastic job. Of course, all remaining errors are my sole responsibility. Thanks to him, there should not be too many left. The typescript was prepared by Christel Korten-Michels, Martina Horn, Marianne Weis and Doris Schindler under sometimes hectic conditions. I thank them all.

Saarbrücken, April 1984 Kurt Mehlhorn

Contents Vol. 2: Graph Algorithms and NP-Completeness

IV. Algorithms on Graphs

In this chapter we treat efficient algorithms for many basic problems on graphs: topological sorting and transitive closure, connectivity and biconnectivity, least cost paths, least cost spanning trees, network flow problems and matching problems and planarity testing. Most of these algorithms require methods for the systematic exploration of a graph. We will introduce such a method in section 4 and then specialize it to breadth first and depth first search.

IV. 1. Graphs and their Representation in a Computer

A directed graph $G = (V,E)$ consists of a set $V = \{1,2,\ldots,|V|\}$ of nodes and a set $E \subseteq V \times V$ of edges. A pair $(v,w) \in E$ is called an edge from v to w. Throughout this chapter we set $n = |V|$ and $e = |E|$.
Two methods for storing a graph are customary.

a) Adjacency matrix: A graph $G = (V,E)$ is represented by a $|V| \times |V|$ boolean matrix $A_G = (a_{ij})_{1 \le i,j \le n}$ with

$$a_{ij} = \begin{cases} 1 & \text{if } (i,j) \in E \\ 0 & \text{if } (i,j) \notin E \end{cases}$$

The storage requirement of this representation is clearly $\Theta(n^2)$.

b) Adjacency lists: A graph $G = (V,E)$ is represented by n linear lists. The i-th list contains all nodes j with $(i,j) \in E$. The headers of the n lists are stored in an array. The storage requirement of this representation is $O(n + e)$. The lists are not necessarily in sorted order.

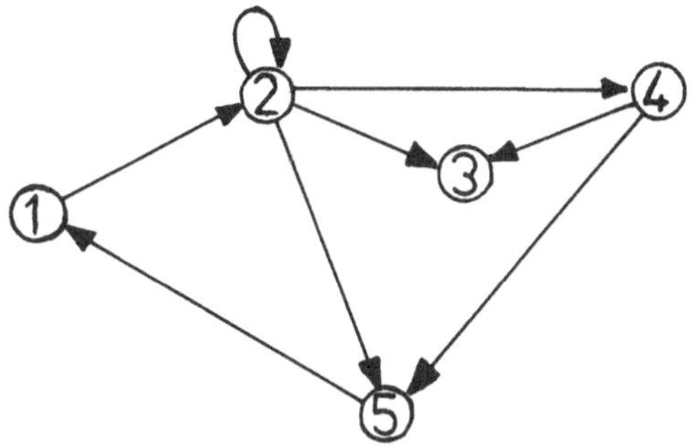

$$\begin{pmatrix} 0 & 1 & 0 & 0 & 0 \\ 0 & 1 & 1 & 1 & 1 \\ 0 & 0 & 0 & 0 & 0 \\ 0 & 0 & 1 & 0 & 1 \\ 1 & 0 & 0 & 0 & 0 \end{pmatrix}$$

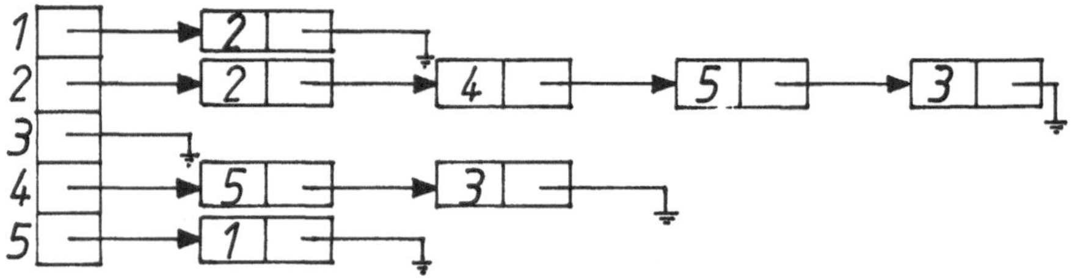

The above example shows a graph, and its representation by adjacency matrix and adjacency lists.

Since $0 \le e \le n^2$ we conclude that the adjacency list represention is often much smaller than the adjacency matrix representation and never much larger. Since most graphs which come up in applications are sparse, i.e. $e \ll n^2$, this is an important point to remember. Even more important is the fact that the choice of the representation can have a drastic influence on the time complexity of graph algorithms. We will see in this chapter that many graph problems can be solved in linear time $O(n + e)$ if the adjacency list representation is used. However, any algorithm using the matrix representation must have running time $\Omega(n^2)$. For this reason we will always use the adjacency lists except when explicitely stated otherwise (chapter V).

In more detail, the adjacency list representation is based on the following declarations:

```
type node = record name : [1 ..n];
                        :
                   next : ↑ node
            end
```

and

ADLHEAD : <u>array</u> [1 ..n] of ↑ node

Array ADLHEAD contains the heads of the adjacency lists. The elements of the adjacency lists are of type node, each element representing an edge. In some cases these elements will contain additional information, e.g. the length of an edge, a pointer to the reverse edge in an undirected graph, ...

We need some more definitions. Let $G = (V,E)$ be a digraph. A path from v to w, $v, w \in V$, is a sequence $v_0, v_1, \ldots, v_k$ of nodes such that $v_0 = v$, $v_k = w$ and $(v_i, v_{i+1}) \in E$ for $0 \le i < k$; k is the length of the path. Note that there is always the path of length zero from v to v. A path is simple if $v_i \neq v_j$ for $0 \le i < j < k$. A cycle is a path from v to v. If, in addition, the path is simple then the cycle is simple. A graph is acyclic if it contains no non-trivial cycle. Let $T \subseteq E$. We write $v \xrightarrow[T]{}^{*} w$ iff there is a path from v to w using only edges in T.

The indegree of a node v is the number od edges ending in v, $indeg_G(v) = |\{w; (w,v) \in E\}|$. Similarly, the outdegree of v is the number of edges starting in v, $outdeg_G(v) = |\{w; (v,w) \in E\}|$.

A digraph $G' = (V',E')$ is a subgraph of $G = (V,E)$ if $V' \subseteq V$ and $E' \subseteq E$. If $G = (V,E)$ is a digraph and $V' \subseteq V$ then the subgraph induced by V' is $(V', E \cap (V' x V'))$. $G - V'$ denotes the subgraph induced by $V - V'$. If $V' = \{v\}$ is a singleton then we write $G - v$ instead of $G - \{v\}$.

A digraph $A = (V,T)$ is a directed forest if A is acyclic and $indeg_A(v) \le 1$ for all $v \in V$. A node v with $indeg_A(v) = 0$ is called a root of the forest. Note that a directed forest has at least one root. If $A = (V,T)$ is a directed tree then $|T| = |V| - 1$. Also, there is a unique path from the root r to any node v of a directed tree. Finally, if v is any node of a directed tree then the subtee A_v rooted at v is the subgraph induced by the descendants of v, i.e. A_v is the subgraph induced by $\{w; v \xrightarrow[T]{}^{*} w\}$.

Let $G = (V,E)$ be a digraph. A directed forest $A = (V,T)$ with $T \subseteq E$ is called a spanning forest of G. If A is a tree then it is called a spanning tree of G.

An undirected graph (or simply graph) is a digraph $G = (V,E)$ with a symmetric relation E, i.e. $(v,w) \in E$ iff $(w,v) \in E$. In a graph the indegree of a node is always equal to its outdegree and is simply called the degree of the node. An undirected graph is called acyclic if it contains no simple cycles of length at least three (Note that an "undirected" edge between v and w always gives rise to a simple cycle, namely v,w,v). An acyclic undirected graph is called an undirected forest.

IV. 2. Topological Sorting and the Representation Problem

A topological sort of a digraph $G = (V,E)$ is a mapping $ord: V \to \{1,\dots,n\}$ such that for all edges $(v,w) \in E$ we have $ord(v) < ord(w)$. Clearly, if a graph G has a topological sort then G is acyclic. The converse is also true and is easily proved by induction on the number of nodes. So suppose, $G = (V,E)$ is acyclic. If $n = |V| = 1$ then G has a topological sort. If $n > 1$ then G must have a node v with indegree 0. (Such a node can be found by starting at an arbitrary node w and walking back edges. Since the graph is acyclic no node is entered twice in this process, and hence the process terminates. It terminates in a node with indegree 0). Deleting v leaves us with an acyclic graph G' with one less node. G' has a topological sort and so does G.

Actually, the argument given above, describes an algorithm for computing the mapping ord.

```
(1)  G_current ← G; COUNT ← 0;
(2)  while G_current has at least one node with no predecessor
(3)  do    let v be a node with no predecessor;
(4)        COUNT      ← COUNT + 1;
(5)        ORD[v]     ← COUNT;
(6)        G_current  ← G_current - v
(7)  od;
(8)  if    G_current is nonempty
(9)  then  cyclic else acyclic fi
```

The correctness of this algorithm is immediate from the preceding discussion. With respect to complexity the crucial lines are lines (3) and (6). How do we find a node with indegree 0 efficiently in line (3)? A brute force approach would be a complete search of graph $G_{current}$. Since such a search would take time at least $\Omega(n)$ the entire algorithm would be $\Omega(n^2)$ at best.

A better approach is to look at the interdependence of lines (3) and (6). In line (6) node v and all edges leaving v are deleted. Exactly the indegrees of the other endpoints are changed. This suggests to use an array INDEG[1 .. n] to store the current indegree of all nodes. Array INDEG is updated in line (6). In line (3) we need to know one node with indegree 0; the indegree of a node can only become zero in line (6) and it is easy to detect that fact there. It is therefore wise to keep all nodes with indegree 0 in $G_{current}$ in a set ZEROINDEG.

The following refinement of our algorithm makes use of the variables INDEG: array [1 .. n] of integer and ZEROINDEG: subset of V. The graph $G_{current}$ is not stored explicitely. Rather it is the subgraph of G induced by the nodes which have not received a number ord yet. ZEROINDEG contains the points of zero indegree in $G_{current}$ and INDEG contains the indegree of all nodes in $G_{current}$. Initially $G_{current}$ = G and so INDEG should be initialized to the indegrees in G. This can be done efficiently by traversing all adjacency lists.

Algorithm: Topological sort

```
(1.1)   COUNT ← 0;
(1.2)   ZEROINDEG ← ∅; for all i ∈ V do INDEG[i] ← 0 od;
(1.3)   for all i ∈ V
(1.4)   do for all j ∈ V with (i,j) ∈ E
(1.5)      do INDEG[j] ← INDEG[j] + 1
(1.6)      od
(1.7)   od;
(1.8)   for all i ∈ V
(1.9)   do if INDEG[i] = 0 then add i to ZEROINDEG fi
(1.1o)  od;
(2)     while ZEROINDEG ≠ ∅
(3.1)   do let v be any node in ZEROINDEG;
(3.2)      delete v from ZEROINDEG;
(4)        COUNT ← COUNT + 1;
(5)        ORD[v] ← COUNT;
(6.1)      for all w ∈ V with (v,w) ∈ E
(6.2)      do INDEG[w] ← INDEG[w] - 1;
(6.3)         if INDEG[w] = 0
```

```
(6.4)       then add w to ZEROINDEG fi;
(6.5)    od
(7)   od ;
(8)   if COUNT < n
(9)   then Halt ("graph is cyclic") else Halt ("graph is acyclic") fi
```

It remains to specify an implementation for set ZEROINDEG. On this set the following operations are performed: Insertion, deletion of an unspecified element, and test for emptiness. In chapter I we saw that implementing ZEROINDEG by a stack or by a queue will allow us to execute each one of these operations in time O(1). We prefer the stack for its simplicity and higher efficiency, so ZEROINDEG is a stack of elements of V (stack *of* [1.. n]).

Finally, we have to explain lines (1.4) and (6.1) in more detail. They are realized by stepping through the adjacency list corresponding to nodes i and w respectively and take time proportional to the outdegree of those nodes. A detailed program for lines (1.4) and (1.5) is given by (p is of type ↑node):

```
p ← ADJHEAD[i];
while p ≠ nil
do j ← p↑.name;
   INDEG[j] ← INDEG[j] + 1 ;
   p ← p↑.next
od
```

We are now in a position to determine the performance of our algorithm for topological sorting. Line (1) takes time O(1), lines (1.2) and lines (1.8) - (1.10) take O(n). Execution of (1.4) and (1.5) for a fixed i takes time $O(\text{outdeg}_G(i))$ and hence lines (1.3) - (1.7) take time O(n + e). Altogether, initialization takes time O(n + e).

The main loop is executed O(n) times and hence the total time spent in lines (3.1), (3.2), (4) and (5) is O(n). For a fixed v, lines (6.1) - (6.4) take time $O(\text{outdeg}_G(v))$. Since every node v is deleted from ZEROINDEG at most once total running time of that loop is O(n + e). This shows that the running time of the entire algorithm is O(n + e).

Theorem 1: A topological sort of digraph $G = (V,E)$ can be computed in linear time $O(n + e)$.

Proof: By the discussion above. □

Next we will show that getting the graph as a matrix will doom any algorithm to inefficiency.

Theorem 2: Any algorithm for topological sorting which gets the digraph as an adjacency matrix has running time $\Omega(n^2)$.

Proof: Consider the behaviour of any such algorithm on the empty graph, i.e. on the all zero matrix. Suppose there is a pair i,j of nodes, $i \neq j$, such that the algorithm neither inspects a_{ij} nor a_{ji}. Then we could change both entries to one and the algorithm would still return with a topological sort. However, the graph is cyclic after adding edges (i,j) and (j,i). This shows that the algorithm has to inspect at least half of the entries of the matrix and hence has running time $\Omega(n^2)$. □

We saw that a topological sort of an acyclic graph can be computed in linear time. Given the mapping ord: $V \to \{1,\ldots,|V|\}$ it is then easy to reorder the adjacency lists in increasing order as follows: Generate all pairs $\{(ord(v), ord(w));\ (v,w) \in E\}$ and sort them by bucket sort according to the second component and then according to the first component. This takes time $O(n + e)$ and generates the adjacency lists in sorted order.

IV. 3. Transitive Closure of Acyclic Digraphs

Let $G = (V,E)$ be a digraph. Digraph $G^* = (V,E^*)$ is the reflexive, transitive closure of G if $(v,w) \in E^*$ if and only if there is a path from v to w in G. In this section we present an algorithm for computing the transitive closure of an acyclic digraph; the algorithm is extended to general digraphs in section 6. We will assume that the acyclic digraph is topologically sorted, i.e. $(i,j) \in E$ implies $i < j$ and that the adjacency lists are sorted in increasing order. We saw in the previous section that this can be achieved in linear time $O(n + e)$.

The idea for the algorithm is very simple. We step through the nodes of

G in decreasing order. Suppose that we consider node i. Then for every $j > i$ we have already computed the set of nodes reachable from j, $REACH[j] = \{k;\ j \to^* k\}$. Then

$$REACH[i] = \{i\} \cup (\cup\{REACH[j]\ ;\ (i,j) \in E\})$$

This suggests to step through the nodes j with $(i,j) \in E$ and to compute the union of the sets REACH[j]. We will see that this is a costly process. It can be improved somewhat as follows. We step through nodes j with $(i,j) \in E$ in <u>increasing</u> order. When edge (i,j) is encountered, we will first test whether $j \in$ REACH[i] already. If this is the case then there must be a node $h \neq j$ with $i \to h \to^* j$ and hence $REACH[h] \supseteq REACH[j]$ and thus we do not have to add REACH[j] to REACH[i]. This observation will lead to considerable savings in many cases. Here is the complete algorithm.

```
(1)  BREACH ← ∅;                     -- BREACH is a bitvektor
(2)  for i from n downto 1
(3)  do REACH[i] ← BREACH ← {i}      -- REACH[i] is a linear list
(4)     for all j with (i,j) ∈ E    -- in increasing order!!
(5)     do if j ∉ BREACH
(6)        then for all k ∈ REACH[j]
(7)             do if k ∉ BREACH
(8)                then add k to BREACH and REACH[i]
(9)                fi
(1o)            od
(11)       fi
(12)    od;
(13)    for all k ∈ REACH[i]
(14)    do delete k from BREACH
(15)    od
(16) od
```

There is one subtle point about this algorithm, the two faces of set REACH[i]. REACH[i] is kept as a linear list and as a bitvektor BREACH. We initialize both of them to {i} in time O(1) in line (3). Note that BREACH is empty prior to the first execution of the loop and that this is ensured for later executions by lines (13) to (15). In lines (4)-(12) we step through the directdescendants of i in increasing order. Remember that the adjacency lists are sorted. The tests in line (5) and (7) take time O(1) since BREACH is a bitvektor. If $j \notin$ BREACH in line (5) then BREACH[j] is added to REACH[i] and BREACH in time $O(|REACH[j]|)$. In lines (13) to (15) BREACH is reduced to the empty set in time $O(|REACH[i]|)$.

<u>Definition:</u> Let $G = (V,E)$ be an acyclic digraph. Let $E_{red} = \{(i,j) \in E;$ there is no path of length at least two from i to j in G$\}$, let $G_{red} = (V,E_{red})$, and let $e_{red} = |E_{red}|$. G_{red} is called the reduction of G.

<u>Lemma 1:</u> Let $G = (V,E)$ be an acyclic digraph

a) $G^* = G^*_{red}$

b) the algorithm correctly computes the reflexive transitive closure

c) if lines (6) - (10) are executed for (i,j) then $(i,j) \in E_{red}$.

<u>Proof:</u> a) G^*_{red} is certainly a subgraph of G^*. In order to prove the converse consider any $(i,j) \in E^*$. Let $i_o,i_1,\ldots,i_k$ be a path of maximal length from $i = i_o$ to $j = i_k$. Then $(i_\ell,i_{\ell+1}) \in E_{red}$ for all ℓ and hence $(i,j) \in E^*_{red}$.

b) It is obvious that our algorithm computes a subset of the transitive closure. Suppose that it computes a proper subset. Then let i be maximal such that there exists h with $i \to^* h$ and h is never added to REACH[i]. Consider a maximal length path $i_o,\ldots,i_k$ from $i = i_o$ to $h = i_k$. Then $h \in$ REACH[i_1] by definition of i. Also $(i_o,i_1) \in E$. If the test in line (5) is executed with $j = i_1$ then $j \notin$ BREACH because there is no path of length at least two from i_o to i_1; otherwise the path would not be of maximal length. Hence h is added to REACH[i] in line (8).

c) Suppose that $(i,j) \in E - E_{red}$. Then there exists h with $(i,h) \in E_{red}$ and $h \underset{E}{\to^*} j$. Hence j is added to REACH[i] when edge (i,h) is considered in loop (4) - (12). □

<u>Theorem 1:</u> The reflexive, transitive closure of an acyclic digraph $G = (V,E)$ can be computed in time $O(n\ e_{red}) = O(n^3)$.

<u>Proof:</u> Lines (13) to (15) are executed once for each edge of E^* and hence the total time spent in these lines is $O(e^*)$. Lines (4) and (5) are executed for each edge of G and hence take time $O(e)$. Lines (6) to (10) are executed for each edge $(i,j) \in E_{red}$ and take time

$O(|REACH[j]|)$ for a fixed edge (i,j). Hence the total time spent in lines (6) to (10) is $\sum_{(i,j)\in E_{red}} O(|REACH[j]|)$. In the remaining lines we spend time O(n). Hence the total running time is

$$O(n + e + e^* + \sum_{(i,j)\in E_{red}} |REACH[j]|) = O(e_{red} \cdot n). \qquad \square$$

Of course, $e_{red} \le e$. Unfortunately, $e_{red} = e = \Theta(n^2)$ is possible. Consider $V = \{1,\ldots,n\}$ and $E = \{(i,j),\ i \le n/2 < j\}$. However, in general e_{red} is considerably smaller than e. We can support this claim by an analysis of random graphs. We postulate the following model of random acyclic digraph on n nodes. Let $\varepsilon(n)$ be a real between 0 and 1.

Edge (i,j) is present with probability $\varepsilon(n)$ for $i < j$. Events $(i,j) \in E$ are independent.

Theorem 2: a) The expected outdegree of a node in the reduction of an n node random acyclic digraph is $\le (1 - (1 - \varepsilon(n)^2)^{n-1})/\varepsilon(n) = O(\sqrt{n})$.

b) The expected running time of our algorithm on a n node random acyclic digraph is $O(n^{5/2})$.

Proof: a) Let i be any fixed node and let $\varepsilon = \varepsilon(n)$. Let $X_j(G)$ be the following random variable

$$X_j(G) = \begin{cases} 1 & \text{if } (i,j) \in E_{red} \\ 0 & \text{otherwise} \end{cases}$$

Then the expected outdegree of node i in G_{red} is $E(\sum_j X_j)$. We can estimate $E(X_j)$ as follows. If X_j is one, then $(i,j) \in E$ and for all h, $i < h < j$, either $(i,h) \notin E$ or $(h,j) \notin E$. Hence the probability that $(i,j) \in E_{red}$ is bounded by $\varepsilon\ (1 - \varepsilon^2)^{j-i-1}$. Thus $E(X_j) \le \varepsilon\ (1 - \varepsilon^2)^{j-i-1}$ and hence the expected outdegree of i is bounded by

$$\sum_{j=i+1}^{n} \varepsilon\ (1 - \varepsilon^2)^{j-i-1} \le \sum_{j=0}^{n-2} \varepsilon\ (1 - \varepsilon^2)^{j}$$

$$\le (1 - (1 - \varepsilon^2)^{n-1})/\varepsilon$$

It remains to prove that $(1 - (1 - \varepsilon^2)^{n-1})/\varepsilon \le \sqrt{n}$. This is obvious for $\varepsilon \ge 1/\sqrt{n}$. So let us assume $\varepsilon < 1/\sqrt{n}$. Then by the binomial theorem

$$1 - (1 - \varepsilon^2)^{n-1} = (n - 1)\,\varepsilon^2 - \binom{n-1}{2}\varepsilon^4 + \binom{n-1}{3}\varepsilon^6 - \ldots$$

$$\leq n \cdot \varepsilon^2$$

since $-\binom{n-1}{2i}(\varepsilon^2)^{2i} + \binom{n-1}{2i+1}(\varepsilon^2)^{2i+1} \leq 0$ for $\varepsilon < 1/\sqrt{n}$ and $i \geq 1$. Hence $(1 - (1 - \varepsilon^2)^{n-1})/\varepsilon \leq n \cdot \varepsilon \leq \sqrt{n}$.

b) We infer from part a) that the expected size of E_{red} is $O(n^{3/2})$ and hence the expected running time of our algorithm is $O(n^{5/2})$ by theorem 1. □

A closer look at the proof of theorem 2 reveals that the expected running time is $O(n^2)$ for dense graphs, i.e. $\varepsilon(n) = \varepsilon > 0$ for all n. As $\varepsilon(n)$ becomes smaller running time goes up and reaches its peak for $\varepsilon(n) \approx 1/\sqrt{n}$. For even smaller $\varepsilon(n)$ running time will go down again. This has to be seen in contrast to worst case running time which is $O(n^3)$.

In the remainder of this section we describe an improved transitive closure algorithm for acyclic digraphs.

<u>Definition:</u> Let $G = (V,E)$ be an acyclic digraph. A chain decomposition of G is a partition $V_1,\ldots,V_k$ of V such that V_i is a path for all i, $1 \leq i \leq k$. Integer k is called the width of the decomposition.

Recall that we assumed G to be topologically sorted. In a chain decomposition every V_i is a chain, i.e. if $V_i = \{v_1 < v_2 < \ldots < v_n\}$ then $(v_i, v_{i+1}) \in E$. The following figure shows a graph and a chain decomposition of width 3.

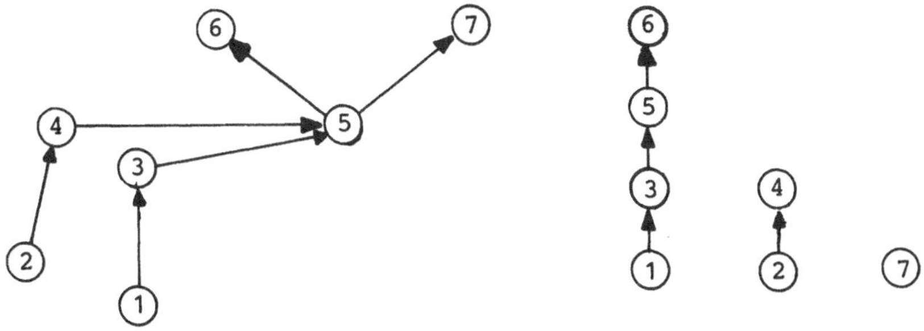

A chain decomposition of an acyclic graph is easily constructed in time O(n+e). We describe one particular algorithm now and show later that it decomposes a random graph into an expected number of at most $\min(n, 1 + 2 \log n/(-\log(1-\varepsilon)))$ chains.

```
(1)   S ← V;
(2)   while S ≠ ∅
(3)   do C ← ∅                          -- we start to construct chain C
(4)      let x ∈ S be minimal;
(5)      delete x from S and add x to C;
(6)      while ∃y ∈ S : (x,y) ∈ E
(7)      do let y be minimal with y ∈ S and (x,y) ∈ E;
(8)         delete y from S and add y to C
(9)         x ← y
(1o)     od
(11)     output chain C
(12) od
```

Set S is realized as a bit vector. Then loop (6) - (1o) takes time O(outdeg(x)) for fixed x. Hence total time spent in lines (6) - (1o) is O(n + e). Line (4) is implemented by sliding a pointer p across bit vector S. All elements to the left of p are not in S. Then total time spent in line (4) is O(n) since p is slided once across vector S.

<u>Lemma 2:</u> A chain decomposition of an acyclic graph G = (V,E) can be constructed in time O(n + e). Furthermore, the expected width of the chain decomposition constructed by the algorithm above is at most $\min(n, 1 + 2 \log n/(-\log(1-\varepsilon)))$ for an n node random graph.

<u>Proof:</u> The bound on the running time is immediate from the preceding discussion. So let us turn to the analysis of the expected width of the decomposition. Let G be an n node graph. Let $V_1(G), V_2(G), \ldots, V_k(G), k = k(G)$, be the chain decomposition constructed for G. We have to derive a bound on the expected value of k(G). In a first step we compute the expected size of $V_1(G)$.

<u>Lemma 3:</u> $E(|V_1(G)|) = 1 + \varepsilon(n-1)$, here $E(|V_1(G)|)$ is the expectation of the cardinality of $V_1(G)$.

Proof: Let us compute the probability that $|V_1(G)| = m$. If $|V_1(G)| = m$ then there are vertices $v_1 = 1, v_2, v_3, \ldots, v_m$ such that $(v_i, v_{i+1}) \in E$ for $1 \le i < m$ and $(v_i, h) \notin E$ for $v_i < h < v_{i+1}$ and $1 \le i \le m$ (let $v_{m+1} = n + 1$). Hence $\text{prob}(V_1(G) = \{1, v_2, v_3, \ldots, v_m\}) = \varepsilon^{m-1}(1-\varepsilon)^{n-m}$ and further

$$E(|V_1(G)|) = \sum_{m \ge 0} \text{prob}(|V_1(G)| = m)m$$

$$= \sum_{m \ge 1} \binom{n-1}{m-1} \varepsilon^{m-1}(1-\varepsilon)^{n-m} m$$

$$= \sum_{m \ge 0} \binom{n-1}{m} \varepsilon^m (1-\varepsilon)^{n-1-m}(m+1)$$

$$= 1 + \varepsilon(n-1) \sum_{m \ge 1} \binom{n-2}{m-1} \varepsilon^{m-1}(1-\varepsilon)^{n-2-(m-1)}$$

$$, \text{ since } \binom{n-1}{m} m = (n-1)\binom{n-2}{m-1}$$

$$= 1 + \varepsilon(n-1)$$ □

Before we proceed, we need some additional notation. For $t \ge 0$, let $c_t = \sum_{i=0}^{t-1} (1-\varepsilon)^i$ and let $s_t = \text{prob}(|V_1(G)| + \ldots + |V_t(G)| < n)$, i.e. s_t is the probability that the width of the chain decomposition is at least $t + 1$.

Lemma 4: For all t: $E(|V_1| + \ldots + |V_t|) \ge \varepsilon n c_t + s_t c_t$.

Proof: Let $n_t = E(|V_1| + \ldots + |V_t|) = E(|V_1|) + \ldots + E(|V_t|)$. Then $n_{t+1} - n_t = E(|V_{t+1}|)$. Since removal of $V_1, \ldots, V_t$ turns a random graph into a random graph, we infer from lemma 3

$$n_{t+1} - n_t = \sum_{m=0}^{n-1} \text{prob}(|V_1| + \ldots + |V_t| = m)(1 + \varepsilon(n-m-1))$$

$$= \sum_{m=0}^{n} \text{prob}(|V_1| + \ldots + |V_t| = m)(1 + \varepsilon(n-m-1))$$

$$- (1 - s_t)(1 + \varepsilon(n-n-1))$$

$$= 1 + \varepsilon(n-1) - (1 - s_t)(1 - \varepsilon) - \varepsilon n_t$$

Thus

$$n_{t+1} = (1 - \varepsilon)n_t + 1 + \varepsilon(n - 1) - (1 - s_t)(1 - \varepsilon)$$

or by repeated substitution

$$n_{t+1} = (1 + \varepsilon(n - 1)) \sum_{i=o}^{t} (1 - \varepsilon)^i - \sum_{i=o}^{t} (1- s_i)(1 - \varepsilon)^{t+1-i}$$

Next note that $1 = s_o \geq s_1 \geq s_2 \geq s_3 \geq \ldots$ and hence

$$n_{t+1} \geq (1 + \varepsilon(n - 1))\, c_{t+1} - (1 - s_{t+1}) \sum_{i=o}^{t} (1 - \varepsilon)^{t+1-i}$$

$$= \varepsilon n c_{t+1} + s_{t+1}c_{t+1}$$ □

Lemma 4 can be used to derive bounds for s_t.

Lemma 5: Let $\varepsilon > 0$, $\delta > 0$. Then $s_t \leq \delta$ for $t \geq (\log \delta/n)/\log(1 - \varepsilon)$

Proof: Note first that

$$n_t = \sum_{m=o}^{n} \text{prob}(|V_1| + \ldots + |V_t| = m)m$$

$$\leq (n - 1)s_t + n(1 - s_t) = n - s_t$$

Combining this inequality with lemma 4 we obtain

$$n - s_t \geq \varepsilon n c_t + s_t c_t$$

or

$$s_t(1 + c_t) \leq (1 - \varepsilon c_t)n = (1 - \varepsilon)^t n.$$

since $c_t = (1 - (1 - \varepsilon)^t)/\varepsilon$. For $t \geq (\log \delta/n)/\log(1 - \varepsilon)$ we conclude further

$$s_t(1 + c_t) \leq \delta$$

and hence $s_t \leq \delta$ since $c_t \geq 0$. □

The proof of lemma 2 is now easily completed. Recall that s_t is the probability that the width of the decomposition is at least $(t + 1)$. Hence we have the following bound for $E(k(G))$, the expected width of the chain decomposition of a random graph, for all t

$$E(k(G)) \leq t(1 - s_t) + s_t n \leq t + s_t n$$

Let $\delta = 1/n$. Then $s_t \leq 1/n$ provided that $t \geq (\log 1/n^2)/\log(1 - \varepsilon)$ and hence

$$E(k(G)) \leq 1 + 2 \log n/(- \log(1 - \varepsilon))$$

Also $k(G) \leq n$ always.

It remains to show how we can use a chain decomposition to speed up the computation of the transitive closure. Let $G = (V,E)$ be an acyclic graph and let $V_1,\ldots,V_k$ be a chain decomposition of G. The crucial observation is that it suffices to compute $REACH[h,i] = \min\{j \in V_h;\ i \to^* j\}$, $1 \le h \le k$ and $1 \le i \le n$. For $j \in V$ let $CH[j] = h$ where $j \in V_h$. Given a chain decomposition it is trivial to compute array CH in time O(n). Also

$$REACH[h,i] = i \qquad \text{if} \qquad h = CH[i]$$

and $REACH[h,i] = \min\{REACH[h,j];\ (i,j) \in E\}$ if $h \neq CH[i]$. Again it is easy to see that it suffices to take the minimum over all edges in E_{red}. This leads to the following algorithm:

```
(1)  for 1 ≤ i ≤ n, 1 ≤ h ≤ k do REACH[h,j] ← ∞ od;
(2)  for i from n downto 1
(3)      for (i,j) ∈ E                     -- in increasing order!!
(4)      do if j < REACH[CH[j],j]
(5)         then for h, 1 ≤ h ≤ k
(6)              do REACH[h,i] ← min(REACH[h,i], REACH[h,j]) od
(7)         fi
(8)      od
(9)      REACH[CH[i],i] ← i;
(1o) od
```

<u>Lemma 6:</u> The algorithm above computes $REACH[h,i] = \min\{j; j \in V_h \text{ and } i \to^* j\}$, $1 \le h \le k$, $1 \le i \le n$, in time $O((n+e_{red})k + e)$.

<u>Proof:</u> Correctness is shown by induction on i, starting with i = n. The base of the induction is obvious. For the induction step note first that certainly $REACH[h,i] \ge \min\{j \in V_h;\ i \to^* j\}$ and that lines (5) and (6) are certainly executed if $(i,j) \in E_{red}$. Let $\ell = \min\{j \in V_h;\ i \to^* j\}$. If $h = CH[i]$ and hence $\ell = i$ then line (9) correctly computes REACH[h,i]. If $h \neq CH[i]$ then let j be such that $(i,j) \in E_{red}$ and $j \to^* \ell$. Then $\ell \le REACH[h,j]$ by induction hypothesis and hence $\ell \le REACH[h,i]$ by lines (5) and (6).
The cost of the algorithm outside lines (5) and (6) is clearly $O(e + nk)$. Also lines (5) and (6) are executed only if $(i,j) \in E_{red}$. This can be seen as follows. If lines (5) and (6) are executed for edge (i,j) then there can be no ℓ such that $i \to \ell \to^* j$. Hence $(i,j) \in E_{red}$. Thus the total cost of lines (5) and (6) is $O(e_{red}k)$. □

From array REACH it is now trivial to compute E^* in time $O(e^*)$ by observing that for all i

$$\{j;\ (i,j) \in E^*\} = \bigcup_{1 \le h \le k} \{v \in V_h;\ v \ge \text{REACH}[h,i]\}$$

We summarize in

<u>Theorem 3:</u> a) The improved algorithm computes the transition closure of an acyclic digraph in time $O(e + (n + e_{red})k)$, where k is the width of the decomposition produced by the decomposition algorithm.

b) The improved algorithm computes the transitive closure of a random acyclic digraph in time

$$O(e^* + \min(\varepsilon n^3,\ n^2 \log n,\ (n/\varepsilon^2)\log n) = O(n^2 \log n)$$

<u>Proof:</u> a) follows immediately from lemmas 2 to 6.

b) Since $n \le E(e_{red})$ it suffices to bound the expected value of $e_{red}k$. Let $k_o = 1 + 4 \log n/(-\log(1 - \varepsilon))$ and let $A = \{G;\ k(G) \le k_o\}$ and $B = \{G;\ k(G) \ge k_o\}$. Then

$$\begin{aligned} E(e_{red}k) &= \sum_G \text{prob}(G)\ e_{red}(G)\ k(G) \\ &= \sum_{G\in A} \text{prob}(G)\ e_{red}(G)\ k(G) + \sum_{G\in B} \text{prob}(G)\ e_{red}(G)\ k(G) \\ &\le \min(n,k_o) \sum_{G\in A} \text{prob}(G)\ e_{red}(G) + n^3 \sum_{G\in B} \text{prob}(G) \\ &\le \min(n,k_o)\ E(e_{red}(G)) + 1 \end{aligned}$$

since $\sum_{G\in B} \text{prob}(G) \le 1/n^3$ by lemma 5 with $\delta = 1/n^3$.

$$\le 1 + \min(n,k_o)[(1 - (1 - \varepsilon^2)^{n-1})/\varepsilon]\,n$$

since $E(e_{red}(G)) \le [(1 - (1 - \varepsilon^2)^{n-1})/\varepsilon]\,n$ by theorem 2a. For the remainder of the proof we have to distinguish three cases.

<u>Case A:</u> $\varepsilon \le (\log n)/n$. Then $E(e_{red}(G)) \le n^2\varepsilon$ by theorem 2a and hence $E(e_{red}(G)\ k(G)) \le n^3\varepsilon$.

Case B: $(\log n)/n \le \varepsilon \le 1/\sqrt{n}$. Then $E(e_{red}(G)) \le n^2\varepsilon$ by theorem 2a and $k_0 \le 1 + 4 \log n/\varepsilon$. Hence $E(e_{red}(G)\ k(G)) = O(n^2 \log n)$.

Case C: $1/\sqrt{n} \le \varepsilon$. Then $E(e_{red}(G)) \le n/\varepsilon$ and $k_0 \le 1 + 4 \log n/\varepsilon$. Hence $E(e_{red}(G)\ k(G)) = O((n/\varepsilon^2)\log n)$. □

We can see from theorem 3 that the improved algorithm is indeed a considerable improvement over the basic algorithm. The expected running time of the improved algorithm is $O(n^2 \log n)$, in contrast to $O(n^{2.5})$ for the basic algorithm. Moreover, worst case running time is $O(e_{red}k)$ in constrast to $O(e_{red}n)$.

IV. 4. Systematic Exploration of a Graph

A basic requirement for most graph algorithms is the systematic exploration of a graph starting at some node s (or at some set of nodes S). The basic idea is quite simple.

Suppose we have visited some set S of nodes already; initially S = {s}. Also some of the edges incident to nodes in S have been used. In each step the algorithm selects one of the unused edges incident to a node in S and explores it, i.e. the edge is marked used and the other endpoint of the edge is added to S. The algorithm terminates when there are no unused edges incident to nodes in S left.

```
S ← {s};
mark all edges unused;
while there are unused edges leaving nodes in S
do    choose any v ∈ S and an unused edge (v,w) ∈ E;
      mark (v,w) used;
      add w to S
od
```

Lemma 1: Let G = (V,E) be a digraph. Then S = {v; there is a path from s to v in G} upon termination of the algorithm.

Proof: If a node is added to S then it is certainly reachable from s. Suppose now that v is reachable from s, i.e. there is a path $v_0,\ldots,v_k$ from s to v. We show by induction on i that v_i is added to S. Since $s = v_0$ this is certainly true for $i = 0$. Suppose now v_i is in S but v_{i+1} is not. Then edge (v_i,v_{i+1}) is unused and incident to a node in S. As long as this condition prevails the algorithm cannot terminate and hence v_{i+1} must be added to S. □

We face two major decisions at this point. How to represent set S and which edge to choose for exploration. We concentrate on the first question for a moment. Actually, the algorithm does not only need to know set S but also a subset $\tilde{S}$ of S consisting of all nodes which still have outgoing unused edges. Using S and $\tilde{S}$ our basic exploration algorithm can be reformulated as follows.

```
proc Explorefrom(s);
    S ← {s};
    S̃ ← {s};
    while S̃ ≠ ∅
    do   choose some node v ∈ S̃;
         let (v,w) be the next unused edge out of v;
         if  (v,w) does not exist
         then delete v from S̃
         else if w ∉ S then add w to S;
                            add w to S̃
                       fi
         fi
    od
end
```

We still have not solved the representation question for sets S and $\tilde{S}$. On set S the operations Insert, Member and Set_to_empty_set are executed, on set $\tilde{S}$ the operations Empty?, Insert, Selectsome, Select_and_ Delete_some and Set_to_empty_set are executed. We saw in chapter I that a boolean array is a good representation for S, operations Insert and Member cost O(1) time units and Set_to_empty_set costs O(n) time units. For set $\tilde{S}$ we use either a stack or a queue. Then all operations on $\tilde{S}$ take O(1) time units.

We also need to explain line (6) in more detail. We use a pointer p[i] into the i-th adjacency list for each i. Initially this pointer points to the first entry of the i-th adjacency list. In the course of the algorithm, the elements of the i-th list which are to the left of the pointer are used and the elements to the right or at the pointer are unused. Then line (6) is equivalent to reading the element pointed at by p[v] and advancing p[v] one position. Then lines (6) to (8) can be expanded to

```
if p[v] = nil
then delete v from S̃
else w ← p[v]↑.name;
     p[v] ← p[v]↑.next;
     if w ∉ S then ...
```

We are now in the position to determine the efficiency of procedure Explorefrom.

Lemma 2: A call Explorefrom(s) (not counting the cost of initializing S in line (2)) costs $O(n_s + e_s)$ time units where $n_s = |V_s| = |\{v;$ there is a path from s to v$\}|$ and e_s is the number of edges in the subgraph induced by V_s.

Proof: One execution of the body of the while-loop takes O(1) units of time. In each iteration either an edge is used up or an element is deleted from $\tilde{S}$. Since each node in V_s is added exactly once to $\tilde{S}$ (the test in line (9) avoids repetitions) the total time spent in the while-loop is $O(n_s + e_s)$. □

We will now put procedure Explorefrom to its first use: determining the connected components of an undirected graph.

Definition: An undirected graph G = (V,E) is connected if for every $v,w \in V$ there is a path from v to w. A connected component of an undirected graph G is a maximal (with respect to set inclusion) connected subgraph of G. □

The problem of determining the connected components of a graph often comes up in the following disguise. V is a set and $E \subseteq V \times V$ is a relation on V. Then the reflexive, symmetric, transitive closure of E is an equivalence relation. Determine the equivalence classes of this relation. In the language of graphs this amounts to determining the connected components of the graph $G = (V, \{(v,w);\ (v,w) \in E \text{ or } (w,v) \in E\})$.

In an undirected graph the set of nodes reachable from s form a connected component. This observation leads us to the following theorem.

Theorem 1: The connected components of an undirected graph can be found in linear time $O(n + e)$.

Proof: We embed our procedure Explorefrom in the following program.

```
S ← ∅;
for all v ∈ V do p[v] ← ADJHEAD[v] od;
for all v ∈ V
do  if  v ∉ S then Explorefrom(v) fi od;
```

and change line (2) in procedure Explorefrom from $S \leftarrow \{s\}$ to $S \leftarrow S \cup \{s\}$.

We infer from Lemma 2 that the cost of a call Explorefrom(v) is proportial to the size of the connected component containing v. Since Explorefrom is called exactly once for each connected component the total running time is $O(n + e)$.

In what sense does this program determine the connected components of a graph? All nodes of a component are visited during one call of Explorefrom. A list of the nodes of each component can be obtained as follows. Let COMP be a variable of type set of nodes (realized by a stack). COMP is initialized to singleton set {v} before call Explorefrom(v) and the instruction add w to COMP is added in line (10) of Explorefrom. Then COMP contains all nodes of the component v is in after return from Explorefrom(v). □

The reader should convince himself that the running time of the program given in the proof above is linear even in the case of a digraph. What does the program do?

Depending on the representation of set $\tilde{S}$, stack or queue, we have two versions of procedure Explorefrom at our hands. They are known under the names <u>depth first search</u> ($\tilde{S}$ is a stack) and <u>breadth first search</u> ($\tilde{S}$ is a queue). In depth first search exploration always proceeds from the last node visited which still has unused edges, in breadth first search it proceeds from the first node visited which still has unused edges.

In either case Explorefrom steps through the adjacency list of each node in a strictly sequential manner; the order of the edges on the adjacency lists has no influence on running time.

In section 5 we will take a closer look at depth first search. In section 6 we will apply depth first search to various connectivity problems. In section 7 we will apply breadth first search to distance type problems.

IV. 5. A Close Look at Depth First Search

In this section we will take a detailed look at depth first search of directed and undirected graphs. In the depth first search version of procedure Explorefrom set $\tilde{S}$ is handled as a stack. It is convenient to make that stack implicit by formulating depth first search as a recursive procedure DFS. The parameter of DFS will always be an element of $\tilde{S}$. We will now rewrite the algorithm of section 4.

```
proc DFS(v : V);
     for all w with (v,w) ∈ E
     do if w ∉ S
        then add w to S;
             [add (v,w) to T]
             COUNT1 ← COUNT1 + 1; DFSNUM[w] ← COUNT1;
             DFS(w);
             COUNT2 ← COUNT2 + 1; COMPNUM[w] ← COUNT2;
        else [if v →*_T w then add (v,w) to F fi;
              if w →*_T v then add (v,w) to B
                          else add (v,w) to C fi;      ]
        fi
     od
end
```

```
begin
S ← ∅; COUNT1 ← 0;  COUNT2 ← 0;
[ T ← F ← B ← C ← ∅;]
for all v ∈ V
do if v ∈ S then add v to S;
                 COUNT1 ← COUNT1 + 1; DFSNUM[v] ← COUNT1;
                 DFS(v);
                 COUNT2 ← COUNT2 + 1; COMPNUM[v] ← COUNT2
             fi
od
end
```

Several remarks are in order at this point. We have fleshed out our basic algorithm in two respects. First of all, we number the nodes in two different ways. The first numbering DFSNUM is with respect to calling time of procedure DFS, the second numbering is with respect to completion time of procedure DFS. Second of all, we partition the edges of the graph into four classes: the tree edges T, the forward edges F, the backward edges B and the cross edges C. The partitioning process is only done conceptually (this fact is indicated by enclosing the corresponding statements in brackets), it will facilitate the discussion of depth first search.

In the following example tree edges are drawn solid (-), back edges are drawn dashed (- - -), cross edges are drawn wiggled (〰) and forward edges are drawn dash-dotted (-•-•). Name (an element of {a,b,c,d,e}), depth first search and completion numbers are indicated in each node in that order. Nodes are explored in the order a,d,e,c,b. In our examples we will always draw tree edges upward and order the sons of a node (via tree edges) in increasing order of DFSNUM from left to right.

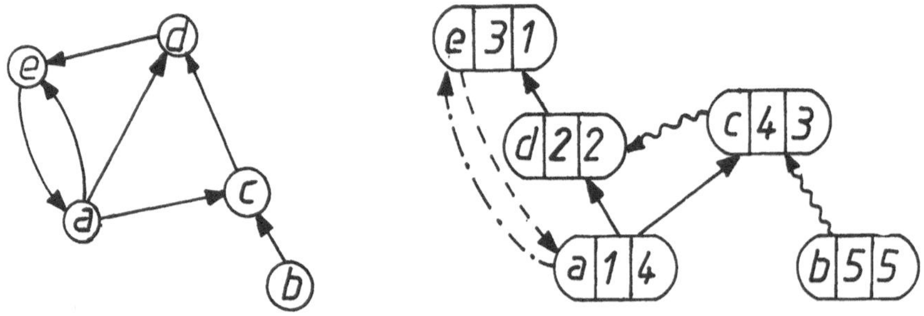

Lemma 1: Let G = (V,E) be a directed graph. Then a depth-first-search on G takes time $O(n + e)$.

Proof: A call DFS(v) costs $O(\text{outdeg}_G(v))$ units of time; this accounts for the time spent in the body of DFS but does not account for further recursive calls. Since a node v is always added to S prior to the call DFS(v) and no node is ever removed from S DFS is called for every node at most once. Hence the total time spent outside DFS is clearly $O(n)$. □

Next we will state some important properties of depth-first-search.

Lemma 2: Let G = (V,E) be a digraph and let T,F,B,C, DFSNUM and COMPNUM be defined by a depth-first-search on G.

a) sets T,F,B,C form a partition of E

b) A = (V,T) is a spanning forest of G

c) $v \xrightarrow[T]{*} w$ iff DFSNUM[v] ≤ DFSNUM[w] and COMPNUM[w] ≤ COMPNUM[v]

d) $(v,w) \in T \cup F$ iff DFSNUM[v] ≤ DFSNUM[w] and $(v,w) \in E$

e) $(v,w) \in B \cup C$ iff DFSNUM[v] > DFSNUM[w] and $(v,w) \in E$

f) if nodes v,w,z are such that $v \xrightarrow[T \cup F]{*} w$, $(w,z) \in B \cup C$ and $\neg (v \xrightarrow[T]{*} z)$ then DFSNUM[z] < DFSNUM[v]. Furthermore, if $(w,z) \in C$ then COMPNUM[z] < COMPNUM[v].

Proof: a) Immediate from the definition of DFS and the fact that each edge is handled exactly once during the depth first search of graph G.

b) When edge (v,w) is added to T in line (5) of DFS then w was added to S in line (4) and v was already in S. This shows that $\text{indegree}_A(z) \le 1$ for all $z \in V$ and that A is acyclic.

c) ⇒ : if $(v,w) \in T$ then call DFS(w) is started in line (7) of DFS(v) and hence DFSNUM[v] ≤ DFSNUM[w]. Also call DFS(w) is completed before call DFS(v) and hence COMPNUM[w] ≤ COMPNUM[v]. The general claim follows by induction on the length of the tree path from v to w.

⇐ : A node v gets its DFSNUM (COMPNUM) when call DFS(v) is started (completed). Hence DFSNUM[v] ≤ DFSNUM[w] and COMPNUM[w] ≤ COMPNUM[v] implies that call DFS(v) is started before and completed after call DFS(w). Hence call DFS(w) is nested within call DFS(v) and thus $v \xrightarrow[T]{*} w$ since an edge (u,z) is added to T in line (5) iff DFS(z) is called in line (7) of DFS(u).

d) ⇒ : if $(v,w) \in T \cup F$ then $v \xrightarrow[T]{}{}^{*} w$ by definition of T and F and hence DFSNUM[v] ≤ DFSNUM[w] by part c).

⇐ : Consider the point of time when edge (v,w) is handled in DFS(v). Either exploration of that edge will lead to call DFS(w) and hence $(v,w) \in T$ or $v = w$ or $v \neq w$ and DFS(w) was called before edge (v,w) was handled. In the first two cases we are done. Consider the third case. Since DFSNUM[v] < DFSNUM[w] call DFS(w) was started after call DFS(v), but before edge (v,w) is handled in call DFS(v). Hence call DFS(w) is nested within call DFS(v) and therefore $v \xrightarrow[T]{}{}^{*} w$ by part b). Thus $(v,w) \in F$ in this case.

e) Immediate from parts a) and d). Note that $T \cup F = E - (B \cup C)$ by part a).

f) The situation is visualized in the following diagram.

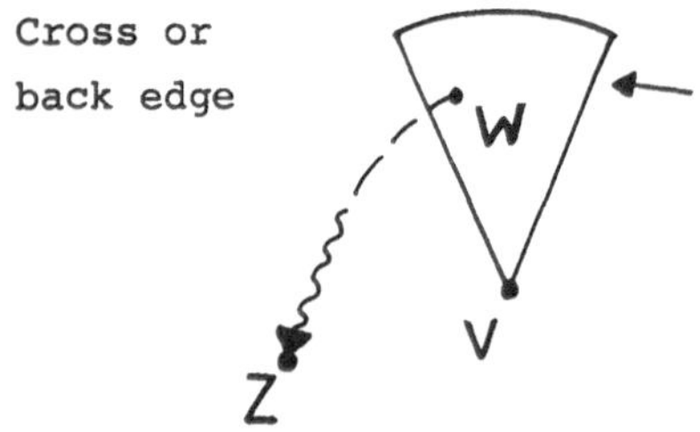

Since $v \xrightarrow[T]{}{}^{*} w$ we have DFSNUM[v] ≤ DFSNUM[w] (part c) and since $(w,z) \in B \cup C$ we have DFSNUM[z] ≤ DFSNUM[w] (part e). If DFSNUM[z] < DFSNUM[v] then we are done. Assume otherwise, i.e. DFSNUM[v] ≤ DFSNUM[z]. Since $\neg (v \xrightarrow[T]{}{}^{*} z)$ call DFS(z) is not nested within call DFS(v). Since it is started after call DFS(v) is started, it must be started after call DFS(v) is completed. In particular, when edge (w,z) is handled in call DFS(w), call DFS(z) has not been started yet. So exploration of edge (w,z) will lead to call DFS(z) and hence $(w,z) \in T$, a contradiction. So DFSNUM[z] < DFSNUM[v].

Assume now that $(w,z) \in C$ and hence $\neg (z \xrightarrow[T]{}{}^{*} w)$ and hence $\neg (z \xrightarrow[T]{}{}^{*} v)$. Part c) implies COMPNUM[z] < COMPNUM[v]. □

It is worthwile to restate the content of lemma 3 in an informal way.

In our drawings of depth first search tree edges are always directed upwards and the sons via tree edges of nodes are ordered according to increasing depth first search number from left to right. Then forward edges go from nodes to their descendants with respect to tree edges, backward edges go from nodes to their ancestors and cross edges go from right to left. Also the depth first search (completion) number of a node is smaller (larger) than those of its tree desdencants. Cross edges go from larger to smaller depth first search and completion numbers. Finally, if (u,w) is a back edge then all nodes which are completed between u and w are descendants of w.

In undirected graphs the situation is simpler; there are no cross edges and every forward edge is the reversal of a backward edge.

Lemma 3: Let G = (V,E) be an undirected graph without self-loops and let T,F,B,C be defined by a depth first search on G.

a) $C = \emptyset$

b) $(v,w) \in B$ iff $(w,v) \in T \cup F$ for every edge $(v,w) \in E$.

c) If G is connected then A = (V,T) is a tree.

Proof: a) (Indirect). Assume $C \neq \emptyset$. Let $(v,w) \in C$ be the first edge which was added to C in the depth first search of G. By lemma 2,f call DFS(w) is completed when edge (v,w) is handled in call DFS(v). Since graph G is undirected, edge (v,w) was explored in DFS(w) and since (v,w) is the first edge added to C we must have $(w,v) \in T \cup F \cup B$. In either case we have $w \underset{T}{\rightarrow^*} v$ or $v \underset{T}{\rightarrow^*} w$. Hence (v,w) is not added to C, a contradiction.

b) Since $C = \emptyset$ by part a) this is an immediate consequence of lemma 2, parts a), d) and e).

c) If A = (V,T) were not a tree but a proper forest, then A contains at least two trees A_1 and A_2. Since G is connected there must be edges between A_1 and A_2. Since back edges and forward edges run parallel to paths of tree edges such edges must be cross edges. However, depth first search on an undirected graph does not produce cross edges and hence A must be a single tree. □

IV. 6. Strongly-Connected and Biconnected Components of Directed and Undirected Graphs

We will describe linear time algorithms to determine the strongly-connected components of a digraph and the biconnected components of an undirected graph. Both algorithms are based on depth first search.

Definition: a) A digraph $G = (V,E)$ is strongly connected if $v \to^* w \to^* v$ for all $v,w \in V$.

b) A strongly connected component of a digraph G is a maximal strongly connected subgraph. □

The problem of determining the strongly connected components of a digraph often comes up in the following disguise. V is a set and E a relation on V. Two elements $v,w \in V$ are called equivalent if $v \to^* w$ and $w \to^* v$. The equivalence classes of this equivalence relation are just the s.c.c.'s (strongly connected components) of $G = (V,E)$. Furthermore, shrinking the equivalence classes (s.c.c.'s) to single points leaves us with a partial order (an acyclic graph). In the following example there are

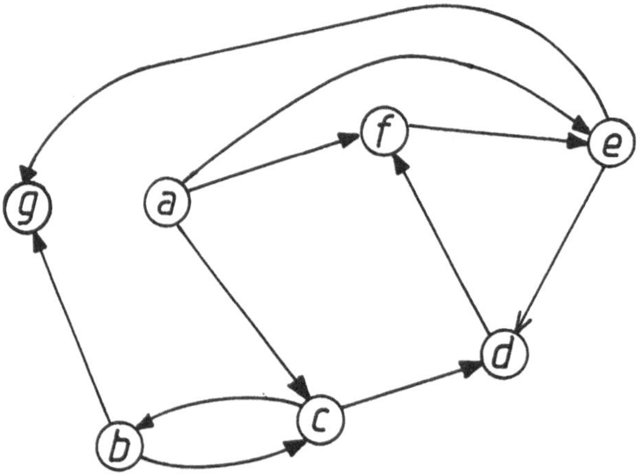

four strongly connected components, namely {a}, {g}, {b,c} and {e,f,d}. A depth first search of G could yield the following structure: the nodes are visited in the order a,c,b,g,d,f,e.

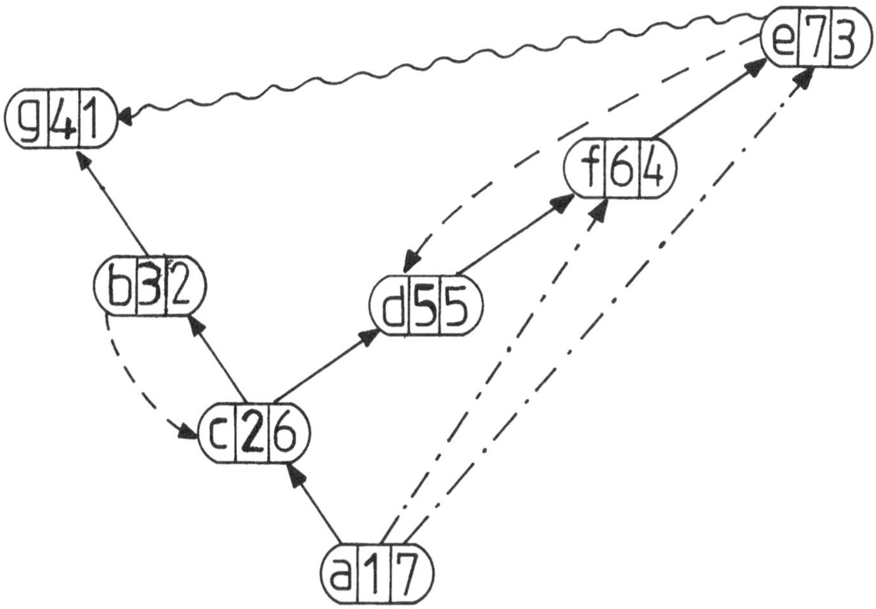

The first s.c.c. which is completely visited during the search, i.e. all calls DFS(v) for v a node of the component are completed, is {g}. When DFS(g) is completed, there are no edges leaving the subtree A_g and none of the edges which go into the component {g} have been explored at this moment (except for the tree edge (b,g)). The first feature will be (almost) our test for completion of a s.c.c., the second feature allows us to reduce the problem. We can conceptually delete the component {g} and determine the components of a simpler graph. The second completed s.c.c. is {d,e,f}. Again, note that the only edge into the component which has been explored is the tree edge (c,d). However, there are edges leaving the subtree A_d, namely the cross edge (e, g). But this edge ends in a previously completed s.c.c.. We will now make these observations precise.

A node v is called the root of a s.c.c. if its DFSNUM is the smallest of all nodes in the s.c.c., i.e. the root of the s.c.c. is the first node of the s.c.c. which is reached during the search. In the following lemma we will first show that all elements of a s.c.c. are tree descendants of the root of the s.c.c. and so justify the name root. A precise characterization of the nodes contained in a s.c.c. is given in part b): all tree descendants of the root which are not descendants of another root. Finally part c) characterizes the roots of s.c.c.'s in terms of DFS. We observed in our example that v is a root of a s.c.c. if all edges leaving the subtree A_v end in previously completed s.c.c.. By IV. 5. lemma 2,f there is a simple test, whether edge (w,z) where $w \in A_v$ leaves tree A_v: namely DFSNUM[z] < DFSNUM[v]. Roots of s.c.c. can therefore be recognized by computing the lowest point (the point with the smallest DFSNUM) reachable from a node whilst staying inside the s.c.c. of the node. This is made precise in part c.

Lemma 1: Let G = (V,E) be a digraph and let T,F,B,C, DFSNUM and COMPNUM be defined by a depth first search on G.

a) Let G' = (V',E') be a s.c.c. of G and let $v \in V'$ be its root. Then $v \xrightarrow[T]{*} w$ for all $w \in V'$ and v is the node with largest COMPNUM in V'.

b) Let G' = (V',E') be a s.c.c. of G and let v be its root. Then $w \in V'$ iff the path of tree edges from v to w does not go through a root of a s.c.c. different from v.

c) For $v \in V$ let $CUR_v = \{w \in V;\ COMPNUM[r] \geq COMPNUM[v]$ where r is the root of the s.c.c. containing w$\}$ and let

$$\begin{aligned} LOWPT[v] = \min\ (&\{DFSNUM[v]\} \cup \\ &\cup \{DFSNUM[z];\ (v,z) \in B \cup C \text{ and } z \in CUR_v\} \\ &\cup \{LOWPT[u];\ (v,u) \in T\}) \end{aligned}$$

Then LOWPT[v] = DFSNUM[v] iff v is the root of a s.c.c..

Proof: a) Node v is the first node in V' reached by the search. Before call DFS(v) is completed all nodes reachable from v have been explored by the search. Hence $v \xrightarrow[T]{*} w$ and COMPNUM[w] ≤ COMPNUM[v] for all $w \in V'$.

b) "⇒": Let $w \in V'$. Then $v \xrightarrow[T]{*} w$ by part a). Furthermore $z \in V'$ for all nodes z on the path of tree edges from v to w, since $v \xrightarrow[T]{*} z \xrightarrow[T]{*} w \xrightarrow{*} v$. Hence there can be no root different from v on the path of tree edges from v to w.

"⇐": Suppose $v \xrightarrow[T]{*} w$ and $w \notin V'$. Let r be the root of the s.c.c. containing w. Then $r \xrightarrow[T]{*} w$ by part a) and hence either $r \xrightarrow[T]{*} v$ or $v \xrightarrow[T]{+} r$. If

$r \xrightarrow[T]{*} v$ then $w \in V'$ since $r \xrightarrow[T]{*} v \xrightarrow[T]{*} w \rightarrow^* r$, a contradiction. Hence $v \xrightarrow[T]{+} r$.

c) It suffices to show the following two claims:

Claim 1: LOWPT[v] $\geq$ DFSNUM[r], where r is the root of the s.c.c. containing v.

Claim 2: If v is not the root of a s.c.c. then LOWPT[v] < DFSNUM[v].

Proof of claim 1: (By induction on COMPNUM[v]). We distinguish three cases according to the definition of LOWPT.

Case 1: LOWPT[v] = DFSNUM[v]: in this case claim 1 is immediate from the definition of root of a s.c.c..

Case 2: LOWPT[v] = DFSNUM[z] < DFSNUM[v] for some z with $(v,z) \in B \cup C$ and $z \in CUR_v$. Let r be the root of the s.c.c. containing z. Then $r \xrightarrow[T]{*} z$ by part a) and hence DFSNUM[r] $\leq$ DFSNUM[z] $\leq$ DFSNUM[v]. Also COMPNUM[r] $\geq$ COMPNUM[v] (since $z \in CUR_v$) and hence $r \xrightarrow[T]{*} v$ by IV. 5. lemma 2,c. Thus $r \xrightarrow[T]{*} v \xrightarrow[B\cup C]{} z \rightarrow^* r$ and so r,v and z belong to the same s.c.c.. In particular, r is the root of the s.c.c. containing v. This proves DFSNUM[r] $\leq$ DFSNUM[z] = LOWPT[v].

Case 3: LOWPT[v] = LOWPT[u] < DFSNUM[v] for some u with $(v,u) \in T$. Then COMPNUM[u] < COMPNUM[v] and hence the I.H. applies to u. Let r_u (r_v) be the root of the s.c.c. containing u (v). Then by part b) either $r_u = r_v$ or $r_u = u$; in either case we have $r_v \xrightarrow[T]{*} r_u$ and hence DFSNUM[r_v] $\leq$ DFSNUM[r_u] $\leq$ LOWPT[u]. The last inequality follows from the induction hypothesis.

Proof of claim 2: If v is not the root of a s.c.c. then let $v_0, v_1, v_2, \ldots, v_k$ be a path from $v = v_0$ to the root $r = v_k$ of the s.c.c. containing v. Since $v \neq r$ and $r \xrightarrow[T]{*} v$ by part a) there must be a minimal i such that $\neg (v \xrightarrow[T]{*} v_i)$. Then $v \xrightarrow[T]{*} v_{i-1}$, $(v_{i-1}, v_i) \in B \cup C$, DFSNUM[$v_i$] < DFSNUM[v] (by IV. 5. lemma 2,f) and LOWPT[v] $\leq$ LOWPT[v_{i-1}] (by definition of LOWPT). Therefore it suffices to show that

$v_i \in CUR_{v_{i-1}}$ because this will imply $LOWPT[v_{i-1}] \leq DFSNUM[v_i]$. Note first that v_i and $v = v_0$ belong to the same s.c.c. and hence r is also the root of s.c.c. containing v_i. From $r \underset{T}{\to^*} v \underset{T}{\to^*} v_{i-1}$ we conclude $COMPNUM[v_{i-1}] < COMPNUM[r]$ and hence $v_i \in CUR_{v_{i-1}}$. □

Lemma 1 provides us with a characterization of the roots of the s.c.c.'s (the nodes v with LOWPT[v] = DFSNUM[v]) and the s.c.c.'s themselves (all tree descendants of the root which are not descendants of other roots). Also part c) of the lemma describes a method for computing LOWPT[v] from the LOWPT's of the sons of v and the DFSNUM's of the endpoints of back and cross edges out of v. In order to compute function LOWPT we must be able to distinguish edges in B ∪ C from edges in T and edges in F and we must be able to test whether the endpoint of a cross or back edge belongs to CUR_v. The first task is solved by IV. 5. lemma 2, namely $(v,w) \in B \cup C$ iff DFSNUM[w] < DFSNUM[v]. Edges in T are distinguished from the edges in F by the fact that they lead to recursive calls of DFS. The second problem is solved by maintaining set CURRENT in the algorithm where CURRENT = {w; w was reached by the search and DFS(r), where r is the root of the s.c.c. containing r, is not completed}. Whenever an edge $(v,w) \in B \cup C$ is explored, node w has certainly been reached previously by the search. So a test $w \in$ CURRENT is equivalent to a test $w \in CUR_v$ in computing LOWPT[v]. Finally, whenever the root v of a s.c.c. is found, i.e. LOWPT[v] = DFSNUM[v], we have to be able to enumerate the nodes in the s.c.c. with root v. The s.c.c. with v consists of all nodes w such that $v \underset{T}{\to^*} w$ (and hence DFSNUM[v] ≤ DFSNUM[w]) and which were not enumerated in previously found s.c.c.'s.. Thus the s.c.c. with root v consists of all points w in CURRENT with DFSNUM[w] ≥ DFSNUM[v]. Our discussion leads to the following algorithm for computing the s.c.c.'s of a digraph.

```
(1) begin S ← ∅; COUNT1 ← 1;
(2) CURRENT ← ∅;
(3) for all v ∈ V
(4) do  if v ∉ S then add v to S;
(5)                   add v to CURRENT;
(6)                   COUNT1 ← COUNT1 + 1;
(7)                   DFSNUM[v] ← COUNT1;
(8)                   DFS(v)
```

```
(9)              fi
(10) od
(11) end
```

where

```
(12) proc DFS(v : V);
(13)      LOWPT[v] ← DFSNUM[v];
(14)      for all w with (v,w) ∈ E
(15)      do  if w ∉ S
(16)          then add w to S;
(17)               add w to CURRENT;
(18)               COUNT1 ← COUNT1 + 1;
(19)               DFSNUM[w] ← COUNT1;
(2o)               DFS(w);
(21)               LOWPT[v] ← min(LOWPT[v], LOWPT[w])
(22)          fi;
(23)          if DFSNUM[w] < DFSNUM[v] and w ∈ CURRENT
(24)          then LOWPT[v] ← min(LOWPT[v], DFSNUM[w])
(25)          fi;
(26)      od;
(27)      if LOWPT[v] = DFSNUM[v]
(28)      then delete all nodes w with DFSNUM[w] ≥ DFSNUM[v] from CURRENT
(29)      fi
(30) end
```

Let us reconsider the example from the beginning of the section. Just prior to execution of line (27) of call DFS(d) the situation is as follows:

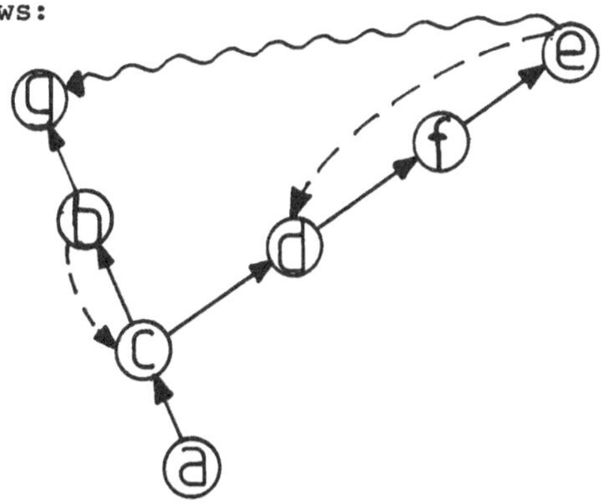

	DFSUM	LOWPT
a	1	1
b	3	2
c	2	2
d	5	5
e	7	5
f	6	5
g	4	4

CURRENT = {a,c,b,d,f,e}

In line (28) of DFS(d) we remove d,f,e from CURRENT. Then the flow of control returns to line (20) of DFS(c) and LOWPT[c] is not changed in line (21). Then in line (28) of DFS(c) nodes c and b are removed from CURRENT.

Theorem 1: The strongly connected components of a digraph can be found in time O(n + e).

Proof: The correctness of our algorithm is almost immediate from lemma 1. Function LOWPT is computed as in lemma 1,c. We initialize LOWPT[v] to DFSNUM[v] in line (13) and update it for every tree edge (v,w) in line (21) and for every cross or back edge in lines (23)-(25). Also CURRENT always contains exactly those nodes w which where reached by the search and such that DFS(r) is not completed where r is the root of the s.c.c. containing w. This is true after initializing CURRENT in line (2). Whenever a node is reached by the search it is added to CURRENT (line (5) and (17)), and whenever a root of a s.c.c. is found all nodes in the s.c.c. are deleted from CURRENT (in line (28)).

Next we discuss the running time of our algorithm. On set CURRENT the following operations are executed: Initialize-to-Empty-Set (line (2)), Insert (lines (5) and (17)), Member (line (23)) and Deleting all elements w with DFSNUM[w] ≥ DFSNUM[v] from CURRENT (line (28)). The last operation is non-standard. A crucial observation is the fact that nodes are added to CURRENT in increasing order of DFSNUM's. Hence if we realize CURRENT by a pushdown store then the Delete operations in line (28) take time proportional to the number of elements deleted. Since every node belongs to exactly one s.c.c. the total time spent in line (28) will be O(n). However, the membership test in line (23) cannot be done efficiently when CURRENT is implemented as a pushdown store, a boolean array is the structure called for. The solution is to represent CURRENT twice: once as a pushdown store and once as a boolean array. Then line (2) takes O(n), lines (5), (17) and (28) take O(1) for each element inserted or deleted and line (23) takes O(1). Since every node is inserted into and deleted from CURRENT exactly once the total time spent on manipulating set CURRENT is O(n + e). The time spent in the remaining lines of the program is O(n + e) by IV. 5. lemma 1. □

We gave a recursive definition of LOWPT in lemma 1. There is an equivalent explicite definition

$$\text{LOWPT}[v] = \min(\{\text{DFSNUM}[v]\} \cup \{\text{DFSNUM}[z];\ \text{there is } w \text{ with } v \underset{T}{\to^*} w \text{ and } (w,z) \in B \cup C \text{ and } z \in CUR_v\})$$

This non-recursive definition of LOWPT will be useful in our discussion of biconnected components of undirected graphs to which we turn next.

<u>Definition:</u> a) A connected undirected graph $G = (V,E)$ is biconnected if $G - v$ is connected for every $v \in V$.

b) A biconnected component (b.c.c.) of an undirected graph is a maximal biconnected subgraph.

c) A point $a \in V$ is an articulation point of G if $G - a$ is not connected. □

We start with a simple observation about biconnected components. Let $G_1 = (V_1,E_1),\ldots,G_m = (V_m,E_m)$ be the biconnected components of undirected graph $G = (V,E)$. Then $E = E_1 \cup\ldots\cup E_m$ and $E_i \cap E_j = \emptyset$ for $i \neq j$. For every edge $(v,w) \in E$ the graph consisting of points v and w and the single edge (v,w) is biconnected, and hence contained in one of the biconnected components of G. Thus $(v,w) \in E_i$ for some i. It remains to show $E_i \cap E_j = \emptyset$ for $i \neq j$. Assume o.w., say $(v,w) \in E_i \cap E_j$ for some $i \neq j$. Since G_i and G_j are maximal biconnected subgraphs the subgraph $G' = (V_i \cup V_j, E_i \cup E_j)$ is not biconnected. Thus there must be a point $a \in V_i \cup V_j$ such that $G' - a$ is not connected. Let x and y be points in different components of $G' - a$. Since $G_i - a$ and $G_j - a$ are connected we must have $x \in V_i$ and $y \in V_j$ (or vice versa). Since a cannot be equal to both v and w we may assume $v \neq a$. Since $G_i - a$ ($G_j - a$) is connected there is a path from x to v (y to v) in $G_i - a$ ($G_j - a$). Thus there is path from x to y in $G' - a$, a contradiction. We have thus shown that the b.c.c.'s of a graph form a partition of the edges of the graph. One further observation about b.c.c.'s will be useful in the sequel. If there is a simple cycle through nodes v,w then v and w belong to the same b.c.c.. In the following example there are four b.c.c.'s,

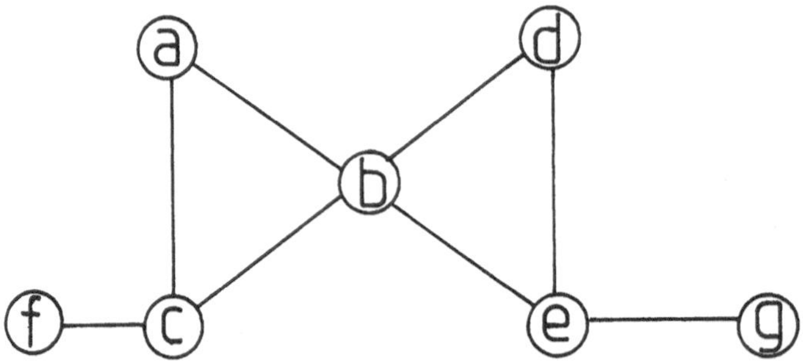

namely {f,c}, {a,b,c}, {e,g} and {b,d,e}. The articulation points are c,e and b. A depth first search of G could yield the following structure; nodes are explored in the order a,b,c,f,d,e,g.

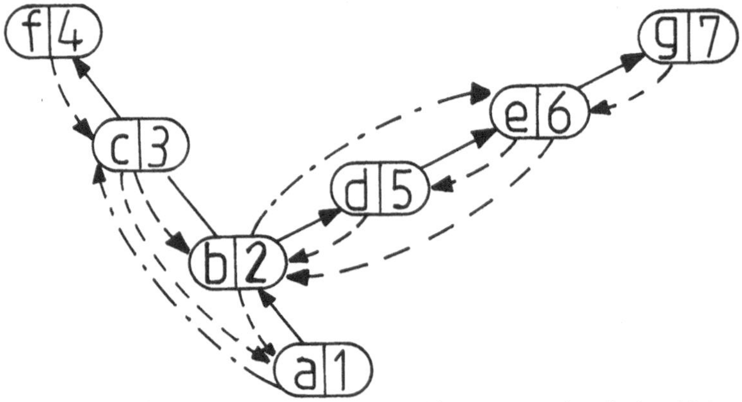

The biconnected components are easily recognized in this picture. The first edge of each b.c.c. which is explored is a tree edge; call the endpoint of that tree edge the center of the component (the node with the next to smallest DFSNUM in the b.c.c.). All backedges out of the subtree rooted at the center of a b.c.c. end in or above the father node of the center. The father of the center is always an articulation point and the b.c.c. with center v consists of the father of v and the nodes which are reachable from v via tree edges without going through another center. In our example the centers of the four components are f,g,d and b. The b.c.c. with center d consists of b = FATHER[d], and descendants d and e of d.

Formally, we define the center of a b.c.c. as the node with the next to smallest DFSNUM in the b.c.c.. The observations above suggest to use a strategy very similar to the one used for s.c.c.'s namely to compute a function LOWPT

$$LOWPT[v] = \min(\{DFSNUM[v]\} \cup \{DFSNUM[z];\ \text{there is } w \text{ such that } v \underset{T}{\rightarrow^*} w \underset{B}{\rightarrow} z\})$$

<u>Lemma 2:</u> Let G = (V,E) be a connected undirected graph without self-loops, let T,F,B and DFSNUM be determined by a depth first search on G and let LOWPT and FATHER be defined as above.

a) $LOWPT[v] \le DFSNUM[FATHER[v]]$ for all v with $DFSNUM[v] \ge 2$.

b) v is the center of a b.c.c. iff $LOWPT[v] = DFSNUM[FATHER[v]]$ and $DFSNUM[v] \ge 2$.

c) Let G' = (V',E') be a b.c.c. with center v. Then $V' = \{FATHER[v] \cup w;\ v \underset{T}{\rightarrow^*} w$ and there is no center different from v on the path from v to w$\}$.

d) $$LOWPT[v] = \min(\{DFSNUM[v]\} \cup \{DFSNUM[z];\ (v,z) \in B\} \cup \{LOWPT[u];\ (v,u) \in T\}) \text{ for all } v \in V$$

<u>Proof:</u> a) If $DFSNUM[v] \ge 2$ then FATHER[v] exists and edge (v, FATHER[v]) is a back edge. Hence $LOWPT[v] \le DFSNUM[FATHER[v]]$.

b) ⇒: Let v be the center of a b.c.c.. Then certainly $DFSNUM[v] \ge 2$. Suppose $LOWPT[v] = DFSNUM[u] < DFSNUM[FAHTER[v]]$. Then there is a path $v \underset{T}{\rightarrow^*} w \underset{B}{\rightarrow} u$ for some w. Also u is a tree ancestor of v and since $u \ne FATHER[v]$ also of FATHER[v]. Hence u, FATHER[v], v and w lie on a

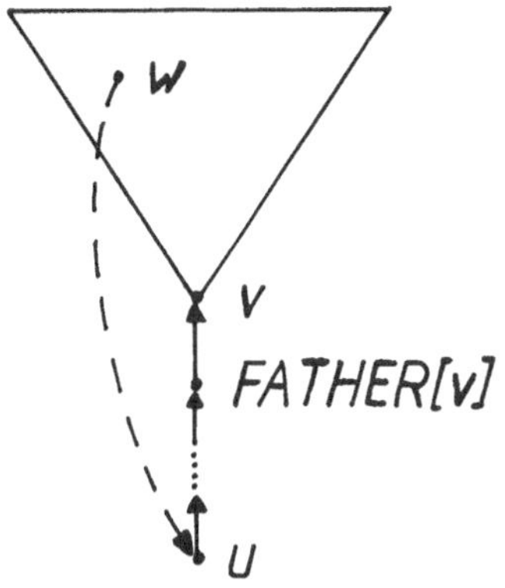

simple cycle and hence all belong to the same b.c.c.. This b.c.c. contains at least two nodes, namely u and FATHER[v], whose DFSNUMbers are smaller than v's number, a contradiction.

$\Leftarrow$: Suppose DFSNUM[v] $\geq$ 2 and LOWPT[v] = DFSNUM[FATHER[v]]. Consider the b.c.c. G' = (V',E') containing edge (FATHER[v],v). We will show that v is the center of G'. Assume the existence of u $\in$ V', u $\neq$ FATHER[v] and DFSNUM[u] < DFSNUM[v]. Since G' - FATHER[v] is connected there must be a simple path $v_o,..,v_k$ from $v = v_o$ to $v_k = u$ avoiding node FATHER[v]. Let v_i be the first node on that path which is not a descendant of v, i.e. $v \xrightarrow[T]{}^* v_{i-1}$ and $\neg(v \xrightarrow[T]{}^* v_i)$. Then edge (v_{i-1},v_i) must be a backedge and hence LOWPT[v] $\leq$ DFSNUM[v_i] by definition of LOWPT. Furthermore, since v_i is a tree ancestor of v_{i-1} and since v_i is not a tree

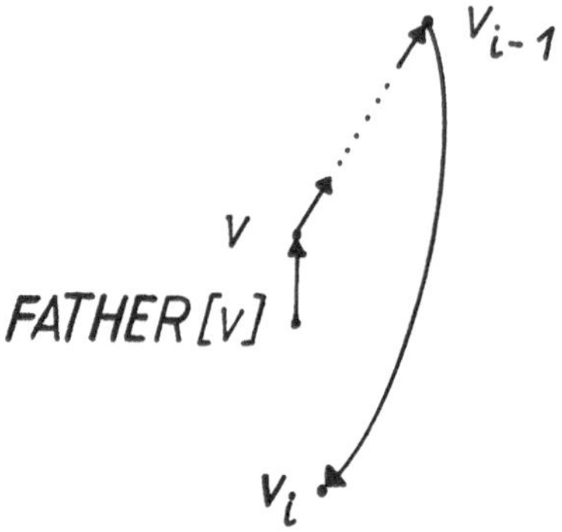

descendant of v and $v_i \neq$ FATHER[v], v_i must be a proper ancestor of FATHER[v]. Hence DFSNUM[v_i] < DFSNUM[FATHER[v]], a contradiction.

c) Let G' = (V',E') be a b.c.c. with center v. In the proof of part b) it was shown that FATHER[v] $\in$ V'. Also by the definition of center DFSNUM[v] < DFSNUM[w] for all w $\in$ V' - {v, FATHER[v]}. Since G' - FATHER[v] is connected all points w $\in$ V' - {v, FATHER[v]} are reached by the search before DFS(v) is completed. None of them is reached before DFS(v) is started and hence $v \xrightarrow[T]{}^* w$ for all w $\in$ V' - FATHER[v]. This proves V' $\subseteq$ FATHER[v] $\cup$ $\{w;\ v \xrightarrow[T]{}^* w\}$.

Next suppose $v \xrightarrow[T]{}^* z$ and z $\notin$ V'. Let c be the center of the b.c.c. G'' containing edge (FATHER[z], z). Then $c \xrightarrow[T]{}^* z$ by the first part of the proof of part c) and hence either $v \xrightarrow[T]{}^* c$ or $c \xrightarrow[T]{}^* v$. c = v is impossible since $z \notin V$. In the first case we are done. So suppose $c \xrightarrow[T]{*} v$. Since G" - FATHER[v] is connected (FATHER[v] might not even be a node of G") there must be a path $v_o,..,v_k$ from $v = v_o$ to $c = v_k$ avoiding FATHER[v]. Let v_i be the first node of that path which is not a descendant of v. As in the proof of part b) one shows LOWPT[v] $\leq$ DFSNUM[v_i] $<$ DFSNUM[FATHER[v]], a contradiction. This completes the proof of part c).

d) Immediate from the definition of LOWPT. □

Lemma 2 directly leads to an algorithm for finding the biconnected components of an undirected graph; in fact we can use our algorithm for strongly connected components with only three minor changes.

Change 1: Drop " and w ∈ CURRENT" from line (23).

Change 2: Change lines (27) and (28) to

(27') <u>if</u> DFSNUM[v] ≥ 2 and LOWPT[v] = DFSNUM[FATHER[v]]

(28') <u>then</u> delete all nodes w with DFSNUM[w] ≥ DFSNUM[v] from CURRENT (these nodes together with FATHER[v] form the b.c.c. with center v).

Change 3: Insert line (19a) just prior to call DFS(w) in line (20).

(19a) FATHER[w] ← v;

It is immediate from lemma 2,d that LOWPT is computed correctly and hence the centers of the b.c.c.'s are identified correctly in lines (27'). If v is a center then all tree descendants of v which are still on CURRENT, i.e. are not descendants of another center, together with FATHER[v] form the biconnected component with center v.

Finally, note that no membership testing on set CURRENT is done now and so it suffices to represent CURRENT as a pushdown store.

<u>Theorem 2:</u> The biconnected components of an undirected graph can be determined in time O(n + e).

<u>Proof:</u> Immediate from theorem 1 and the preceeding discussion. □

In our example we have LOWPT[f] = 3, LOWPT[g] = 6, LOWPT[e] =

LOWPT[d] = 2 and LOWPT[c] = LOWPT[b] = LOWPT[a] = 1. The first center encountered is f. Just prior to execution of line (27') in DFS(f) the content of CURRENT is a,b,c,f. In line (28') f is deleted. Then d,e and g are added to CURRENT and so prior to execution of (27') in DFS(g) the content of CURRENT is a,b,c,d,e,g. In line (28') g is removed. The next center found is d and so d and e will be removed. Finally, center b is found and c and b are removed in line (28 ') of DFS(b).

We close this section with an application of the s.c.c. algorithm to computing the transitive closure of digraphs. Let G = (V,E) be a digraph. Let $V_1,V_2,\dots,V_k$ be the (node sets of the) s.c.c.'s of G. Let G' = (V',E') be defined by

$$V' = \{V_1,\dots,V_k\}$$

$$E' = \{(V_i,V_j);\ \text{there are } v \in V_i,\ w \in V_j \text{ such that } (v,w) \in E\}$$

Then G' = (V',E') is an acyclic digraph. Let G'* = (V',E'*) be the transitive closure of G'. Then G = (V,E*) where

$$E^* = \{(v,w) \in E;\ v \in V_i,\ w \in V_j \text{ and } (V_i,V_j) \in E'^* \text{ for some i and j}\}$$

is the transitive closure of G. The process described above is easily turned into an algorithm. First, determine $V_1,\dots,V_k$ in time $O(n + e)$. Second, construct G' in time $O(n + e)$. Finally, compute the transitive closure of G' by the methods described in IV.3. in time $O(k^3)$. Finally, E* can be computed in time $e^* = |E^*|$ from G'*. We summarize in

<u>Theorem 3:</u> Let G = (V,E) be a digraph. Then the transitive closure of G can be computed in time $O(n + e^* + k^3)$ where e* is the number of edges in the transitive closure and k is the number of s.c.c.'s of G.

IV. 7. Least Cost Paths in Networks

A network N is a directed graph G = (V,E) together with a cost function $c : E \to \mathbb{R}$. We are interested in determining the least cost path from a fixed vertex s (the source) to all other nodes (the singlė source problem) or from each node to every other node (the all pairs problem). The latter problem is also treated in chapter V.

A path p from v to w is a sequence $v_0,v_1,\dots,v_k$ of nodes with $v = v_0$,

$w = v_k$ and $(v_i, v_{i+1}) \in E$ for $0 \le i < k$. The length of the path p is k and the cost c(p) of the path is $\sum_{i=0}^{k-1} c(v_i, v_{i+1})$. The cost of the path of length 0 is 0. The path above is simple if $v_i \neq v_j$ for $0 \le i < j < k$. We define the cost $\mu(u,v)$ of the least cost path from u to v by

$$\mu(u,v) = \inf \{c(p);\ p \text{ is a path from u to v}\}$$

, the infimum over the empty set being ∞.

<u>Example:</u> In the example we have $\mu(a,e) = 1$,

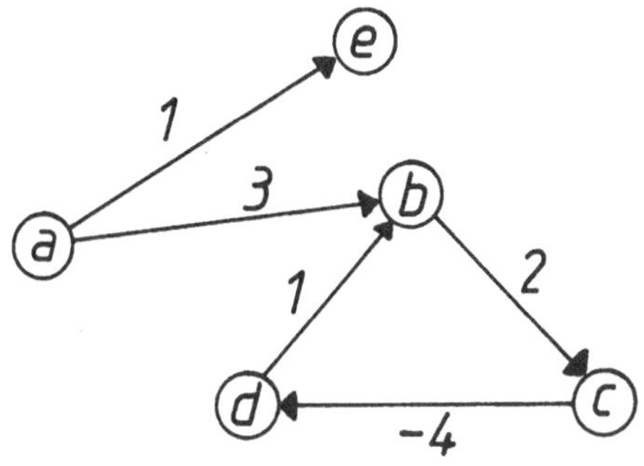

$\mu(e,a) = +\infty$, $\mu(a,b) = \mu(a,c) = \mu(a,d) = -\infty$ (Note that the path $ab(cdb)^i$ from a to b has length $1 + 3i$ and cost $3 - i$).

We will concentrate on the single source problem first, i.e. we are given a network $N = (V,E,c)$, $c : E \to \mathbb{R}$, and a node $s \in V$ and we have to determine $\mu(s,v)$ for all $v \in V$. Our algorithm for this problem is based on the following observation: The costs $\mu(s,v)$ certainly satisfy the triangle inequalities

$$\forall (u,v) \in E \quad \mu(s,u) + c(u,v) \ge \mu(s,v)$$

, i.e. a path from s to v which consists of a least cost path from s to u followed by the edge (u,v) can certainly be of no smaller cost than the least cost path from s to v. Furthermore, for every $v \neq s$ there must be at least one edge $(u,v) \in E$ such that $\mu(s,u) + c(u,v) = \mu(s,v)$, namely, let (u,v) be the last edge on a least cost path from s to v.

These observations lead to the following algorithm for determining least cost paths. We start with a function COST[v], $v \in V$, which overestimates $\mu(s,v)$; e.g. COST[s] = 0 and COST[v] = $+\infty$ for $v \neq s$ will do. Then we look for an edge (u,v) such that COST does not satisfy the triangle inequality with respect to edge (u,v), i.e. COST[u] + c(u,v) < COST[v]. Whenever such an edge is found we use it to reduce COST[v] to COST[u] + c(u,v).

In the following algorithm we not only compute the costs of the least cost paths but also the paths themselves, i.e. PATH[v] contains a path of cost COST[v] from s to v stored as a sequence of nodes. We use (s) to denote the path of length zero from s to s and we use PATH[u] cat v for extending a path from s to u to a path from s to v

```
(1)  COST[s] ← 0; PATH[s] ← (s);
(2)  for all v ∈ V, v ≠ s do  COST[v] ← ∞;
(3)                           PATH[v] ← undefined
(4)                        od;
(5)  while ∃(u,v) ∈ E : COST[u] + c(u,v) < COST[v]
(6)  do choose any edge (u,v) ∈ E with COST[u] + c(u,v) < COST[v];
(7)     COST[v] ← COST[u] + c(u,v);
(8)     PATH[v] ← PATH[u] cat v
(9)  od
```

The algorithm above is nondeterministic. Any edge violating the triangle inequality can be chosen in line (6). We will show that the correctness of the algorithm does not depend on the sequence of choices made, but the running time depends very heavily on it.

Let $N_n = (V_n, E_n, c_n)$ be the following network.

$$V_n = \{v_i, u_i, s_i;\ 0 \le i < n\} \cup \{s_n\}$$

$$E_n = \{(s_{i+1}, v_i),\ (s_{i+1}, u_i),\ (v_i, s_i),\ (u_i, s_i);\ 0 \le i < n\} \text{ and}$$

$c_n : E_n \to \mathbb{R}$ with

$$c_n((s_{i+1}, u_i)) = c_n((u_i, s_i)) = c((v_i, s_i)) = 0$$

$c_n((s_{i+1}, v_i)) = 2^i$. Also $s = s_n$.

(The figure shows N_3)

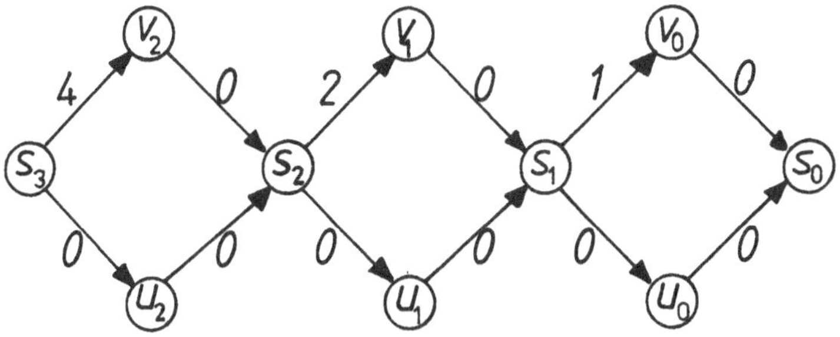

If the edges are chosen in the order (s_n,u_{n-1}), (u_{n-1},s_{n-1}), (s_n,v_{n-1}), (s_{n-1},u_{n-2}), (u_{n-2},s_{n-2}), (s_{n-1},v_{n-2}), ... in line (6) then the body of the while loop is executed exactly $|V_n| - 1 = 3n$ times.

Consider now the following inductively defined sequence S_n of choices. On N_1 we use $S_1 = (s_1,v_0), (v_0,s_0), (s_1,u_0), (u_0,s_0)$ of length 4 and on N_n we use $S_n = (s_n,v_{n-1}), (v_{n-1},s_{n-1})\ S_{n-1} (s_n,u_{n-1}), (u_{n-1},s_{n-1})\ S_{n-1}$ of length $|S_n| = 4 + 2 \cdot |S_{n-1}| = 4 \cdot (2^n - 1)$. Note that after using edges $(s_n,v_{n-1}), (v_{n-1},s_{n-1}), S_{n-1}$ we will have COST$[s_n] = 0$, COST$[u_{n-1}] = \infty$, and COST$[v] = 2^{n-1}$ for all other nodes v. Choosing edges (s_n,u_{n-1}), (u_{n-1},s_{n-1}) will reduce COST$[s_{n-1}]$ to zero. We can now run through sequence S_{n-1} again.

Lemma 1: a) $\mu(s,v) > -\infty$ for all $v \in V$ iff the algorithm terminates.

b) If the algorithm terminates then $\mu(s,v) =$ COST [v] for all $v \in V$ after termination.

Proof: a) "$\Rightarrow$": The following claim is easily proved by induction on the number of iterations of the loop.

Claim: Before any execution of line (6) the following is true: PATH[v] is a path of cost COST[v] from s to v and if PATH[v] $= (v_0,\ldots,v_k)$ then for all $i < k$ we have that $(v_0,\ldots,v_i)$ was the content of PATH$[v_i]$ previously.

Proof: Immediate from the formulation of the algorithm. □

We will show now that PATH[v] is always a simple path from s to v if $\mu(s,v) > -\infty$. Since the number of simple paths is finite this implies termination.

Assume to the contrary that PATH[v] may be a non-simple path from s to v, i.e. PATH[v] = $(v_0,\dots,v_i,\dots,v_j,\dots,v_k)$ and $u = v_i = v_j$ for some $i < j$. Then $p_1 = (v_0,\dots,v_i)$ as well as $p_2 = (v_0,\dots,v_i,\dots,v_j)$ was content of PATH[u] at some point during the execution of the algorithm. Also $c(p_2) < c(p_1)$ since COST[u] goes down whenever PATH[u] is changed. However, $c(p_2) - c(p_1)$ is the cost of the cycle $v_i,\dots,v_j$. So the graph contains a cycle of negative cost. Going around that cycle a large number of times we can make the cost of a path to v as small as want. Hence $\mu(s,v) = -\infty$, a contradiciton. This shows that PATH[v] is always a simple path.

"$\Leftarrow$": When the algorithm terminates we obviously have COST[v] $> -\infty$ for all $v \in V$ after termination. Hence this direction follows from part b).

b) Suppose that the algorithm terminates and $\mu(s,v) <$ COST[v] for some $v \in V$ after termination. Then there must be a path $p = (v_0,\dots,v_k)$ from $s = v_0$ to $v = v_k$ with cost $c(p) <$ COST[v]. Let $p_i = (v_0,\dots,v_i)$ be the prefix of p leading from s to v_i, $0 \le i < k$. There must be a minimal i such that $c(p_i) <$ COST[v_i] after termination. Since $c(p_0) = 0$ and COST[v_0] ≤ 0 (recall $s = v_0$) we deduce $i \ge 1$, and thus COST[v_{i-1}] $= c(p_{i-1})$ after termination. This implies

$$\begin{aligned} \text{COST}[v_i] > c(p_i) &= c(p_{i-1}) + c(v_{i-1},v_i) \\ &= \text{COST}[v_{i-1}] + c(v_{i-1},v_i) \end{aligned}$$

and hence the algorithm does not terminate because the triangle inequality for edge (v_{i-1},v_i) is violated. □

Lemma 1 states that the algorithm will terminate with the correct costs whenever $\mu(s,v) > -\infty$ for all $v \in V$. However, we have also seen that the sequence of choices made in line (6) has a crucial influence on the running time. Also we have to say more about the test in line (5). How do we find out that some edge violates the triangle inequality?

Note first that when the loop is entered for the first time only the edges out of s are candidates for selection in (6). Assume now that whenever an edge (u,v) is selected in (6) we will also check all other edges (u,v') out of u for satisfaction of the triangle inequality. Then the edges out of u do not have to be checked again until COST [u] is reduced. This observation leads to the following refinement of our basic algorithm.

```
(1)  COST[s] ← 0; U ← {s};
(2)  for all v ≠ s do  COST[v] ← + ∞ od;
(3)  while U ≠ ∅
(4)  do co if u ∉ U then COST[u] + c(u,v) ≥ COST[v] for all (u,v) ∈ E;
(5)     select any u ∈ U and delete u from U;
(6)     for all (u,v) ∈ E
(7)     do if COST[u] + c(u,v) < COST[v]
(8)        then COST[v] ← COST[u] + c(u,v);
(9)             add v to U;
(10)       fi
(11)    od
(12) od
```

Our main problem still remains: which point u to select from U in line (5). The following lemma states that U always contains at least one perfect choice: a node with COST[u] = $\mu(s,u)$.

Lemma 2: a) If $v \notin U$ then COST[v] + c(v,w) $\geq$ COST[w] for all $(v,w) \in E$.

b) Let $\infty > \mu(s,v) > -\infty$ and let $v_0,\ldots,v_k$ be a least cost path from $s = v_0$ to $v = v_k$. If COST[v] > $\mu(s,v)$ then there is an i, $0 \leq i < k$, such that $v_i \in U$ and COST[v_i] = $\mu(s,v_i)$.

c) If $\mu(s,v) > -\infty$ for all $v \in V$ then either $U = \emptyset$ or there exists $u \in U$ with COST[u] = $\mu(s,u)$.

d) If a node u with COST[u] = $\mu(s,u)$ is always chosen in line (5) then the body of the loop is executed at most n times.

Proof: a) (By induction on the number of executions of the while loop). The claim is certainly true before the first execution of the loop. Now suppose that $v \notin U$ after execution of the body. Then either $v \notin U$ before execution and then COST[v] has not changed and COST[w] for $w \neq v$ was not increased in the body of the loop and hence COST[v] + c(v,w) ≥ COST[w] by induction hypothesis or $v \in U$ before execution and then edge (v,w) was considered in lines (7) and (8) and hence COST[v] + c(v,w) ≥ COST[w] by the algorithm.

b) Let $i = \min \{j;\ COST[v_{j+1}] > \mu(s,v_{j+1})\}$. Then $i < k$ since $COST[v_k] > \mu(s,v_k)$ by assumption and $i \geq 0$ since $\mu(s,s) = 0$ (note that $\mu(s,s) < 0$ would imply $\mu(s,v) = +\infty$ or $\mu(s,v) = -\infty$ for all $v \in V$) and hence $\mu(s,s) = COST[s]$. Since $i \geq 0$ we have $COST[v_i] = \mu(s,v_i)$. If v_i were not in U then by part a) $\mu(s,v_{i+1}) = \mu(s,v_i) + c(v_i,v_{i+1})$ $= COST[v_i] + c(v_i,v_{i+1}) \geq COST[v_{i+1}]$, a contradiction to the definition of i. Thus $v_i \in U$.

c) Let $v \in U$ be arbitrary. If $COST[v] = \mu(s,v)$ then we are done. Otherwise there is a node $u \in U$ on the least cost path from s to v with $COST[u] = \mu(s,u)$ by part b).

d) If a node u with $COST[u] = \mu(s,u)$ is always chosen in line (5) then no node can reenter U after leaving U, since COST[u] is reduced whenever a node is added to U. Hence every node is deleted at most once from U; i.e. the body of the loop is executed at most n times. □

Lemma 2 states that U always contains at least one perfect choice for the selection process in line (5). Unfortunately, there is no known efficient method for making the perfect choice in the case of arbitrary real costs. We treat two special cases: acyclic networks (the underlying graph is acyclic) and non-negative networks ($c : E \rightarrow \mathbb{R}_{\geq 0}$ assigns non-negative costs to every edge). In these cases we obtain O(e) and O(e log n) algorithms respectively. In the general case we can only make sure that a good choice is made every O(n) iterations of the loop. This will lead to an $O(e \cdot n)$ algorithm.

IV. 7.1 Acyclic Networks

Let $G = (V,E)$ be an acyclic graph and $c : E \rightarrow \mathbb{R}$ be a cost function on the edges. We assume that G is topologically sorted, i.e. $V = \{1,\dots,n\}$ and $E \subseteq \{(i,j);\ 1 \leq i < j \leq n\}$ and $s = 1$. We saw in section 2 that a graph can be topologically sorted in time $O(n + e)$. We replace line (5) by

(5') select and delete $u \in U$ with u minimal

Then u is always a perfect choice, i.e. $COST[u] = \mu(s,u)$ when u is selected from U. By lemma 2 there must be a node $v \in U$ on the least cost path from s to u with $COST[v] = \mu(s,v)$. Since the graph is topologically sorted we must have $v \le u$ and hence $v = u$ by the definition of u.

Rule (5') steps through the nodes of G in increasing order. We can therefore do away with set U completely and rewrite the algorithm as

```
(1)  COST[1] ← 0;
(2)  for v ≥ 2 do COST[v] ← + ∞ od;
(3)  for u from 1 to n - 1
(4)  do for all (u,v) ∈ E
(5)     do COST[v] ← min (COST[v], COST[u] + c(u,v))
(6)     od
(7)  od
```

__Theorem 1:__ In acyclic graphs the single source least cost paths problem can be solved in time $O(n + e)$.

__Proof:__ Topological sorting takes time $O(n + e)$. The algorithm above clearly runs in time $O(n + e)$. □

IV. 7.2 Non-negative Networks

A network $N = (V,E,c)$ is non-negative if $c : E \to \mathbb{R}_{\ge 0}$ assigns non-negative costs to every edge. In this case we replace line (5) by

(5") select and delete $u \in U$ with $COST[u]$ minimal

Then u is always a perfect choice, i.e. $COST[u] = \mu(s,u)$ when u is selected from U. By lemma 2 there must be a node $v \in U$ on the least cost path from s to u with $COST[v] = \mu(s,v)$. Since u is selected we have $COST[u] \le COST[v]$ and since v is on the least cost path from s to u and edge costs are non-negative we have $\mu(s,v) \le \mu(s,u)$. Therefore $COST[u] \le COST[v] = \mu(s,v) \le \mu(s,u)$ and since $COST[u] \ge \mu(s,u)$ by the proof of lemma 1 we even have $COST[u] = \mu(s,u)$.

How should we implement set U? What operations are required on set U?

In line (5") we need to select and delete $u \in U$ with COST[u] minimal. This suggests to store set $\{(COST[u], u);\ u \in U\}$ in a priority queue PQ according to costs (cf. III.5.3.1.) in addition to having the costs stored in array COST[1..n]. Then line (5") corresponds to operation Min and Deletemin on priority queue PQ. The test in line (7) takes time O(1) using array COST. Lines (8) and (9) take time O(1) to change array COST. In addition, they require us to change priority queue PQ. If v is not in U then we have to add COST[v] to PQ, if v is in U then we have to reduce COST[v] from its old value to its new value. The latter operation requires that we can quickly find COST[v] in PQ given v. A good solution is to have an array P[1..n] of pointers to elements of PQ. We have P[v] = nil if $v \notin U$ and P[v] points to COST[v] in PQ if $v \in U$. In summary, the following operations (cf. III.5.3.1.) are required on PQ:

Min, Deletemin	line (5")
Insert, Demote*	lines (8) and (9)

We saw in section III.5.3.1. that Min, Deletemin take time O(a log n/log a) and Insert, Demote* take time O(log n/log a) if PQ is realized as an unordered (a,2a)-tree for integer $a \ge 2$. What is a good choice of a? Note that loop (3) - (12) is executed at most n times since no vertex is added to U twice by our choice of line (5"). Hence line (5") is executed at most n times. Moreover, lines (7) to (9) are executed at most once for each edge $(u,v) \in E$. Hence the total running time of the algorithm is

$$O(an \log n/\log a + e \log n/\log a)$$

Theorem 2: The single source least cost path problem on networks with non-negative edge costs can be solved in time

a) $O(n^2)$
b) $O(e \log n)$
c) $O(e \log n/\max(1, \log e/n))$

Proof: a) Choose a = n. In this case priority queue PQ is just a duplicate of array COST and is not needed at all. Also, array P is reduced to a bit vector. Finally, $u \in U$ with COST[u] minimal is determined by a complete scan of array COST.

b) Choose a = 2.

c) Choose a = max(2, e/n). □

It is worthwhile to look at theorem 2 for some particular values of e. If e = O(n) then running time is O(n log n), if $e = n^{1+1/k}$ then running time is O(ek). In particular, running time on dense graphs is linear.

In some applications edge costs are known to be drawn from some restricted domain, say from the set of integers between 0 and M. In this case priority queue PQ has to handle only M + 1 distinct values.

Lemma 3: If $c(u,v) \in \mathbb{N}_0$, $c(u,v) \le M$ for all $(u,v) \in E$ then $|COST[u] - COST[v]| \le M$ for all $u,v \in U$.

Proof: Let $u \in U$ be such that COST[u] is minimal and let $v \in U$ be arbitrary. Since $v \in U$ there must be $w \notin U$ (and hence $COST[w] \le COST[u]$) such that $COST[v] \le COST[w] + c(w,v) \le COST[u] + M$. □

Since PQ always contains values in range [a..a + M] for some integer a, we can efficiently store PQ as follows:

1) integer a

2) for $0 \le i \le M$ a list $L[i] = \{v \in U;\ COST[v] = a + i\}$

3) set $\{i;\ L[i] \ne \emptyset\}$.

We discuss two realizations of set $A = \{i;\ L[i] \ne \emptyset\}$ in more detail. The obvious implementation for set A is an implicit one, namely the array L[0..M] of headers for lists L[i]. With this implementation line (5") takes time O(M) and lines (7) to (9) take time O(1). Thus total running time is O(e + nM). A less obvious implementation is to use the fast priority queue of III.8.2. to store set A. With this implementation lines (5"), (7) to (9) take time O(log log M) each. Thus total running time is O((n + e)log log M).

Theorem 3: If $c(v,w) \in \mathbb{N}_0$, $c(v,w) \le M$ for all $(v,w) \in E$ then the single source least cost path problem can be solved in time O(min(e + nM, (n + e)log log M)).

Proof: Immediate from the discussion above. □

We will now turn to the one pair least cost path problem. Let $N = (V,E,c)$ be a network with non-negative edge costs and let s,t be two vertices of N. We want to compute $\mu(s,t)$, the cost of a least cost path from s to t. Of course, we can use our algorithms for the single source least cost path problem to compute $\mu(s,t)$. However, sometimes we can do better. In some applications, e.g. heuristic search in AI, wire routing in VLSI, branch and bound methods for solving optimization problems, one has estimates $g: V \to \mathbb{R}_+ \cup \{0\}$ for the cost of a path from $v \in V$ to t.

Definition: a) $g: V \to \mathbb{R}_+ \cup \{0\}$ is called estimator if for all $v \in V$:

(*) $\mu(s,v) + g(v) \le \min\{c(p);\ p \text{ is a path from s to t which goes through } v\}$

b) g is consistent if $g(v) \le c(v,w) + g(w)$ for every edge $(v,w) \in E$. □

Example: Let V be a set of points in the plane. Let E represent a set of streets between these points and let $c(v,w)$ be the length of the road from v to w. Assume that $c(v,w) \ge dist_2(v,w)$ where $dist_2(v,w)$ is the Euclidian distance of points v and w. Then $g(v) = dist_2(v,t)$ is a consistent estimator. □

Estimators can be used to direct the search for the least cost path from s to t. We replace line (5) by

(5"). Let $u \in U$ be such that COST[u] + g(u) is minimal

Example continued: Consider the following grid graph with all edge costs being 1. If we use $g_1 \equiv 0$ then all nodes shown are added to U and in the worst case also deleted. If we use $g_2(v) = dist_2(v,t)$ then only the nodes in the hatched region are ever removed from U. □

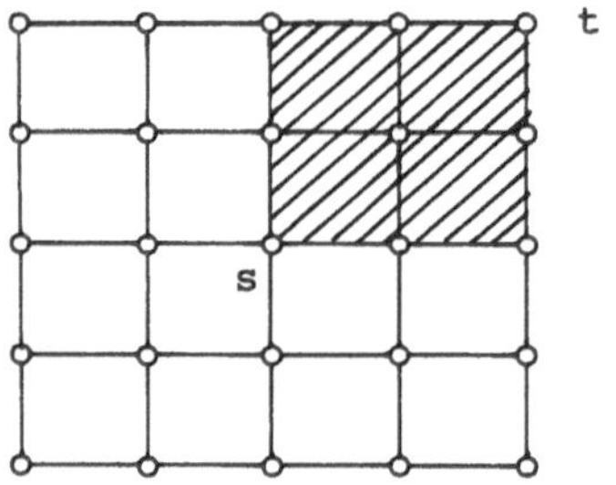

We can infer from this example that a good estimator can focus the search. This is made precise in

Theorem 4: a) Let $g: V \to \mathbb{R}$ be an estimator. Then $COST[t] = \mu(s,t)$ when t is removed from U. In addition, no node is removed twice from U when g is consistent.

b) Let $g_1, g_2: V \to \mathbb{R}$ be estimators. Let R_i, $i = 1,2$, be the set of nodes removed from U when estimator g_i is used. Then $R_1 \subseteq R_2$ if $g_i(v) > g_2(v)$ for all $v \in V - \{t\}$.

Proof: a) Let $v \in V$ be arbitrary and let p be a least cost path from s to v. When v is removed from U there is $u \in U$ such that u lies on p and $COST[u] = \mu(s,u)$ by lemma 2.

Let us apply this observation for $v = t$. We have

$$\mu(s,t) = c(p) \geq \mu(s,u) + g(u) = COST[u] + g(u)$$

since g is an estimator. Also $g(t) = 0$ since g is an estimator and hence $\mu(s,t) + g(t) \geq COST[u] + g(u) \geq COST[t] + g(t)$ since we assumed that t was removed prior to u. Thus $COST[t] = \mu(s,t)$ when t is removed from U.

Assume now that g is consistent and hence $g(u) \leq \mu(u,v) + g(v)$. We conclude further that $COST[v] + g(v) \leq COST[u] + g(u) = \mu(s,u) + g(u) \leq \mu(s,u) + \mu(u,v) + g(v) = \mu(s,v) + g(v) \leq COST[v] + g(v)$. (The first inequality holds since v is removed before u). Thus $COST[v] = \mu(s,v)$ when v is removed from U.

b) Assume otherwise, i.e. $R_1 - R_2 \neq \emptyset$. Let $v \in R_1 - R_2$ be arbitrary. We use Alg_i to denote our algorithm with estimator g_i and $COST_i[v]$ to denote the value of COST[v] when Alg_i terminates. Let p be a least cost path from s to v. Since Alg_2 never removes v from U there must be node u such that $COST_2[u] = \mu(s,u)$, $u \in U$ and u lies on p when Alg_2 terminates. We have

$$\begin{aligned} COST_2[u] + g_2(u) &= \mu(s,u) + g_2(u) \\ &< \mu(s,u) + g_1(u) \\ &\leq \mu(s,t) \end{aligned}$$

since g_1 is an estimator. Thus $COST_2[u] + g_2(u) < \mu(s,t) = COST_2[t] = COST_2[t] + g_2(t)$. Thus Alg_2 removes u from U instead of t, a contradiction. □

Theorem 4 has to be interpreted with care. Part a) states that the use of an estimator does not impede correctness and that the use of a consistent estimator does not impede efficiency. Part b) formulates a containment between sets, i.e. if $g_1(v) > g_2(v)$ for all $v \neq t$ then every node removed from U under use of g_1 will also be removed when g_2 is used. However, if g_1 is not consistent then nodes might be removed several times from U and hence the number of loop iterations might actually be larger when g_1 is used. If g_1 is consistent then part b) can be strengthened to $N_1 \leq N_2$ where N_i is the number of removals from U when estimator g_i is used.

IV. 7.3 General Networks

We will now treat the case of general networks $N = (V,E,c)$, $c: E \to \mathbb{R}$. In this case there is no known efficient method for always making a perfect choice. However, if U is organized as a queue, then between any subsequent selection of any one node we will have made one perfect choice.

More precisely, U is implemented as a queue UQ and a boolean array UB. We use UQ in order to select elements in line (4) on a first in-first out basis. Furthermore, we use the boolean array representation of U in order to test in line (11) whether v is already present in U and if not to add v to the end of the queue. The complete algorithm reads as follows:

```
(1)  COST[s] ← 0; UQ ← ∅; add s to the end of UQ;
     UB[s] ← true; COUNT[s] ← 0;
(2)  for all v ≠ s do COST[v] ← + ∞; COUNT[v] ← 0; UB[v] ← false od;
(3)  while UQ ≠ ∅
(4)  do let u be the first element in UQ;
(5)     COUNT[u] ← COUNT[u] + 1;
(6)     if COUNT[u] ≥ n + 1 then goto Exit fi;
(7)     delete u from UQ; UB[u] ← false;
(8)     for all (u,v) ∈ E
```

```
(9)      do if COST[u] + c(u,v) < COST[v]
(1o)        then COST[v] ← COST[u] + c(u,v);
(11)             if  ¬UB[v]
(12)             then add v to the end of UQ;
(13)                  UB[v] ← true
(14)             fi
(15)        fi
(16)     od;
(17) od
(18) Exit: if COUNT[v] = n + 1 for some v ∈ V
(19)        then "cycle of negative cost exists"
(2o)        else "COST[v] = μ(s,v) for all v ∈ V"
```

We have added the array of counters in order to ensure termination even in the presence of cycles of negative costs. We still have to argue that the counters do not impede correctness. Queue UQ is implemented as described in I.V., i.e. either by a linear list or by an array.

Theorem 5: In general networks the single source least cost path problems can be solved in time O(ne).

Proof: By virtue of the counters each node (except for maybe one) is selected at most n times in line (4). Whenever node v is chosen the time spent in lines (4) - (16) is O(outdegree(v)). Hence the total running time of the loop (4) - (17) is $n \cdot \sum_{v \in V} O(\text{outdegree}(v)) = O(n \cdot e)$. The cost of the statements outside the loop is clearly O(n). It remains to show correctness. We prove

Claim: Assume $\mu(s,u) > -\infty$ for all $u \in V$. Let v be arbitrary. Then v is selected at most n times in line (4).

Proof: Let U_i be set U when v is removed for the i-th time from U. Then U_i contains at least one element, say u_i, with $COST[u_i] = \mu(s,u_i)$ (lemma 2,c). Since U is organized as a queue u_i is deleted from U before v is deleted for the (i+1)-th time. Since u_i will never be added to U again (lemma 2,d), we have $i \le n$. □

In exercise 15 it is shown that the time bound may be improved to $O(k_{max} \cdot e)$ where k_{max} is the maximal length (number of edges) of a least cost path from s to any $v \in V$. In exercise 16 the algorithm above is related to dynamic programming. Alternative approaches to the single source least cost path problem are discussed in exercises 18 and 19. A fast algorithm for planar graphs is described in section IV.10..

Another improvement can be made for almost acyclic graphs. Let $G = (V,E)$ be a graph and let $V = V_1 \cup \ldots \cup V_k$ be the partition of V into strongly connected components. We order the SCC's such that $(v,w) \in E$, $v \in V_i$, $w \in V_j$ implies $i \le j$. Also we split the adjacency lists in two parts, the cyclic and the acyclic part. For each node $v \in V_i$, the cyclic part contains all edges (v,w) with $w \in V_i$, and the acyclic part contains all edges (v,w) with $w \in V_j$, $j > i$. We can now modify our algorithm as follows. There are k queues $UQ_1,\ldots,UQ_k$ one for each SCC. In line (4) we always select the first element, say u, of the first (smallest index) non-empty queue. Then in line (8) we only step through the cyclic part of u's adjacency list. Once a queue UQ_i becomes empty we step through the acyclic parts of the adjacency lists of all nodes $v \in V_i$ and update the costs of the other endpoints. An argument similar to the one used in the proof of theorem 5 shows that $v \in V_k$ is selected at most $|V_k|$ times from UQ_k (provided that $\mu(s,v) > -\infty$ for all v). Hence the running time is bounded by

$$O(e + \sum_{j=1}^{k} |V_j| \cdot |E_j|)$$

where (V_j,E_j), $1 \le j \le k$, are the scc's of graph G. If the scc's are small then this is a considerable improvement over theorem 5. Also note that the modified algorithm will work in linear time on acyclic networks.

<u>Theorem 6:</u> Let $N = (V,E,c)$ be a network and let (V_j,E_j), $1 \le j \le k$, be the strongly connected components of $G = (V,E)$. Then the single source least cost path problem can be solved in time

$$O(e + \sum_{j=1}^{k} |V_j|\ |E_j|)$$

IV. 7.4 The All Pairs Problem

We now extend the solution of the previous section to a solution of the all pairs least cost path problem; an alternative solution can be found in chapter V.

Let $N = (V,E,c)$ be a network. Suppose that we have a function $\alpha : V \to \mathbb{R}$ such that

$$\forall (u,v) \in E : \alpha(u) + c(u,v) \geq \alpha(v)$$

Consider cost function $\bar{c} : E \to \mathbb{R}$ with

$$\bar{c}(u,v) = \alpha(u) + c(u,v) - \alpha(v)$$

for all $(u,v) \in E$. Then $\bar{c}$ is a non-negative cost function. Let $\bar{\mu}(x,y)$ be the cost of the least cost path from x to y with respect to cost function $\bar{c}$. There is a very simple relation between μ and $\bar{\mu}$.

<u>Lemma 4:</u> Let μ and $\bar{\mu}$ be defined as above. Then $\bar{\mu}(x,y) = \mu(x,y) + \alpha(x) - \alpha(y)$.

<u>Proof:</u> Let $p = (v_o,\ldots,v_k)$ be any path from $x = v_o$ to $y = v_k$. Then

$$\bar{c}(p) = \sum_{i=o}^{k-1} \bar{c}(v_i,v_{i+1})$$

$$= \sum_{i=o}^{k-1} (\alpha(v_i) + c(v_i,v_{i+1}) - \alpha(v_{i+1}))$$

$$= \alpha(v_o) + \sum_{i=o}^{k-1} c(v_i,v_{i+1}) - \alpha(v_k)$$

$$= c(p) + \alpha(x) - \alpha(y)$$

Since p was an arbitrary path from x to y we infer $\bar{\mu}(x,y) = \mu(x,y) + \alpha(x) - \alpha(y)$. □

Lemma 4 tells us that we can reduce a general least cost path problem to a non-negative least cost path problem if we know a function α with the required properties. But solving one single source problem will give us (essentially) a function, namely $\mu(s,v)$, with the desired properties. There is only one problem we have to cope with: $\mu(x,v)$ might be infinite and the α's are required to be real. We will overcome this difficulty by augmenting the network as described below.

Theorem 7: The all pairs least cost path problem can be solved in time $O(n \cdot e \frac{\log n}{\max(1, \log(e/n))})$.

Proof: Let $N = (V,E,c)$ be a network and let $s \in V$ be arbitrary. In a first step we will extend N to a network $N' = (V,E',c')$ by adding some edges, namely $E' = E \cup \{(s,v);\ v \in V,\ v \neq s\}$ and

$$c'(u,v) = \begin{cases} c(u,v) & \text{if } (u,v) \in E \\ \text{large} & \text{if } (u,v) \in E' - E \end{cases}$$

where large $= \sum_{(u,v) \in E} |c(u,v)|$. Let $\mu(x,y)$ and $\mu'(x,y)$ be the cost of the least cost path from x to y in N and N' respectively. Then $\mu'(s,v) < +\infty$ for all $v \in V$ by virtue of the augmentation. Also N' con-contains a cycle of negative cost iff N contains a cycle of negative cost. This can be seen as follows: If N' contains a cycle of negative cost, then N' contains a simple cycle of negative cost. Let $v_o, \ldots, v_k$ where $v_o = v_k$ be a simple cycle of negative cost. Then each edge of E' is used at most once in this cycle. It cannot contain an edge of $E' - E$ because then the length of the cycle were at least large $- \sum_{(u,v) \in E} |c(u,v)| \geq 0$. Hence N contains a cycle of negative cost.

Next we use the algorithm of section 6.3. to find out whether N' (and hence N) has a cycle of negative cost and if not to determine $\mu(s,v)$ for all $v \in V$. In the first case the algorithm stops, in the second case we use $\alpha(v) = \mu(s,v)$ to transform the all pairs problem on a general network into a set of n single source problems on a non-negative network. Using the methods of 7.2. we obtain the time bound

$$O(e \cdot n + n \cdot e(\log n)/\max(1, \log(e/u))) \qquad \square$$

IV. 8. Minimum Spanning Trees

Let $N = (V,E,c)$ be an undirected network, i.e. (V,E) is an undirected graph and c is symmetric ($c(v,w) = c(w,v)$ for all $(v,w) \in E$). A tree $A = (V,T)$ with $T \subseteq E$, $|T| = n - 1$ is called a spanning tree of N. The cost of spanning tree A is $c(A) = \sum_{(v,w)\in T} c(v,w)$. It is a minimum spanning tree (least cost spanning tree) if $c(A) \le c(A')$ for all other spanning trees A'.

Example: A network and one of its minimum spanning trees.

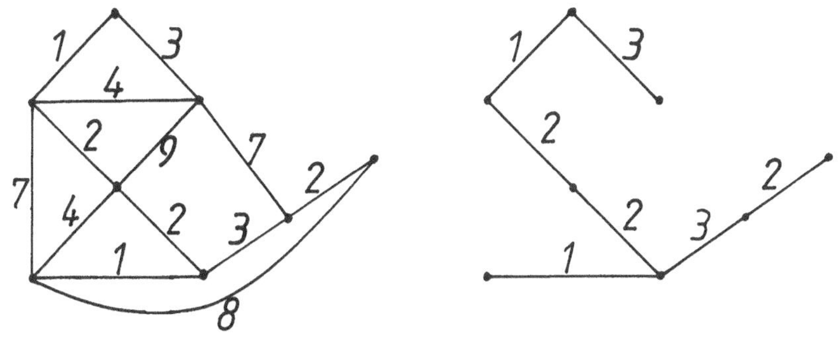

The following algorithm is a common skeleton for many algorithms for computing minimum spanning trees.

(1) **for** all $i \in V$ **do** $V_i \leftarrow \{i\}$; $T_i \leftarrow \emptyset$ **od**;
(2) **do** $n - 1$ **times**
(3) choose any non-empty V_i;
(4) choose $(v,w) \in E$ such that $v \in V_i$, $w \notin V_i$ and $c(v,w) \le c(v',w')$ for all $(v',w') \in E$ with $v' \in V_i$, $w' \notin V_i$;
(5) let j be such that $w \in V_j$;
(6) $V_i \leftarrow V_i \cup V_j$; $V_j \leftarrow \emptyset$;
(7) $T_i \leftarrow T_i \cup T_j \cup \{(v,w)\}$; $T_j \leftarrow \emptyset$
(8) **od**

Lemma 1: The algorithm above computes a minimum spanning tree.

Proof: We show by induction on $m = |T_1| + |T_2| + \dots + |T_n|$ that there is a minimum spanning tree $A = (V,T)$ with $T_i \subseteq T$ for all i. If $m = 0$ then there is nothing to show. So let us turn to the induction step. By induction hypothesis there is a minimum spanning tree with $T_i \subseteq T$ for all i. Let $(v,w) \in E$ be the edge chosen in line (4). If $(v,w) \in T$ then we are done. If $(v,w) \notin T$ then $(V, T \cup \{(v,w)\})$ contains a cycle. Hence there must be an edge $(v',w') \in T$ such that $v' \in V_i$, $w' \notin V_i$. We have $c(v,w) \le c(v',w')$ by the choice of (v,w). Hence $T - \{(v',w')\} \cup \{(v,w)\}$ is also a minimum spanning tree. Finally, case $m = n - 1$ implies the correctness of the algorithm. □

Various details are to be filled in. What set V_i should we choose in line 3, how do we find (v,w) in line (4) and how do we represent sets V_i. Let us resolve the latter problem first. We use the union-find data structure of section III.8.3. to represent sets V_i. Then line (6) is a Union operation (and we do n - 1 of those) and testing whether both endpoints of edge $(v,w) \in E$ belong to the same V_i corresponds to two Finds. Since this test has to be done at most once for every edge $(v,w) \in E$ the number of Finds is O(e). Thus the total cost of handling sets V_i is $O(e\ \alpha(e,n))$ where α was defined in section III.8.3..

The former questions are harder to resolve. We discuss three strategies: considering edges in order of increasing weight, always growing component V_1 and growing components uniformly.

Theorem 1: a) Let $E = \{e_1, e_2, \ldots\}$ be sorted according to cost, i.e. $c(e_1) \le c(e_2) \le \ldots$. Then a minimum spanning tree can be constructed in time $O(e\ \alpha(e,n))$.

b) A minimum spanning tree can be constructed in time O(e log n).

Proof: a) We replace lines (3) and (4) by

(3') let (v,w) be the next edge on E;
(4') while v and w belong to the same component
(4") do let (v,w) be the next edge on E od ;

Correctness of this refinement is immediate from lemma 1. Also the bound on the running time follows directly from the discussion above.

b) follows from part a) and the fact that we can sort the set of edges in time O(e log e) = O(e log n). □

We show next that we can improve upon theorem 1 for dense graphs.

Theorem 2: A minimum spanning tree can be constructed in time $O(e \log n / \max(1, \log(e/n)))$.

Proof: We always choose V_1 in line (3), i.e. we grow the spanning tree starting at node 1. In order to facilitate the selection of edge (v,w) in line (4) we maintain a priority queue PQ for set $\{(c(w),v,w); w \notin V_1\}$ ordered according to c(w) where $c(w) = \min\{c(u,w); u \in V_1\}$ and v is such that c(w) = c(v,w). With this definition line (4) corresponds to operation Deletemin on priority queue PQ. Suppose that edge (v,x) is chosen in line (4). In line (6) we have to add point x to V_1 and we have to update priority queue PQ. More precisely, for every edge $(x,w) \in E$ with $w \notin V_1$ we have to check whether $c(x,w) < c(w)$ and if so we have to change element (c(w), ,w) of PQ to (c(x,w),x,w). In order to do this efficiently we use an array P[1..n] of pointers. Pointer P[w] points to element (c(w), ,w) on PQ if $w \notin V_1$ and is nil otherwise. With the help of array P[1..n] line (6) reduces to O(deg(x)) operations Demote* (cf. III.5.3.1.) on priority queue PQ. Thus the cost of constructing a minimum spanning tree is the cost of n Deletemin operations and O(e) Demote* operations on PQ.

If we realize PQ as an (a,2a)-tree (cf. III.5.3.1.) with a = max(2,e/n) then the cost of a Delete is O(log n/log a). Hence total cost is O(e log n/log(e/n)). □

Theorem 2 is most significant for dense graphs. If $e = n^{1+1/k}$ for $k \in \mathbb{N}$ then running time is O(k e). For sparse graphs, say e = O(n), running time is O(n log n). Can we do better for sparse graphs? We close this section with a brief description of an O(n log log n) algorithm. This algorithm is based on two ideas, a strategy for growing components uniformly and a special purpose priority queue.

Put sets $V_1, V_2, \ldots, V_n$ into a queue Q and replace lines (3) and (6) by

(3") let V_i be the first element of queue Q

and

(6"a) delete V_i and V_j from Q;
(6"b) $V_i \leftarrow V_i \cup V_j$; $V_j \leftarrow \emptyset$;
(6"c) add V_i to the end of Q;

The selection strategy described above selects components in a round-robin fashion. For the analysis we conceptually divide the algorithm into stages. Stages are defined as follows. We add a special marker to the end of Q initially and start stage 0. Whenever the special marker appears at the front of queue Q we finish a stage, move the marker to the end of the queue, and start the next stage.

Lemma 2: a) All sets selected at line (3'') in stage k have size at least 2^k and all sets produced in line (6"b) have size at least 2^{k+1}

b) the number of stages is at most log n.

Proof: a) We use induction on k. The claim is clearly true for k = 0. If V_i is chosen in stage k > 0 and combined with V_j then V_i and V_j were created in stage k - 1 and hence have size at least 2^k each by induction hypothesis. Thus $|V_i \cup V_j| \geq 2^{k+1}$

b) the algorithm terminates when a set of size n is produced in line (6). Hence the maximal stage number k must satisfy $2^{k+1} \leq n$. □

Lemma 2 has an important consequence. Call a point v active during an iteration of loop (2) - (8) if v belongs to component V_i selected in line (3''). Then any node v can be active at most once in a stage and hence can be active at most log n times by lemma 2b. In other words, any fixed node v has to be considered at most log n times in line (4).

We can use this fact to derive another O(e log n) algorithm as follows:

In line (4) we look at all nodes $v \in V_i$ and determine the least cost edge (v,w) with $w \notin V_i$. This can certainly be done in time O(deg(v)). Since a node is active at most log n times the total cost of this algorithm is $O(\sum_v \deg(v) \log n) = O(e \log n)$.

In order to obtain an O(e log log n) algorithm we need two additional concepts: shrinking the graph and a special purpose priority queue. Suppose that we execute the algorithm above for log log n stages; this will take O(e log log n) time units and builds up components of at least $2^{\log\log n} = \log n$ vertices each; let $V_1,\ldots,V_m$, $m \leq n/\log n$, be the components after stage log log n. Define network $N' = (V',E',c')$ as follows. $V' = \{1,\ldots,m\}$; $E' = \{(i,j);\ \exists\, v \in V_i,\ w \in V_j$ such that $(v,w) \in E\}$ and $c'(i,j) = \min\{c(v,w);\ v \in V_i,\ w \in V_j\}$. N' can be constructed from N in time O(e); cf. exercise 2. It remains to compute a minimum spanning tree of N'. For every node v of N' we divide the edges incident to v into deg(v)/log n groups of log n edges each. We sort each group for a cost of O((log n)log log n) time units per group. Thus total preprocessing time is O(e log log n).

In line (4) we proceed as follows. For every node $v \in V_i$ we inspect every group. For every group we inspect edges in order of increasing cost and throw away edges which do not lead outside V_i. After this process we are left with $\lceil deg(v)/log\ n \rceil$ edges leading from v to nodes outside V_i. In time $O(\lceil deg(v)/log\ n \rceil)$ we can certainly find the one of minimal cost. Thus the cost of finding minimum cost edges ouf of v is O(1 + deg(v)/log n + number of discarded edges) per stage. Since every edge is discarded at most once, since there are only log n stages and since N' has only n/log n nodes total cost is O(n + e). We have

Theorem 3: A minimum cost spanning tree of an undirected network can be computed in time O(e log log n).

Proof: By the discussion above. □

A final improvement can be made for planar networks. In a planar graph we always have $e \le 3n - 2$, cf. IV.10, lemma 2. Suppose that we apply the shrinking process after every stage. Let N_i be the network after stage i. Then N_i is planar and hence $e_i \le 3n_i - 2$ where e_i (n_i) is the number of edges (nodes) of network N_i. Also stage i + 1 takes $O(e_i)$ time units and N_{i+1} can be constructed from N_i in time $O(e_i)$. Thus total cost is $\sum_{i=1}^{\log n} O(e_i) = O(\sum_{i=1}^{\log n} n_i) = O(\sum_{i=1}^{\log n} n/2^i) = O(n)$.

Theorem 4: Let N = (V,E,c) be a planar undirected network. Then a minimum cost spanning tree can be computed in time O(n).

IV. 9. Maximum Network Flow and Applications

IV. 9.1 Algorithms for Maximum Network Flow

A directed network N = (V,E,c) consists of a directed graph G = (V,E) and a capacity function $c: E \to \mathbb{R}_+$. Let $s,t \in V$ be two designated vertices, the source s and the sink t. A function $f: E \to \mathbb{R}$ is a legal (s,t)-flow function (or legal flow for short) if it satisfies

a) the capacity constraints, i.e. $0 \le f(e) \le c(e)$ for all $e \in E$

b) the conservation laws, i.e. $\sum_{e \in in(v)} f(e) = \sum_{e \in out(v)} f(e)$ for all nodes $v \in V - \{s,t\}$. Here in(v) (out(v)) is the set of edges leaving (entering) v.

If $f: E \to \mathbb{R}$ is a legal flow function then $val(f) = \sum_{e \in out(s)} f(e) - \sum_{e \in in(s)} f(e)$ is the flow value of f. The maximum network flow problem is to compute a legal flow function with maximum flow value. In this section we will describe two algorithms for achieving this goal. On the way we will derive a powerful combinatorial result: the max flow - min cut theorem.

Definition: An (s,t)-cut is a partition S,T of V, i.e. $V = S \cup T$, $S \cap T = \emptyset$, such that $s \in S$, $t \in T$. The capacity of cut (S,T) is given by

$$c(S,T) = \sum_{e \in E \cap (S \times T)} c(e)$$ □

The capacity of a cut (S,T) is thus the total capacity of all edges going from S to T. The easy direction of the min cut - max flow is given by:

Lemma 1: Let f be a legal flow and let (S,T) be an (s,t)-cut. Then

$$val(f) \le c(S,T)$$

Proof: We have

$$val(f) = \sum_{e \in out(s)} f(e) - \sum_{e \in in(s)} f(e)$$

$$= \sum_{v \in S} [\sum_{e \in out(v)} f(e) - \sum_{e \in in(v)} f(e)]$$

since the conservation law holds for all $v \in S - \{s\}$.

$$= \sum_{e \in E \cap (S \times T)} f(e) - \sum_{e \in E \cap (T \times S)} f(e)$$

since every edge $e = (u,v) \in E \cap (S \times S)$ is counted twice, positively since $e \in out(u)$ and negatively since $e \in in(v)$

$$\leq c(S,T)$$

since $f(e) \leq c(e)$ for all $e \in E \cap (S \times T)$ and $f(e) \geq 0$ for all $e \in E \cap (T \times S)$. □

Most algorithms for maximum network flow work iteratively and are based on the concept of augmenting path , i.e. they start with any legal initial flow, say the flow function which is zero everywhere, and then use augmenting paths to increase flow. In the following example we use edge label a/b to denote capacity a and flow b. There are three

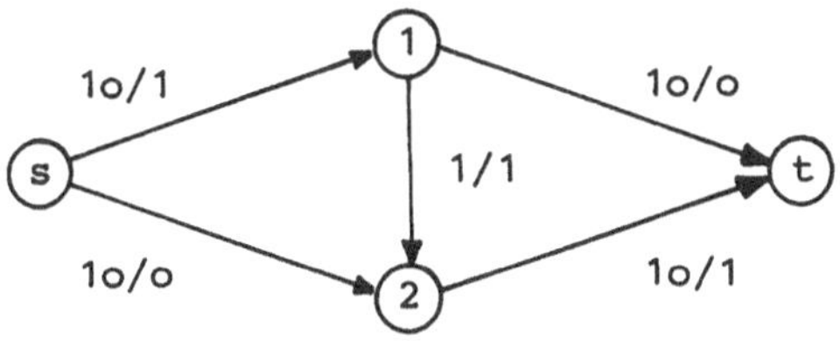

augmenting paths in this example; s,1,t with bottleneck value 9, s,2,t with bottleneck value 9, and s,2,1,t with bottleneck value 1. Paths s,1,t and s,2,t can be used to increase the flow value by 9 in an obvious way. Usage of path s,2,1,t is more subtle. We might send one additional unit from s to 2. This frees us from the obligation to push one unit from 1 to 2 and we can therefore send this unit directly from 1 to t. Augmentation algong path s,2,1,t changes the flow into

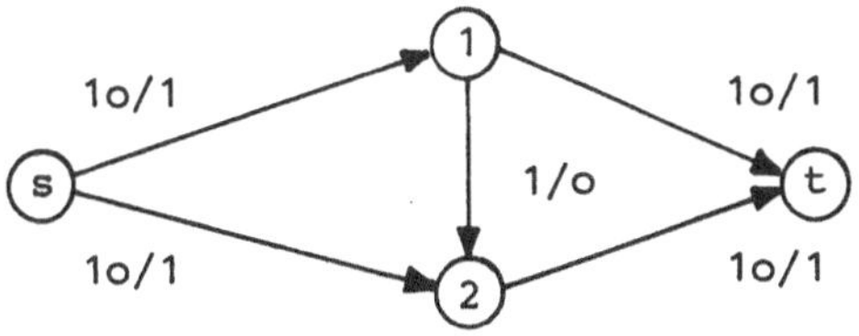

All shortest (=minimum cardinality) augmenting paths are captured in the layered (augmenting) network LN which is defined with respect to legal flow function f as follows.

Let $E_1 = \{(v,w);\ (v,w) \in E \text{ and } f(e) < c(e)\}$ and let

$E_2 = \{(w,v);\ (v,w) \in E \text{ and } f(e) > 0\}$, i.e. edges in E_1 can be used to push flow forward and edges in E_2 can be used to push flow backward. If $e = (v,w) \in E$ then we use e_1 to denote edge $(v,w) \in E_1$ (if it is there) and e_2 to denote edge $(w,v) \in E_2$ (if it is there). Also $\bar{c}: E_1 \cup E_2 \to \mathbb{R}$ is given by $\bar{c}(e_1) = c(e) - f(e)$ for $e_1 \in E_1$ and $\bar{c}(e_2) = f(e)$. Note that $E_1 \cup E_2$ is a multiset. In our first example we obtain (edges in E_1 are drawn solid and edges in E_2 are drawn dashed):

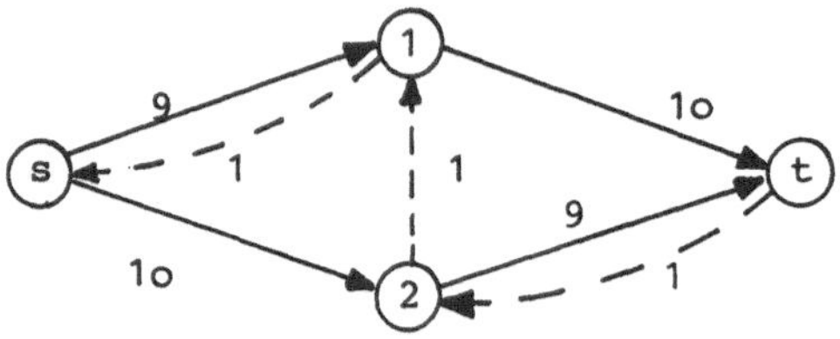

Next, let $V_o = \{s\}$, let

$$V_{i+1} = \{w \in V - (V_1 \cup \ldots \cup V_i);\ \exists\, v \in V_i\ (v,w) \in E_1 \cup E_2\}$$

for $i \geq 0$, and let $\bar{V} = \bigcup_{i \geq 0} V_i$. Then $LN = (\bar{V}, (E_1 \cup E_2) \cap \bigcup_{i \geq 0} (V_i \times V_{i+1}), \bar{c})$ is the layered network with respect to flow function f. In our example we obtain

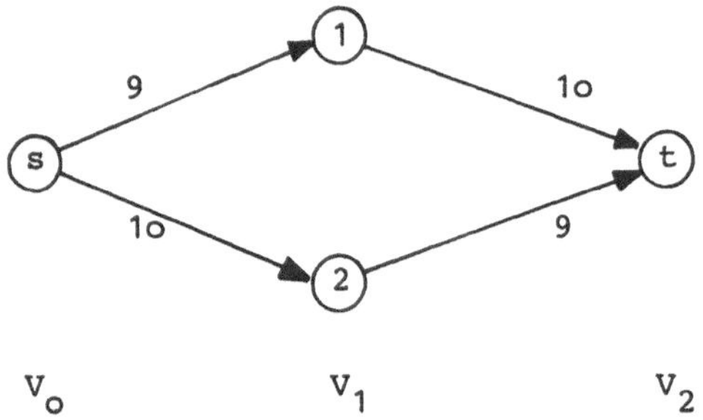

Any path from s to t in the layered network is an augmenting path and can be used to increase flow. More generally, we have

<u>Lemma 2:</u> Let f be a legal (s,t)-flow in network N and let $LN = (\bar{V}, \bar{E}, \bar{c})$ be the layered network with respect to f.

a) f is a maximal flow iff $t \notin \bar{V}$

b) Let $\bar{f}$ be a legal (s,t)-flow in LN. Then $f_1: E \to \mathbb{R}$ with

$$f_1(e) = f(e) + \bar{f}(e_1) - \bar{f}(e_2)$$

is a legal flow in N with flow value val(f) + val($\bar{f}$).

Proof: b) We have to show that f_1 satisfies the capacity constraints and the conservation law. Let $e \in E$ be arbitrary. Then

$$\begin{aligned} 0 &\le f(e) - \bar{f}(e_2) && \text{since } f(e_2) = \bar{c}(e_2) \ge \bar{f}(e_2) \\ &\le f_1(e) && \text{since } \bar{f}(e_1) \ge 0 \\ &\le f(e) + \bar{f}(e_1) && \text{since } \bar{f}(e_2) \ge 0 \\ &\le c(e) && \text{since } \bar{f}(e_1) \le \bar{c}(e_1) = c(e) - f(e) \end{aligned}$$

, i.e. f_1 satisfies the capacity constraints. Next, let $v \in V - \{s,t\}$ be arbitrary. Then

$$\sum_{e \in out(v)} f_1(e) - \sum_{e \in in(v)} f_1(e)$$

$$= \sum_{e \in out(v)} f(e) - \sum_{e \in in(v)} f(e) + \Big[\sum_{e \in out(v)} \bar{f}(e_1) + \sum_{e \in in(v)} \bar{f}(e_2)\Big]$$

$$- \Big[\sum_{e \in in(v)} \bar{f}(e_1) + \sum_{e \in out(v)} \bar{f}(e_2)\Big] = 0 + 0$$

since f and $\bar{f}$ satisfy the conservation laws. Note that $e_2 \in E_2$ emanates from node v if $e \in in(v)$ and that e_2 ends in node v if $e \in out(v)$.

Finally, the flow value of f_1 is clearly val(f) + val($\bar{f}$).

a) "⇒": If $t \in \bar{V}$ then there is a path from s to t in the layered network. Let p be any such path and let $\varepsilon > 0$ be the minimal capacity of any edge of p. Then there is clearly a flow of value ε in LN, namely $\bar{f}(e) = \varepsilon$ for all edges e of p and $\bar{f}(e) = 0$ otherwise. Hence f is not maximal by part b).

"⇐": Let $S = \bar{V}$ and let $T = V - S$. Then $s \in S$ and $t \in T$, i.e. (S,T) is an (s,t)-cut. Furthermore, $(E_1 \cup E_2) \cap (S \times T) = \emptyset$ since no node of T is added to the layered network. Thus $f(e) = c(e)$ for $e \in S \times T$ and $f(e) = 0$ for $e \in T \times S$. We conclude that the last inequality in the proof of lemma 1 turns into an equality and hence val(f) = c(S,T). Since val(f') ≤ c(S,T) for any legal flow f' we infer that f is a flow with maximal flow value. □

It seems that we have not gained very much. In order to increase the flow through network N we have to find a (large) legal flow through layered network LN. Fortunately, an approximation to the maximal flow in LN is good enough. More precisely, it suffices to compute a blocking flow in LN.

Definition: A legal flow $\overline{f}$ in layered network LN is blocking if for every path $s = v_0 \xrightarrow{e_1} v_1 \xrightarrow{e_2} v_2 \rightarrow \ldots \xrightarrow{e_k} v_k = t$ from s to t at least one of the edges is saturated, i.e. $\overline{f}(e_i) = \overline{c}(e_i)$ for at least one i, $1 \le i \le k$. □

We can now outline the basic maximum flow algorithm.

```
(1)  let f(e) ← 0 for all e ∈ E;
(2)  construct layered network LN = (V̄,Ē,c̄) from f;
(3)  while t ∈ V̄
(4)  do find a blocking flow f̄ in LN;
(5)     update f by f̄ as described in lemma 2,b;
(6)     construct layered network LN from f
(7)  od
```

Two questions arise: How can we find a blocking flow in a layered network and how many iterations are required? We turn to the second question first.

Definition: Let f be a (non-maximal) legal flow in N and let LN be the layered network for f. Then k, where $t \in V_k$, is called the depth of LN.

Lemma 3: Let k_i be the depth of the layered network used in the i-th iteration, i = 1,2,... . Then $k_i > k_{i-1}$ for $i \ge 2$.

Proof: Let LN_i be the layered network used in the i-th iteration. In LN_i there is a path p of length k_i from s to t.

$$s = v_0 \xrightarrow{e_1} v_1 \xrightarrow{e_2} v_2 \xrightarrow{e_3} \ldots \longrightarrow v_{k_i-1} \xrightarrow{e_{k_i}} v_{k_i} = t$$

For $0 \le j \le k_i$, let d_j be the length (= number of edges) of the shortest path from s to v_j in LN_{i-1}, i.e. v_j belongs to the d_j's layer of LN_{i-1}.

If v_j is not a node of LN_{i-1} then $d_j = \infty$.

<u>Claim:</u> For all $i \geq 2$:

a) If there is an edge from v_{j-1} to v_j in LN_{i-1} then $d_j = d_{j-1} + 1$.

b) If there is no edge from v_{j-1} to v_j in LN_{i-1} then $d_j \leq d_{j-1}$

c) $k_{i-1} < k_i$

<u>Proof:</u> a) is immediate since network LN_{i-1} is layered, i.e. if v_{j-1} belongs to the d_{j-1}'s layer and there is an edge from v_{j-1} to v_j in LN_{i-1} then v_j belongs to layer $d_{j-1} + 1$.

b) Let us assume for the sake of contradiction that $d_j \geq d_{j-1} + 1$. Let $f_{i-1}(f_i)$ be the flow in network N which gives rise to the construction of layered network $LN_{i-1}(LN_i)$. Then $f_{i-1}(v_{j-1}, v_j) = c(v_{j-1}, v_j) > f_i(v_{j-1}, v_j)$ if $(v_{j-1}, v_j) \in E$ or $f_{i-1}(v_j, v_{j-1}) = 0 < f_i(v_j, v_{j-1})$ if $(v_j, v_{j-1}) \in E$ because $(v_{j-1}, v_j) \notin \bar{E}_{i-1}$ and $(v_{j-1}, v_j) \in \bar{E}_i$. In either case we conclude that $(v_j, v_{j-1}) \in \bar{E}_{i-1}$ and hence $d_{j-1} = d_j + 1$. Thus $d_j = d_{j-1} - 1 \leq d_{j-1}$, a contradiction.

c) Since $v_0 = s$ and hence $d_0 = 0$ we conclude $d_j \leq j$ from parts a) and b). Also, $d_j = j$ for all $j \leq k_i$ is only possible if edge e_j from v_{j-1} to v_j is present in LN_{i-1} for all $j \geq 1$. Thus $d_j = j$ for all $j \leq k_i$ implies that there is some path p from s to t which exists in LN_{i-1} and LN_i. This contradicts the fact that f_i is obtained from f_{i-1} by "adding" a blocking flow with respect to layered network LN_{i-1}.

We conclude that $d_j < j$ for some $j < k_i$ and hence $d_{k_i} < k_i$ by parts a) and b). We can now complete the proof of the claim and the lemma by observing that $k_{i-1} = d_{k_i}$. □□

<u>Corollary 1:</u> The number of iterations is at most n.

<u>Proof:</u> Let k_i be the depth of the layered network used in the i-th iteration, $i \geq 1$. Then $k_1 \geq 1$ since $s \neq t$, $k_{i-1} < k_i$ by lemma 3 and $k_i \leq n$ for all i. Hence the number of iterations is at most n. □

Better bounds on the number of iterations can be derived for restricted networks. In particular, we will derive considerably smaller bounds for 0 - 1 networks in section IV.9.2.. It remains to design efficient algorithms for constructing blocking flows in layered networks. We will first describe an $O(n^2)$ algorithm and then an $O(e(\log n)^2)$ algorithm.

Let $LN = (V,E,c)$ be a layered network, i.e. $V = \bigcup_{0\le i\le k} V_i$ for some k, $E \subseteq \bigcup_{0\le i<k} (V_i \times V_{i+1})$, $V_0 = \{s\}$ and $c: E \to \mathbb{R}_+$. We may assume w.l.o.g., i.e. the condition can be enforced in linear time by simple graph exploration, that every node $v \in V$ is reachable from s and that t can be reached from all nodes. In particular, $V_k = \{t\}$ in this case. The $O(n^2)$ algorithm is based on the concept of potential of a node. Let f be a legal flow and let $v \in V$. The potential of node v with respect to flow f is given by

$$PO(v) = \min[\sum_{e\in out(v)} c(e) - f(e), \sum_{e\in in(v)} c(e) - f(e)]$$

, i.e. the potential of node v is the maximal possible increase in flow through node v. Also

$$PO^* = \min\{PO(v);\ v \in V\}$$

is the minimal potential of any node in V. It is now quite simple to increase the flow by PO*. Let v be any node with PO(v) = PO*. Starting at node v we forward PO* additional units from node v through higher layers to node t and we suck PO* additional units of flow into node v through lower layers. Forwarding flow is done as follows. We proceed layer by layer, starting at the layer containing v. When we consider layer V_ℓ we have determined a subset $S_\ell \subseteq V_\ell$ of nodes which hold an additional amount of PO* units of flow, i.e. $PO^* = \sum_{x\in S_\ell} S(x)$ where S(x) is the excess of flow available in node $x \in S_\ell$. We consider the nodes in S_ℓ in turn and push their excess of flow into the next layer. Since $PO^* \le PO(w)$ for all w no node can receive more flow than he can handle. We continue in this fashion until we pushed the additional flow all the way to t . Similarly, we work our way back from node v towards source s and suck PO* additional units of flow into the network. In this way we increase the flow by PO* units. After having done so, we simplify the network by deleting saturated edges, and useless nodes, i.e. nodes which are not connected to either s or t, and edges incident upon useless nodes. Note that at least node v will be deleted from the network (Remark: Note that it would simplify the algorithm if we would forward the additional flow starting at s. Correctness would not be impeded, however efficiency might suffer). If the network is not empty after simplification we repeat the process. Since simplification deletes at least one node from the network the number of iterations is clearly O(n).

We will next describe the algorithm in more detail. We assume that for every node $v \in V$ the set of ingoing and outgoing edges are ordered in some way. Also set $S_\ell \subseteq V_\ell$ is realized as a bit vector and a linear list. In this way we can test $v \in S_\ell$, add to S_ℓ and delete some element from S_ℓ in time O(1). In addition, we store for every node $x \in X$ the excess (deficit) of flow available at node x in S[x]. The following procedure FORWARD is basic for the algorithm; it forwards flow from node x into the next layer. There is a symmetric procedure SUCK which sucks flow into node x from the previous layer.

```
(1)  proc FORWARD(x,S,h);
     --   x is a node in layer V_h and there are S units of
     --   additional flow available in x. These S units are
     --   pushed into nodes in layer V_{h+1}
(2)  while S > 0
(3)  do let e = (x,y) be the first edge out of x;
(4)     delta ← min(S,c(e) - f(e));
(5)     increase flow along e by delta, add y to S_{h+1} (if it is not
        already there), increase S[y] by delta, and decrease c(e) by
        delta;
(6)     S ← S - delta;
(7)     if c(e) = 0 then delete e from the graph fi
(8)  od;
(9)  remove x from S_h and set S[x] to zero;
(10) if (out(x) = ∅ and x ≠ t) or (in(x) = ∅ and x ≠ s)
(11) then add x to set DEL fi
(12) end
```

In set DEL we collect all nodes which have to be deleted from the network because either they cannot be reached from s or t cannot be reached from them. The running time of a call to FORWARD is O(1 + # of edges deleted in line (7)), because in every execution of the loop body (except maybe the last) an edge is deleted and since the cost outside the loop is clearly O(1). The complete algorithm for computing a blocking flow is given by:

```
(1)  for all x ∈ V do S[x] ← 0 od;
(2)  for all ℓ, 0 ≤ ℓ ≤ k do S_ℓ ← ∅ od;
(3)  DEL ← ∅;
(4)  while LN is not empty
(5)  do compute PO[v] for all v ∈ V, let PO* = min{PO[v]; v ∈ V} and
        let v ∈ V_ℓ be such that PO* = PO[v];
(6)     S[v] ← PO*; S_ℓ ← {v};
(7)     for h from ℓ to k - 1
(8)     do for x ∈ S_h do FORWARD(x,S[x],h) od od;
(9)     S[v] ← PO*; S_ℓ ← {v};
(10)    for h from ℓ step - 1 to 1
(11)    do for x ∈ S_h do SUCK(x,S[x],h) od od;
(12)    SIMPLIFY(DEL)
(13) od
```

Procedure SIMPLIFY(DEL) removes all nodes (and edges incident to them) in DEL from the network. Also if some other node z looses its last ingoing (outgoing) edge during this process then z is also deleted. It is easy to see that SIMPLIFY can be implemented to run in time proportional to the number of nodes and edges removed from the graph; an algorithm similar to the algorithm used for topological sorting will do. The details are left to the reader (exercise 27).

Theorem 2: Let LN be a layered network. Then a blocking flow can be computed in time $O(n^2)$.

Proof: a) Correctness of the algorithm follows from the fact that nodes (edges) are removed only if all paths from s to t through that node (edge) are blocked.

The cost of lines (1) - (3) is clearly O(n). Also, loop (4) - (13) is executed O(n) times since at least one node, namely v, is removed from the graph in line (12). The cost of an execution of the loop body outside the calls to FORWARD, SUCK and SIMPLIFY is clearly O(n) and hence $O(n^2)$ if summed over all O(n) iterations. Since the cost of a call to FORWARD(SUCK) is O(1 + # deleted edges), since FORWARD(SUCK) is called at most once for each node during an execution of the loop body and since every edge is deleted at most once the total cost of all calls to FORWARD(SUCK) is $O(n^2 + e) = O(n^2)$. Finally the total cost of all calls to SIMPLIFY is O(e). □

The algorithm can be made to run faster in (0 - 1)-networks, i.e. networks where $c(e) = 1$ for all $e \in E$. Exercise 28 describes an implementation with running time O(e). We will later describe a simpler O(e) algorithm for computing blocking flows in (0 - 1)-networks.

Theorem 3: Let $N = (V,E,c)$, $s,t \in V$ be a network. Then a maximum flow from s to t can be computed in time $O(n^3)$.

Proof: A maximum flow can be computed by O(n) applications of the blocking flow algorithm to layered networks. Construction of the layered network and computation of a blocking flow takes time $O(n^2)$. The time bound follows. □

It is now easy to derive the min-cut max-flow theorem.

Theorem 4: Let $N = (V,E,c)$, $s,t \in V$ be a network. Let fmax be the maximal flow value of any (s,t)-legal flow function and let cmin be the minimal capacity of all (s,t)-cuts. Then

$$\text{fmax} = \text{cmin}$$

Proof: Note first that cmin exists because there are only a finite number of (s,t)-cuts. Also, fmax exists because we have an $O(n^3)$ algorithm to compute a maximal flow from s to t. It remains to show fmax = cmin. We have fmax $\le$ cmin by lemma 1. Finally, let f be a flow function with val(f) = fmax. If we construct the layered network with respect to f then t is not added to the network. Lemma 2, a shows how to construct an (s,t)-cut (S,T) such that fmax = val(f) = c(S,T). Since c(S,T) $\ge$ cmin, this proves fmax $\ge$ cmin. □

Our second algorithm for computing flows is based on DFS and is particularly well suited for sparse networks, i.e. $e \ll n^2$. The basic idea is quite simple. Starting at s we construct a path by always taking the first edge out of every node until we either reach t or reach a dead-end v, i.e. a node v with $out(v) = \emptyset$ and $v \neq t$. In the second case we back up one node, delete all edges leading into v from the graph and continue. In the first case we compute the bottle neck capacity ε of the path, i.e. the minimal capacity of any edge on the path, increase the flow along the path by ε, and delete all saturated edges from the graph. Having done so, we construct the next path starting at node s.

Theorem 5: The algorithm above constructs a blocking flow in a layered network in time O(en). In a (0-1)-network it runs in time O(e).

Proof: Correctness is obvious. The bound on the running time is derived as follows. Observe first, that a path from s to t is constructed in time O(k + # of edges found to be ending in dead-ends) and that at least one edge on the path is saturated by increasing the flow. Hence at most O(e) paths are constructed for a total cost of O(ke + e) = O(en).

One additional observation is needed for (0-1)-networks. In (0-1)-networks all edges on the constructed path are satured and hence the cost of constructing a path from s to t is proportional to the number of deleted edges. The claimed bound follows. □

We will next describe an improved implementation of the algorithm above which reduces the time bound to $O(e(\log n)^2)$. In the algorithm above, whenever we succeed in constructing a path from s to t we saturate some (in general only a few) of its edges, delete the saturated edges and then forget everything about the constructed path. A more economical way to proceed is to keep the remnants of the path as path fragments (PFs). In the example below we split

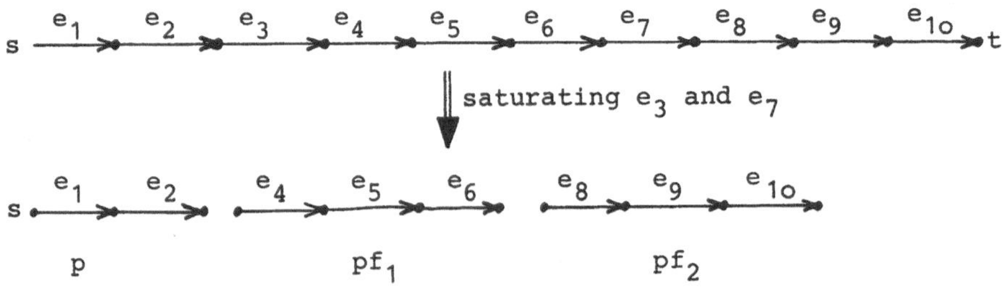

the path into three PFs p, pf_1 and pf_2. We will always use p to denote the path fragment starting in s. We will maintain the invariant that at most one PF goes through every node v, i.e. that there is at most one PF pf such that v is a node of pf but not the last node of pf. In other words the Pfs form a forest with edges directed towards the roots We can now start to construct a new path from s to t starting at the last vertex last(p) of Pf p.

There are four ways of changing path p. If there is a path fragment which goes through last(p), say pf, then we split pf at last(p) and concatenate one of the parts to p. If last(p) is the first vertex of pf then splitting is trivial.

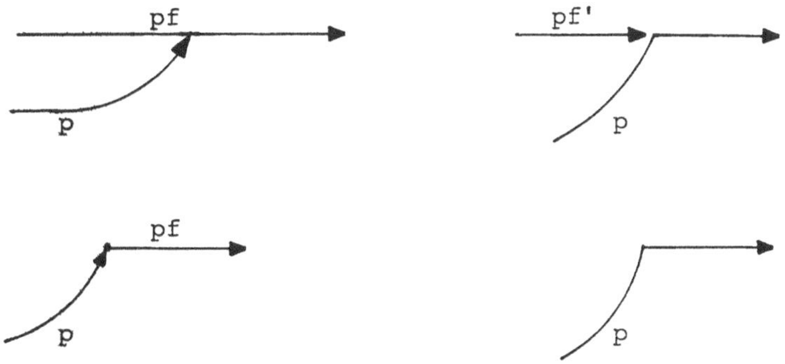

If there is an unblocked edge out of last(p) then we add this edge to p If last(p) is a dead end, i.e. neither is there a PF going through last(p) nor is there an unblocked edge leaving last(p), then we shrink p by deleting its last edge. Finally, if last(p) = t then we saturate some of p's edges and split p into path fragments. The details are as follows.

```
(1)  p ← path consisting of s only;
(2)  while s is not a dead-end
(3)  do extend p by adding an unblocked edge out of last(p);
(4)     while a PF pf goes through last(p)
(5)     do split pf at last(p) into pf', pf" and compute the capacities
           of pf', pf" (pf' ends in last(p), pf" starts in last(p));
(6)        concatenate pf" to the end of p and update p's capacity
(7)     od;
(8)     if last(p) = t
(9)     then increase the flow along p by the capacity of p, split p
             into PFs by deleting all saturated edges, compute the
```

capacities of the fragments and let p be the fragment starting in s.

(1o) fi;

(11) while last(p) is a dead-end and $s \neq$ last(p)

(12) do delete the last edge from p and update p's capacity

(13) od

(14) od

There are two points which we have to address at this point. Do we maintain the invariant and can we always execute line (3)?

Lemma 4: The following holds at all times during execution of the algorithm:

a) For every node v there is at most one path fragment going through v.

b) Whenever line (3) has to be executed there is an unblocked edge out of last(p) and no PF goes through last(p).

Proof: (by induction on the number of steps executed).
Claims a) and b) are certainly true prior to the first execution of the loop body. Suppose now that a) and b) hold prior to execution of line (3). We will show that a) and b) hold at the end of the loop body. Since b) holds line (3) can be executed and execution of line (3) does not impede the truth of part a). Execution of lines (4) - (7) certainly does not either. Before executing line (8) we know that no PF goes through last(p). We claim that this is also true after executing lines (8) and (9). The claim is obvious if last(p) $\neq$ t. If last(p) = t then we reset p to an initial segment p' of p. Since the edge on p which emanates from last(p') is saturated in (9) and since a) holds we conclude that no PF goes through last(p'). Thus a) holds prior to execution of line (11) and no PF goes through last(p) at this point. Execution of lines (11) - (13) certainly does not affect a). Also they ensure that no PF goes through last(p) (this fact is an invariant of line (12) because of a)) and that either last(p) = s or there is an unblocked edge out of last(p). Thus b) and a) hold prior to the next execution of line (3) because of the test in line (2). □

Lemma 4 implies correctness of the algorithm. Let us turn to efficiency next. We need to discuss two points: how to represent path fragments such that the various operations on them can be done fast and how to derive bounds on the number of executions of various statements.

Path fragments are stored as balanced trees. More precisely, we store the edges of a PF in the leaves of a (2,4)-tree in the natural order: Then every vertex z of the tree represents a path pf(z) in the network, namely the path comprised of the edges stored in the subtree rooted at z. We store two informations about path pf(z) in vertex z: f(z) (flow) and c(z) (capacity). The flow field f(z) indicates that f(z) units of flow have been pushed through pf(z) without distributing these units over the subpaths. Thus, if e is an edge of the network, the flow through e is given by Σ f(z) where the summation is over all vertices z on the path from the leaf representing edge e (note that this leaf is uniquely defined by lemma 4a) to the root of the tree representing the path fragment containing e. Field c(z) is the minimal residual capacity (= capacity - flow) of any edge in pf(z) ignoring the flows associated with proper ancestors of z. Thus

$$c(z) = \min_{e \in pf(z)} [c(e) - \sum_{y \in ver(e,z)} f(y)]$$

where ver(e,z) is the set of vertices of the tree path from the leaf representing e to z (e and z included). In particular, if z is the root of a tree then c(z) is the residual capacity of pf(z); i.e. c(z) and no more additional units of flow can be pushed through pf(z).

<u>Lemma 5:</u> a) If pf_1 and pf_2 are path fragments with last(pf_1) = first(pf_2) then pf_1 and pf_2 can be concatenated in time O(log n).

b) Let pf be a PF represented as a balanced tree and let v be a node of pf. Then pf can be split at v in time O(log n). Also if the residual capacity of pf is zero then a saturated edge of pf can be located in time O(log n).

<u>Proof:</u> For both parts we need to push flow information into trees. If z is a vertex with sons z_i, i = 1,2,... then

$$(f(z_i),\ c(z_i)) \leftarrow (f(z_i) + f(z),\ c(z_i) - f(z))$$
$$(f(z),\ c(z)) \leftarrow (0, c(z))$$

is a consistent change of the information fields associated with vertices $z, z_1, z_2, \ldots$. Also, it pushes flow from vertex z into the subpaths represented by nodes z_i, $i = i,2,\ldots$.

a) Let T_i of height h_i be the tree representing pf_i, $i = 1,2$. Assume w.l.o.g. that $h_1 \le h_2$. Then we concatenate T_1 and T_2 by first pushing flow down the left spine of T_2 for $h_2 - h_1 + 1$ levels and then concatenating T_1 and T_2 as described in section III.5.. Note that the flow and capacity field of the vertices affected by the operation are easily computed. More precisely, the flow field is set to zero and the capacity field is set to the minimum residual capacity of the sons. This shows that T_1 and T_2 can be concatenated in time $O(|h_2 - h_1| + 1)$.

b) Let T represent path fragment pf and let v be a node in pf. Note first, that v corresponds to a "gap" between two leaves of T in a natural way. Let e be the edge (leaf) following v in pf. We prepare the split by tracing the tree path from e to the root to T and then pushing flow down this path. This changes the flow field of all vertices on the tree path to zero and therefore they can be safely removed. Splitting is completed by a sequence of concatenates as in ordinary (2,4)-trees.

Finally, we need to show how to find a saturated edge if the residual capacity of pf is zero. Push flow from the root z of T into its sons. Then $0 = c(z) = \min(c(z_i))$ where z_i ranges over the sons of z. Therefore one of the sons has a zero capacity field. Continuing in this fashion we find a saturated edge in time $O(\log n)$. □

Lemma 6: A single execution of line (3), (5), (6) and (12) takes time $O(\log n)$. A single execution of line (9) takes time $O(d \log n)$ where d is the number of edges deleted in line (9).

Proof: Immediate from lemma 5. Note that line (3) can be thought of constructing a path fragment consisting of a single edge and concatenating it with p. □

We are now (almost) in a position to determine the running time of the improved algorithm. Note first that the total time spent outside lines (4) - (7) is $O(e \log n)$ because line (3) is executed at most e times and therefore the number of executions of the loop body is at most e, because the total number of edges deleted in lines (9) and (12) is at most e, and because the cost of handling an edge is O(log n) by lemma 6. It remains to bound the cost arising in lines (4) - (7), i.e. we need to bound the number of executions of lines (5) and (6). Call this number K. We show K = O(e log n) in a two step process. In the first step we rephrase the problem of bounding K as a game problem (which bears great similarity to the union-find problem studied in III.8.3.) and in the second step we derive a bound on the number of moves in the game. The argument will be similar to the one used in section III.8.3..

For step one we conceptually assign non-negative integers to path fragments as follows. Path fragment p (starting at s) never has a number assigned to it. When p is split in line (9) in path fragments p, pf_1, pf_2, ... , pf_k (in this order from s to t) then we assign integer L + i to pf_i, $1 \le i \le k$, where L is the largest integer given to a PF prior to that point. Also if we split PF pf into pf', pf" and concatenate pf" to p, then pf' inherits pf's number provided that pf' is non-trivial. We use num(pf) to denote the number assigned to PF pf. We clearly have $1 \le \text{num(pf)} \le e$ for all path fragments pf since new numbers are assigned only in line (9) and assigning a new number corresponds to deleting an edge. We need one more property of path fragment numbers.

If pf_1 and pf_2 are PFs then pf_1 <u>points to</u> pf_2 if pf_2 goes through last(pf_1). We have

<u>Lemma 7:</u> At all times during the execution:

a) If pf is a PF then pf points to at most one other PF.

b) If pf_1 points to pf_2 and $pf_2 \neq p$ then $\text{num}(pf_1) < \text{num}(pf_2)$.

<u>Proof:</u> a) Follows directly from lemma 4a since there is at most one path fragment going through last(pf) by that lemma.

b) Is shown by induction on execution time. New path fragments are created in lines (5) and (9). Line (9) certainly keeps b) true since "large" numbers are assigned to the newly created path fragments and since the newly created path fragments do not point to any other path fragments by part a). Line (5) keeps b) true since pf' inherits num(pf), since pf' is a subpath of pf, and since pf' points to p after its creation and therefore to no other path fragment by part a. □

We can now view our algorithm as manipulating a set $S \subseteq \{(x,y);\ 1 \le x < y \le e\}$ of pairs, namely $S = \{(num(p), num(q));$ p,q are PFs and p points to q$\}$. Set S is manipulated in stages, where a stage corresponds to a single execution of the body (3) - (14) of the main loop. Thus the number of stages is at most e. In a stage we remove a number of pairs in lines (4) - (7), say (x_1,y_1), (x_2,y_2), ... , (x_k,y_k) and $k \ge 0$. These pairs form a chain, i.e. $y_1 = x_2, y_2 = x_3, \ldots, y_{k-1} = x_k$, because if

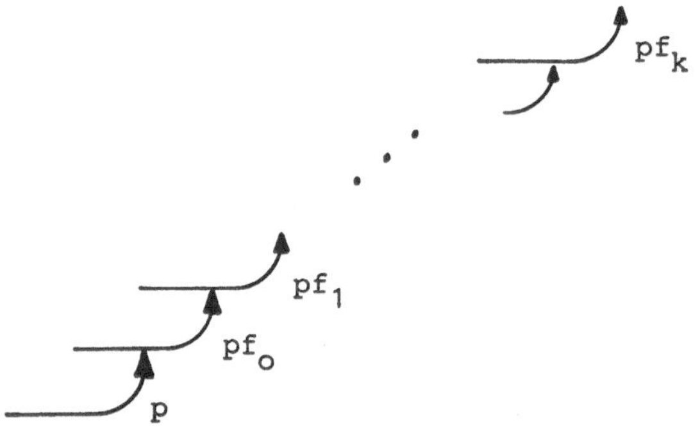

$y_i = num(pf_i)$, $x_1 = num(pf_0)$ then pf_i must point to pf_{i+1}, $0 \le i < k$, and p must point to pf_0 prior to line (3). Thus $K \le D + e$ where D is the number of pairs removed in lines (4) - (7). In a stage we add some pairs to S in line (9). If $(x,y) = (num(pf_1), num(pf_2))$ is a pair added in line (9) then $y = num(pf_2)$ is a "new" number. In particular, if pair (x,y) was deleted at some previous stage and pair (u,v) was deleted at the same stage then $y > v$.

Readers familiar to the union-find problem, section III.8.3., should see a similarity at this point. Consider the union-find data structure with path compression but without the weighted union rule. If one numbers nodes as they are created then upward links correspond to pairs (x,y) with $x < y$. Also path compression removes a chain of pairs and adds some new pairs with "large" second component.

<u>Theorem 6:</u> Let N and M be integers. Consider a process operating on set $S \subseteq \{(x,y);\ 1 \le x < y \le M\}$ in N stages. Initially, S is a set of pairs

satisfying $(x,y) \in S$, $(x,y') \in S \Rightarrow y = y'$. In each stage a chain (x_1,x_2), $(x_2,x_3),\ldots,(x_{k-1},x_k)$ of pairs is removed from S and some set of pairs (x,y) is added to S. Added pairs (x,y) satisfy

(1) If (x,y) is added to S then no (x,y') is currently in S nor did (x,y) ever belong to S previously.

(2) If (x,y') for some y' was deleted at some previous (including the present) stage and pair (u,v) was deleted at the same stage then $y \geq v$.

Then at most $(N + M)\lceil \log M \rceil$ pairs are removed from S.

<u>Proof:</u> The proof is based on the following idea. If we delete a large chain $(x_1,x_2),\ldots,(x_{k-1},x_k)$ at some stage then all pairs (x_i,y) added later on must satisfy $y > x_k$. Therefore all these edges must have a large reach $y - x_i$. But no pair can have reach exceeding M and hence this cannot happen too often. The details are as follows.

Let F be the set of pairs deleted. We divide F into classes according to the "reach" of the edges in F, namely

$$M_i = \{(x,y) \in F;\ 2^i \leq y - x < 2^{i+1}\},\ 0 \leq i \leq \lceil \log M \rceil - 1.$$

Furthermore, let

$$L_i = \{(x,y) \in M_i;\ \text{no}(u,v) \in M_i \text{ with } v > y \text{ is removed from S at the same stage as } (x,y)\}.$$

Note that the definitions make sense since no pair can be added twice to S by property (1).

<u>Claim 1:</u> $|L_i| \leq N$.

<u>Proof:</u> Obvious, since the edges removed at a stage form a chain and since there are only N stages. □

<u>Claim 2:</u> For all x and i there is at most one y such that $(x,y) \in M_i - L_i$.

<u>Proof:</u> Assume (x,y_1), $(x,y_2) \in M_i - L_i$ where $y_1 < y_2$. When (x,y_1) was

removed from S a pair $(u,v) \in M_i$ with $v > y_1$ was also removed from S at the same stage, since $(x,y_1) \notin L_i$.

Since the set of pairs removed at a stage form a chain we also have $y_1 \le u$. Next observe that $y_2 \ge v$ by property (2). Thus

$$y_2 - x \ge v - x \ge v - u + y_1 - x \ge 2^i + 2^i = 2^{i+1}$$

since (x,y_1), $(u,v) \in M_i$ and hence $v - u \ge 2^i$ and $y_1 - x \ge 2^i$. We conclude that $(x,y_2) \notin M_i$, a contradiction. □

The proof is now easily completed.

$$|F| = \sum_{i=0}^{\lceil \log M \rceil - 1} |M_i - L_i| + |L_i| \le (M + N) \lceil \log M \rceil .$$

since $|M_i - L_i| \le M$ by claim 2 and $|L_i| \le N$ by claim 1. □

Theorem 7: a) Let LN be a layered network with n nodes and e edges. Then a blocking flow can be computed in time $O(e(\log n)^2)$.

b) Let $N = (V,E,c)$, $s,t \in V$ be a network with n nodes and e edges. Then a maximal (s,t)-legal flow can be computed in time $O(en(\log n)^2)$.

Proof: a) Theorem 6 ($M = N = e$) implies that the number of executions of lines (5) and (6) is $O(e \log n)$. Thus total running time is $O(e(\log n)^2)$ by lemma 6 and the discussion following it.

b) follows from part a) and Corollary 1. □

Theorem 6 can be used to show an $O((n+m)\log(n+m))$ bound on the cost of n unions and m finds when path compression is used but the weighted union rule is not used (cf. chapter III).

Theorem 7 can be improved slightly. Sleator/Tarjan (Sleator 8o) have shown that a clever use of dynamic weighted trees (cf. III.6.) instead of balanced trees reduces the cost of blocking flow computations to $O(e \log n)$ and hence the cost of the maximum flow problem to $O(en \log n)$. Finally, the algorithm above can be used to compute the maximal flow in an (s,t)-planar network in time $O(n \log n)$, exercise 29.

IV. 9.2 (0,1)-Networks, Bipartite Matching and Graph Connectivity

In this section we will specialize the network flow algorithms to (0,1)-networks, or more generally bounded networks, and then apply it to compute maximum matchings in bipartite graphs and to compute the vertex connectivity of graphs.

Definition: Let $d \in \mathbb{N}$. A network $N = (V,E,c)$ is d-bounded if $c(e) \in \{1,2,\dots,d\}$ for all $e \in E$. A 1-bounded network is mostly called (0,1)-network.

If we apply any of our maximum flow algorithms to d-bounded networks then all intermediate flows f computed are integer, i.e. $f(e) \in \mathbb{N}_0$ for all $e \in E$. In particular, the maximum flow is integer. We observed already that a blocking flow in a (0,1)-network can be computed in linear time. More generally, we have

Lemma 8: Let N be a d-bounded network. Then a blocking flow can be computed in time $O(de)$.

Proof: Use the proof of theorem 5 and observe that an edge can be used at most d times in any path from s to t. □

From lemma 8 we conclude that maximum flows in d-bounded networks can be computed in time $O(den)$. Actually, a much better holds and can be shown by a more careful analysis of our network flow algorithms. More precisely, we show improved bounds on the number of phases needed by the algorithm.

Let $N = (V,E,c)$ be a network. Let $s,t \in V$ and let f be a legal flow. Let $E_1 = \{(v,w);\ f(v,w) < c(v,w)\}$ and let $E_2 = \{(w,v);\ f(v,w) > 0\}$; cf. the definition of layered network. Let $AN = (V,E_1 \dot\cup E_2,\bar{c})$ where $\bar{c}(v,w) = c(v,w) - f(v,w)$ for $(v,w) \in E_1$ and $\bar{c}(w,v) = f(v,w)$ if $(w,v) \in E_2$ and $E_1 \dot\cup E_2$ is the disjoint union of E_1 and E_2. Then constructing the layered network with respect to N and f is the same as constructing the layered network with respect to AN and the flow function which is zero everywhere.

Lemma 9: Let N be a network and let fmax be the value of a maximal (s,t)-flow. Let f be any legal (s,t)-flow, let AN be defined as above and let $\overline{\text{fmax}}$ be the value of a maximal (s,t)-flow in AN. Then

$$\text{fmax} = \overline{\text{fmax}} + \text{val}(f)$$

<u>Proof:</u> Let (S,V-S) be any (s,t)-cut. We use c(S,V-S) and $\bar{c}$(S,V-S) to denote the capacity of cut(S,V-S) with respect to N and AN respectively. We have

$$\bar{c}(S,V-S) = \sum_{v\in S, w\in V-S} \bar{c}(v,w)$$

$$= \sum_{v\in S, w\in V-S} [(c(v,w) - f(v,w)) + f(w,v)], \text{ definition of } \bar{c}$$

$$= c(S,V-S) - \sum_{v\in V, w\in V-S} (f(v,w) - f(w,v))$$

$$= c(S,V-S) - \text{val}(f).$$

We conclude from this that $\overline{\text{cmin}}$ = cmin - val(f) where cmin and $\overline{\text{cmin}}$ are the minimum capacities of any (s,t)-cut in N and AN respectively. An application of theorem 4 (min cut = max flow) completes the proof. □

Lemma 9 tells us that the augmenting network AN has the potential of increasing flow to its maximum value. The layered network captures all shortest (s,t)-paths in AN.

<u>Lemma 1o:</u> Let N be a d-bounded network. Then the number of phases ist at most $3d^{1/3}n^{2/3}$.

<u>Proof:</u> Let fmax be the value of a maximum (s,t)-flow. If fmax $< d^{1/3}n^{2/3}$ then the claim is true since every phase increases flow by at least one. So let us assume fmax $\geq d^{1/3}n^{2/3}$. Consider the phase, say the ℓ-th phase, which increases flow to at least fmax $- (d^{1/2}n)^{2/3}$. Then there are at most $d^{1/3}n^{2/3}$ phases after phase ℓ since every phase increases flow by at least one. We complete the proof by showing that $\ell \leq 2d^{1/3}n^{2/3}$, i.e. that flow value fmax $- d^{1/3}n^{2/3}$ was reached in at most $2d^{1/3}n^{2/3}$ phases. Since the depth of the layered network grows by at least one in every phase (lemma 3), it suffices to show that d_ℓ, the depth of layered network LN used in phase ℓ, is at most $2d^{1/3}n^{2/3}$. Let

$LN = (V_0 \cup V_1 \cup \ldots \cup V_k, \bar{E}, \bar{c})$, where $k = d_\ell$, $V_0 = \{s\}$, $t \in V_k$, and $\bar{E} \subseteq \bigcup_i (V_i \times V_{i+1})$ be the layered network used in phase ℓ. LN is constructed with respect to flow f.

Let $W_i = V_0 \cup \ldots \cup V_i$, $0 \le i < k$. Then $(W_i, V-W_i)$ is an (s,t)-cut and hence $\bar{c}(W_i, V-W_i) \ge \overline{fmax} = fmax - val(f) \ge d^{1/3}n^{2/3}$ by the proof of lemma 9. Next observe that all edges of AN which emanate in W_i and end in $V - W_i$ actually start in V_i and end in V_{i+1} by the way layered network LN is defined. Hence $\bar{c}(W_i, V-W_i) \le 2d\,|V_i|\,|V_{i+1}|$ since there are at most $2 \cdot |V_i|\,|V_{i+1}|$ edges from V_i to V_{i+1} (the two comes from the fact that $(v,w) \in E_1$ and $(v,w) \in E_2$ is possible). Thus $|V_i|\,|V_{i+1}| \ge (n/d)^{2/3}/2$ and hence $|V_i| + |V_{i+1}| \ge (n/d)^{1/3}$ for $0 \le i < k$. Summing this inequality for i, $0 \le i < k$, we obtain

$$2|V| \ge k(n/d)^{1/3}$$

or

$$k \le 2d^{1/3}n^{2/3}$$ □

<u>Theorem 8:</u> Let N be a d-bounded network. Then a maximum flow can be computed in time $O(d^{4/3}n^{2/3}e)$.

<u>Proof:</u> Immediate from lemmas 8 and 10. □

A restricted form of (0,1)-networks is particularly important, simple (0-1)-networks.

<u>Definition:</u> A network N = (V,E,c) is <u>simple</u> if $indeg(v) \le 1$ or $outdeg(v) \le 1$ for all $v \in V$. □

<u>Theorem 9:</u> Let N = (V,E,c) be a simple (0,1)-network. Then a maximum flow can be computed in time $O(n^{1/2}e)$.

<u>Proof:</u> A phase of the network flow algorithm takes time O(e) by theorem 5. It therefore suffices to show that the number of phases is $O(n^{1/2})$. We use an argument similar to lemma 10.

Let fmax be the value of a maximum (s,t)-flow. If $fmax < n^{1/2}$ then there is nothing to show. If $fmax \ge n^{1/2}$ then consider the phase, say the ℓ-th phase, which increases flow to $fmax - n^{1/2}$. Then there are at most $n^{1/2}$ phases after phase ℓ. It remains to show that the layered network LN used in phase ℓ has depth at most $n^{1/2}$.

Let f be the legal (s,t)-flow obtained by our algorithm just prior to phase ℓ and let AN be the augmenting network with respect to f. We claim that AN is a simple network. This can be seen as follows. Let $v \in V$ be arbitrary. Assume that indegree(v) = 1, the case outdegree(v) = 1 being similar. If f(e) = 0 for in(v) = {e} and hence f(e') = 0 for all $e' \in$ out(v) then v has certainly indegree one in AN. If f(e) = 1 for in(v) = {e} and hence f(e') = 1 for exactly one $e \in$ out(v) then v has also indegree at most one in AN. This follows from the fact that the direction of e and e' is reversed for constructing the augmenting network. Thus AN is a simple network.

By lemma 9, AN allows an (s,t)-flow of fmax - val(f) $\geq n^{1/2}$. Consider a maximum (s,t)-flow $\overline{f}$ in AN. We may assume that $\overline{f}$ is integer, i.e. $\overline{f}(\overline{e}) \in \{0,1\}$ for all edges of AN. Since AN is a simple network, $\overline{f}$ defines $val(\overline{f}) \geq n^{1/2}$ paths from s to t which have no common vertex other than s and t. Hence any one of these paths can have at most $n^{1/2}$ intermediate nodes. This shows that the layered network used in phase ℓ has depth at most $n^{1/2}$.

We have thus shown that the number of phases is $O(n^{1/2})$ and hence total running time is $O(n^{1/2}e)$. □

We close this section with two applications of simple (0,1)-network flow: bipartite matching and graph connectivity.

Let G = (V,E) be an undirected graph. A <u>matching</u> M is a set of edges $M \subseteq E$ such that no two edges $e_1, e_2 \in M$, $e_1 \neq e_2$, share an end point. A maximal matching is a matching of maximal cardinality. An undirected graph G = (V,E) is <u>bipartite</u> if there is a partition V_1, V_2 of V such that $E \subseteq V_1 \times V_2$. In bipartite graphs, the nodes of V_1 (V_2) are often called girls (boys). Then $(v,w) \in E$ can be interpreted as "girl v can go along with boy w". Matching in arbitrary graphs allows for homosexuality.

<u>Theorem 1o:</u> Let $G=(V_1 \cup V_2, E)$, $E \subseteq V_1 \times V_2$, be a bipartite graph. A maximal matching can be computed in time $O(n^{1/2}e)$.

Proof: Define a simple (0-1)-network $N = (V_1 \cup V_2 \cup \{s,t\}, \bar{E}, c)$ as follows. Add two nodes s and t, connect s to all vertices in V_1, direct all edges in E from V_1 to V_2 and connect all vertices in V_2 to t. Also assign capacity one to all edges. Then integer-valued flows in N are in one-to-one correspondance to matchings in G. (The following figure

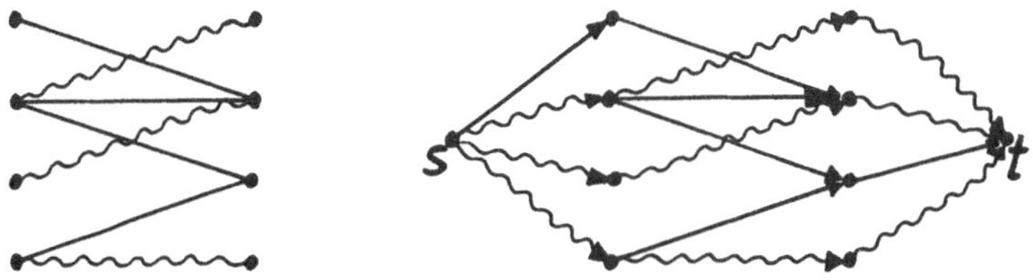

shows a matching and the corresponding flow by wiggled edges). By theorem 9 a maximum flow in N can be computed in time $O(n^{1/2}e)$. □

We will next turn to vertex connectivity of undirected graphs. Let $G = (V,E)$ be an undirected graph and let $a,b \in V$ be such that $(a,b) \notin E$. Set $S \subseteq V - \{a,b\}$ is an (a,b) vertex separator if every path from a to b passes through a vertex of S. In other words a and b belong to different connected components of $G - S$. The minimum cardinality of any (a,b) vertex seperator is denoted by $N(a,b)$.

Lemma 11: Let $G = (V,E)$ be an undirected graph and let $a,b \in V$ be such that $(a,b) \notin E$. Then $N(a,b)$ can be computed in time $O(n^{1/2}e)$.

Proof: Construct a simple (0-1)-network $N = (\bar{V},\bar{E},\bar{c})$ as follows. Let $V' = \{v';\ v \in V\}$ and $V'' = \{v'';v \in V\}$; let $\bar{V} = V' \cup V''$, and let $\bar{E} = \{(v',v'');\ v \in V\} \cup \{(v'',w'), (w'',v');\ (v,w) \in E\}$. Finally, let $\bar{c}(v',v'') = 1$ for $v \in V$ and let $\bar{c}(v'',w') = \bar{c}(w'',v') = \infty$ for $(v,w) \in E$. The construction is illustrated by the following figure. (see next page).

Claim: $N(a,b)$ is equal to the maximum flow from a", the source, to b', the sink, in network N.

Proof: "≤": Let $(A,\bar{V} - A)$ be a minimal (a",b') cut in network N. Let $S = \{v;\ v' \in A,\ v'' \in \bar{V} - A\}$. Then clearly $\bar{c}(A,\bar{V} - A) \geq |S|$. Also, S is a vertex separator and hence $|S| \geq N(a,b)$. This can be seen as follows.

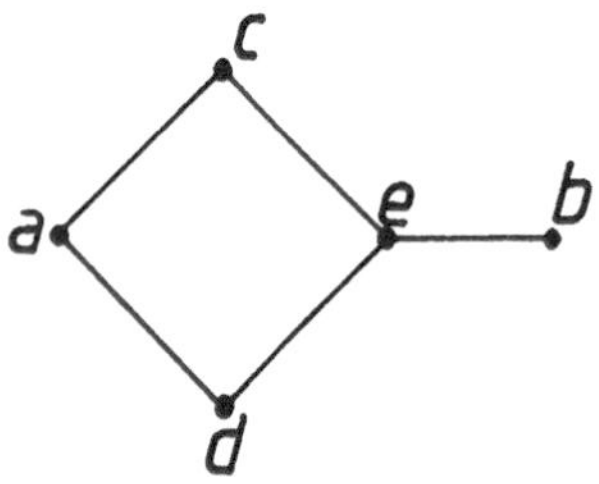

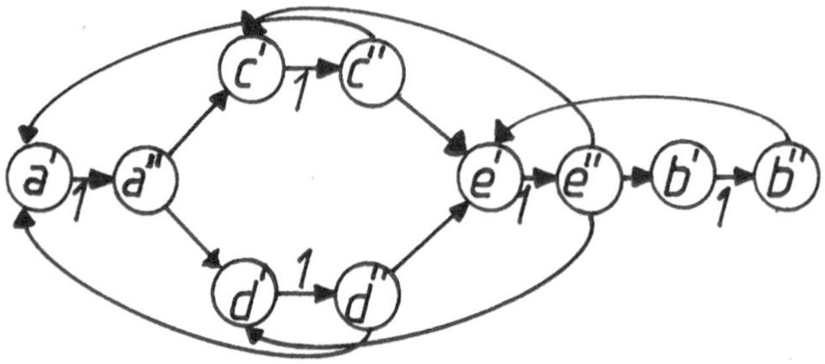

Let $a = v_0, v_1, \ldots, v_k = b$ be a path from a to b in G. Consider path $v_0'', v_1', v_1'', v_2', \ldots v_{k-1}'', v_k'$ from a" to b' in N. At least one of its edges must go across the cut defined by A. It cannot be one of the edges (v_i'', v_{i+1}') because these edges have capacity ∞ and cut $(A, \overline{V} - A)$ has finite capacity. Note that cut $(A, \overline{V} - A)$ has finite capacity because it is a minimal cut and since there are cuts, e.g. $A = \{a''\} \cup (V' - \{b'\})$, of finite capacity.

"$\geq$": Let $S \subseteq V - \{a,b\}$ be an (a,b) vertex separator with $|S| = N(a,b)$. Define $A = \{x \in \overline{V};$ x can be reached from a" without using an edge (s',s'') for $s \in S\}$. Then $b' \notin A$ and hence $(A, \overline{V} - A)$ is an (a",b')-cut of network N. Also, $v' \in A$ implies $v'' \in S$ for $v \in V - S$. Hence $c(A, \overline{V} - A) = |S| = N(A,B)$.

It is now easy to see that the maximal flow from a" to b' does not change if we change all capacities to 1. We obtain a simple (0,1)-network in this way. A maximal flow in this network and hence N(a,b) can be computed in time $O(n^{1/2}e)$ by theorem 9. □

The <u>vertex connectivity</u> c of an undirected graph G = (V,E) is the minimal connectivity number of any pair of unconnected vertices. More precisely,

$$c = \begin{cases} n - 1 & \text{if G is complete} \\ \min\{N(a,b);\ (a,b) \notin E\} & \text{otherwise} \end{cases}$$

<u>Theorem 11:</u> Let G = (V,E) be an undirected graph and let c be its vertex connectivity.

a) c can be computed in time $O(cn^{3/2}e) = O(n^{1/2}e^2)$.

b) Let $\varepsilon > 0$ and assume $e \le n^2/4$. Then there is a randomized algorithm computing c in expected time $O((-\log\varepsilon)n^{3/2}e)$ with probability of error at most ε.

Proof: Both parts are based on the following simple observation.

Claim 1: Assume $c < n - 1$. Let $c = N(x,y)$ for some nodes $x,y \in V$ and let S, $|S| = c$, be an (x,y)-vertex separator. Then $c = \min\{N(a,b);\ b \in V\}$ for all $a \in V - S$.

Proof: G - S consists of at least two components. Let b be a node which does not belong to the same component as a. Then S separates a from b and hence $N(a,b) \le |S| = c$. Thus $c = N(a,b)$ by definition of c. □

a) The claim above suggests the following algorithm. Let $v_1, v_2, v_3, \ldots, v_n$ be some ordering of V.

```
(1)  C ← ∞; i ← 1;
(2)  while C ≥ i
(3)  do c_i ← min{N(v_i,v); v ∈ V};
(4)     C ← min(C,c_i); i ← i + 1
(5)  od
```

Correctness of this algorithm can be seen as follows. We have $c = \min\{c_1, c_2, \ldots, c_{c+1}\}$ by the claim above. Also $C \ge c$ and $C = \min\{c_1, \ldots, c_i\}$ always. The algorithm terminates with $c \le C < i$ and hence $C = c$. Also $C = c$ whenever $i \ge c + 1$. Thus $c + 1$ iterations suffice.

Running time is determined by line (3). Single execution of line (3) takes time $O(n^{3/2}e)$ by lemma 11. Hence total running time is $O(cn^{3/2}e)$. Finally, observe that $c \le \min\{\deg(v);\ v \in V\} \le 2e/n$ since $\sum_{v \in V} \deg(v) = 2e$.

b) Since $c \le 2e/n$, cf. the proof of part a, and $e \le n^2/4$ by assumption we have $c \le n/2$.

Claim 2: Choose $a \in V$ at random. Then

$$\text{Prob}(c > \min\{N(a,b);\ b \in V\}) \le 1/2$$

Proof: This is almost immediate from claim 1. Let S be defined as in claim 1. Then $|S| \le n/2$ and

$$\text{Prob}(c > \min\{N(a,b); b \in V\}) \le \text{Prob}(a \in S) \le 1/2. \qquad \square$$

Claim 2 suggests the following randomized algorithm for computing c.

(1) $k \leftarrow -\log \varepsilon$; $C \leftarrow \infty$;
(2) do k times
(3) choose $a \in V$ at random;
(4) $C \leftarrow \min(C, \min\{N(a,b); b \in V\})$
(5) od

Running time of this algorithm is clearly $O((-\log \varepsilon)n^{3/2}e)$. Also, the probability that $C > c$ upon termination, is at most $(1/2)^k = \varepsilon$ by claim 2. □

IV. 9.3 Weighted Network Flow and Weighted Bipartite Matching

A weighted network flow problem is given by $N = (V,E,cap,cost)$ and nodes $s,t \in V$. Here $cap: E \to \mathbb{R}_+$ gives the capacity of an edge (we used c instead of cap so far) and $cost: E \to \mathbb{R}$ is the cost of transporting one unit of flow across an edge. Throughout this section we assume that capacities are integers. Let f be a legal (s,t)-flow. Then the cost of f is given by

$$cost(f) = \sum_{e \in E} f(e)\ cost(e).$$

The weighted network flow problem is then to compute a legal (s,t)-flow with maximal flow value and (among these) minimal cost. More generally, we might look for a flow function f with $val(f) = v$ for some predefined v and minimal cost. We will see in this section that a minimal cost flow with flow value v can be computed in time $O(ve(\log n)/\log(e/n))$. At the end of this section we will apply this result to weighted bipartite matching and derive an $O(ne(\log n)/\log(e/n))$ algorithm for it.

The theory of weighted network flow is a natural extension of the theory of ordinary network flow. Let N = (V,E,cap,cost) be a network, $s,t \in V$ and let $f: E \to \mathbb{R}$ be a legal (s,t)-flow. We define the augmenting network with respect to N and f as in the previous section. More precisely, $AN = (V,\bar{E},\overline{cap},\overline{cost})$, where $\bar{E} = E_1 \cup E_2$ and $E_1 = \{e \in E;\ f(e) < cap(e)\}$ and $E_2 = \{(w,v);\ (v,w) = e \in E \text{ and } f(e) > 0\}$. For $e \in E$ we use e_i to denote the edge corresponding to e in E_i, $i = 1,2$. Also

$$\overline{cap}(\bar{e}) = \begin{cases} cap(e) - f(e) & \text{if } \bar{e} = e_1 \\ f(e) & \text{if } \bar{e} = e_2 \end{cases}$$

and

$$\overline{cost}(\bar{e}) = \begin{cases} cost(e) & \text{if } \bar{e} = e_1 \\ -\,cost(e) & \text{if } \bar{e} = e_2 \end{cases}$$

Our first lemma connects minimality in cost with the presence of cycles of negative cost in the augmenting network.

<u>Lemma 12:</u> Let f be a legal (s,t)-flow with val(f) = v and let AN be the augmenting network with respect to f. Then f has minimal cost among all (s,t)-flows with value v iff there is no cycle of negative cost in AN.

<u>Proof:</u> "⇒" (indirect): It is clear that a negative cost cycle can be used to decrease the cost of f without changing the flow value.

"⇐" (indirect): Assume that f does not have minimal cost, i.e. there is a legal (s,t)-flow g with val(g) = val(f) and cost(g) < cost(f). Let $AN = (V,\bar{E},\overline{cap},\overline{cost})$ be the augmenting network with respect to f. Consider $h: \bar{E} \to \mathbb{R}$ defined by

$$h(\bar{e}) = \begin{cases} \max(0,\ g(e) - f(e)) & \text{if } e = e_1 \\ \max(0,\ f(e) - g(e)) & \text{if } e = e_2 \end{cases}$$

<u>Claim 1:</u> h is a legal (s,t)-flow in AN with val(h) = 0 and $\overline{cost}(h) < 0$.

<u>Proof:</u> We show first that h has negative cost. Note that for all $e \in E$ we have $h(e_1)\ \overline{cost}(e_1) + h(e_2)\ \overline{cost}(e_2) = (g(e) - f(e))\ cost(e)$ and hence

$$\overline{\text{cost}}(h) = \sum_{\bar{e}\in\bar{E}} h(\bar{e})\ \overline{\text{cost}}(\bar{e})$$

$$= \sum_{e\in E} [h(e_1)\ \overline{\text{cost}}(e_1) + h(e_2)\ \overline{\text{cost}}(e_2)]$$

$$= \sum_{e\in E} (g(e) - f(e))\ \text{cost}(e)$$

$$= \text{cost}(g) - \text{cost}(f) < 0$$

We show next that h satisfies the conservation laws. Note that for all $e \in E$ $h(e_1) - h(e_2) = g(e) - f(e)$ and hence for all $v \in V$ ($\overline{\text{out}}(v)$ is the set of edges emanating from v in AN and similarly for $\overline{\text{in}}(v)$):

$$\sum_{\bar{e}\in\overline{\text{out}}(v)} h(\bar{e}) - \sum_{\bar{e}\in\overline{\text{in}}(v)} h(\bar{e}) = \sum_{e\in\text{out}(v)} (h(e_1)-h(e_2)) - \sum_{e\in\text{in}(v)} (h(e_1)-h(e_2))$$

$$= \sum_{e\in\text{out}(v)} (g(e)-f(e)) - \sum_{e\in\text{in}(v)} (g(e)-f(e))$$

$$= [\sum_{e\in\text{out}(v)} g(e) - \sum_{e\in\text{in}(v)} g(e)] - [\sum_{e\in\text{out}(v)} f(e) - \sum_{e\in\text{in}(v)} f(e)]$$

$$= \begin{cases} 0 - 0 & \text{if } v \neq s,t \\ \text{val}(g) - \text{val}(f) & \text{if } v = s \\ -\text{val}(g) + \text{val}(f) & \text{if } v = t \end{cases}$$

In any case, this shows that h satisfies the conservation laws and that $\text{val}(h) = 0$. Finally, it is trivial to see that h satisfies the capacity constraints. □

Flow function h has zero flow and negative cost. It is intuitively clear, that h is circular in some sense. More precisely, we show that h can be decomposed in a set of flows around cycles. It is then easy to conclude that one of the cycles must have negative cost.

<u>Claim 2:</u> There are $h_1, h_2, \ldots, h_m: \bar{E} \to \mathbb{R}_{\geq 0}$, $m \leq e$, such that

1) $h(\bar{e}) = \sum_i h_i(\bar{e})$ for all $\bar{e} \in \bar{E}$

2) For every i there is a directed cycle $w_0, w_1, \dots, w_k = w_0$ in AN such that $h_i(w_j, w_{j+1}) = h_i(w_\ell, w_{\ell+1})$ for $0 \le j < \ell < k$, and $h_i(\bar{e}) = 0$ for edges not on the cycle.

Proof: (By induction on the number k of edges $\bar{e} \in \bar{E}$ with $h(\bar{e}) \neq 0$). If $k = 0$ then there is nothing to prove. So let us assume $k \ge 0$. Let v_0 be any node such that there is edge $(v_0, v_1) \in \bar{E}$ with $h(v_0, v_1) \neq 0$. Since $\sum_{\bar{e} \in out(v_1)} h(\bar{e}) = \sum_{\bar{e} \in in(v_1)} h(\bar{e})$ and $h(\bar{e}) \ge 0$ for all $\bar{e} \in \bar{E}$ there must be v_2 such that $(v_1, v_2) \in \bar{E}$ with $h(v_1, v_2) \neq 0$. Continuing in this fashion we construct a path $v_0, v_1, v_2, \dots, v_m$ in AN with $v_m = v_j$ for some $j < m$.

We take $v_j, v_{j+1}, \dots, v_m$ as the desired cycle and define $h_1 \colon E \in \mathbb{R}_{\ge 0}$ by $h_1(v_\ell, v_{\ell+1}) = \min\{h(v_\ell, v_{\ell+1});\ j \le \ell < m\}$ for $j \le \ell < m$ and $h_i(\bar{e}) = 0$ for all edges $\bar{e}$ not on the cycle.

Finally, let $h' = h - h_1$. Then h' is a legal (s,t)-flow with flow value 0. Also there is one less edge with $h'(\bar{e}) \neq 0$. □

The proof of lemma 12 is now readily completed. We have $\overline{cost}(h) = \sum_i \overline{cost}(h_i)$ and hence $\overline{cost}(h_i) < 0$ for some i, $1 \le i \le m$. Let C be the cycle underlying h_i and let ε be the flow along the edges of C. Then $\overline{cost}(h_i) = \varepsilon\, \overline{cost}(C)$ whre $\overline{cost}(C)$ is the cost of cycle C interpreted as a path in network AN. □

Lemma 12 can be used to design an algorithm for minimizing cost without changing the flow value (exercise 32). More importantly, we can use lemma 12 to show that augmentation along minimum cost paths does not destroy cost minimality.

Lemma 13: Let f be a minimal cost flow with $val(f) = v$ and let $AN = (V, \bar{E}, \overline{cap}, \overline{cost})$ be the augmenting network with respect to f. Let p be a minimum cost path from s to t in AN, let f' be a legal (s,t)-flow in AN which is non-zero only along p (i.e. f' sends some units of flow from s to t along p). Then f'' where

$$f''(e) = f(e) + f'(e_1) - f'(e_2) \qquad \text{for all } e \in E$$

is a minimum cost flow of value $val(f) + val(f')$.

Proof: f" is certainly a legal (s,t)-flow with value val(f) + val(f'). A formal proof can be given along the lines of lemma 2b). It remains to show that f" has minimal cost. Assume otherwise. Then there is a negative cost cycle C in the augmenting network AN" constructed with respect fo f". We will derive a contradiction as follows.

If cycle C exists in AN then f was not optimal, a contradiction. So C cannot exist in AN, i.e. there is at least one edge (v,w) on path p such that C uses this edge in reverse direction. Let (v,w) be the first such edge.

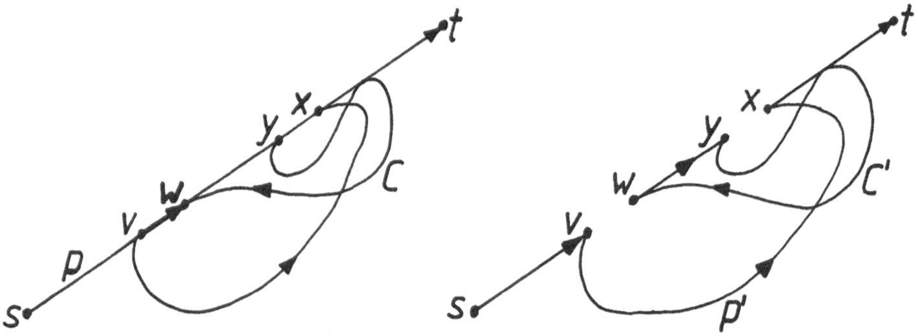

Let path p' from s to t be constructed as follows. Follow p from s to v, then follow C until C intersects p for the next time, say in point x, then follow from x to t. Let cycle C' be constructed as follows: Follow p from w to y, where y is the point following x on cylce C, and then follow C from y to w. Note that $\overline{\text{Cost}}(p') + \overline{\text{Cost}}(C') = \overline{\text{Cost}}(p) + \overline{\text{Cost}}(C)$ since the cost of edge (v,w) is the negative of the cost of edge (w,v). Continuing in this fashion we obtain an (s,t)-path p" from s to t in AN and a cycle C" such that $\overline{\text{cost}}(p") + \overline{\text{cost}}(C") = \overline{\text{cost}}(p) + \overline{\text{cost}}(C)$ and p" and C" use no edge in reverse order. Thus C" is a cycle in network AN. Since $\overline{\text{cost}}(C) < 0$ we either have $\overline{\text{cost}}(C") < 0$, a contradiction to the optimality of f, or $\overline{\text{cost}}(p") < \overline{\text{cost}}(p)$, a contradiction to the fact, that p is a least cost path from s to t in AN. □

Lemma 13 gives rise to a minimum cost flow algorithm.

(1) let f(e) = 0 for all e ∈ E;
(2) while val(f) < v
(3) do let AN be the augmenting network with respect to f;
(4) let p be a least cost path from s to t in AN;

(5) let ε be the minimal capacity of any edge in p;
(6) increase the flow along p by min(ε, v - val(f))
(7) od

Theorem 12: Let N = (V,E,cap,cost), s,t $\in$ V be a network with integer capacities and let v $\in \mathbb{R}_+$. Then a minimum cost flow with value v (if it exists) can be computed in time O((1 + v)ne).

Proof: Correctness of the algorithm above is immediate from lemma 13. Single execution of the loop body takes time O(e), lines (3), (5) and (6), plus O(ne) for line (4). The time bound for line (4) follows from IV.7.3., theorem 5. Finally, since capacities are integer, flow is increased by at least one in every iteration (except maybe the last). Thus total running time is O((1 + v)ne). □

In line (4) of the above algorithm one has to solve single source least costs. In section IV.7.4. we saw that arbitrary edge costs can sometimes be transformed into non-negative edge costs by means of a potential function. More precisely, we proceeded as follows. Given a weighted graph (V,E,cost), and s $\in$ V we computed dist(s,v), the length of the shortest path from s to v. We used dist(s,v) as a potential function and turned all edge costs by

$$\widetilde{\text{cost}}(v,w) = \text{cost}(v,w) + \text{dist}(s,v) - \text{dist}(s,w)$$

into non-negative edge costs. A similar approach works here.

Let AN be the augmenting network with respect to minimal cost flow f and let p be a minimal cost path from s to t in AN. After increasing flow along p we obtain flow f'. Let AN' be the augmenting network with respect to f'. Then AN and AN' are very similar. The only difference is that some edges of path p are removed from, and the reverse of some edges of path p are added to AN to obtain AN'. Also if a reverse edge is added then its cost is the negative of the cost of the edge. Let dist(s,v) be the cost of the least cost path from s to v in AN. We claim that we can use dist(s,v) as a potential function for least cost path computations in network AN'.

Lemma 14: Let AN' = (V,E',cap',cost') and let dist(s,v) be the cost of a least cost path from s to v in AN, v $\in$ V. Let

$$\widetilde{cost}(v,w) = cost'(v,w) + dist(s,v) - dist(s,w)$$

for all $(v,w) \in E'$. Then $\widetilde{cost}(v,w) \geq 0$ for all $(v,w) \in E'$.

Proof: We distinguish two cases: Edge (v,w) is the reverse of an edge of path p or it is not. If it is not then $cost'(v,w) = \overline{cost}(v,w)$ where $\overline{cost}$ is the cost function of network AN and the claim is true since distances satisfy the triangle inequality. If (v,w) is the reverse of edge (w,v) and (w,v) belongs to p then $dist(s,v) = dist(s,w) + \overline{cost}(w,v)$ since p is a least cost path and $cost'(v,w) = -\overline{cost}(w,v)$ by definition of AN'. Hence $\widetilde{cost}(v,w) = 0$. □

Lemma 14 almost implies that we only have to solve single source least cost path problems with non-negative edge costs in line (4). However, there is still a small problem to resolve. If we transform edge costs as described in lemma 14, then we compute $\widetilde{dist}(s,v)$, the least cost of a path from s to v in AN' with respect to cost function $\widetilde{cost}$, in line (4). However, we need to know dist'(s,v), the least cost of a path from s to v in AN' with respect to cost function cost', in order to able to transform edge costs for the next iteration. This difficulty is easily resolved. Note that

$$\begin{aligned}\widetilde{dist}(s,v) &= dist'(s,v) + dist(s,s) - dist(s,v)\\ &= dist'(s,v) - dist(s,v)\end{aligned}$$

for all $v \in V$. Hence dist'(s,v) is easily computed from $\widetilde{dist}(s,v)$ and dist(s,v). We summarize in

Theorem 13: Let N = (V,E,cap,cost), $s,t \in V$ be a network with integer capacities and let $v \in \mathbb{R}_+$. Then a minimum cost flow from s to t with value v can be computed in time $O(ve(\log n)/\max(\log(e/n),1))$.

Proof: Immediate from the discussion above, and IV.7.2. theorem 2. □

We close this section with a short discussion of weighted bipartite matching. Let $G = (V_1 \cup V_2, E)$, $E \subseteq V_1 \times V_2$, be a bipartite (undirected) graph and let cost: $E \to \mathbb{R}_+$ be a cost function. If $M \subseteq E$ is a matching then the cost of M is defined by

$$cost(M) = \sum_{e \in M} cost(e)$$

Theorem 14: Let $G = (V_1 \cup V_2, E)$, cost: $E \to \mathbb{R}_+$ be a weighted bipartite graph and let $v \le n$, $v \in \mathbb{N}$. Then a matching of cardinality v (if it exists) and minimal cost can be computed in time

$O(ne(\log n)/\max(1,\log(e/n)))$.

Proof: The proof is very similar to the proof of theorem 1o. Define network $N = (\{s,t\} \cup V_1 \cup V_2, \overline{E}, \overline{cap}, \overline{cost})$ by $\overline{E} = (\{s\} \times V_1) \cup E \cup (V_2 \times \{t\})$, $\overline{cap}(\overline{e}) = 1$ for all $\overline{e} \in E$ and $\overline{cost}(\overline{e}) = cost(\overline{e})$ for $\overline{e} \in E$ and $cost(\overline{e}) = 0$ for $\overline{e} \in \overline{E} - E$. Then matchings and flows are in one-to-one correspondence and hence a matching of cardinality v and minimal cost can be computed in time $O(ne(\log n)/\max(1,\log(e/n)))$ by theorem 13. □

IV. 1o. Planar Graphs

This section is devoted to planar graphs. We treat three topics. The main topic is a linear time O(n) algorithm for testing planarity. We will then turn to the planar separator theorem which opens the family of planar graphs to divide and conquer algorithms. Finally, we desribe one particular algorithm based on that paradigm: a single source shortest path algorithm for planar graphs.

Let $G = (V,E)$ be an undirected graph. G is planar iff there exists a mapping of the vertices and edges of the graph into the plane such that each vertex is mapped into a distinct point, each edge (v,w) is mapped onto a simple curve connecting the images of v and w, and mappings of distinct edges have only the images of their common endpoints in common. A mapping which satisfies these conditions is called a planar embedding of G. We use $\hat{G}$ to denote a planar embedding of G. The following figure shows two planar embeddings of a graph.

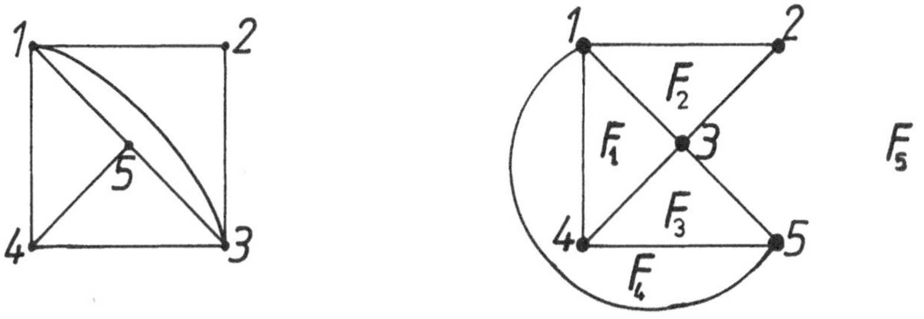

Let $\hat{G}$ be a planar embedding of graph G. Removal of $\hat{G}$ from the plane splits the plane into connected open regions, the faces of $\hat{G}$. One face of $\hat{G}$ is unbounded; it is called the outer region. Every face is enclosed by a path of edges of the graph. We will say that the edges and nodes of this path border the face. The following lemma is helpful.

Lemma 1: Let $\hat{G}$ be any planar embedding of a graph G, let F be a face of $\hat{G}$ and let p be the path enclosing F. Then there is an embedding $\hat{\hat{G}}$ of G in which path p encloses the outer face.

Proof: $\hat{G}$ is an embedding of G into the plane. Choose any point x in the interior of face F and identify the plane with the field of complex numbers, point x corresponding to number O. Then mapping $z \to 1/z$ applied to $\hat{G}$ generates embedding $\hat{\hat{G}}$. □

It is well known that planar graphs are necessarily sparse.

Lemma 2: Let $G = (V,E)$ be a planar graph. Then $e \le 3n - 6$ for $n \ge 3$.

Proof: We prove the lemma for triangulated planar graphs first. A planar graph is triangulated if it has an embedding where every face is a triangle, i.e. is adjacent to (the images of) exactly three edges. For triangulated planar graphs we can relate the number of edges, vertices, and faces.

Claim: Let $\hat{G}$ be an embedding of a triangulated planar graph.

a) Then $n + f = e + 2$ where n,e,f is the number of nodes, edges and faces respectively.

b) $e = 3n - 6$ for $n \ge 3$.

Proof: a) We use induction on n. The claim is clearly true for $n \le 3$. Suppose now that $n > 3$. Let v be any node of G, let d be the degree of v and let $v_1,\dots,v_d$ be the neighbours of v. Since every face of $\hat{G}$ is a triangle, we conclude that $d \ge 3$ and that edges $(v_1,v_2),(v_2,v_3),\dots,$ $(v_{d-1},v_d),(v_d,v_1)$ exist, for some appropriate ordering of the neighbours of v.

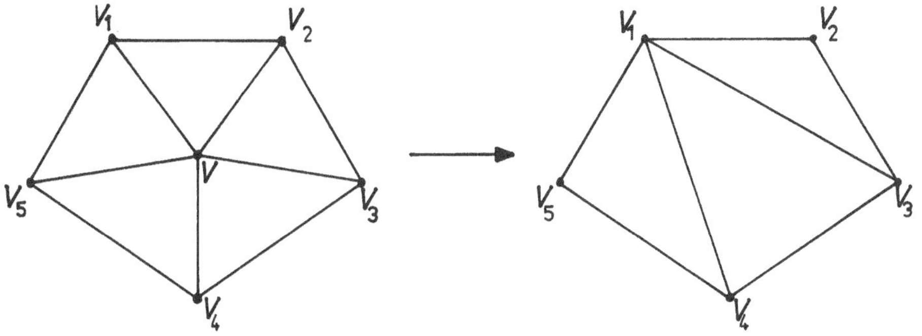

Construct $\hat{G}'$, the planar embedding of a triangulated planar graph G' as follows: Remove v and all edges incident to v and add edges $(v_1,v_3),\ldots,(v_1,v_{d-1})$. Let n',e',f' be the number of nodes, edges, faces respectively of $\hat{G}'$. Then n' = n - 1, e' = e - 3 and f' = f - 2. Also n' + f' = e' + 2 by induction hypothesis. Hence n - 1 + f - 2 = e - 3 + 2 or n + f = e + 2.

b) Since every face is bounded by exactly three edges and since every edge is adjacent to exactly two faces we have 3f = 2e provided that $n \geq 3$. Hence n + 2/3e = e + 2 or e = 3n - 6 by part a). □

Extension to arbitrary planar graphs is quite simple now. Let $\hat{G}$ be the embedding of a planar graph. We can add edges to $\hat{G}$ until every face of $\hat{G}$ is a triangle. Hence $e \leq 3n - 6$ for all planar graphs provided that $n \geq 3$. □

Lemma 2 is helpful in two respects. Firstly, it implies that an O(n + e) algorithm is really an O(n) algorithm and secondly it implies that a planar graph has a large fraction of nodes of small degree. More precisely, let n_d be the number of nodes of degree at most d. Then $(n - n_d)(d + 1) \leq 2e$ since at least $n - n_d$ nodes have degree d + 1 or more. Thus $(n - n_d)(d + 1) \leq 6n - 12$ by lemma 2 and hence $n_d \geq (n(d - 5) + 12)/(d + 1)$. In particular, there is always at least one node of degree at most 5, i.e. $n_5 \geq 1$, and at least 14% of nodes have degree at most 6. The fact that a large number of nodes have small degree can sometimes be used to design divide and conquer algorithms for planar graphs. One such algorithm is treated in the section on Voronoi diagrams and searching planar subdivisions in chapter VIII.3..

We will now describe a linear time planarity testing algorithm. Since a graph is planar iff its biconnected components (cf. section 6) are we can restrict attention to biconnected graphs. Also we can restrict ourselves to graphs with $e \le 3n - 6$ by lemma 2. The planarity testing algorithm is an extension of depth first search. In the sequel we will always identify nodes with their DFS number. Suppose that we perform a DFS on $G = (V,E)$ and divide the edges of G into tree edges and backward edges (cf. section 5). More precisely, let T be the set of tree edges and let B be the set of backward edges which are not reversals of tree edges. In this way every edge in E becomes either a tree edge or (exclusive) a backward edge, i.e. $E = T \cup B$, $T \cup B = \emptyset$. Note that this notation differs slightly from the one used in section 5. There, reversals of tree edges were also called backward edges. Suppose also that we identify a cycle C starting in the root of the DFS-tree and consisting of tree edges followed by one backward edge. Such a cycle exists since G is biconnected. We call such a cycle a spine cycle of G. The underlying path of tree edges is called spine path. Consider the other edges emanating from the nodes on the cycle. With every such edge e we associate a segment S(e) as follows. If e is a backward edge then S(e) is just e. If $e = (x,y)$ is a tree edge with x a node on cycle C and y not a node on cycle C then S(e) consists of the subgraph spanned by the set $V(e) = \{z;\ y \underset{T}{\rightarrow^*} z\}$ of nodes reachable from y by tree edges and all backward edges emanating from a node in V(e) and ending in a node on cycle C (which is then an ancestor of x). We also need to talk about the set of attachments A(e) of segment S(e) to cycle C. If $e = (x,y)$ and e is a backward edge then $A(e) = \{x,y\}$ and if e is a tree edge then $A(e) = \{x\} \cup \{u;\ (z,u) \text{ is a backward edge and } u \underset{T}{\rightarrow^*} x \underset{T}{\rightarrow} y \underset{T}{\rightarrow^*} z\}$.

In our example (see next page), cycle C runs from 1 to 9 by tree edges and then back to node 1. There are four segments with respect to C associated with edges (9,1o), (7,5), (7,13) and (6,4). Set A((9,1o)) consists of nodes 9,8,7 and 5. □

We test planarity of G in a two step process. We first test whether C + S(e), the graph consisting of cycle C and segment S(e), is planar for every edge e emanating from cycle C. For this test we will use the algorithm recursively. In a second step we then try to merge the embeddings found in step one. The merging process only needs to look at the set of attachments of the different segments emanating from S and how they interact. In our example, segments S((7,5)) and S((6,4)) have to be embedded on different sides of C because these segments "interlace".

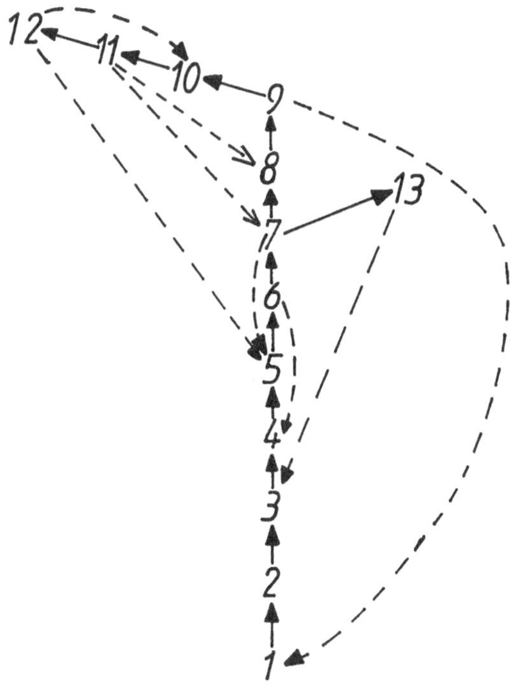

We will next describe the theory behind both steps in more detail. Let C be a cycle, let e = (x,y) be an edge emanating from cycle C, and let A(e) be the set of attachments of segment S(e). Let w_o = min A(e), i.e. w_o is an ancestor of all other nodes in A(e). Also let (z,w_o) be a backward edge where z is a node of segment S(e).

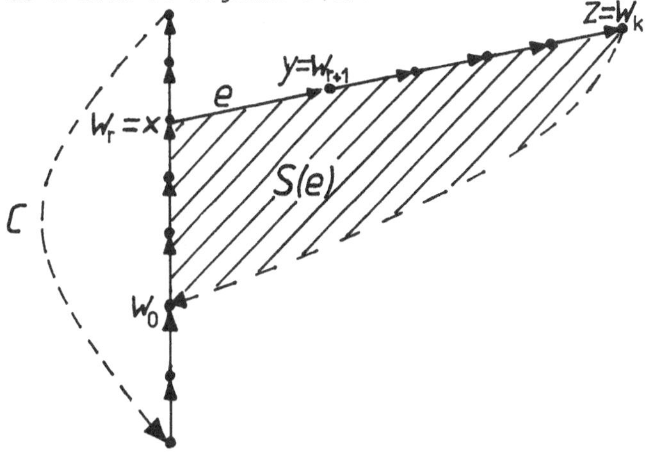

Then a spine cycle SC(e) of segment S(e) consists of the tree path $w_o, w_1, \ldots, w_k$ from w_o to $z = w_k$ followed by backward edge (w_k, z). Then $x = w_r$, $y = w_{r+1}$ for some r. Tree path $w_r, w_{r+1}, \ldots, w_k$ is called the spine of segment S(e). The spine cycle of segment S(e) will play the role of cycle C in the recursive application of the algorithm. The following concept is crucial:

Segment S(e) is <u>strongly planar</u> iff there is an embedding of S(e) + SC(e) such that the tree path from w_o to $w_r = x$ borders the outer face. Recursive application of the planarity testing algorithm is justified by:

<u>Lemma 3:</u> For all edges e emanating from C we have: C + S(e) is planar iff S(e) is strongly planar.

<u>Proof:</u> "⇒". Consider any embedding of C + S(e). Cycle C divides the plane into a bounded and a unbounded region. We may assume w.l.o.g. that edge e = (x,y) lies in the unbounded region. Hence all of S(e) must lie in the unbounded region since every node of S(e) is reachable from y without passing through a node of C. If we remove the part of cycle C between x and w_o then we have the desired embedding of S(e) + SC(e).

"⇐". Given an embedding of S(e) + SC(e) which has the property stated we can clearly add the missing part of C to obtain an embedding of C + S(e). □

We need to straighten out the relationship between planarity and strong planarity at this point. Let G = (V,E) be a biconnected graph and let node 1 be the root of a DFS spanning tree. Suppose now that we add (conceptually) a self-loop at node 1 to graph G. Then S(e), where e is the only (since G is biconnected) tree edge out of node 1, is the entire graph G. Also G is planar iff S(e) is strongly planar with respect to the self-loop. This follows from the fact that the tree path from w_o to x referred to in the definition of strong planarity consists of a single node, namely node 1, and that every face can be made the outer face by lemma 1. This discussion shows that we can restrict ourselves to testing strong planarity. Note that a test for strong planarity was required in lemma 3.

For step 2 we need the concept of <u>interlacing</u>. Let e and e' be edges emanating from cycle C. Then segments S(e) and S(e') interlace if either there are nodes $x < y < z < u$ on cycle C such that $x,z \in A(e)$ and $y,u \in A(e')$ or $A(e)$ and $A(e')$ have three points in common. Clearly,

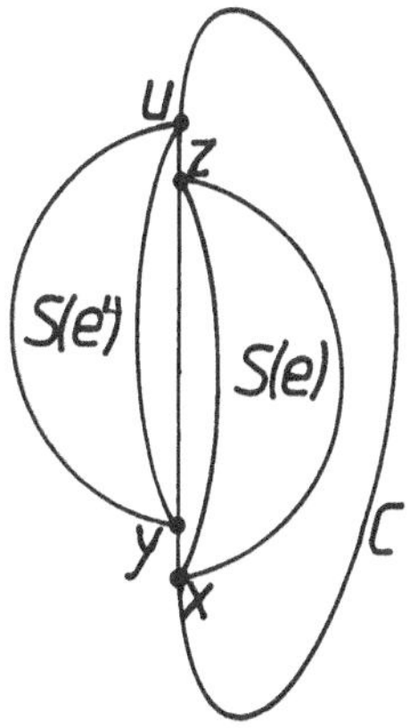

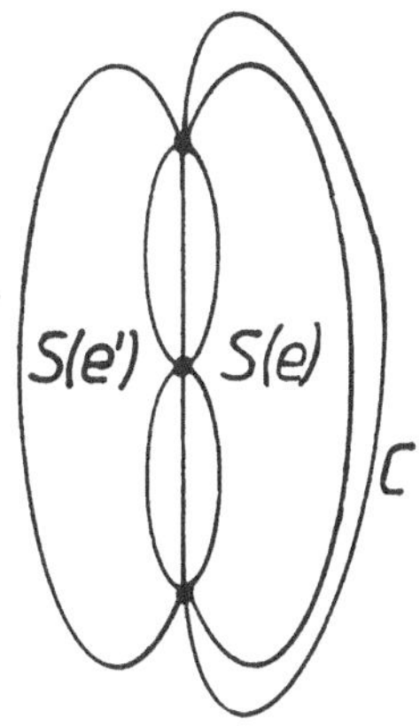

interlacing segments cannot be embedded on the same side of C. The interlacing graph IG(C) with respect to cycle C is defined as follows: The nodes of IG(C) are the segments S(e) where e emanates from C. Also S(e) and S(e') are connected by an edge iff S(e) and S(e') interlace. In our example we have the following interlacing graph. This graph is

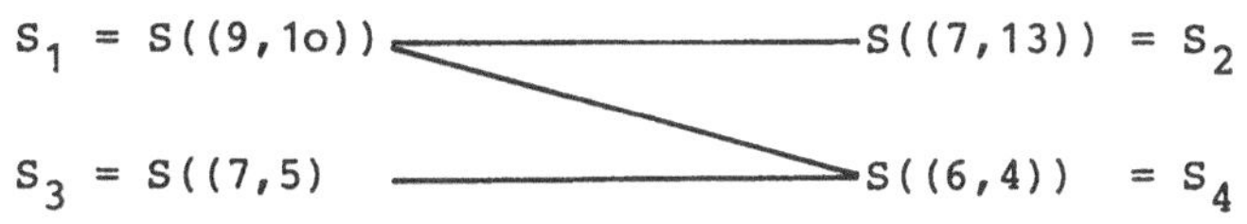

bipartite with segments S_1 and S_3 forming one of the sides of the bipartite graph. Note also that the planar embedding of our example graph shown above has S_1 and S_3 on one side of C and S_2 and S_4 on the other side of cycle C.

<u>Lemma 4:</u> Let C' be the spine cycle of some segment $S(e_o)$, i.e. $C' = w_o \underset{T}{\rightarrow} w_1 \rightarrow \dots \underset{T}{\rightarrow} w_k \underset{B}{\rightarrow} w_o$ and $e_o = (w_r, w_{r+1})$ for some r (cf. the figure preceding lemma 3). Let $e_1,\dots,e_m$ be the edges leaving the spine of $S(e_o)$, i.e. they leave the cycle in nodes w_j, $r < j \le k$. Then $C' + S(e_o)$ is planar iff $S(e_i)$ is strongly planar for all i, $1 \le i \le m$, and IG(C') is bipartite, i.e. there is a partition {L,R} of $\{S(e_1),\dots,S(e_m)\}$ such that no two segments in L(R) interlace. Moreover, segment $S(e_o)$ is strongly planar if in addition for every connected component B of IG(C'): either $\{w_1,\dots,w_{r-1}\} \cap \bigcup_{S(e) \in B \cap L} A(e) = \emptyset$ or $\{w_1,\dots,w_{r-1}\} \cap \bigcup_{S(e) \in B \cap R} A(e) = \emptyset$.

Proof: "⇒": Segments $S(e_i)$, $1 \le i \le m$, are strongly planar by lemma 3. Consider any planar embedding of $C' + S(e_o) = C' + S(e_1) + \ldots + S(e_m)$. Let $L = \{S(e_i);\ S(e_i)$ is embedded inside cycle C', $1 \le i \le m\}$ and let R be the remaining segments. Then no two segments in L (R) interlace because interlacing segments have to be embedded on different sides of C'. Hence IG(C') is bipartite. Finally, assume that $S(e_o)$ is strongly planar. Consider an embedding of $C' + S(e_o)$ which witnesses the strong planarity of $S(e_o)$, i.e. tree paths $w_o \rightarrow w_1 \rightarrow w_2 \rightarrow \ldots \rightarrow w_r$ borders the outer face. Then no segment $S(e_i)$, $1 \le i \le m$, which is embedded outside C' can have an attachment in $\{w_1,\ldots,w_{r-1}\}$ and hence

$$\{w_1,\ldots,w_{r-1}\} \cap \bigcup_{S(e)\in R} A(e) = \emptyset.$$

"⇐". The proof of this direction is postponed. It will be given in lemma 5,d below. □

Lemma 4 suggests an algorithm for testing strong planarity. In order to test strong planarity of segment $S(e_o)$, test strong planarity of segments $S(e_i)$, $1 \le i \le m$, construct the interlacing graph and test for the conditions stated in lemma 4. Unfortunately, the size of the interlacing graph might be quadratic and therefore we cannot afford to construct the interlacing graph explicitely. Rather, we compute the connected components (and their partition into left and right side) of IG(C') iteratively by considering segment after segment. More precisely, we will first consider all segments emanating from w_k, then all segments starting at $w_{k-1},\ldots$. For each w_j we will consider the edges emanating from w_j in the following order. The motivation for this order becomes clear in the proof of lemma 5,b below. Let $e = (w_j,z)$ and $e' = (w_j,u)$ be edges starting in w_j. Then e is considered before e' if either (<u>if</u> e ∈ B <u>then</u> z <u>else</u> LOWPT1[z]) < (<u>if</u> e' ∈ B <u>then</u> u <u>else</u> LOWPT1[u]) or these quantities are equal and either e is a backward edge or LOWPT2[z] ≥ w_j. Ties are broken arbitrarily. Functions LOWPT1 and LOWPT2 are defined by

$$\text{LOWPT1}[v] = \min(\{v\} \cup \{z;\ v \xrightarrow[T]{}{}^{*} w \xrightarrow[B]{} z \text{ for some } w \in V\})$$

and let

$$\text{LOWPT2}[v] = \min(\{v\} \cup \{z;\ v \xrightarrow[T]{}{}^{*} w \xrightarrow[B]{} z \text{ for some } w \in V \text{ and } z \neq \text{LOWPT1}[v]\}).$$

LOWPT1[v] is the lowest node reachable from v by a sequence of tree edges followed by one backward edge. Since G is assumed to be biconnected we have LOWPT1[v] < v for all v ≠ 1. LOWPT2[v] is the second lowest node reachable from v in this way, if there is one. The default value for both functions is v. Functions LOWPT1 and LOWPT2 are easily computed during DFS since

$$\text{LOWPT1}[v] = \min(\{v\} \cup \{z;\ (v,z) \in B\} \cup \{\text{LOWPT1}[w];\ (v,w) \in T\})$$

and

$$\begin{aligned}\text{LOWPT2}[v] = \min(\{v\} &\cup \{z;\ (v,z) \in B \text{ and } z \neq \text{LOWPT1}[v]\}\\ &\cup \{\text{LOWPT1}[w];\ (v,w) \in T,\ \text{LOWPT1}[v] \neq \text{LOWPT1}[w]\}\\ &\cup \{\text{LOWPT2}[w];\ (v,w) \in T\})\end{aligned}$$

These equations suggest to compute LOWPT1 and LOWPT2 by two separate applications of DFS. In a first application of DFS one computes LOWPT1 and in a second application one computes LOWPT2 knowing already LOWPT1. We leave it to the reader to show that one DFS suffices to compute both functions.

Having computed LOWPT1 and LOWPT2 we can now reorder adjacency lists using bucket sort. Let $c : E \to \mathbb{R}$ be defined by

$$c(v,w) = \begin{cases} 2w & \text{if } (v,w) \in B \\ 2\ \text{LOWPT1}[w] & \text{if } (v,w) \in T \text{ and LOWPT2}[w] \geq v \\ 2\ \text{LOWPT1}[w] + 1 & \text{if } (v,w) \in T \text{ and LOWPT2}[w] < v \end{cases}$$

We want to reorder adjacency lists according to non-decreasing order of c. We can do so in linear time by bucket sort. Have 2n initially empty buckets. Step through the edges of G one by one and throw edge (v,w) into bucket c(v,w). After having done so we go through the buckets in decreasing order. When edge (v,w) is encountered we add (v,w) to the front of v's adjacency list.

In our example, the edges out of node 7 are ordered (7,8), (7,13), (7,5) and the edges out of node 11 are ordered (11,12), (11,7), (11,8).

From now on, we assume that adjacency lists are reordered in the way described above. Then spine paths and spine cycles of segments can be found very easily. Consider segment $S(e_o)$ where $e_o = (x,y)$. Start in node y and construct a path by always taking the first edge out of every node until a backward edge is encountered. This path is easily seen to be a spine path of segment $S(e_o)$.

We resume the discussion of how to deal with the interlacing graph now. As in lemma 4, C' is the spine cycle of some segment $S(e_o)$, i.e. $C' = w_o \underset{T}{\rightarrow} w_1 \underset{T}{\rightarrow} \cdots \underset{T}{\rightarrow} w_k \underset{B}{\rightarrow} w_o$ and $e_o = (w_r, w_{r+1})$ for some r. Let $e_1,\ldots,e_m$ be the edges leaving the spine of $S(e_o)$ <u>in order</u>, i.e. the edges leaving w_k are considered first and for each w_j the edges are ordered as described above. Let $IG_i(C')$ be the subgraph of $IG(C')$ spanned by $S(e_1),\ldots,S(e_i)$. If $IG_i(C')$ is non-bipartite then so is $IG(C')$ and hence $S(e_o)$ is not strongly planar. If $IG_i(C)$ is bipartite then every connected component (= block) of $IG_i(C)$ is. If B is a block of $IG_i(C)$ then we use LB, RB to denote the partition of B induced by the bipartite graph.

Our next goal is to describe how the blocks of $IG_{i+1}(C)$ can be obtained from the blocks of $IG_i(C)$. Let $e_{i+1} = (v_j, z)$. For every block B of $IG_i(C)$ let

$$ALB = \{w_h;\ h < j \text{ and } w_h \in A(e) \text{ for some } S(e) \in LB\}$$

be the set of attachments (below v_j) of segments in LB. ARB is defined similarly.

<u>Lemma 5:</u> If $IG_i(C')$ is bipartite, then

a) there is some ordering of the blocks of $IG_i(C)$, say $B_1, B_2, \ldots, B_h, B_{h+1}, \ldots$ such that

$$\max(ALB_\ell \cup ARB_\ell) \le \min(ALB_{\ell+1} \cup ARB_{\ell+1})$$

for $1 \le \ell < h$ and $ALB_\ell = ARB_\ell = \emptyset$ for $\ell \ge h$.

b) $IG_{i+1}(C')$ is bipartite iff for all ℓ, $1 \le \ell \le h$, either $\max ALB_\ell \le LOWPT1'[z]$ or $\max ARB_\ell \le LOWPT1'[z]$. Here, $LOWPT1'[z] = z$ if $e_{i+1} = (v_j, z)$ is a backward edge and $LOWPT1'[z] = LOWPT1[z]$ otherwise.

c) If $IG_{i+1}(C')$ is bipartite then the blocks of $IG_{i+1}(C)$ can be obtained as follows: Assume w.l.o.g. that max $ALB_\ell \le LOWPT1'[z]$ for all ℓ (this can always be achieved by interchanging LB and RB for some blocks B). Let $d = \min\{\ell;\ \max ARB_\ell > LOWPT1'[z]\}$. Then the blocks of $IG_{i+1}(C)$ are $B_1,\dots,B_{d-1}, B_d \cup \dots \cup B_h \cup \{S(e_{i+1})\}, B_{h+1},\dots$.

d) If $IG_{i+1}(C')$ is bipartite and $S(e_\ell)$, $1 \le \ell \le i+1$, are strongly planar then there is a planar embedding of $C' + S(e_1) + \dots + S(e_{i+1})$ such that all segments in $\bigcup_\ell LB_\ell$ are embedded inside C' and all segments in $\bigcup_\ell RB_\ell$ are embedded outside C'.

<u>Proof:</u> We use induction on i. For $i = 0$ there is little to show. $IG_0(C')$ is empty and $IG_1(C')$ consists of a single node. This shows a), b) and c). For part d) we only have to observe that $S(e_1)$ can be embedded inside as well as outside C' (if $S(e_1)$ is strongly planar).

So let us turn to the case $i > 0$. We will show parts b), c), a) and d) in this order.

b) "⇒". Note first that it suffices to show the following

<u>Claim 1:</u> If max $ALB_\ell > LOWPT1'[z]$ then there is a segment $S(e) \in LB_\ell$ such that $S(e)$ and $S(e_{i+1})$ interlace.

Suppose we have shown the claim. If there were ℓ, $1 \le \ell \le h$, such that max $ALB_\ell > LOWPT1'[z]$ and max $ARB_\ell > LOWPT1'[z]$ then $S(e_{i+1})$ interlaces with a segment $S(e) \in LB_\ell$ and a segment $S(e') \in RB_\ell$. Since $S(e)$ and $S(e')$ belong to the same block there is a path from $S(e)$ to $S(e')$ in $IG_i(C)$. Since $IG_i(C)$ is bipartite this path necessarily has odd length. Together with edges $S(e) - S(e_{i+1}) - S(e')$ we obtain an odd length cycle in $IG_{i+1}(C)$. Hence $IG_{i+1}(C)$ is non-bipartite, a contradiction. It remains to show claim 1.

<u>Proof of claim 1:</u> Let $v = LOWPT1'[z]$. Since max $ALB_\ell > v$ there must be a segment $S(e) \in LB_\ell$ such that $w \in A(e)$ for some w with $v \xrightarrow[T]{+} w \xrightarrow[T]{+} w_j$. Edge e emanates from node w_p for some $p \ge j$.

<u>Case 1:</u> $p > j$. Then $v \xrightarrow[T]{+} w \xrightarrow[T]{+} w_j \xrightarrow[T]{+} w_p$, $v, w_j \in A(e_{i+1})$ and $w, w_p \in A(e)$. Hence segments $S(e)$ and $S(e_{i+1})$ interlace (cf. figure 1).

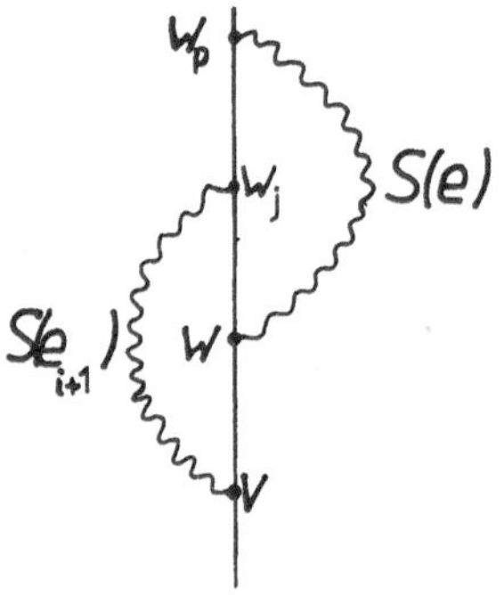

figure 1

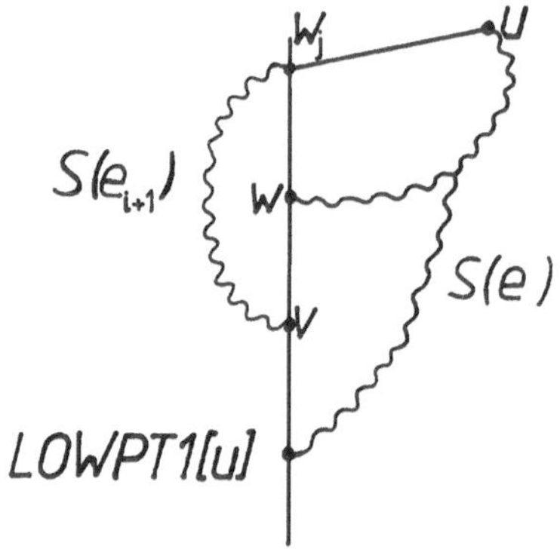

figure 2

Case 2: $p = j$. Let $e = (w_j,u)$. Since e is considered before e_{i+1} and hence $LOWPT1'[u] \le v$, edge e cannot be a backward edge (If it were a backward edge then $LOWPT1'[u] = u = w > v$, a contradiction). Hence e is a tree edge and $LOWPT1'[u] = LOWPT1[u]$.

Case 2.1: $LOWPT[u] < v$. Then $LOWPT1[u] \xrightarrow[T]{}^{+} v \xrightarrow[T]{}^{+} w \xrightarrow[T]{}^{+} w_j$, $LOWPT1[u]$, $w \in A(e)$ and $v,w_j \in A(e_{i+1})$. Hence segments $S(e)$ and $S(e_{i+1})$ interlace (cf. figure 2).

Case 2.2: $LOWPT1[u] = v$. Since $w \in A(e)$ we have $LOWPT2[u] < w_j$. Since e is considered before e_{i+1} edge e_{i+1} cannot be a backward edge. Rather, it must be a tree edge and we must have $LOWPT2[z] < w_j$. If $LOWPT2[z] \neq LOWPT2[u]$, say $LOWPT2[z] \xrightarrow[T]{}^{+} LOWPT2[u]$, then we have $v \xrightarrow[T]{}^{+} LOWPT2[z] \xrightarrow[T]{}^{+} LOWPT2[u] \xrightarrow[T]{}^{+} w_j$, $v, LOWPT2[u] \in A(e)$, and $LOWPT2[z]$, $w_j \in A(e_{i+1})$. Hence $S(e_{i+1})$ and $S(e)$ interlace (cf. figure 3). If $LOWPT2[z] = LOWPT2[u]$ then $A(e)$ and $A(e_{i+1})$ have three points in common and hence $S(e_i)$ and $S(e_{i+1})$ interlace (cf. figure 4)(see next page).

"$\Leftarrow$". Assume now that $\max ALB_\ell \le LOWPT1'[z]$ or $\max ARB_\ell \le LOWPT1'[z]$ for all ℓ, $1 \le \ell \le h$. By interchanging LB_ℓ and RB_ℓ, if necessary, we can achieve that $\max ALB_\ell \le LOWPT1'[z]$ for all ℓ, $1 \le \ell \le h$.

Claim 2: Let $S(e) \in \bigcup_\ell LB_\ell$ be arbitrary. Then $S(e)$ and $S(e_{i+1})$ do not interlace.

Proof: We have $A(e_{i+1}) \subseteq \{w;\ LOWPT1'[z] \xrightarrow[T]{}^{*} w \xrightarrow[T]{}^{*} w_j\}$ and $A(e) \subseteq \{w;\ w \xrightarrow[T]{}^{*} LOWPT1'[z]$ or $w_j \rightarrow^{*} w\}$. Hence $S(e)$ and $S(e_{i+1})$ do not interlace. □

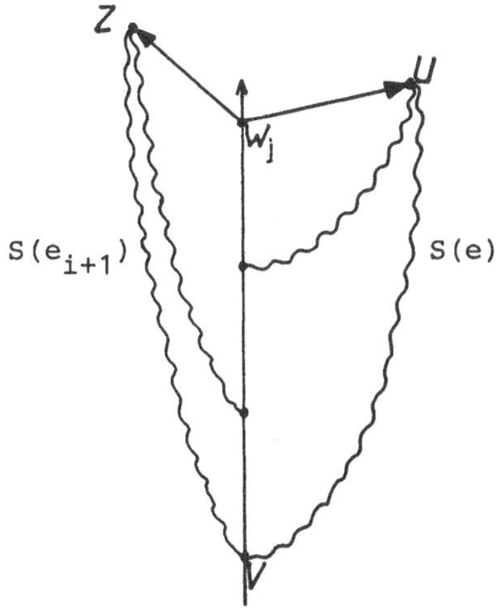

figure 3

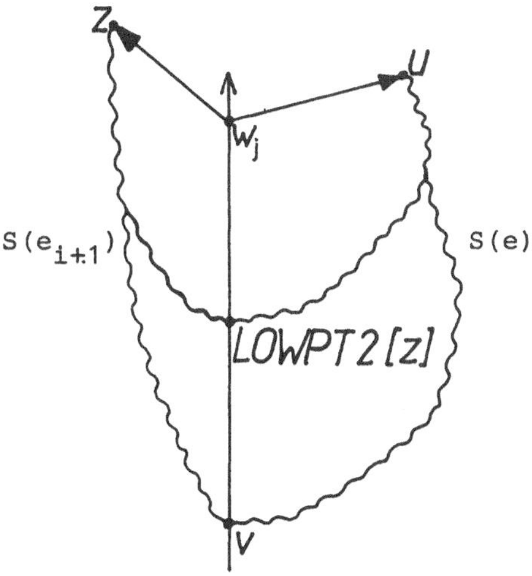

figure 4

The bipartiteness of $IG_{i+1}(C')$ follows directly from claim 2 because it is safe to add $S(e_{i+1})$ to the "left side" of the interlacing graph.

c) Assume that $IG_{i+1}(C')$ is bipartite. Then for all ℓ, $1 \le \ell \le h$, $\max ALB_\ell \le LOWPT1'[z]$ or $\max ARB_\ell \le LOWPT1'[z]$ by part b). By interchanging LB_ℓ and RB_ℓ, if necessary, we can achieve $\max ALB_\ell \le LOWPT1'[z]$ for all ℓ. Let $d = \min\{\ell;\ \max ARB_\ell > LOWPT1'[z]\}$.

Claim 3: For all ℓ: there is a segment $S(e) \in RB_\ell$ such that $S(e)$ and $S(e_{i+1})$ interlace iff $d \le \ell \le h$.

Proof: "⇐". Let $d \le \ell \le h$. Then

$$
\begin{aligned}
LOWPT1'[z] &< \max ARB_d && \text{,by definition of } d \\
&\le \min ARB_\ell && \text{,by induction hypothesis, part a) and } d \le \ell \\
&\le \max ARB_\ell && \\
&< w_j && \text{,since } \ell \le h
\end{aligned}
$$

and hence there is a segment $S(e) \in RB_\ell$ such that $S(e)$ and $S(e_{i+1})$ interlace by claim 1.

"⇒". (Indirect). Let $\ell < d$ or $\ell > h$ and let $S(e) \in RB_\ell$. Then $A(e) \subseteq \{w;\ w_j \underset{T}{\to^*} w\}$ if $\ell > h$ and $A(e) \subseteq \{w;\ w_j \underset{T}{\to^*} w$ or $w \underset{T}{\to^*} LOWPT1[z]\}$ if $\ell < d$. The former inclusion follows from the definition of h, the latter inclusion follows from the definition of d, and part a) of the induction hypothesis. Also from $A(e_{i+1}) \subseteq \{w;\ LOWPT1'[z] \underset{T}{\to^*} w \underset{T}{\to^*} w_j\}$ and hence $S(e)$ and $S(e_{i+1})$ do not interlace.

□

We conclude from claims 2 and 3 that $S(e_{i+1})$ is connected to segments in blocks $B_d,\ldots,B_h$. Hence the blocks of $IG_{i+1}(C)$ are $B_1,\ldots,B_{d-1}$, $B_d \cup \ldots \cup B_h \cup \{S(e_{i+1})\}$, $B_{h+1},\ldots,$. Let $B = B_d \cup \ldots \cup B_h \cup \{S(e_{i+1})\}$ be the new block. Then B can be partitioned into LB and RB where $LB = \bigcup_{d\le\ell\le h} LB_\ell \cup \{S(e_{i+1})\}$ and $RB = \bigcup_{d\le\ell\le h} RB_\ell$. Moreover, $\max RB_d \le \min RB_{d+1} \le \max RB_{d+1} \le \ldots \le \min RB_h \le \max RB_h$ by part a) and $\max LB_d \le \min LB_{d+1} \le \max LB_{d+1} \le \ldots \le \min LB_h \le \max LB_h \le \min A(e_{i+1})$ by part a) and the assumption that $\max ALB_\ell \le LOWPT1'[z] = \min A(e_{i+1})$ for all ℓ, $1 \le \ell \le h$.

a) follows immediately from part c). The ordering of blocks of $IG_{i+1}(C)$ given in part c) satisfies the conditions required in part a). This follows immediately from the discussion closing the proof of part c).

d) Assume that $IG_{i+1}(C')$ is bipartite and that $S(e_\ell)$, $1 \le \ell \le i+1$, are strongly planar. Let $B'_1, B'_2,\ldots$ be the blocks of $IG_{i+1}(C')$. By part c) we have $B'_1 = B_1,\ldots,B'_{d-1} = B_{d-1}$, $B'_d = B_d \cup \ldots \cup B_h \cup \{S(e_{i+1})\}$, $B'_{d+1} = B_{h+1},\ldots$ where $B_1,B_2,\ldots$ are the blocks of $IG_i(C)$. Moreover, $LB'_\ell = LB_\ell$, $RB'_\ell = RB_\ell$ for $\ell < d$, $LB'_{d+\ell} = LB_{h+\ell}$, $RB'_{d+\ell} = RB_{h+\ell}$ for $\ell \ge 0$ and $LB'_d = \bigcup_{d\le\ell\le h} LB_\ell \cup \{S(e_{i+1})\}$ and $RB'_d = \bigcup_{d\le\ell\le h} RB_\ell$. By induction hypothesis there is a planar embedding of $C' + S(e_1) + \ldots + S(e_i)$ such that all segments in $\bigcup_\ell LB_\ell$ are embedded inside C and all segments in $\bigcup_\ell RB_\ell$ are embedded outside C. By the proof of claim 2 no segment $S(e) \in \bigcup_\ell LB_\ell$ has an attachment w which lies strictly between LOWPT1'[z] and w_j. Thus there is a face F (inside C) such that the tree path from LOWPT1'[z] to w_j is part of the boundary of F. All attachments of $S(e_{i+1})$ lie between LOWPT1'[z] and w_j inclusive. Moreover, $S(e_{i+1})$ is strongly planar and hence there is a planar embedding of $C' + S(e_{i+1})$ where the tree path from LOWPT1'[z] to w_j borders the outer face. We can add this embedding to the embedding of $C' + S(e_1) + \ldots + S(e_i)$

by putting it inside face F. In this way we obtain a planar embedding of C' + S(e_1) + ... + S(e_{i+1}). This finishes the proof of lemma 5.

In the diagram below we illustrate how segment S(e_{i+1}) can be added to the embedding of C' + S(e_1) + ... + S(e_i). □

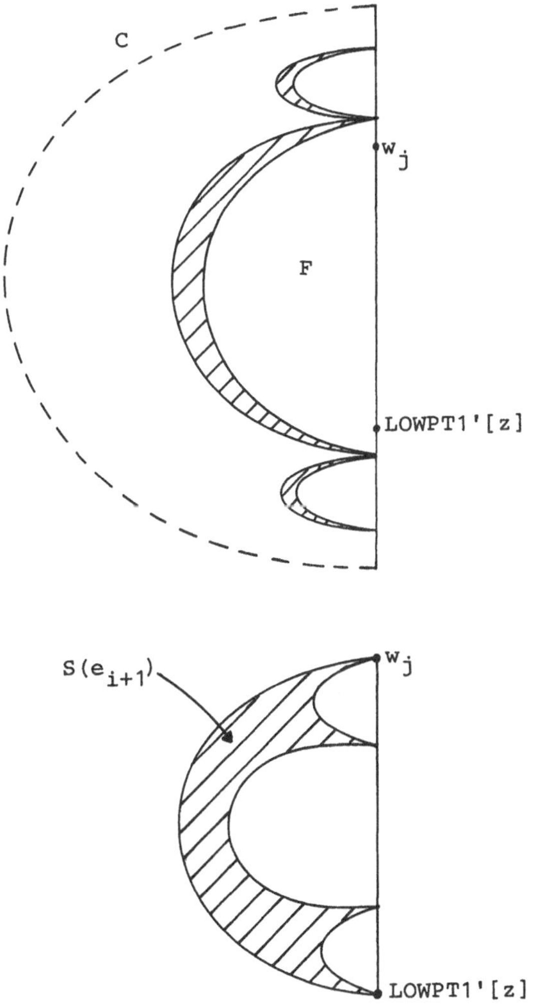

We illustrate lemma 5 on our example. Let C' be the cycle which runs from node 1 to node 9 along tree edges and then back to node 1. There are four segments emanating from this cycle: S_1 = ((9,1o)), S_2 = S((7,13)), S_3 = S((7,5)) and S_4 = S((6,4)). All four segments are strongly planar. When segment S_2 = S((7,13)) is considered, we have: $IG_1(C')$ has one block B_1 consisting of segment S_1. Say S_1 belongs to RB_1. Then $ARB_1 = \emptyset$ and $ALB_1 = \{5\}$. Lemma 5,b is satisfied and hence $IG_2(C')$ is bipartite. We have d = 1 in lemma 5,c and hence $IG_2(C')$ has only block B_1, say $LB_1 = \{S_2\}$ and $RB_1 = \{S_1\}$. Then $ALB_1 = \{3\}$ and $ARB_1 = \{5\}$ when S_3 is considered. $IG_3(C')$ is bipartite and has two blocks B_1 and B_2, say $LB_1 = \{S_2\}$, $RB_1 = \{S_1\}$, $RB_2 = \{S_3\}$. Then $ALB_1 = \{3\}$, $ARB_1 = \{5\}$, $ARB_2 = \{5\}$, $ALB_2 = \emptyset$ when S_4 is considered. S_4 forces us to merge blocks B_1 and B_2, i.e. d = 1 in lemma 5,c, and hence $IG_4(C')$ has only one block B_1. Moreover $LB_1 = \{S_2, S_4\}$ and $RB_1 = \{S_1, S_3\}$.

From lemma 5 is it now easy to derive an efficient way of dealing with the interlacing graph. Suppose that we processed edges $e_1, \ldots, e_i$ and want to process edge e_{i+1} next. At this point we keep blocks $B_1, \ldots, B_h$ in a stack where h is defined as in lemma 4. Also for each ℓ, $1 \le \ell \le h$, we keep multi-sets ALB_ℓ and ARB_ℓ in a doubly linked list. Sets ALB_ℓ and ARB_ℓ are <u>ordered</u> according to DFS number. From the stack position corresponding to B_ℓ we have pointers to the front and back end of lists ALB_ℓ and ARB_ℓ.

The test for bipartiteness of $IG_{i+1}(C)$ given in lemma 5b is now easily implemented.

```
ℓ ← h + 1;
while max(ALB_{ℓ-1} ∪ ARB_{ℓ-1}) > LOWPT1'[z]
do if ALB_{ℓ-1} is non-empty and max ALB_{ℓ-1} > LOWPT1'[z]
   then interchange LB_{ℓ-1} and RB_{ℓ-1} fi;
   if ALB_{ℓ-1} is non-empty and max ALB_{ℓ-1} > LOWPT1'[z]
   then IG_{i+1}(C') is not bipartite and hence the graph can be declared
        non-planar
   fi;
   ℓ ← ℓ - 1
od;
d ← ℓ
```

The running time of this algorithm is clearly O(h - d + 1). Also, it correctly computes d as defined in lemma 5,c. The new blocks of $IG_{i+1}(C)$ are now easily formed.

ALB ← ARB ← ∅;
for ℓ from d to h
do ALB ← ALB concatenated with ALB_ℓ;
   ARB ← ARB concatenated with ARB_ℓ
od;
ALB ← ALB concatenated with $(A(e_{i+1}) - \{w_j\})$;
pop $B_h, \ldots, B_d$ from the stack;
add B to the stack

Again the running time of this algorithm is clearly O(h - d + 1) provided we are given $(A(e_{i+1}) - \{w_j\})$. Also it correctly computes lists ALB and ARB. Note that these lists are ordered by the remark ending the proof of lemma 5,c.

We can now give the complete planarity testing algorithm.

(0) procedure STRONGLYPLANAR (e_0: edge);
-- tests whether segment $S(e_0)$, e = (x,y), is strongly planar.
-- If so, it returns the ordered (according to DFS number) list of
-- attachments of $S(e_0)$ excluding x.
(1) find the spine path of segment $S(e_0)$ by starting in node y and always taking the first edge on every adjacency list until a backward edge is encountered. This back edge leads to node w_0 = LOWPT1'[y]. Let $w_0, \ldots, w_r$ be the tree path from v_0 to $x = w_r$ and let $w_{r+1} = y, \ldots, w_k$ be the spine path constructed above.
(2) let S be an empty stack of blocks;
(3) for j from k downto r + 1
(4) do for all edges e' (except the first) emanating from w_j
(5)   do STRONGLYPLANAR (e_j);
(6)   let $A(e_j)$ be the ordered list of attachments of $S(e_j)$ as returned by a successful call STRONGLYPLANAR (e_j);
(7)   update stack S as described above
(8)   od;
(9)   let B_h be the top entry in stack S;
(1o)   while $\max(ALB_h \cup ARB_h) = w_{j-1}$

```
(11)     do remove node w_{j-1} from ALB_h and ARB_h;
(12)        if ALB_h and ARB_h become empty
(13)        then pop B_h from the stack; h ← h - 1 fi
(14)     od;
(15) od;
     -- if control reaches this point then IG(C') is bipartite. We will
     -- now test for strong planarity and compute A(e_o).
(16) L ← ∅;       -- an empty list
(17) for ℓ from 1 to h
(18) do if max ALB_ℓ ≥ w_1 and  max ARB_ℓ ≥ w_1
(19)    then declare S(e_o) not strongly planar and stop fi;
(2o)    L ← L concatenated with (ALB_ℓ and ARB_ℓ) or (ARB_ℓ and ALB_ℓ)
            whatever order is appropriate
(21) od ;
(22) return L
(23) end
```

Lemma 6: The algorithm above tests strong planarity in linear time.

Proof: Observe first that line (1) determines the spine path of segment $S(e_o)$ in time proportional to the length of the spine path. Next we argue that bipartiteness of IG(C') is tested correctly. The correctness of loop (4) - (8) is immediate from the discussion following lemma 5. Suppose now that we processed all edges emanating from w_j. In order to prepare for processing the edges emanating from w_{j-1} we only have to delete all occurrences of w_{j-1} on lists ALB_ℓ and ARB_ℓ. This is done in lines (9) - (15). Note that all occurrences of w_{j-1} must be in the top entries of stack S by lemma 5a. Hence lines (9) - (15) work correctly. When control reaches line (16) interlacing graph IG(C') is bipartite. Moreover, lists ALB, ARB for blocks B in the stack contain exactly the attachments of segments $S(e_i)$ strictly below w_r. We can now complete the test for strong planarity by implementing the condition given in lemma 4. It states that for all blocks B of IG(C') either

$\{w_1,\dots,w_{r-1}\} \cap \bigcup_{S(e)\in LB} A(e) = \emptyset$ or $\{w_1,\dots,w_{r-1}\} \cap \bigcup_{S(e)\in RB} A(e) = \emptyset$.

This test is carried out in line (18). Also if $S(e_o)$ is strongly planar, then the ordered set of attachments of $S(e_o)$ below x is correctly collected in line (2o). This finishes the proof of correctness.

It remains to analyse running time. Note first that STRONGLYPLANAR is called at most once for every edge. Also every edge belongs to at most one spine path. Hence total time spent in lines (1), (2), (3), (4), (5) (not counting the time spent within the recursive call) (6), (8), (9) and (16) is O(e). Let us look at line (7) next. Observe that line (7) is executed once for each edge. Also at most one block is pushed on stack S in one execution of line (7), and execution time of line (7) is proportional to the number of entries removed from stack S. Since only e elements are added to stacks S altogether, only e elements can be removed and hence total time spent in line (7) is O(e). The same argument shows that total time spent in lines (16) - (21) is O(e), because the time spent in these lines is proportional to the number of elements removed from stacks S in these lines. It remains to consider lines (9) - (14). Only endpoints of backward edges are placed on lists ALB and ARB. No backward edge is placed twice on a list and every backward is removed at most once. Hence the total cost of lines (9) - (14) is O(e). □

<u>Theorem 1:</u> Let G = (V,E) be a graph. Then planarity of G can be tested in time O(n).

<u>Proof:</u> If $e > 3n - 6$ then G is non-planar. If $e \le 3n - 6$ then we can divide G into its biconnected components in time O(e) = O(n). For each biconnected component we can test strong planarity and hence planarity in linear time. Also a graph is planar iff its biconnected components are. □

At this point we arrived at an O(n) algorithm for testing planarity. Suppose now that G = (V,E) is a planar graph. Does a successful planarity test also tell us something about a planar embedding? In particular, does it determine the faces of a possible planar embedding? We will show that it does.

A planar graph G = (V,E) together with a cyclic ordering σ of the edges incident to any node $v \in V$ is a <u>planar map</u> if there is a planar embedding of G such that cyclic ordering σ agrees with the clockwise ordering of the edges in the embedding. The example (see next page) shows a planar map (think of the adjacency lists as circular lists) and a corresponding embedding. The faces of a planar map are easily determined by the following algorithm. Declare all edges unused initially.

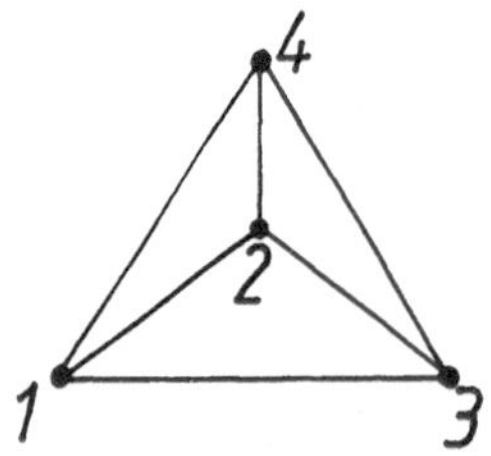

1: (1,2), (1,3), (1,4)
2: (2,4), (2,3), (2,1)
3: (3,1), (3,2), (3,4)
4: (4,2), (4,1), (4,3)

```
while there are unused edges
do let e = (u_o,v) be any unused edge; let x = u_o;
   declare e used in the direction from u_o to v;
   while v ≠ u_o
   do let e' = (v,w) be the edge following (v,x) in the cyclic order-
      ing of edges around v;
      declare e' used in the direction from v to w;
      x ← v; v ← w
   od
od
```

The running time of this algorithm is linear because every edge is traversed exactly twice, once in each direction.

We show next how the planarity testing algorithm can be used to turn a planar graph into a planar map. Let $G = (V,E)$ be a planar map. Consider an application of the planarity testing algorithm to graph G. Let C' be the spine cycle of some segment $S(e_o)$ and let $e_1,\dots,e_m$ be the edges emanating from the spine path. The planarity testing algorithm computes the blocks (and their partition into sides) of IG(C'). More precisely, it computes a mapping α: $\{S(e_1),\dots,S(e_m)\} \to \{L,R\}$ such that no two segments with the same label interlace. Mapping α can be computed as follows. Let B be the block of IG(C') which contains S(e). Algorithm STRONGLYPLANAR computes B iteratively. Construction of B is certainly completed when B is popped from stack S. Let $\alpha(S(e)) = R$ if $S(e) \in RB$ at that point of time and let $\alpha(S(e)) = L$ otherwise. With this extension, algorithm STRONGLYPLANAR computes mapping α in linear time.

Suppose now that we know mapping α. Run algorithm STRONGLYPLANAR again. When segment S(e) has to be added to the planar embedding, add it as given by α. In this way, no flipping of sides ever takes place. Also the proof of lemma 5d shows us how segment $S(e_{i+1})$ can be placed with respect to previously placed segments. Thus when $S(e_{i+1})$ is added to the planar embedding all edges which attach $S(e_{i+1})$ to the spine cycle of $S(e_o)$ can be inserted into the correct position in the cyclic ordering of edges around nodes on the path of tree edges in C'. More precisely, let father[w] be such that (father[w],w) $\in$ T. Then any edge which attaches $S(e_{i+1})$ to C' at point w can be inserted immediately after (before) tree edge (father[w],w) in the cyclic ordering. We summarize in

Theorem 2: Let G = (V,E) be a planar graph. Then G can be turned into a planar map (G,σ) in linear time. Moreover, the faces of (G,σ) can be determined in linear time.

Planar graphs have more structure than general graphs and are therefore in many respects computationally simpler than general graphs. The planar separator theorem (theorem 3 below) makes planar graphs amenable to divide and conquer algorithms. It states that a planar graph can be split into about equal sized subgraphs by the removal of only $O(\sqrt{n})$ nodes.

Theorem 3: Let G = (V,E) be a planar graph and let $w: V \to \mathbb{R}_{\geq 0}$ be a weight function on the vertices of G. Let $W = \sum_{v \in V} w(v)$ be the total weight of G. Then there is a partition A,S,B of V such that

1) $W(A) = \sum_{v \in A} w(v) \leq 2W/3$, $W(B) \leq 2W/3$

2) $|S| \leq 4\sqrt{n}$

3) S separates A from B, i.e. $E \cap (A \times B) = \emptyset$

4) Partition A,S,B can be constructed in time O(n).

Proof: Assume first that G is connected. Let $s \in V$ be arbitrary and let $L(t) = \{v;\ v \in V$ and the shortest path from s to v has length $t\}$ for $t \geq 0$. Then $L(0) = \{s\}$. Let r be maximal such that $L(r) \neq \emptyset$. Add empty levels $L(-1) = L(r+1) = \emptyset$ for the sake of convenience.

Let t_1 be such that

$$W(L(0) \cup \ldots \cup L(t_1 - 1)) \leq W/2 \leq W(L(0) \cup \ldots \cup L(t_1))$$

, let $t_0 \le t_1$ be such that $|L(t_0)| + (t_1 - t_0) < 2\sqrt{n}$ and let $t_2 > t_1$ be such that $|L(t_2)| + (t_2 - t_1 - 1) < 2\sqrt{n}$.

<u>Claim 1:</u> t_0, t_1 and t_2 exist.

<u>Proof:</u> The existence of t_1 is obvious. If $t_1 < \sqrt{n}$ then we can choose $t_0 = -1$. If $t_1 \ge \sqrt{n}$ then $|L(t_1 - \sqrt{n})| + \ldots + |L(t_1)| \le n$ and hence $|L(t_0)| < \sqrt{n}$ for some t_0, $t_1 - \sqrt{n} \le t_0 \le t_1$. Thus $|L(t_0)| + t_1 - t_0 < 2\sqrt{n}$. In either case we have shown the existence of t_0. The existence of t_2 is shown similarly. □

Let us take a closer look at $W(L(t_0 + 1) \cup \ldots \cup L(t_2 - 1))$. If this weight is at most $2W/3$ then let $S = L(t_0) \cup L(t_2)$, let A be the heaviest of the three sets $L(0) \cup \ldots \cup L(t_0 - 1)$, $L(t_0 + 1) \cup \ldots \cup L(t_2 - 1)$, $L(t_2 + 1) \cup \ldots \cup L(r)$ and let B the union of the remaining two sets. Then $W(A) \le 2W/3$ and $W(B) \le 2W/3$.

Let us assume now that $W(L(t_0 + 1) \cup \ldots \cup L(t_2 - 1)) > 2W/3$. Construct planar graph G' as follows. Delete levels t_2 and above from the graph and shrink all nodes in levels t_0 and below to a single node, i.e. replace all nodes in levels t_0 and below by a single node and connect this node to all nodes in $L(t_0 + 1)$. The planarity of G' can be seen as follows. Consider a planar embedding of G and identify a tree of paths from s to all nodes in $L(t_0 + 1)$. Then delete all nodes in levels t_0 and below, make s the new node and draw the new edges along the tree paths. Note that graph G' has a spanning tree with radius $t_2 - t_0 - 1$, i.e. the newly constructed node is the root and all other nodes have distance at most $t_2 - t_0 - 1$ from the root.

Claim 2: Let $G = (V,E)$ be a connected planar graph having a spanning tree of radius r and let $w: V \to \mathbb{R}_{\ge 0}$ be a weight function. Then there is a partition A,S,B of V such that $W(A) \le 2W/3$, $W(B) \le 2W/3$, $|S| \le 2r + 1$, S contains the root of the spanning tree, and S separates A from B. Moreover, partition A,S,B can be found in time $O(n)$.

Suppose that we have shown claim 2. Clearly, all steps of the proof preceeding claim 2 can be carried out in linear time, i.e. the construction of levels $L(0), L(1), \ldots, L(r)$, determination of t_0, t_1 and t_2, and construction of G'. By claim 2 we can find a partition A',S',B' of the nodes of G' such that S' contains at most $2(t_2 - t_0 - 1) + 1$ nodes one of which is the node which replaced levels t_0 and below. Let $S = L(t_0) \cup L(t_2) \cup (S' - \{\text{new node}\})$. Then

$$|S| \le |L(t_0)| + |L(t_2)| + 2(t_2 - t_0)$$

$$= |L(t_0)| + 2(t_1 - t_0) + |L(t_2)| + 2(t_2 - t_1 - 1) + 2$$

$$\le 2\sqrt{n} - 1 + 2\sqrt{n} - 1 + 2 = 4\sqrt{n}$$

Removal of S from G splits G into sets $L(0) \cup \ldots \cup L(t_0 - 1)$, A',B', $L(t_2 + 1) \cup \ldots \cup L(r)$ none of which has weight exceeding 2W/3. It is easy to form sets A and B from these four sets such that $W(A) \le 2W/3$ and $W(B) \le 2W/3$. Moreover, partition A',S',B' and hence partition A,S,B can be found in linear time.

Proof of Claim 2: If there is $v \in V$ with $w(v) \ge W/3$ then let S consist of v and the root of the spanning tree, let $A = \emptyset$ and let $B = V - S$. Clearly, partition A,S,B has all properties desired.

So let us assume next that $w(v) < W/3$ for all $v \in V$. Extend G to a planar map $\hat{G}$; this can be done in time $O(n)$ by theorem 2. Add edges to $\hat{G}$ such that every face becomes a triangle. Let T be a spanning tree of G of radius at most r. Every non-tree edge of G forms a simple cycle with some of the tree edges. This cycle has length at most $2r + 1$ if the root belongs to the cycle and has length at most $2r-1$ otherwise. Every such cycle separates its inside from its outside. It therefore suffices to show that there is one such cycle such that neither inside nor outside has weight exceeding 2W/3. More precisely, if e is a non-tree edge, let C(e) by the cycle defined by e, let WC(e) be the weight of cycle C(e), i.e. $WC(e) = \sum_{v \in C(e)} w(v)$ and let WI(e) be the weight of the nodes in the inferior of C(e).

In our example (see next page)(tree edges are shown solid, non-tree edges are shown dashed) we have for e = (2,6), C(e) = (2,1,5,7,6), $WC(e) = w(2) + w(1) + w(5) + w(7) + w(6)$ and $WI(e) = w(3) + w(4)$.

We have to show that there is a non-tree edge e such that $WI(e) \le 2W/3$ and $WI(e) + WC(e) \ge W/3$. The following program computes WI(e), WC(e), and C(e) for (all) non-tree edges e. We assume that C(e) is stored as

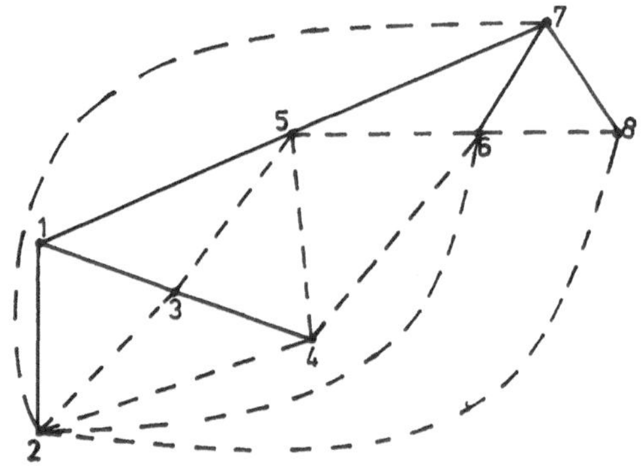

a doubly linked list. The program makes use of procedure CYCLE which computes C(e), WI(e) and WC(e) for non-tree edge e. The body of CYCLE is basically a case distinction according to the type of edges in the triangle inside C(e) with edge e. This case distinction is illustrated in the figures below. In the main program CYCLE is called at most once for every non-tree edge e.

```
begin for all non-tree edges e do WC(e) ← undefined od;
      for all non-tree edges e
      do if WC(e) is undefined then CYCLE(e) fi od
end
```

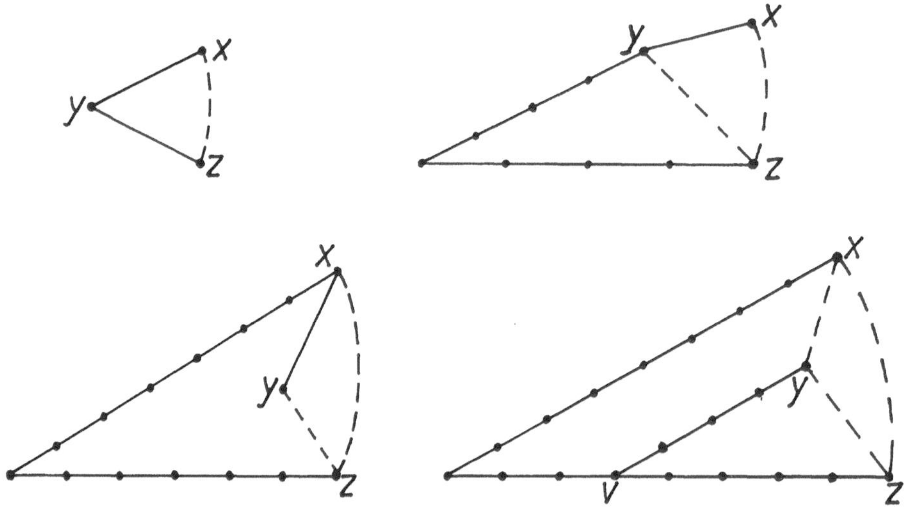

where procedure CYCLE is given by

<u>procedure</u> CYCLE (e: non-tree edge);
-- computes C(e) as a doubly linked list and weights WI(e) and WC(e);
-- stops computation if C(e) is desired cycle
let e = (x,z), and let y be the third node of the triangle inside C(e) which has e as an edge;

<u>Case 1:</u> (x,y) and (y,z) are tree edges. Then triangle (x,y,z) is cycle C(e) and hence C(e) ← (x,y,z), WI(e) ← 0 and WC(e) ← w(x) + w(y) + w(z).

<u>Case 2:</u> (x,y) is a tree edge, and (y,z) is not. Moreover, edge (x,y) lies on cycle C(e), i.e. y is closer to the root of the spanning tree than x.

CYCLE((y,z));
C(e) ← x concatenated with C((y,z));
WC(e) ← WC((y,z)) + w(x);
WI(e) ← WI((y,z));

<u>Case 3:</u> (x,y) is a tree edge, (y,z) is not, and edge (x,y) does not lie on cycle C(e), i.e. y is farther away from the root of the spanning tree than x.

CYCLE((y,z));
C(e) ← C((y,z)) minus node y;
WC(e) ← WC((y,z)) - w(y);
WI(e) ← WI((y,z)) + w(y)

<u>Case 4:</u> Neither (x,y) nor (y,z) are tree edges.

CYCLE((x,y));
CYCLE((y,z));
let p be path from y to C(e) including y and excluding v where v is the node on C(e) where p meets C(e). v is the last common node on cycles C((y,z)) and C((x,y)) and p is the set of nodes preceeding v;
C(e) ← (C((x,y)) minus p) concatenated with (C((y,z)) minus p);
WC(e) ← WC((x,y)) + WC((y,z)) - 2W(p) - w(z);
WI(e) ← WI((x,y)) + WI((y,z)) + W(p);
<u>end of case-distinction</u>;

<u>if</u> WI(e) ≤ 2W/3 and WC(e) + WI(e) ≥ W/3
<u>then</u> stop and exhibit C(e) as the desired cycle <u>fi</u>
<u>end</u>

It remains to show that some call of CYCLE finds a cycle with the desired properties and to analyse the running time. We show first that running time is linear. Note first that CYCLE is called once for every non-tree edge e. Also the cost of a call to CYCLE is O(1) if case 1,2 or 3 is taken in the body and it is O(|p|) in case 4 where |p| is the number of nodes on path p. Also 2|p| nodes are deleted from cycles C((x,y)) and C((y,z)) when cycle C(e) is formed in the latter case. Since at most two tree edges are added to cycles in a single execution of cases 1 to 3 the total number of nodes deleted in case 4 must be O(n). Thus the total cost of either case is O(n) and hence total running time is O(n).

Finally, we have to show that a cycle with the desired properties is found. We will show first that there is a non-tree edge e with WC(e) + WI(e) ≥ W/3. Since every face of $\hat{G}$ is a triangle, so is the outer face. Let e_1, e_2, e_3 be the edges bordering the outer face. At least one of them is a non-tree edge, say $e_1,..,e_i$ are non-tree edges for some i, 1 ≤ i ≤ 3. Then $\sum_{j=1}^{i} WC(e_j) + WI(e_j) \geq W$ since every node of G lies inside or on some of the cycles $C(e_j)$, j = 1,..,i. Thus $WC(e_j) + WI(e_j) \geq W/3$ for some j, 1 ≤ j ≤ i.

We can now exhibit edge e such that C(e) has the desired properties. Let e be a non-tree edge such that WC(e) + WI(e) ≥ W/3 and either case 1 is taken for e or WC(e') + WI(e') < W/3 for all non-tree edges e' such that CYCLE(e') is called by CYCLE(e). Edge e exists since there are edges with WC(e) + WI(e) ≥ W/3 and since case 1 is taken for at least one edge. If case 1 is taken then WI(e) = 0 and we are done. If case 2 is taken then WI(e) = WI(e') < W/3 and we are done. If case 3 is taken then WI(e) + WC(e) = WI(e') + WC(e') which is impossible. If case 4 is taken, let e_1 and e_2 be the two non-tree edges for which CYCLE is called. We have.

$$\begin{aligned} WI(e) &= WI(e_1) + WI(e_2) + W(p) \\ &\leq WI(e_1) + W(p) + WI(e_2) + W(p) \\ &\leq WI(e_1) + WC(e_1) + WI(e_2) + WC(e_2) \\ &\leq 2W/3 \end{aligned}$$

and hence C(e) is the desired cycle.

We have now proved theorem 3 for connected graphs. If G is unconnected, let $G_1, G_2, \dots, G_k$ be the connected components. If $W(G_i) \le 2W/3$ for all i then a partition with $S = \emptyset$ is possible. If $W(G_i) \ge 2W/3$ for some i then split G_i as described above and then proceed as in the former case.

□

An important corollary of theorem 3 is obtained in the unit cost case.

Corollary 4: Let G = (V,E) be a planar graph. Then there is a partition A,S,B of V such that

1) $|A| \le 2n/3$, $|B| \le 2n/3$
2) $|S| \le 4\sqrt{n}$
4) S separates A from B
4) Partition A,S,B can be found in time O(n).

Proof: Immediate from theorem 3 with $w(v) = 1$ for all $v \in V$.

We close this section with an application of the planar separator theorem. Let N = (V,E,c) with $c: E \to \mathbb{R}$ be a directed planar network and let $s \in V$ be a designated node. As in section 7 we will study the problem of computing $\mu(s,v)$, the cost of a least cost path from s to v, for any node $v \in V$. In section 7.3 we saw how to solve this problem in time $O(ne) = O(n^2)$ for planar networks. A better algorithm can be obtained by applying the separator property of planar graphs.

Theorem 5: The single source least cost path problem on planar networks can be solved in time $O(n^{1.5} \log n)$

Proof: Let N = (V,E,c) with $c: E \to \mathbb{R}$ be a planar directed network and let $s \in V$ be a designated node. We want to compute $\mu(s,v)$ for all nodes $v \in V$. The algorithm is as follows.

(1) Compute a partition V_1, S, V_2 as given by the planar separator theorem. Let $S \leftarrow S \cup \{s\}$ and let N_i be the subnetwork induced by $V_i \cup S$ for i = 1,2.

(2) Compute $\mu_1(t,v)$ for $t \in S$ and $v \in V_1 \cup S$. Here $\mu_1(t,v)$ is the cost

of a least cost path from t to v in subnetwork N_1. Similary, compute $\mu_2(t,v)$ for $t \in S$ and $v \in V_2 \cup S$. The details of this step are spelled out below.

(3) Define network $\bar{N} = (S, S \times S, \bar{c})$ by $\bar{c}(r,t) = \min\{\infty, \mu_1(r,t), \mu_2(r,t)\}$. Compute $\bar{\mu}(s,t)$ for all $t \in S$ where $\bar{\mu}(s,t)$ is the cost of a least cost path from s to t in network $\bar{N}$.

(4) for $v \in V_i \cup S$, $i = 1,2$, output $\mu(s,v) = \min_{t \in S} \{\bar{\mu}(s,t) + \mu_i(t,v)\}$.

The correctness of this algorithm is fairly easy to see. It follows from

Claim 1: a) $\bar{\mu}(s,t) = \mu(s,t)$ for all $t \in S$

b) $\mu(s,v) = \min\{\bar{\mu}(s,t) + \mu_i(t,v);\ t \in S\}$ for $v \in V_i$, $i = 1,2$.

Proof: a) Edges of $\bar{N}$ correspond to least cost paths in subnetworks N_i, $i = 1,2$. Thus $\bar{\mu}(s,t) \ge \mu(s,t)$ since every path in $\bar{N}$ gives rise to a path in N by replacing edges of $\bar{N}$ by paths in N. Also $\bar{\mu}(s,t) \le \mu(s,t)$ since a least cost path from s to t in N can be decomposed into sub-paths running completely within N_i, $i = 1,2$.

b) follows immediately from part a). □

It remains to describe the details of the implementation. For step 1 we use the algorithm described in corollary 4 above; it yields partition V_1, S, V_2 with $|V_1| \le 2n/3$, $|V_2| \le 2n/3$ and $|S| \le 5\sqrt{n}$ (We use 5 instead of 4 because node s is added to S). For step 3 we use the algorithm described in section 7.3.; it runs in time $O(|S|^3) = O(n^{1.5})$. Step 4 is also easily done in time $O(n^{1.5})$. It remains to describe step 2 in detail. We do so for subnetwork N_1.

(2.1) Compute $\mu_1(s,v)$ for all $v \in V_1 \cup S$ using the algorithm recursively. This takes time $T(|V_1 \cup S|)$ where $T(n)$ is the running time of the algorithm on an n node graph.

(2.2) Use the solution of step (2.1) to make all edge costs non-negative as described in section 7.4. Compute $\mu_1(t,v)$ for $t \in S$,

$v \in V_1 \cup S$ in time $O(|S|\ n_1 \log n_1) = O(n^{1.5} \log n)$ using the methods described in section 7.4. and 7.2.. Here $n_1 = |V_1 \cup S|$.

We conclude that the cost of step 2 is $T(n_1) + T(n_2) + O(n^{1.5} \log n)$ where $n_i = |V_i \cup S|$, $i = 1,2$. Altogether we have the following recurrence for $T(n)$

$$T(n) \le cn^{1.5} \log n \qquad \text{for } n < 1500$$

$$T(n) \le \max_{\substack{n_1+n_2 \le n+5\sqrt{n} \\ n_1,n_2 \le 4n/5}} \{T(n_1) + T(n_2) + dn^{1.5} \log n\} \qquad \text{for } n \ge 1500$$

Here c,d are appropriate constants, $n_1 = |V_1 \cup S| \le 2n/3 + 5\sqrt{n} \le 4n/5$ for $n \ge 1500$, $n_2 = |V_2 \cup S|$ and $n_1 + n_2 \le n + |S| \le n + 5\sqrt{n}$. $T(n)$ is clearly a non-decreasing function. Let $U(n) = T(n)/n$. Then

$$U(n) \le cn^{0.5} \log n \qquad \text{for } n < 1500$$

and

$$U(n) \le \max_{\substack{n_1+n_2 \le n+5\sqrt{n} \\ n_1,n_2 \le 4n/5}} \{(n_1/n)U(n_1) + (n_2/n)U(n_2) + dn^{0.5} \log n\}$$

$$\le \max_{n_1+n_2 \le n+5\sqrt{n}} \{((n_1+n_2)/n)U(4n/5) + dn^{0.5} \log n\}$$

$$\le (1 + 5/\sqrt{n})U(4n/5) + d\sqrt{n} \log n$$

for $n \ge 1500$. Let $k = k(n) = \lceil \log(n/1500)/\log(5/4) \rceil$ and $f(n) = d\sqrt{n} \log n$. Then

$$U(n) \le \sum_{i=0}^{k} \left[\prod_{j=0}^{i-1} (1 + 5/\sqrt{(4/5)^j n})\right] f((4/5)^i n)$$

for $n \ge 1500$.

<u>Claim 2:</u> $\prod_{j=0}^{i-1} (1 + 5/\sqrt{(4/5)^j n}) \le a$ for all $i \le k$ and some constant a.

Proof: We have

$$\prod_{j=0}^{k-1} (1 + 5/\sqrt{(4/5)^j n}) = e^{\sum_{j=0}^{k-1} \ell n(1 + 5/\sqrt{(4/5)^j n})}$$

$$\leq e^{\sum_{j=0}^{k-1} 5/\sqrt{(4/5)^j n}} \qquad \text{since } \ell n(1 + x) \leq x$$

$$\leq e^{5/\sqrt{(4/5)^k n} \sum_{j=1}^{k} (\sqrt{4/5})^j}$$

$$\leq a$$

for some constant a since $\sum_{j=1}^{\infty} (\sqrt{4/5})^j$ converges and since $1500 \geq (4/5)^k n \geq (4/5) \cdot 1500$. Constant a can be chosen as 3. □

Substituting into the upper bound for U(n) we obtain

$$U(n) \leq \sum_{i=0}^{k} a \cdot f((4/5)^i n)$$

$$\leq \sum_{i=0}^{k} a \cdot d \sqrt{(4/5)^i n} \log n$$

$$= O(\sqrt{n} \log n)$$

This proves that $T(n) = nU(n) = O(n^{1.5} \log n)$. □

Other applications of the planar separator theorem can be found in exercises 34 to 41.

IV. 11. Exercises

1) Let $G = (V,E)$ be a digraph. Let $G^{rev} = (V,E^{rev})$ be obtained from G by reversing all edges, i.e. $E^{rev} = \{(w,v);\ (v,w) \in E\}$. Show: Given the adjacency list representation of G one can compute the adjacency list representation of G^{rev} in time $O(n + e)$.

2) A multi-graph is given by a set V of nodes, a set K of edges and functions, $a,b: K \to V$. An edge $k \in K$ runs from $a(k)$ to $b(k)$. The underlying graph $G = (V,E)$ is defined by $E = \{(a(k),\ b(k));\ k \in K\}$, i.e. parallel edges are eliminated. Show: Given the adjacency list representation of a multi-graph, i.e. for every i a linear list containing <u>multi-set</u> $\{b(k);\ k \in K \text{ and } a(k) = i\}$, one can compute the adjacency list representation of G in time $O(|V| + |K|)$. (Hint: Use bucket sort to sort multi-set $\{(a(k);\ b(k));\ k \in K\}$ into lexicographic order).

3) Let $G = (V,E)$ be an acyclic digraph and let $\bar{G} = (V,\bar{E})$ be any acyclic digraph with the same transitive closure as G, i.e. $G^* = \bar{G}^*$. Show:

a) $E_{red} \subseteq \bar{E}$ where E_{red} is defined in section IV.3.

b) Conclude from part a) that G_{red} is the minimal graph (with respect to set inclusion) with a fixed transitive closure.

4) Let $G = (V,E)$ be an acyclic digraph. Show that one can compute G_{red} in time $O(ne_{red})$.

5) Show that one can use procedure Explorefrom of section 4 to compute the transitive closure of an arbitrary digraph in time $O(ne)$.

6) Let G be a context-free grammar. For sentential form α let $First_1(\alpha)$ be the set of terminal symbols a such that $\alpha \to^* a\beta$ for some β.

a) Show how to use procedure Explorefrom to compute $First_1(\alpha)$ if G contains no ε-rules.

b) Modify your solution to part a) such that ε-rules can also be handled.

7) Is the algorithm for strongly connected components still correct if line (24) is changed to

<u>then</u> LOWPT[v] ← min(LOWPT[v], LOWPT[w])

8) Let G = (V,E) be an undirected graph. G' = (V,E') is a minimal biconnected extension of G if $E \subset E'$, G' is biconnected, and $|E'|$ is a small as possible. Develop an algorithm to compute minimal biconnected extensions. (Hint: Solve the problem for trees G first. Extend to general graphs as follows. Let $V_1,\ldots,V_k$ be the b.c.c.'s of G. Define a graph with node set $V_1,\ldots,V_k$ and edges (V_i,V_j) iff $V_i \cap V_j \neq \emptyset$. This graph is a tree).

9) Derive a bound g(n) on the maximal number of iterations of the basic least cost path algorithm (cf. the beginning of section IV.7.) on a network on n nodes. Design networks where the algorithm might actually need (close to) g(n) iterations.

1o) Extend all least cost path algorithms such that they not only compute the least cost of a path but also the path itself. Running times should not change (Hint: Have array Pred[1..n]; whenever COST[v] is changed when considering edge (u,v) set Pred[v] to u. Then array Pred stores a tree of least cost paths after termination).

11) Let $\ell p(s,v) = \max\{c(p);\ p \text{ is a path from } s \text{ to } v\}$. Derive algorithms for computing $\ell p(s,v)$ for all $v \in V$ under various assumptions about the underlying network.

12) (Extension of 7.2., theorem 4). Let g_1,g_2 be estimators and let $g_1(v) \geq g_2(v)$ for all $v \in V$. Let R_i be the set of nodes removed from U when estimator g_i is used. Then $R_1 - R_2 \subseteq \{v;\ \mu(s,v) + g_1(v) = \mu(s,t)\}$ provided that g_1 is consistent.

13) Construct an instance of a least cost path problem and an estimator g such that some nodes are removed from U more than once.

14) Consider the following well-known "15-puzzle". The board consists of a 3 by 3 square with 8 1 by 1 tokens numbered 1 to 8 arranged on the board. One square of the board is empty. The goal is arrange the tokens into ascending order.

7	3	1
2	8	
4	6	5

a) Formulate this puzzle as a path finding problem. What are the nodes and what are the edges of the graph?

b) Use the path-finding algorithm of section 7.2. to find a solution. Use the following three estimators: constant zero, number of tokens out of place, total distance of tokens from their final position.

15) Show that the algorithm of section 7.3. has running time $O(k_{max}\ e)$ where k_{max} is the length (number of edges) of the longest least cost path form s to any $v \in V$.

16) For $v \in V$ let $COST_i[v] = \min\{c(p);$ p is a path from s to v of length (number of edges) at most i$\}$, $i \geq 0$. Show how to compute array $COST_i[1..n]$ from array $COST_{i-1}[1..n]$ in time $O(e)$. Conclude that the single source least cost path problem can be solved in time $O(ne)$. Relate this algorithm to the algorithm described in section 7.3.. Relate the algorithm of this exercise to dynamic programming in general.

17) It is a good idea to realize set U as a stack instead of a queue in the algorithm of section 7.3.? Is it a good ideal to replace the array COUNT[1..n] of counters by a single counter COUNT which counts iterations of the loop?

18) Let $N = (V,E,c)$, $c: E \to \mathbb{R}$ be a network. Let $E_p = \{(v,w) \in E;$ $c(v,w) \geq 0\}$ and let $E_n = \{(v,w) \in E;\ c(v,w) < 0\}$. If N has no negative cycles then (V,E_n) is acyclic. Show that one can solve a single source least cost path problem by repeatedly (at most n times) solving the problem for $N_p = (V,E_p,c)$ and $N_n = (V,E_n,c)$. Here function COST as computed by one algorithm is used as input to the other algorithm. Show that this idea leads to a $O(\min(ne + n^{2+1/k}, (n^2 + ne)\log n))$ algorithm for arbitrary integer k.

19) Consider the following algorithm for solving the single source least cost path problem. Let $E = \{e_1,\ldots,e_m\}$. Use the basic algorithm of the beginning of section 7. Go through the elements of E in <u>cyclic</u> order and check for the triangle inequality. Prove that this algorithm runs in time $O(ne)$.

2o) Design and analyse algorithms for maximum cost spanning trees.

21) Let $N = (V,E,c)$ be a network and let $s,t \in V$. Let f be a legal flow function. Show

$$val(f) = \sum_{e \in in(t)} f(e) - \sum_{e \in out(t)} f(e)$$

22) Let f be a legal (s,t)-flow in network N. Define the augmenting network AN with respect fo f by AN = $(V,E_1 \cup E_2,\bar{c})$ where E_1,E_2 are defined as in the definition of layered network. Note that AN captures <u>all</u> augmenting paths while LN captures only the minimum length augmenting path.

a) Construct AN for the example at the beginning of section 9.1..

b) Show that an analog of lemma 2 is true with AN instead of LN.

c) Define the concept of blocking flow and depth for augmenting networks. Does lemma 3 stay true? (Hint: check part b) of the claim in lemma 3 carefully).

23) Let N = (V,E,c) be a network with integral capacities, i.e. $c: V \rightarrow \mathbb{N}$. Let vmax be the maximal value of any legal (s,t)-flow in N. Show that vmax augmentations suffice to construct a maximal flow, where an augmentation can be done along any augmenting path.

24) Show that O(log vmax) augmentations suffice under the assumptions of exercise 23 if augmentation is always done along an augmenting path of maximal capacity.

25) Design efficient algorithms for each of the following versions of the max flow problem by reducing it to the standard version

a) the nodes, as well as the arcs, have capacities

b) there are many sources and sinks

c) the network is undirected

d) there are both upper and lower bounds on the value of the flow through each arc.

26) In the $O(n^2)$ algorithm for computing a blocking flow in a layered network we first determined a node v with PO(v) = PO* and then "forwarded" and "backwarded" flow starting at v.

a) Show that the algorithm stays correct if we only forward flow, but start at node s.

b) Can you still prove the $O(n^2)$ time bound?

27) Describe an algorithm for procedure SIMPLIFY in detail.

28) Adapt the $O(n^2)$ blocking flow algorithm for (0,1)-networks. Avoid recomputation of PO[v] for all $v \in V$ in line (5). Instead, compute PO[v] once and update it as edges incident to v are removed in procedures FORWARD, SUCK and SIMPLIFY. Also have an array L[1..e] of linear lists. In list L[i] store all nodes v with PO[v] = i. Keep a pointer in this list pointing to the leftmost non-empty list. Move this pointer to the right in order to find min{PO[v]; $v \in V$} in line (5), move it to the left when potentials are updated. Show that the total number of moves of the pointer is O(e). Conclude that a blocking flow in a (0,1)-network can be computed in time O(e).

29) A network N = (V,E,c), $s,t \in V$ is (s-t)-planar if (V,E) is a planar graph and if s and t border the same face of the planar graph. Consider an embedding of (V,E) where s and t border the outer face. In this

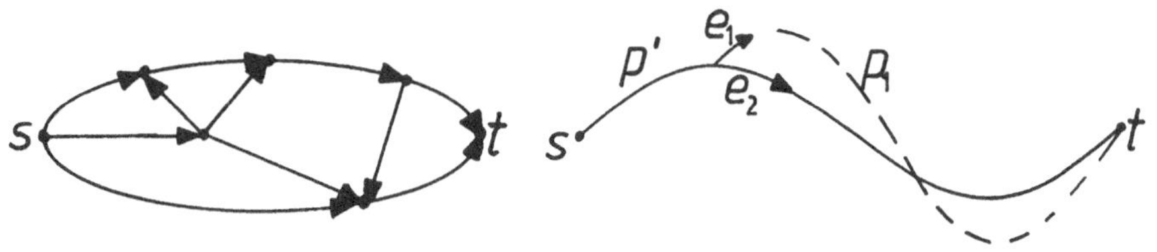

situation there is a natural order on the set of paths from s to t. (Path p_1 is above path p_2 if $p_1 = p'e_1p''$ and $p_2 = p'e_2p'''$ and e_1 is "above" e_2; cf. the figure above). Let $p_1,p_2,p_3,\ldots,p_m$ be the set of paths from s to t ordered according to being above.

a) Construct a blocking flow by first saturating an edge of p_1, then an edge of $p_2,\ldots$. Show that the constructed flow is maximal (Hint: let c_1 be the capacity of p_1; show that there is a maximal flow which sends c_1 units across every edge of p_1. Assume otherwise. Let p_1 consist of edges $e_1,e_2,\ldots,e_k$. Let f be a maximal flow function such that

$f(e_1),\ldots,f(e_i) \geq c_1$, $f(e_{i+1}) < c_1$ and no maximal flow f' satisfies $f'(e_1),\ldots,f'(e_i) \geq c_1$ and $f'(e_{i+1}) > f(e_{i+1})$. Then $c_1 - f(e_{i+1})$ units must be transported from v to t along some path p'. Let $j > i + 1$ be minimal such that $f(e_j) \geq c_1$. (If j does not exist the argument becomes simpler). Then $f(e_j) - f(e_{j-1}) > 0$ units of flow are transported from s to w along some path p". Since the network is assumed to be planar p' and p" must meet in some node, say x. It is now easy to divert flow from the path $v \rightarrow^* x \rightarrow^* w$ to path p_1 thus contradicting the existance of f. This proves that there is a maximal flow which sends c_1 units along every edge of p_1. The correctness proof is now completed by induction).

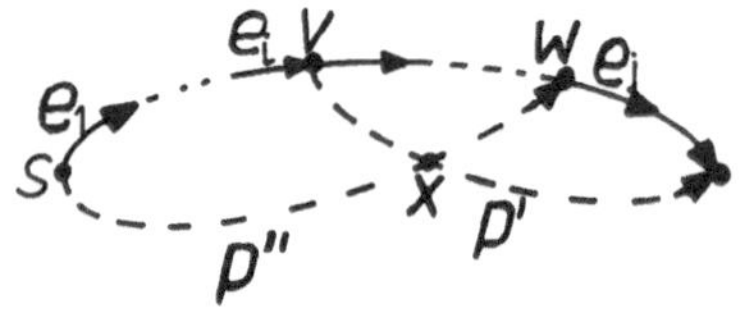

b) Show how to implement the algorithm outlined in part a) in time O(e log n). Hint: Use the blocking flow algorithm described in the text without change. Explain how edges around nodes have to be ordered. Show that lines (5) and (6) are executed at most e times. This follows

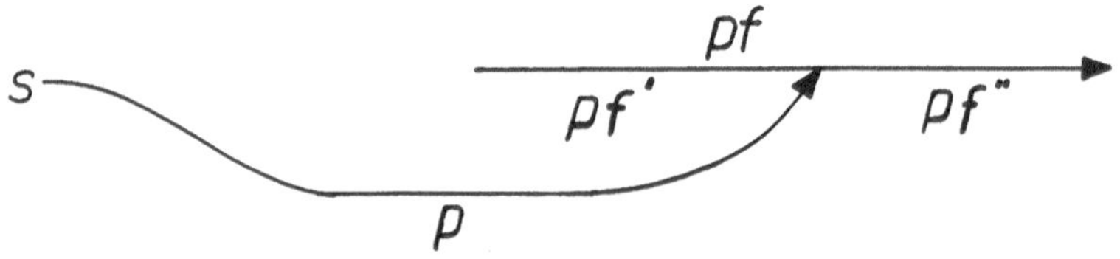

from the observation that p always points into pf from below in lines (4) - (6) and hence pf' can be discarded because it will never happen later on that p points into pf'. This will discard at least one edge except when pf' is trivial, i.e. last(p) = first(pf). However, this can happen only if line (3) was executed immediately before.

3o) A network flow problem with upper and lower bounds is given by a directed graph G = (V,E), source s, sink t and two capacity functions low: $E \rightarrow \mathbb{R}$ and high: $E \rightarrow \mathbb{R}$. A legal (s,t)-flow f must satisfy the conversation laws and the capacity constraints: $low(e) \leq f(e) \leq high(e)$ for all $e \in E$.

a) Show that the problem whether a legal flow exists can be reduced to an ordinary network flow problem (Hint: Let $\overline{V} = V \cup \{\overline{s},\overline{t}\}$, let

$\overline{E} = E \cup (\{\overline{s}\} \times V) \cup (V \times \{\overline{t}\}) \cup \{(s,t), (t,s)\}$ and let $\overline{c}: \overline{E} \to \mathbb{R}_+$ be defined by $\overline{c}(e) = high(e) - low(e)$ for $e \in E$, $\overline{c}(\overline{s},v) = \sum_{e \in in(v)} low(e)$, $\overline{c}(v,\overline{t}) = \sum_{e \in out(v)} low(e)$ and $\overline{c}(s,t) = \overline{c}(t,s) = \infty$.

Show: there is a legal flow iff the maximum flow in the auxiliary network $\overline{N}$ saturates all edges emanating from $\overline{s}$.

b) Show how to compute a maximal flow in a network with upper and lower bounds (Hint: Start with a legal flow as constructed in a) and use augmentation).

31) Let $G = (V_1 \cup V_2, E)$, $E \subseteq V_1 \times V_2$, be a bipartite graph with $|V_1| \le |V_2|$. Show: G has a complete matching M, i.e. $|M| = |V_1|$ if for all $S \subseteq V_1$: $|\{w \in V_2;\ (v,w) \in E$ for some $v \in S\}| \ge |S|$.

32) Let N = (V,E,cap,cost) be a weighted network and let f be a legal (s,t)-flow. Show how to compute a legal (s,t)-flow g from f with val(f) = val(g) and cost(g) minimal. Running time?

33) Let T be an undirected tree where every node has degree at most d. Show that there is a node v of T such that removal of v splits T into subtrees of at most $(d-1)n/d$ nodes each.

34) Let G = (V,E) be a planar graph. Show that there is a partition A,S,B of V such that $|A| \le n/2$, $|B| \le n/2$, $S = O(\sqrt{n})$, and S separates A from B. Moreover A,S,B can be found in linear time.

35) Let A be a symmetric positive definite matrix. Show: If A is the adjacency matrix of a planar graph G = (V,E), i.e. $(i,j) \in E$ iff $a_{ij} \neq 0$, then the linear system $Ax = b$ can be solved in time $O(n^{3/2})$. (Hint: Let V_1, S, V_2 be a partition of V as given by the planar separator theorem; let P be a permutation matrix such that PAP^{-1} has the form

$$\begin{array}{r} V_1 \{ \\ V_2 \{ \\ S \{ \end{array} \left(\begin{array}{c|c|c} A_1 & & A_3 \\ \hline & A_2 & A_4 \\ \hline A_3 & A_4 & A_5 \end{array} \right)$$
$$\qquad\quad \underbrace{\quad}_{V_1} \quad \underbrace{\quad}_{V_2} \quad \underbrace{\quad}_{S}$$

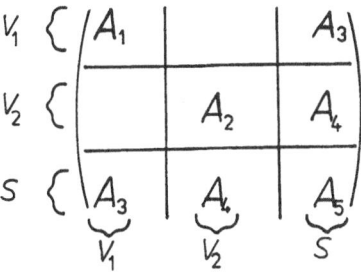

Apply a similar reordering to submatrices A_1, A_2. Use Gaussian elimination on the reordered matrix. Study carefully, which entries of the matrix become non-zero during Gaussian elimination.

36) Let G = (V,E) be a directed planar graph. Show that one can construct a transitive reduction of G, i.e. a smallest graph with the same transitive closure, in time $O(n^{3/2})$. (Hint: Use the planar separator theorem).

37) Let G = (V,E) be a planar graph, let $w: V \to \mathbb{R}_{\geq 0}$ be a weight function, and let $W = \sum_{v \in V} w(v)$. Show that there is a partition A,S,B of V such that $|S| \leq 8\sqrt{n}$, $|A| \leq 2n/3$, $W(A) \leq 2W/3$, $|B| \leq 2n/3$, $W(B) \leq 2W/3$ and S separates A from B. (Hint: Apply theorem 3 to G, then apply corollary 4 to the heavier part).

38) Let G = (V,E) be a planar graph, let $w: V \to \mathbb{R}_{\geq 0}$ be a weight function and let $0 < \varepsilon \leq 1/2$. Show that there is a subset $S \subseteq V$ such that $|S| = O(\sqrt{n/\varepsilon})$ and such that no connected component of G - S has weight exceeding εW. (Hint: Use exercise 37 repeatedly).

39) Let G = (V,E) be a planar graph. A subset $V' \subseteq V$ is independent if $(V' \times V') \cap E = \emptyset$. The problem of deciding whether there is an independent set of size m is NP-complete (cf. chapter VI). Show how to find a nearly maximal independent set fast in planar graphs (Hint: Use exercise 38 with $w(v) = 1$ for all $v \in V$ and $\varepsilon = \log\log n/n$. Find maximal independent sets of all components of G - S by exhaustive search and output the union of these sets. Show that $(|I| - |I^*|)/|I|) = O(1/\sqrt{\log\log n})$ where I is the independent set computed by the algorithm and I* is a maximum independent set. Observe that $|I^*| = \Omega(n)$ since a planar graph has a large number of nodes of small degree).

4o) Show that a maximum independent set of a planar graph can be found in time $2^{O(\sqrt{n})}$ (Hint: split V into V_1, S, V_2 as given by the planar separator theorem. For every $S' \subseteq S$ find a maximal independent set I of the subgraph induced by $V_1 \cup S$ ($V_2 \cup S$) such that $I \cap S = S'$ by recursive application of the algorithm).

41) Show how to find the chromatic number of a planar graph in time $2^{O(\sqrt{n})}$ (Hint: Proceed as in the preceding exercise).

IV. 12. Bibliographic Notes

The algorithm for topological sorting is due to Kahn (62) and Knuth (68). A detailed analysis of the representation problem can be found in Rivest/Vuillemin (75). The $O(ne_{red})$ algorithm for transitive closure of digraphs is taken from Goralcikova/Konbek (79). The analysis for random acyclic digraphs and the improved closure algorithm have not appeared before; they are joint work with K. Simon (Simon (83)). A linear expected time algorithm for random digraphs is described in Schnorr (78). Algorithms for the systematic exploration of a graph (maze) are very old and date back to at least the 19th century. Depth first search was made popular by Tarjan (72) and sections 5 and 6 are taken from his paper.

The presentation of the basic algorithm for least cost paths follows Johnson (77); theorem 2c is also due to him. Theorem 2a is taken from Dijkstra (59). The discussion on the use of estimators in solving one pair least cost path problems is based on Hart/Nilsson/Raphael. An algorithm which solves the all-pair problem on nonnegative networks in expected time $O(n^2 \log n \log^* n)$ is discussed in Bloniarz (8o). The treatment of the general case follows Bellmann (58), Floyd (62) for theorem 5 and exercise 16, Edmonds/Karp (72) for lemma 4, and Johnson (77) for theorem 7 and exercise 18.

The section on minimum spanning trees combines work of Kruskal (56) (theorem 1), Prim (57) and Dijkstra (59) (theorem 2), Yao (75) (theorem 3,4) and Cheriton/Tarjan (76) (theorem 3,4). The paper by Cheriton/Tarjan contains even better algorithms than the ones described in the text.

Many fundamental results on network flow, in particular theorem 4, are due to Ford/Fulkerson (62). The $O(n^3)$ algorithm is taken from Malhotra et al. (78) who refine an algorithm due to Karzanov (74). The $O(n^2e)$ algorithm underlying theorem 5 was invented by Dinic (7o) and then improved to an $O(ne(\log n)^2)$ algorithm by Galil/Naamad (79). An $O(en \log n)$ algorithm was recently described by Sleator/Tarjan (Sleator (79)). Theorem 6 is also taken from Galil/Naamad (79). Section 9.2 on (0-1)-Networks combines work of Even/Tarjan (75)(theorems 8,9,11a), Hopcroft/Karp (75)(theorem 1o) and Becker et al. (82)(theorem 11b). Weighted network flow was treated by Jewell (58), Busacker/Gowen (61)(lemma 13) and Edmonds/Karp (72)(lemma 14). Exercise 29 comes from Itai/Shiloach (79) and Galil/Namaad (79). The linear time planarity testing algorithm is due to Hopcroft/Tarjan 72). The planar separator theorem and many of its applications (exercises 35,37-41) are taken from Lipton/ Tarjan (77,77). The application to least cost path computations is taken from Mehlhorn/Schmidt (83). An $O(n^{3/2})$ algorithm for least cost path computations in planar graphs was described by Tarjan (81). Exercise 36 was proposed by Th. Lengauer.

V. Path Problems in Graphs and Matrix Multiplication

In this chapter we concentrate on path problems in graphs. Typical examples are the problems of computing shortest or longest paths or computing the k shortest path between all pairs of points in a graph. The best known algorithms for these problems differ only slightly. In fact, they are all special cases of an algorithm for solving general path problems on graphs. General path problems over closed semi-rings and Kleene's algorithm for solving them are dealt with in section 1, special cases are then treated in section 2. The algebraic point of view allows us to formulate the connection between general path problems and matrix multiplication in an elegant way: Matrix multiplication in a semi-ring and solution of a general path problem have the same order of complexity. In section 4 we consider fast algorithms for multiplication of matrices over a ring. This is then applied to boolean matrices. Section 7 contains a lower bound on the complexity of boolean matrix product.

V. 1. General Path Problems

Let us recall some notation. Let $G = (V,E)$ with $V = \{v_1,\ldots,v_n\}$ be a digraph. A path p from v_i to v_j is a sequence $w_0,w_1,\ldots w_k$ of nodes with $v_i = w_0$, $v_j = w_k$ and $(w_\ell, w_{\ell+1}) \in E$ for $0 \le \ell \le k-1$. The length of this path is k. Note that there is always the path of length 0 from a node to itself. We use P_{ij} to denote the set of all path from v_i to v_j.

$$P_{ij} = \{p;\ p \text{ is a path from } v_i \text{ to } v_j\}$$

Kleene's algorithm computes set P_{ij} for all i and j in some sense. We describe this algorithm in a very general setting first and apply it to some special cases in section 2. The general framework is provided by closed semi-rings.

Definition: a) A set S with distinguished elements 0 and 1 and binary operations $\oplus$ and $\odot$ is a semi-ring if

1) $(S, \oplus, 0)$ is a commutative monoid, i.e. for all $a,b,c \in S$

$(a \oplus b) \oplus c = a \oplus (b \oplus c)$

$a \oplus b = b \oplus a$

$a \oplus 0 = a$

2) $(S, \odot, 1)$ is a monoid, i.e. for all $a,b,c \in S$

$$(a \odot b) \odot c = a \odot (b \odot c)$$
$$a \odot 1 = 1 \odot a = a$$

3) Multiplication distributes over addition and 0 is a null-element with respect to multiplication, i.e. for all $a,b,c \in S$

$$(a \oplus b) \odot c = (a \odot c) \oplus (b \odot c)$$
$$c \odot (a \oplus b) = (c \odot a) \oplus (c \odot b)$$
$$0 \odot a = a \odot 0 = 0$$

b) A semi-ring is a <u>closed semi-ring</u> if in addition infinite sums exist, i.e. with every family $\{a_i,\ i \in I\}$ of elements of S with countable (finite or infinite) index set I there is a associated an element $\bigoplus_{i\in I} a_i$, its sum. Infinite sums satisfy the following laws:

4) For finite non-empty index set $I = \{i_1, i_2, \ldots, i_k\}$

$$\bigoplus_{i\in I} a_i = a_{i_1} \oplus a_{i_2} \oplus \ldots \oplus a_{i_k}$$

and for empty index set $I = \emptyset$

$$\bigoplus_{i\in\emptyset} a_i = 0$$

5) The result of a summation does not depend on the ordering of the factors, i.e. for every index set I and every partition $\{I_j;\ j \in J\}$ of I

$$\bigcup_{j\in J} I_j = I \text{ and } I_j \cap I_k = \emptyset \text{ for } i \neq k$$

we have

$$\bigoplus_{i\in I} a_i = \bigoplus_{j\in J} \left(\bigoplus_{i\in I_j} a_i \right)$$

6) Multiplication distributes over infinite sums, i.e.

$$\left(\bigoplus_{i\in I} a_i \right) \odot \left(\bigoplus_{j\in J} b_j \right) = \bigoplus_{i\in I} \left(\bigoplus_{j\in J} a_i \odot b_j \right) \qquad \square$$

In exercise 3 we draw some conclusions from these axioms.

Examples: 1) The boolean semi-ring $B = (\{0,1\}, \vee, \wedge, 0, 1)$. The basic operations are boolean or (= addition)

$$\bigvee_{i\in I} a_i = \begin{cases} 1 & \text{there is } i \in I \text{ with } a_i = 1 \\ 0 & \text{otherwise} \end{cases}$$

with neutral element 0 and boolean and (= multiplication) $x \wedge y = \min(x,y)$ with neutral element 1. The boolean semi-ring is the most simple closed semi-ring. We use it to determine the existance of paths between points.

2) The (min,+) semi-ring $(\mathbb{R} \cup \{\infty\} \cup \{-\infty\}, \min, +, \infty, 0)$ of reals with additional elements ∞ and $-\infty$. The operations are infimum, denoted min, with neutral element ∞ and addition with neutral element 0. We define $(-\infty) + \infty = \infty$. Here min corresponds to addition and + corresponds to multiplication. We use the (min,+) semi-ring to compute least cost paths.

Further examples of closed semi-rings can be found in the exercises. Let $G = (V,E)$ be a digraph, let S be a closed semi-ring and let $c: E \to S$ be a labelling of the edges of G by elements of S. We extend c to paths and set of paths. If $p = w_0, w_1, \ldots, w_k$ is a path, then $c(p) = c(w_0,w_1) \odot c(w_1,w_2) \odot \ldots \odot c(w_{k-1},w_k)$; if $k = 0$ then $c(p) = 1$. If P is a set of path then $c(P) = \sum_{p\in P} c(p)$.

<u>Definition</u> (general path problem): Compute $a_{ij} = \sum_{p\in P_{ij}} c(p)$ for all i,j, $1 \le i,j \le n$. □

We need one further operation in closed semi-rings. For $a \in S$ we define the closure a^* of a by $a^* = 1 \oplus a \oplus a^2 \oplus \ldots = \sum_{i\ge 0} a^i$. Here $a^0 = 1$ and $a^{i+1} = a \odot a^i$. Note that $0^* = 1$.

<u>Example:</u> In the boolean semi-ring we have $a^* = 1$ for all a and in the (min,+)- semi-ring of reals we have $a^* = 0$ for $a \ge 0$ and $a^* = -\infty$ for $a < 0$. In both cases, the closure is trivial to compute.

<u>Definition:</u> $P_{ij}^{(k)}$ is the set of paths $p = w_0, w_1, \ldots, w_\ell$ with

(1) $w_o = v_i$, $w_\ell = v_j$, i.e. p goes from v_i to v_j

(2) $w_h = v_{g_h}$ for some $g_h \le k$ and all $1 \le h < \ell$, i.e. all intermediate points on the path are in $\{v_1,\ldots,v_k\}$,

(3) if $i = j > k$ then $\ell > 0$, i.e. the trivial path of length 0 is included in $P_{ij}^{(k)}$ only if $i \le k$. □

With $p = v_i,v_1,v_3,v_j$ we have $p \in P_{ij}^{(3)}$, $p \notin P_{ij}^{(2)}$. Also path $p = v_i \in P_{ii}^{(i)}$ and $p \notin P_{ii}^{(i-1)}$.

Kleene's algorithm is an application of dynamic programming. It computes iteratively, $k = 0,1,2,\ldots,n$, matrices $a_{ij}^{(k)}$, $1 \le i,j \le n$, where

$$a_{ij}^{(k)} = \sum_{p \in P_{ij}^{(k)}} c(p)$$

We derive recursion formulae for computing $a_{ij}^{(k)}$. A path in $P_{ij}^{(o)}$ can have no intermediate point (by part (2) of the definition of $P_{ij}^{(k)}$ and it must have length at least 1 (this is obvious for $i \neq j$ and follows from part (3) of the definition of $P_{ij}^{(k)}$ for $i = j$). Thus all paths in $P_{ij}^{(o)}$ must have length exactly one, i.e. consist of a single edge. Hence

$$a_{ij}^{(o)} = \underline{\text{if}}\ (v_i,v_j) \in E\ \underline{\text{then}}\ c(v_i,v_j)\ \underline{\text{else}}\ 0\ \underline{\text{fi}}$$

Suppose $k > 0$ next. A path $p \in P_{ij}^{(k)}$ either passes through node k or does not. Also if $i = j = k$ then the path of length 0 belongs to $P_{ij}^{(k)}$ and did not belong to $P_{ij}^{(k-1)}$. Thus by property (5) of closed semi-ring

$$\sum_{p \in P_{ij}^{(k)}} c(p) \overset{(5)}{=} \underline{\text{if}}\ i = j = k\ \underline{\text{then}}\ 1\ \underline{\text{else}}\ 0\ \underline{\text{fi}}$$

$$\oplus \sum_{p \in P_{ij}^{(k-1)}} c(p) \oplus \sum_{p \in P_{ij}^{(k)} - P_{ij}^{(k-1)}} c(p)$$

$$= \underline{\text{if}}\ i = j = k\ \underline{\text{then}}\ 1\ \underline{\text{else}}\ 0\ \underline{\text{fi}} \oplus a_{ij}^{(k-1)}$$

$$\oplus \sum_{p\ P_{ij}^{(k)} - P_{ij}^{(k-1)}} c(p)$$

A path $p \in P_{ij}^{(k)} - P_{ij}^{(k-1)}$ has the form $v_i \ldots v_k \ldots v_j$ and must have length at least 2. It can be divided into three parts, an initial segment p' of length at least 1 which leads from v_i to v_k without going through v_k on the way, i.e. $p' \in P_{ik}^{(k-1)}$, a terminal segment p''' of length at least 1 which leads from v_k to v_j without going through v_k on the way, i.e. $p''' \in P_{kj}^{(k-1)}$ and an intermediate segment p'' of length at least 0 which leads from v_k to v_k going through v_k some number $\ell(\ell \geq 0)$ of times, i.e. $p''' \in P_{kk}^{(k)}$. Conversely, if $p' \in P_{ik}^{(k-1)}$, $p'' \in P_{kk}^{(k)}$ and $p''' \in P_{kj}^{(k-1)}$ then path $p'p''p'''$ obtained by concatenating p', p'' and p''' is in $P_{ij}^{(k)} - P_{ij}^{(k-1)}$. It is important to observe here that $P_{ik}^{(k-1)}$ and $P_{kj}^{(k-1)}$ contain only paths of length at least 1. This is obvious for $i \neq k (k \neq j)$ and follows from part (3) of the definition of $P_{ij}^{(k)}$ for $i = k (k=j)$. Thus

$$\sum_{p \in P_{ij}^{(k)} - P_{ij}^{(k-1}} c(p) \overset{(5)}{=} \sum_{p' \in P_{ij}^{(k-1)}} \sum_{p'' \in P_{kj}^{(k-1)}} \sum_{p''' \in P_{kj}^{(k-1)}} c(p') \odot c(p'') \odot c(p''')$$

$$\overset{(6)}{=} \Big(\sum_{p' \in P_{ij}^{(k-1)}} c(p') \Big) \odot \Big(\sum_{p'' \in P_{kk}^{(k)}} c(p'') \Big) \odot \Big(\sum_{p''' \in P_{kj}^{(k-1)}} c(p''') \Big)$$

$$= a_{ij}^{(k-1)} \odot \Big(\sum_{p'' \in P_{kk}^{(k)}} c(p'') \Big) \odot a_{kj}^{(k-1)}$$

A path $p'' \in P_{kk}^{(k)}$ either has length 0 or it is a proper path of length >0 which goes through v_k some number $\ell(\ell \geq 0)$ of times. In the latter case it consists of $\ell + 1$ subpaths in $P_{kk}^{(k-1)}$. Hence

$$\sum_{p'' \in P_{kk}^{(k)}} c(p'') \overset{(5)}{=} c(\text{path of length } 0) \oplus$$

$$\sum_{\ell \geq 0} \sum_{p'' \in P_{kk}^{(k)}} c(p'')$$

ℓ intermediate points of p" are equal to v_k

$$(\underline{6}) \quad 1 \oplus \sum_{\ell \geq 0} \Big(\sum_{p'''' \in P_{kk}^{(k-1)}} c(p'''') \Big)^{\ell+1}$$

$$= \quad 1 \oplus \sum_{\ell \geq 0} (a_{kk}^{(k-1)})^{\ell+1}$$

$$= \quad (a_{kk}^{(k-1)})^{*}$$

In summary, we have

$$a_{ij}^{(k)} = \sum_{p \in P_{ij}^{(k)}} c(p) = a_{ij}^{(k-1)} \oplus (a_{ik}^{(k-1)} \odot (a_{kk}^{(k-1)})^{*} \odot a_{kj}^{(k-1)})$$

$$\oplus \ \underline{\text{if}}\ i = j = k\ \underline{\text{then}}\ 1\ \underline{\text{fi}}$$

The set of recursion equations derived above immediately leads to the following algorithm:

(1) <u>for</u> i,j ∈ {1,...,n}

(2) <u>do</u> $a_{ij}^{(o)} \leftarrow$ <u>if</u> $(v_i,v_j) \in E$ <u>then</u> $c(v_i,v_j)$ <u>else</u> 0 <u>od</u>

(3) <u>for</u> k <u>from</u> 1 <u>to</u> n

(4) <u>do</u> <u>for</u> i,j ∈ {1,...,n}

(5) <u>do</u> $a_{ij}^{(k)} \leftarrow a_{ij}^{(k-1)} \oplus (a_{ik}^{(k-1)} \odot (a_{kk}^{(k-1)})^{*} \odot a_{kj}^{(k-1)})$

(6) <u>if</u> i = j = k <u>then</u> $a_{ii}^{(i)} \leftarrow a_{ii}^{(i)} \oplus 1$ <u>fi</u>

(7) <u>od</u>

(8) <u>od</u>

Since $P_{ij}^{(n)} = P_{ij}$ we have $a_{ij} = a_{ij}^{(n)}$ and the general path problem is solved.

<u>Theorem 1:</u> Kleene's algorithm solves the general path problem in $\odot(n^3)$ semi-ring operations $\oplus, \odot$ and $*$.

<u>Proof:</u> Line (5) is executed once for each triple i,j,k with $1 \le i,j,k \le n$. □

Kleene's algorithm as described above uses $\Theta(n^3)$ storage locations. With a little care this can be reduced to $\Theta(n^2)$ as follows. Note that we left open the order of execution in line (4). Therefore we can replace lines (4) to (6) by:

(4') <u>for</u> $i,j \in \{1,\ldots,n\} - \{k\}$

(5') <u>do</u> $a_{ij} \leftarrow a_{ij} \oplus (a_{ik} \odot a_{kk}^* \odot a_{kj})$ <u>od</u>;

(6') <u>for</u> $i \in \{1,\ldots,n\} - \{k\}$

(7') <u>do</u> $a_{ik} \leftarrow a_{ik} \oplus (a_{ik} \odot a_{kk}^* \odot a_{kk})$ <u>od</u>;

(8') <u>for</u> $j \in \{1,\ldots,n\} - \{k\}$

(9') <u>do</u> $k_j \leftarrow a_{kj} \oplus (a_{kk} \odot a_{kk}^* \odot a_{kj})$ <u>od</u>;

(1o') $a_{kk} \leftarrow a_{kk}^*$

where we use in line (1o') that $1 \oplus a_{kk} \oplus a_{kk}\, a_{kk}^*\, a_{kk} =$
$1 \oplus a_{kk} \oplus a_{kk}^2 \cdot \sum_{i \ge o} a_{kk}^i$

<u>V. 2. Two Special Cases: Least Cost Paths and Transitive Closure</u>

We take a closer look at two applications of the results of the previous section. Further applications can be found in the exercises.

<u>Transitive Closure of Digraphs:</u> Let $G = (V,E)$ be a digraph. Graph $H(G) = (V,E')$ is called transitive closure of G if $(v,w) \in E'$ if and only if there is a path from v to w in G. We use the boolean semi-ring and define

$$c(v,w) = \begin{cases} 1 & \text{if } (v,w) \in E \\ 0 & \text{if } (v,w) \notin E \end{cases}$$

Then $c(p) = 1$ for all paths p and therefore for every set P of paths

$$\sum_{p\in P} c(p) = \begin{cases} 1 & \text{if } P \neq \emptyset \\ 0 & \text{if } P = \emptyset \end{cases}$$

We can thus apply Kleene's algorithm to compute the transitive closure of a graph. Because of $a^* = 1$ for all elements of the boolean semi-ring, line (5) of Kleene's algorithm simplifies to

$$a_{ij}^{(k)} \leftarrow a_{ij}^{(k-1)} \vee (a_{ik}^{(k-1)} \wedge a_{kj}^{(k-1)})$$

where $\wedge$ is boolean and and $\vee$ is boolean or.

Theorem 1: The matrix representation of the transitive closure of a digraph can be computed in time $\Theta(n^3)$ and space $\Theta(n^2)$. □

Theorem 1 by itself is not a big deal. After all, we know already an $O(n \cdot e_{red})$ algorithm from sections IV.3. and IV.6. (e_{red} is the number of edges in a transitive reduction of G). However, we see in section V.5. that theorem 1 can be improved to yield an $O(n^{2.50})$ algorithm.

All Pairs Least Cost Paths: Let $G = (V,E)$ be a digraph and let $\ell: E \rightarrow \mathbb{R}$ be a labelling of the edges with real numbers. We use the (min,+)-semiring of reals. Then

$$\sum_{\substack{p \text{ path from} \\ v \text{ to } w}} \ell(p) = \operatorname{Inf}\{\ell(v,v_1) + \ell(v_1,v_2) + \ldots + \ell(v_k,w);\ p = v,v_1,\ldots,v_k,w \text{ is path from } v \text{ to } w\}$$

is the minimal cost of a path from v to w. We can thus use Kleene's algorithm to solve the all pairs least cost path problem.

Theorem 2: The all pairs least cost path problem can be solved in time $O(n^3)$ and space $O(n^2)$ by Kleene's algorithm. □

Theorem 2 has to be seen in constrast with theorem 7 of section IV.7.4.. There we described an $O(n \cdot e \cdot \log n/\log(e/n)) = O(n^3)$ algorithm for the all pairs least cost path problem. Although the algorithm of IV.7.4. is asymptotically never worse than Kleene's algorithms, it is nevertheless inferior for small n or dense graphs.

V. 3. General Path Problems and Matrix Multiplication

We resume discussion of the general path problem. Let $G = (V,E)$ be a digraph with $V = \{v_1,\dots,v_n\}$, let S be a closed semi-ring and let $c\colon E \to S$ be a labelling of the edges of G by elements of S. We have shown how to compute $\sum_{p\in P_{ij}} c(p)$ for every i and j. By property (5) of closed semi-rings we can rewrite this sum as

$$\sum_{\ell\geq 0} \ \sum_{\substack{p\in P_{ij} \text{ and} \\ p \text{ has length } \ell}} c(p)$$

The inner sum $\sum_{\substack{p\in P_{ij} \text{ and} \\ p \text{ has length } \ell}}$ is now easily represented as a matrix product. Let $A_G = (a_{ij})_{1\leq i,j\leq n}$ be the following matrix

$$a_{ij} = \begin{cases} c(v_i,v_j) & \text{if } (v_i,v_j) \in E \\ 0 & \text{otherwise} \end{cases}$$

Then the sum above is equal to entry (i,j) of the ℓ-th power A_G^ℓ of matrix A_G, more precisely:

<u>Definition:</u> Let M_n be the set of all n by n matrices with elements of closed semi-ring S. Addition and multiplication of matrices are defined as usual, i.e. $(a_{ij}) \oplus (b_{ij}) = (a_{ij} + b_{ij})$ and $(a_{ij}) \odot (b_{jk}) = (\sum_{j=1}^{n} a_{ij} \odot b_{jk})$. We use 0 to denote the all zero matrix and $I = (\delta_{ij})$ to denote the identity matrix, i.e. $\delta_{ij} = 1$ if $i = j$ and $\delta_{ij} = 0$ if $i \neq j$. □

It is easy to see that $(M_n,\oplus,\odot,0,I)$ is a closed semi-ring (exercise 8). We define the powers of matrix $A \in M_n$ as usual:

$$A^0 = I$$
$$A^{k+1} = A \odot A^k$$

and the closure of A by

$$A^* = I \oplus A \oplus A^2 \oplus \dots = \sum_{\ell\geq 0} A^\ell$$

We are now in a position to formalize the connection between the powers of A_G and the labels of paths of a certain length.

Theorem 1: Let $A_G^{\ell} = (a_{ij}^{(\ell)})_{1\leq i,j\leq n}$ be the ℓ-th power of matrix A_G. Then

$$a_{ij}^{(\ell)} = \sum_{\substack{p\in P_{ij} \\ \text{length}(p)=\ell}} c(p)$$

Proof (by induction on ℓ): For $\ell = 0$ and $\ell = 1$ the claim is immediate from the definition of I and A_G. Assume $\ell > 1$. A path p of length ℓ from v_i to v_j consists of an edge, say from v_i to v_k, and a path of length $\ell - 1$ from v_k to v_j. Hence

$$\sum_{\substack{p\in P_{ij} \\ \text{length}(p)=\ell}} c(p) \overset{(5),(6)}{=} \sum_{k=1}^{n} \Big(\sum_{\substack{p'\in P_{kj} \\ \text{length}(p')=\ell-1}} c(v_i,v_k) \circledast c(p') \Big)$$

$$\overset{(6),(7)}{=} \sum_{k=1}^{n} \Big(c(v_i,v_k) \circledast \sum_{\substack{p'\in P_{kj} \\ \text{length}(p')=\ell-1}} c(p')\Big)$$

$$\overset{\text{J.H}}{=} \sum_{k=1}^{n} a_{ik}^{(1)} \circledast a_{kj}^{(\ell-1)}$$

$$= a_{ij}^{(\ell)}$$ □

Corollary 2: Let $A_G^* = (b_{ij})_{1\leq i,j\leq n}$. Then

$$b_{ij} = \sum_{p\in P_{ij}} c(p)$$

Proof: Immediate from theorem 1 and the definition of A_G^*. □

General path problems are thus equivalent to computing the closure of matrix A_G. Kleene's algorithm allows us to compute the closure of a matrix with $\Theta(n^3)$ additions, multiplications and closures of semi-ring elements. The same number of operations is required to multiply two matrices according to the standard method, the highschool method. In the highschool method we multiply two matrices by A and B by computing the scalar product of every row of A with every column of B. We show next, that there is a deeper reason behind the fact, that Kleene's algorithm for computing the closure of a matrix and the highschool method for multiplying matrices have the same complexity.

<u>Theorem 3:</u> If there is an algorithm which computes the closure of an n by n matrix with A(c) additions, multiplications and closure operations of semi-ring elements and if $A(3n) \leq c \cdot A(n)$ for some $c \in \mathbb{R}$ and all $n \in \mathbb{N}$ then there is an algorithm to multiply n by n matrices with $M(n) = O(A(n))$ additions and multiplications.

<u>Proof:</u> Let A and B the two n by n matrices over closed semi-ring S. Let C be the following 3n by 3n matrix.

$$C = \begin{pmatrix} 0 & A & 0 \\ 0 & 0 & B \\ 0 & 0 & 0 \end{pmatrix}$$

The closure C* of C can be computed with $A(3n) \leq c \cdot A(n)$ operations. Since

$$C^2 = \begin{pmatrix} 0 & 0 & A \circledcirc B \\ 0 & 0 & 0 \\ 0 & 0 & 0 \end{pmatrix} \quad \text{and } C^3 = C^4 = \ldots = \begin{pmatrix} 0 & 0 & 0 \\ 0 & 0 & 0 \\ 0 & 0 & 0 \end{pmatrix}$$

we have

$$C^* = \begin{pmatrix} 0 & A & A \circledcirc B \\ 0 & 0 & 0 \\ 0 & 0 & 0 \end{pmatrix}$$

and product $A \circledcirc B$ can be found in the right upper corner of C*. Thus the product of two n by n matrices can be computed with $M(n) = A(3n) \leq c \cdot A(n) = O(A(n))$ operations. □

Let us discuss briefly the assumption $\exists c : A(3n) \leq c \cdot A(n)$. First of all, this assumption stipulates a polynomial bound on the growth of A(n), namely

$$A(n) \le c \cdot A(n/3) \le c^2 \cdot A(n/9) \le \ldots \le c^{\log_3 n} \cdot A(1)$$

for n a power of 3. Thus $A(n) = O(c^{\log_3 n})$. Since we know already how to compute the closure with $O(n^3)$ operations, a polynomial bound on A(n) is not a severe restriction. Secondly, the assumption stipulates a certain "smoothness" of A(n). Function A(n) is not allowed to grow in jumps. Many functions such as n^α, $\alpha \ge 1$, $n^\alpha \cdot \log n$, satisfy the assumption made in theorem 3. Surprisingly, the converse of theorem 3 is also true.

Theorem 4: If the product of two n by n matrices can be computed with M(n) additions and multiplications of semi-ring elements and if $4M(n/2) \le M(n)$ and $M(2n) \le c \cdot M(n)$ for some c and all n then the closure of an n by n matrix can be computed with $A(n) = O(m(n))$ additions, multiplications and closure operations of semi-ring elements.

Proof: We describe a recursive algorithm which uses only $A(n) = O(M(n))$ semi-ring operations. Let X be any n by n matrix over a closed semi-ring. We assume at first that $n = 2^k$ is a power of 2 and extend the result to arbitrary n later on.

For k = 0 and hence n = 1 the closure of matrix X = (x) is simply $x^* = (x^*)$. Thus $A(1) = 1$.

Assume k > 0. We split X into 4 n/2 by n/2 matrices B,C,D and E.

$$X = \begin{pmatrix} B & C \\ D & E \end{pmatrix}$$

and interpret the splitting of X in terms of graphs. Matrix X corresponds to a graph G = (V,E) with $V = \{v_1,\ldots,v_n\}$, $E = V\mathrm{x}V$, and labelling $c: E \to S$ with $c(v_i,v_j) = x_{ij}$. Let $V_1 = \{v_1,\ldots v_{n/2}\}$ and $V_2 = \{v_{n/2+1},\ldots,v_n\}$. Then B describes the labelling of edges which lead from nodes in V_1 to nodes in V_1, C describes the labelling of edges which lead from nodes in V_1 to nodes V_2,...

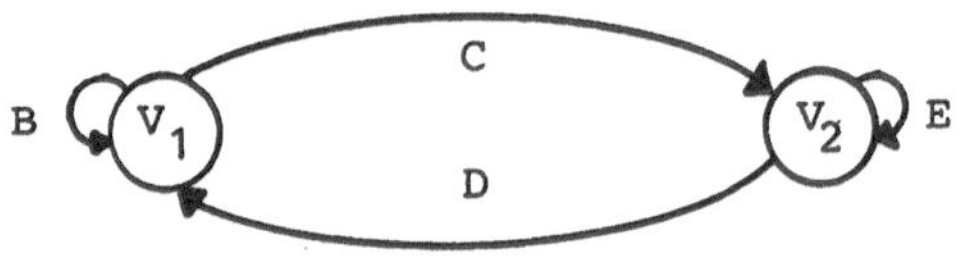

What is the interpretation of matrix

$$X^* = \begin{pmatrix} F & G \\ H & K \end{pmatrix}$$

F is the sum of the labellings of all paths which lead from nodes in V_1 to nodes in $V_1, \ldots$. Let $v, w \in V_1$. A path from v to w has the following form. It begins in v and then goes through some nodes in V_1 using edges in B, then leaves V_1 and enters V_2 via an edge in C, then goes through some nodes in V_2 using edges in D, ... More precisely, we can say that a path from v to w consists of elementary pieces which connect a node in V_1 with another node in V_1 without going through a node in V_1 on the way. Thus an elementary piece is either an edge between two nodes in V_1, i.e. an element of B, or it consists of a single edge in C followed by a path in V_2 consisting of edges in E only, i.e. an element of E*, followed by an edge from V_2 to V_1, i.e. an element of D. Elementary pieces are thus given by $B \oplus (C \odot E^* \odot D)$. Hence

$$F = (B \oplus (C \odot E^* \odot D))^*$$

Similarly,

$$G = F \odot C \odot E^*$$
$$H = E^* \odot D \odot F$$

and

$$K = E^* \oplus (E^* \odot D \odot F \odot C \odot E^*)$$

We leave it to the reader to formally justify these identities. The formulae above suggest the following algorithm for computing F,G,H and K from B,C,D and E.

$$T_1 \leftarrow E^*$$
$$T_2 \leftarrow C \odot T_1$$
$$F \leftarrow (B \oplus (T_2 \odot D)^*)$$
$$G \leftarrow F \odot T_2$$
$$T_3 \leftarrow T_1 \odot D$$
$$H \leftarrow T_3 \odot F$$
$$K \leftarrow T_1 \oplus (T_3 \odot G)$$

Execution of this program requires us to compute the closure of two n/2 by n/2 matrices, six products of n/2 by n/2 matrices and two sums of n/2 by n/2 matrices. If we use the same algorithm recursively then the closure of an n/2 by n/2 matrix can be computed with A(n/2) operations. Summming two n/2 by n/2 matrices takes $(n/2)^2$ additions. Thus

$$A(n) = 2 \cdot A(n/2) + 6M(n/2) + 2(n/2)^2$$

Since $M(n) \geq 4M(n/2)$ and hence $M(n) \geq n^2 M(1) \geq n^2$ this simplifies to

$$A(n) \leq 2 \cdot A(n/2) + 8M(n/2)$$

We show $A(n) \leq 4M(n)$. Since $A(1) = M(1) = 1$ this is certainly true for $n = 1$. If $n = 2^k > 1$ then

$$\begin{aligned} A(n) &\leq 2 \cdot A(n/2) + 8M(n/2) \\ &\leq 16M(n/2) \\ &\leq 4M(n) \end{aligned}$$

by assumption. If n is not a power of two we fill up matrix X with zeroes to matrix $\overline{X}$ of dimension $2^{\lceil \log n \rceil}$

$$\overline{X} = \begin{pmatrix} X & 0 \\ 0 & 0 \end{pmatrix}$$

and compute $\overline{X}^*$. Since

$$\overline{X}^* = \begin{pmatrix} X^* & 0 \\ 0 & 0 \end{pmatrix}$$

we can read off X^* in $\overline{X}^*$. Thus

$$\begin{aligned} A(n) &\leq A(2^{\lceil \log n \rceil}) \\ &\leq 4M(2^{\lceil \log n \rceil}) \\ &\leq 4M(2n) && \text{, since M is non-decreasing} \\ &\leq 4c \cdot M(n) && \text{, by assumption.} \end{aligned}$$

In either case, we have $A(n) = O(M(n))$. □

In theorems 3 and 4 we established that closure of a matrix and matrix product have the same order of complexity. Since matrix product is the more familiar operation we study its complexity in more detail in subsequent sections.

V. 4. Matrix Multiplication in a Ring

We all learned in school how to multiply n by n matrices with $O(n^3)$ arithmetic operations. Surprisingly enough, the naive way of multiplying matrices is not the fastest. As of the writing, the asymptotically fastest algorithm is by Coppersmith and Winograd; their algorithm needs only $O(n^{2.495364})$ arithmetic operations. We describe in this section an $O(n^{2.81})$ algorithm due to Strassen, the first algorithm which actually beat the $O(n^3)$ bound. Strassen's algorithms and all other fast multiplication algorithms for matrices do not work over semi-rings but only in the richer structure of rings.

Definition: An algebraic structure $(S,+,\cdot,0)$ is a ring if

1) $(S,+,0)$ is an abelian group, i.e.

$(a+b) + c = a + (b+c)$	(associativity)
$a + b = b + a$	(commutativity)
$a + 0 = a$	(neutral element)
$\forall a \exists b \; a + b = 0$	(inverses exist)

2) $(S,\cdot)$ is a semi-group, i.e.

$(a\cdot b)\cdot c = a\cdot(b\cdot c)$	(associativity)

3) the distributive laws hold, i.e.

$a\cdot(b+c) = a\cdot b + a\cdot c$

$(b+c)\cdot a = b\cdot a + c\cdot a$ □

Theorem 1: The product of two n by n matrices over a ring can be computed in $O(n^{\log 7})$ ring operations.

Proof: We give a recursive algorithm. Let $n = 2^k$ (the general case is considered later) be a power of two and let A and B be two n by n matrices. We split A and B into 4 n/2 by n/2 matrices each.

$$A = \begin{pmatrix} A_{11} & A_{12} \\ A_{21} & A_{22} \end{pmatrix} \qquad B = \begin{pmatrix} B_{11} & B_{12} \\ B_{21} & B_{22} \end{pmatrix}$$

Then $C = A \cdot B$ can be written as

$$C = \begin{pmatrix} C_{11} & C_{12} \\ C_{21} & C_{22} \end{pmatrix}$$

where
$$\begin{aligned} C_{11} &= A_{11} B_{11} + A_{12} B_{21} \\ C_{12} &= A_{11} B_{12} + A_{12} B_{22} \\ C_{21} &= A_{21} B_{11} + A_{22} B_{21} \\ C_{22} &= A_{21} B_{12} + A_{22} B_{22} \end{aligned}$$

Exactly the same set of formulae defines the product of two 2 by 2 matrices. Note however, that the elements of matrices A,B and C, when considered as 2 by 2 matrices, are not ring elements but large n/2 by n/2 matrices. The following lemma shows, that this difference is inessential.

Lemma 1: Let $m \in \mathbb{N}$ and let S be a ring. Then the set of m by m matrices over S form a ring.

Proof: Exercise 11. □

It remains to describe a fast method for multiplying 2 by 2 matrices. What does fast mean? Note that we want to apply the algorithm recursively, i.e. the elements of the 2 by 2 matrices to be multiplied are themselves large matrices. Therefore, multiplication of ring elements is much more costly than addition in the recursive application of the algorithm. It is therefore important to multiply 2 by 2 matrices with a small number of multiplication of ring elements, in particular to use less than the 8 multiplications used in the school method.

Strassen showed how to multiply two 2 by 2 matrices

$$\begin{pmatrix} a_{11} & a_{12} \\ a_{21} & a_{22} \end{pmatrix} \cdot \begin{pmatrix} b_{11} & b_{12} \\ b_{21} & b_{22} \end{pmatrix} = \begin{pmatrix} c_{11} & c_{12} \\ c_{22} & c_{22} \end{pmatrix}$$

with 7 multiplications and 18 additions and subtractions.

Compute
$$m_1 \leftarrow (a_{12} - a_{22})\,(b_{21} + b_{22})$$
$$m_2 \leftarrow (a_{11} + a_{22})\,(b_{11} + b_{22})$$
$$m_3 \leftarrow (a_{11} - a_{21})\,(b_{11} + b_{12})$$
$$m_4 \leftarrow (a_{11} + a_{12})\,b_{22}$$
$$m_5 \leftarrow a_{11}(b_{12} - b_{22})$$
$$m_6 \leftarrow a_{22}(b_{21} - b_{11})$$
$$m_7 \leftarrow (a_{21} + a_{22})\,b_{11}$$

and then

$$c_{11} \leftarrow m_1 + m_2 - m_4 + m_6$$
$$c_{12} \leftarrow m_4 + m_5$$
$$c_{21} \leftarrow m_6 + m_7$$
$$c_{22} \leftarrow m_2 - m_3 + m_5 - m_7$$

The reader can easily convince himself that this algorithm actually computes the product of 2 by 2 matrices. If we apply this algorithm recursively to compute $C_{11}, C_{12}, C_{21}, C_{22}$ then the following recursion holds for $M(n)$, the number of ring operations required to multiply two n by n matrices by Strassen's algorithm

$$M(1) = 1$$
$$M(n) = 7M(n/2) + 18\,(n/2)^2$$

for n a power of two. This recurrence solves for $n = 2^k$ to

$$M(n) = \sum_{i=o}^{k-1} 7^i \cdot 18 \cdot 2^{(k-i-1)2} + 7^k$$

$$= 7^{k+1} - 6n^2 = 7n^{\log 7} - 6n^2$$

If n is not a power of two we fill up matrices A and B with zeroes until we reach a power of two and compute the product of the padded matrices. This increases n by at most a factor of two. Thus for all n

$$M(n) \le 7(2n)^{\log 7} = 49n^{\log 7} = O(n^{\log 7}) \qquad \square$$

Strassen's method is asymptotically faster than the school method for multiplying matrices. Where is the cross-over point, i.e. from whan n on is Strassen's algorithm superior to the school-method? We restrict ourselves to the case that $n = 2^k$ is a power of two.

The school method requires n^3 multiplications and $n^3 - n^2$ additions for multiplying two n by n matrices. We want to find the smallest k_o such that for all $k \ge k_o$

$$7^{k+1} - 6(2^k)^2 \le 2(2^k)^3 - (2^k)^2$$

A simple calculation shows that $k_o = 10$, i.e. $n = 1024$. This is a little bit disappointing but it also shows how we can improve the recursive algorithm; the school method is faster than Strassen's algorithm for $n \le 1024$. For example, Strassen's algorithm requires 25 operations to multiply 2 by 2 matrices and the school method requires only 12. It is therefore complete nonsense to use recursion all the way down to $n = 2$ in Strassen's algorithm. Where should we stop?

We pose the following question. From what point on is it cheaper to multiply directly by the school method than to use one further step of recursion? Let n be even and let A and B be n by n matrices. We split A and B into 4 matrices of size n/2 by n/2 and multiply A and B with 7 multiplications and 18 additions of n/2 by n/2 matrices. The school method is used to multiply the smaller matrices. The total number of arithmetic operations in this method is:

$$7(2(n/2)^3 - (n/2)^2) + 18(n/2)^2 = 7/4\ n^3 + 11/4\ n^2$$

If the school method is used directly to multiply A and B then

$$2n^3 - n^2$$

arithmetic operations are required. Then

$$7/4\ n^3 + 11/4\ n^2 < 2n^3 - n^2$$

$$\text{iff} \qquad 15/4\ n^2 < 1/4\ n^3 \qquad \text{iff} \qquad 15 < n.$$

We conclude that for even n we should use one more recursive step if $n \geq 16$. Suppose now that n is odd. We split off one column each from matrices A and B, i.e.

$$A = \begin{pmatrix} A_{11} & A_{12} \\ A_{21} & A_{22} \end{pmatrix} \qquad B = \begin{pmatrix} B_{11} & B_{12} \\ B_{21} & B_{22} \end{pmatrix}$$

where A_{11}, B_{11} are n-1 by n-1 matrices, A_{12}, B_{12} are column vectors of length n-1, A_{21}, B_{21} are row vectors of length n-1 and A_{22}, B_{22} are ring elements. If we compute $A \cdot B$ according to the school method then we also multiply $A_{11} \cdot B_{11}$ according to the school method. Recursion applied to product $A_{11} \cdot B_{11}$ saves operations whenever $n-1 \geq 16$. These considerations lead to the following algorithm.

<u>procedure</u> MATMULT (A,B,n);
<u>co</u> A and B are n by n matrices;
<u>if</u> n < 16
<u>then</u> compute A·B according to the classical algorithm
<u>else</u> <u>if</u> n even
  <u>then</u> split A and B into four n/2 by n/2 matrices each and apply
    the formulae given in the proof of theorem 1. Use MATMULT re-
    cursively to multiply n/2 by n/2 matrices.
  <u>else</u> split off one row and column of matrices A and B and apply
    the algorithm recursively to the n-1 by n-1 matrices obtained
    in this way. The remaining products are computed classically.
  <u>fi</u>
<u>fi</u>
<u>end</u>

<u>Theorem 2:</u> Algorithm MATMULT for multiplying n by n matrices has the following properties:

1) for $n < 16$ the algorithm uses the same number of arithmetic operations as the classical algorithm.
2) for $n \geq 16$ MATMULT uses strictly less arithmetical operations than the classical algorithm.
3) MATMULT never uses more than $4.8\, n^{\log 7}$ arithmetical operations.

<u>Proof:</u> 1) and 2) are immediate from the preceding discussion. It remains to prove 3). Let M(n) be the number of arithmetical operations used by MATMULT on n by n matrices. Then

$$M(n) = 2n^2 - n^2 \qquad \text{if } n < 16$$

$$M(n) = 7M(n/2) + (18/4)n^2 \qquad \text{if } n \geq 16 \text{ and } n \text{ even}$$

$$M(n) = 7M((n-1)/2) + (42/4)n^2 - 17n + 15/2 \qquad \text{if } n \geq 16 \text{ and } n \text{ odd}$$

Define $\overline{M}$, $x \in \mathbb{R}_+$, by

$$\overline{M}(x) = 2x^3 - x^2 \qquad \text{if } x < 32$$

$$\overline{M}(x) = 7\overline{M}(x/2) + (42/4)n^2 \qquad \text{if } x \geq 32$$

Then $\overline{M}(n) \geq M(n)$ for all $n \in \mathbb{R}$. This is easily shown by direct calculation for $n < 32$ and by induction for $n \geq 32$. Furthermore

$$\overline{M}(x) = \sum_{i=o}^{k-1} 7^i(42/4)\cdot(x/2^i)^2 + 7^k[2(x/2^k)^3 - (x/2^k)^2]$$

for $x \geq 32$ where $k = \min\{l;\ x/2^{\ell} < 32\}$. This is easily verified by induction. With $k = \lfloor \log x \rfloor - 4 = \log x - t$ for some $t \in [4,5]$ we obtain

$$\overline{M}(x) \leq 7^{\log x}[13(4/7)^t + 2(8/7)^t]$$
$$\leq 4.8 \cdot 7^{\log x}$$

for all $x \geq 32$. For $x < 32$, $\overline{M}(x) \leq 4.8 \cdot 7^{\log x}$ is easily shown directly. □

So far, we have only counted number of arithmetic operations. We neither considered the additional administrative overhead required by Strassen's algorithm nor the difference in complexity of adding and multiplying ring elements. We will now sketch an analysis which takes all these facts into account. Let a be the time required to add two ring elements and let m be the time required to multiply two ring elements. Again we want to compute from what n on a recursion step pays off. We neglect terms of linear order in the sequel. It takes time $n^2a + n^2c_1$ to add two n by n matrices on a RAM; here c_1 is the time required for storage access, index calculations and test for loop exit. Similarly, it takes $n^3m + (n^3-n^2)a + n^3c_2 + n^2c_3$ time units to multiply two n by n matrices according to the classical algorithm. Here c_2 and c_3 are the time required for storage access, index calculations and the test for loop exit in the innermost and next to innermost loop. A recursion step pays off, if

$$7((n/2)^3 m + ((n/2)^3 - (n/2)^2 a + (n/2)^3 c_2 + (n/2)^2 c_3)$$
$$+ 18((n/2)^2 a + (n/2)^2 c_1)$$
$$< n^3 + m (n^3-n^2) a + n^3 c_2 + n^2 c_3,$$

i.e.

$$n > \frac{30a + 36c_1 + 6c_3}{m + a + c_2} .$$

It is beyond the scope of this book to determine constants c_1, c_2, c_3, a, m exactly. Realistic values are $a \le c_2, c_2, c_3, m \le 6a$. Then $n \ge n_0 \approx 40$, which is in good agreement with experiments reported in the literature. We refer the reader to the litarature for a more detailed analysis.

The analysis of Strassen's algorithm offered above is still open for critic. Suppose that we want to multiply two n by n matrices over the integers and that all entries are in the range [O...M-1], i.e. all entries are numbers of at most log M bits. Let us assume further that it takes a(k) (m(k)) time units to add (multiply) k-bit numbers. The assumption here is that it takes one time unit to manipulate a single bit (cf. V. 7. for an exact definition). Then a(k) = O(k) and $m(k) = O(k^2)$ by the classical methods. There are faster methods for multiplying numbers, an $O(k^{\log 3})$ algorithm is discussed in the exercises and an O(k log k loglog k) algorithm can be found in Schönhage/ Strassen. We use $m(k) = O(k^2)$ in the sequel. Then the following question arises. How large do the numbers become in Strassen's algorithm compared with the classical algorithm?

In the classical algorithm we have to perfom n^3 multiplications of log M bit numbers for a cost of $n^3 m(\log M)$. We then have to add numbers in the range $[O...n(M-1)^2]$. Thus the cost of the additions is bounded by $n^3 a(\log n + 2 \log M)$. A more careful analysis allows us to drop the log n term in the bound on the cost of additions (exercise 14). Thus the total cost of the classical method is bounded by $O(n^3 (\log M)^2)$.

What can we say about Strassen's method? The following simple observation is crucial. If $c_{ik} = \sum_j a_{ij} b_{jk}$ and $a_{ij}, b_{jk} \in [O...M-1]$ then $c_{ik} = \sum_j a_{ij} b_{jk} \bmod nM^2$.

The integers mod nM^2 form a ring $\mathbb{Z}_{nM^2}$. We can therefore carry out Strassen's algorithm in the ring $\mathbb{Z}_{nM^2}$ of integers mod nM^2. The cost of an addition or multiplication in that ring is certainly bounded by m(log n + 2 log M) and hence the total cost of Strassen's method is $O(n^{\log 7}(\log n + \log M)^2)$. Thus Strassen's method is asymptotically faster than the classical method not only in number of arithmetical operations but also in number of bit operations.

V. 5. Boolean Matrix Multiplication and Transitive Closure

In this section we apply the results of the previous section to boolean matrix product. Unfortunately, this is not possible directly. The boolean semi-ring $B = (\{0,1\}, \vee, \wedge, 0, 1)$ is not a ring. We have $0 \vee 1 = 1 \vee 1 = 1$, i.e. there is no additive inverse for element 1.

Let A and B be boolean n by n matrices. We want to compute $C = A \otimes B$, the boolean matrix product of A and B. Here $\wedge$ is the multiplicative and $\vee$ is the additive operation.

Since the boolean semi-ring is not a ring we cannot apply the results of the previous section directly. The way out is to look at 0 and 1 as natural numbers and to compute the ordinary product $\hat{C} = A \oplus B$ of A and B. Then

$$c_{ij} = \bigvee_{k=1}^{n} a_{ik} \wedge b_{kj} \qquad \text{and} \qquad \hat{c}_{ij} = \sum_{k=1}^{n} a_{ik} \cdot b_{kj}$$

and hence $c_{ij} = 0$ iff $\hat{c}_{ij} = 0$. We can thus directly translate matrix $\hat{C}$ into matrix C. Natural number 0 corresponds to boolean constant 0 and natural numbers $\neq 0$ correspond to boolean constant 1. We have

Theorem 1: Let A and B be boolean n by n matrices. Then the boolean matrix product of A and B can be computed in $O(n^{\log 7}(\log n)^2) = O(n^{2.82})$ bit operations.

Proof: We have shown at the end of the previous section that the product of 0,1-matrices can be computed with $O(n^{\log 7}(\log n)^2) = O(n^{2.82})$ bit operations. This discussion above shows that this is also true for boolean matrix product.

□

<u>Theorem 2:</u> The closure of an n by n boolean matrix can be computed with $O(n^{\log 7}(\log n)^2)$ bit operations.

<u>Proof:</u> Immediate from theorem 1 and theorem V.3.4.

□

<u>Theorem 3:</u> The transitive closure of a digraph $G = (V,E)$ can be computed with $O(n^{\log 7}(\log n)^2)$ bit operations, $n = |V|$.

<u>Proof:</u> Immediate from theorem 2 and corollary V.3.2.. □

V. 6. (Min,+)-Product of Matrices and Least Cost Paths

We used the (min,+)-semi-ring of reals to deal with least cost path problems. Let A and B be n by n matrices with entries in $[0...M-1] \cup \{\infty\}$. We want to compute $C = A\binom{\min}{+}B$, i.e.

$$c_{ik} = \min_{1 \le j \le n} (a_{ij} + b_{jk})$$

The classical method for computing C takes $O(n^3 \log M)$ bit operations. Again, the results of section V.4. cannot be applied directly because the (min,+)-semi-ring of reals is not a ring.

An asymptotically faster algorithm is based on the following observation. If $a,b \in \mathbb{N}_0$ and $a \neq b$ then $\lim_{x \to 0}(x^a + x^b)/x^{\min(a,b)} = 1$ and hence $\min(a,b) \approx \log(x^a + x^b)/\log x$ for small x.

<u>Lemma 1:</u> Let $b_1,\ldots,b_n \in \mathbb{N}_0$, let $f(x) = \sum_{k=1}^{n} x^{b_k}$ and let $a = \min(b_1,\ldots,b_n)$. Then

$$a = \lceil -(1/m)\log f(2^{-m}) \rceil$$

for any $m > \log n$

<u>Proof:</u> Let $a = b_h$. Then

$$f(2^{-m}) = \sum_{k=1}^{n} 2^{-m\,b_k} = 2^{-m\,a}\,(1 + \sum_{\substack{k=1\\k\neq h}}^{n} 2^{-m(b_k-a)})$$

$$= c\; 2^{-m\,a}$$

for some c with $1 \leq c \leq 1 + (n-1) = n$

Then

$$\lceil -1/m \log f(2^{-m}) \rceil = \lceil a - (\log c)/m \rceil = a$$

since $a \in \mathbb{N}_0$ and $0 \leq (\log c)/m < 1$. □

Based on lemma 1 we can use the following algorithm to compute $C = A(\overset{\min}{+})B$.

(1) Let $m = 1 + \lceil \log n \rceil$. Compute matrices $\hat{A}$ and $\hat{B}$ with

$$\hat{a}_{ij} = \begin{cases} 2^{-m\,a_{ij}} & \text{if } a_{ij} \neq \infty \\ 0 & \text{if } a_{ij} = \infty \end{cases}$$

$$\hat{b}_{ij} = \begin{cases} 2^{-m\,b_{ij}} & \text{if } b_{ij} \neq \infty \\ 0 & \text{if } b_{ij} = \infty \end{cases}$$

(2) Compute $\hat{C} = \hat{A} \cdot \hat{B}$ by Strassen's algorithm.

(3) Compute C from $\hat{C}$ by

$$c_{ij} = \begin{cases} \infty & \text{if } \hat{c}_{ij} = 0 \\ \lceil -(1/m)\log \hat{c}_{ij} \rceil & \text{if } \hat{c}_{ij} \neq 0 \end{cases}$$

<u>Theorem 1:</u> The (min,+)-product of matrices A and B with entries in $[0 \ldots M-1] \cup \{\infty\}$ can be computed with $O(n^{\log 7})$ arithmetical operations on reals and $O(n^{\log 7}(M \log n)^2)$ bit operations.

<u>Proof:</u> m is easily computed from the binary representation of n. Then matrices $\hat{A}$ and $\hat{B}$ can be determined in $O(n^2)$ arithmetical and

$O(n^2 M \log n)$ bit operations. Note that numbers a_{ij} have $O(m \log n)$ bits each. Step (2) clearly takes $O(n^{\log 7})$ arithmetical operations. It takes $O(n^{\log 7}(\log n + M \log n)^2) = O(n^{\log 7}(M \log n)^2)$ bit operations by the discussion at the end of section V.4.. Finally step (3) requires us to take logarithms n^2 times. This can be done as follows.

Lemma 2: Let $x \in \mathbb{R}$, $0 < x < 1$, and let z be the number of leading zeroes in the binary representation of x. Then $\lceil -(1/m)\log x \rceil = 1 + \lfloor z/m \rfloor$

Proof: Note first that

$$- \log x = z + 1 - \delta \qquad \text{for some } \delta,\ 0 \le \delta < 1.$$

Hence

$$-(1/m)\log x = \lfloor z/m \rfloor + (z/m - \lfloor z/m \rfloor) + (1-\delta)/m$$

Also

$$0 < (z/m - \lfloor z/m \rfloor) + (1-\delta)/m \le (m-1)/m + 1/m \le 1$$

and hence

$$\lceil -(1/m \log x \rceil = \lfloor z/m \rfloor + 1 \qquad \square$$

We infer from lemma 2 that step (3) takes $O(n^2)$ arithmetical operations and $O(n^2(\log M + \log\log n)^2)$ bit operations. Note that $z \le M \log n$. Altogether we have shown that $O(n^{\log 7})$ arithmetical operations over the reals and $O(n^{\log 7}(M \log n)^2)$ bit operations suffice. $\square$

Let us compare the classical algorithm with the new algorithm. The classical algorithm is clearly inferior with respect to arithmetical operation. The situation is not so clear with respect to number of bit operations. The classical algorithm uses $O(n^3 \log M)$ bit operations the new algorithm uses $O(n^{\log 7}(M \log n)^2)$. Thus the classical algorithm is superior or at least competitive whenever M is of size $n^{3-\log 7} \approx n^{0.19}$ or larger.

In the boolean case we were able to obtain efficient algorithms for the transitive closure by applying theorem V.3.4.. Is this also true here?

The answer is no! Let us take a closer look at the proof of theorem V.3.4.. In the recursive algorithm described there we have to multiply smaller matrices. In the case of (min,+)-product all entries in these smaller matrices correspond to shortest paths in subgraphs of the given graph. Therefore the entries in these matrices are in the range 0...nM. As above we assume that we start with a matrix with entries in 0...(M-1). Thus the multiplications on the way are extremely costly; their cost may be as large as $O(n^{\log 7}(nM \log n)^2)$ bit operations by theorem 1.

We included this section mostly as a warning. It shows us that saving arithmetical operations may not always correspond to real savings in execution time, if the reduction in arithmetical operations implies a drastic increase in the size of the numbers which have to be handled by the algorithm. The additional time spent on realizing the basic arithmetic operations addition and multiplication then more than compensates the savings in the number of such operations. We conclude that analysing the number of arithmetic steps is not enough; it always has to be accompanied by an analysis of the cost of arithmetic steps.

V. 7. A Lower Bound on the Monotone Complexity of Matrix Multiplication

In this section we will prove a lower bound on the complexity of matrix multiplication in a restricted model of computation: straight-line programs which use only monotone operations. A straight-line program is a program without loops and conditional statements. All programs which we have seen in this chapter are straight-line programs if we restrict ourselves to fixed input size because for fixed input size we can eliminate all loops and procedure calls by explicite duplication of code. Monotone operations preserve the natural ordering on their domain. In the arithmetical case (reals or integers) the operations addition and multiplication are monotone but subtraction is not and in the boolean case the operations AND and OR are monotone but negation is not (The natural ordering is $0 \leq 1$ in the boolean case). We treat the boolean case first and then obtain the lower bound for other cases as a corollary.

<u>Definition:</u> A straight-line program β over set $X = \{x_1,\ldots,x_n\}$ of input variables, $Z = \{z_1,\ldots,z_m\}$ of intermediate variables, and operations AND and OR is a sequence $A_1,\ldots,A_m$ of assignment statements. The j-th assignment statement A_j, $1 \leq j \leq m$, has the form

$$z_j \leftarrow v_{j1} \; op_j \; v_{j2}$$

where $op_j \in \{AND, OR\}$, and $v_{jk} \in X$ or $v_{jk} = z_\ell$ for some $\ell < j$ and $k = 1,2$. If the operation symbol in assignment A_j is AND (OR) then we refer to A_j as an AND (OR)-gate. Integer m is the length of the program program β. □

The semantics of straight-line programs is straightforward. We associate with every variable $v \in X \cup Z$ of a straight-line program a n-ary boolean function $res_{\beta,v} : B^n \rightarrow B$ where $n = |X|$ and $B = \{0,1\}$. Let $\vec{b} = (b_1,\ldots,b_n) \in B^n$ be arbitrary.

If $v \in X$, say $v = x_i$, then $res_{\beta,v}$ is the i-th projection function, i.e.

$$res_{\beta,x_i}(b_1,\ldots,b_n) = b_i$$

If $v \in Z$, say $v = z_j$, and A_j has the form

$z_j \leftarrow v_{j1} \; op_j \; v_{j2}$ then

$$res_{\beta,z_j}(\vec{b}) = res_{\beta,v_{j1}}(\vec{b})\ op_j\ res_{\beta,v_{j2}}(\vec{b})$$

where we took the liberty of using the same symbol op_j for the operation symbol and the operation itself.

Let F be a set of n-ary boolean functions. Then straight-line program β computes F if $F \subseteq \{res_{\beta,v};\ v$ is a variable of $\beta\}$. The complexity of F is the minimal length of any program β which computes it.

<u>Example:</u> Let β be the following program with input variables $a_{11}, a_{21}, b_{11}, b_{12}$.

$$z_1 \leftarrow a_{21} \vee b_{12}$$
$$z_2 \leftarrow z_1 \vee b_{11}$$
$$z_3 \leftarrow z_2 \wedge a_{11}$$

where we used $\wedge$ to denote AND and $\vee$ to denote OR. (Frequently, we suppress the $\wedge$-symbol). Then $res_{\beta,z_2} = a_{21} \vee b_{11} \vee b_{12}$ and $res_{\beta,z_3} = a_{11}a_{21} \vee a_{11}b_{11} \vee a_{11}b_{12}$.

Straight-line programs can be interpreted as circuits, the circuit corresponding to the program above is shown below. The input variables correspond to the input ports

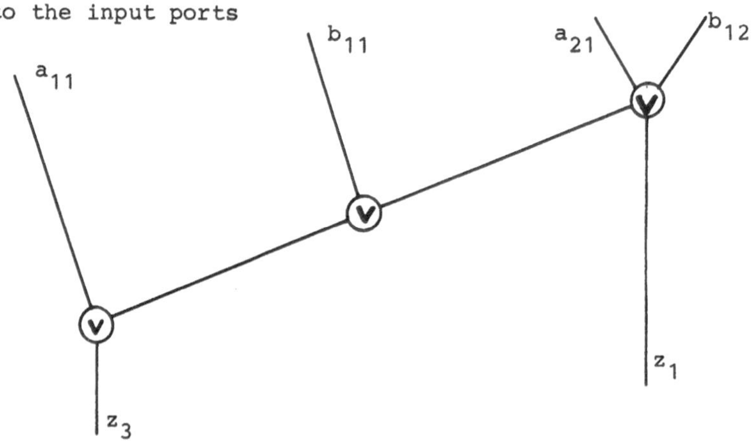

of the circuit and the intermediate variables correspond to outputs of gates.

A boolean function f is <u>monotone</u> if it can be computed by a straight-line program over operation set AND and OR. Equivalently, f is monotone

if it preserves the natural ordering on B: B is ordered by $0 \leq 1$ and B^n is ordered componentwise.
We are interested in boolean matrix multiplication.

Definition: Let $r,p,q \in \mathbb{N}$ and let $A = (a_{ij}), B = (b_{jk})$, $1 \leq i \leq r$, $1 \leq j \leq p$, $1 \leq k \leq q$, be sets of boolean variables. The (r,p,q) boolean matrix product is the following set of rq monotone boolean functions:

$$F = \{\bigvee_{j=1}^{p} (a_{ij} \wedge b_{jk});\ 1 \leq i \leq r,\ 1 \leq k \leq q\} \qquad \square$$

The definition of matrix product suggests the school method for computing it. We will show that the school method is optimal.

Theorem 1:
a) Every monotone straight-line program (= monotone circuit) for the (r,p,q) boolean matrix product contains at least rpq AND-Gates and rq(p-1) OR-gates.
b) The school method for boolean matrix product is the only (up to commutativity and associativity) of AND and OR) program which uses that number of AND- and OR-gates, i.e. the school method is the unique optimal monotone circuit for boolean matrix product.

Proof: The proof of theorem 1 is lengthy. We will first review some basic facts and concepts about boolean functions, then prove two theorems about the structure of optimal monotone circuits and then finally prove the lower bound on matrix multiplication.

Let $f,g: B^n \to B$ be boolean functions. We write $f \leq g$ if $f(b) \leq g(b)$ for all $b \in B^n$. A monomial is a product of input variables. Let m be a monomial. Then m is an implicant of f if $m \leq f$ and it is a prime implicant of f if $m \leq f$ and $m \leq m' \leq f$ implies $m = m'$ for all monomials m'. We use Prim(f) to denote the set of prime implicants of f.

We will now state and prove two theorems about the structure of monotone circuits. We illustrate both theorems on the example given above. We assume that the three assignments given there are part of a program for (r,p,q) boolean matrix product with $r \geq 2$, $p \geq 1$, and $q \geq 2$. We also assume that z_1 and z_3 but not z_2 are used in later statements of the program. We indicated this assumption in the circuit diagram by the two wires leaving the bottom of the diagram.

Theorem 2: Let β be a monotone circuit wich computes F, let v be a variable in β, and let Prim $(res_{\beta,v}) = \{t_o,\dots,t_k\}$.
If there is no monomial t and no function $f \in F$ with $t_o \wedge t \in Prim(f)$ then the following circuit β' also computes F: Circuit β' is obtained from β by replacing every access to variable v by an access to a new variable v' with $res_{\beta',v'} = t_1 \vee \dots \vee t_k$.

Remark: Circuit β' is not necessarily cheaper than circuit β because we might delete only one gate, namely v, but might have to add more than one gate to compute $t_1 \vee \dots \vee t_k$. In our example, $a_{11}\, a_{21}$ is prime implicant of z_3; it is not part of any prime implicant $a_{ij}\, b_{jk}$ of any output function. Hence we can replace all accesses to z_3 by accesses to z_3' with $res_{\beta',z_3'} = a_{11}\, b_{11} \vee a_{11}\, b_{12}$. We can therefore delete gates z_2 and z_3 and replace them by gates which compute $a_{11}\, b_{11} \vee a_{11}\, b_{12}$. We obtain:

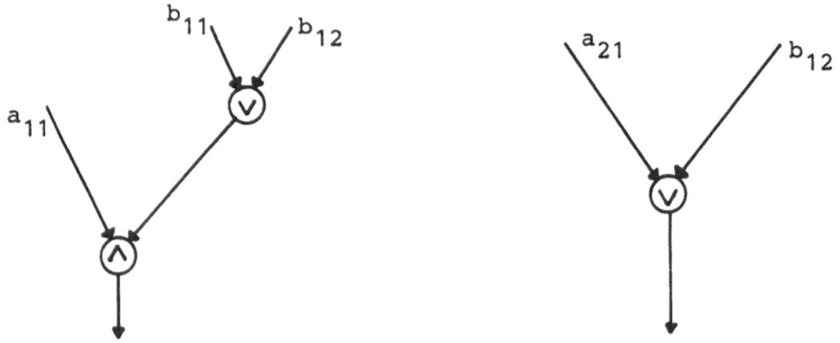

Proof of theorem 2: Let us assume for the sake of contradiction that β' does not compute F, say $f \in F$ is not computed. Then there must be a variable w with $res_{\beta,w} = f$. We conclude from the hypothesis of the theorem that $v \neq w$. Hence w exists also in circuit β' and realizes $f' = res_{\beta',w}$. By monotonicity we have $f' \leq f$ and since f is not computed by β' we even have $f' < f$. Thus there muxt be $b \in B^n$ such that $f'(b) = 0 \neq 1 = f(b)$. Since β and β' only differ in variables v and v' we conclude further that $(t_1 \vee \dots \vee t_n)(b) = 0$ and $t_o(b) = 1$. Hence, if we change the value of any variable which occurs in t_o from 1 to 0 we also change the value of f from 1 to 0 and therefore there is a monomial t with $t_o \wedge t \in Prim(f)$.

Contradiction! □

Consider variable z_3' in our example above. It has prime implicants $a_{11}\, b_{11}$ and $a_{11}\, b_{12}$. Both products have to be computed in any circuit for matrix product but they have to be sent to different outputs. However, separating information is impossible in monotone computations as theorem 3 shows.

Theorem 3: Let v be a variable in a monotone circuit β which computes F. Assume further that $t \wedge t_1,\ t \wedge t_2 \in \mathrm{Prim}(res_{\beta,v})$ for some monomials t, t_1, t_2 and that for all $f \in F$ we have: for all monomials s the inequalities $s \wedge t \wedge t_1 \le f$ and $s \wedge t \wedge t_2 \le f$ imply $s \wedge t \le f$. Then the following circuit β' also computes F. Delete v from β and replace all accesses to v by accesses to v' with $res_{\beta',v'} = t \vee res_{\beta,v}$.

Proof: Let us assume for the sake of contradiction that β' does not compute F, say $f \in F$, is not computed. Let $f = res_{\beta,w}$ for some variable w and let $f' = res_{\beta',w}$ if $w \neq v$. If $w = v$ then let $f' = res_{\beta,v'}$. By monotonicity we have $f \le f'$ and since f is not computed by β' we even have $f < f'$. Let $b \in B^n$ be such that $f(b) = 0 \neq 1 = f'(b)$. Then we must have $res_{\beta,v}(b) = 0$ and $t(b) = 1$.
As before, we conclude that if we change the value of any variable which occurs in t from 1 to 0 then f' changes its value from 1 to 0 and therefore we conclude the existence of a monomial s with $s \wedge t \in \mathrm{Prim}(f')$.
We conclude further from the structure of circuits β and β' that $s \wedge t \wedge t_1$ and $s \wedge t \wedge t_2$ are implicants of f. Hence $s \wedge t$ is implicant of f and hence $f(b) = 1$.
Contradiction! □

In our example we can apply theorem 3 to z_1 and z_3'. Consider z_1 first. Let $f_{ik} = \bigvee_j (a_{ij} \wedge b_{jk})$ be an arbitrary output of boolean matrix product and let s be a monomial with $s \wedge a_{21} \le f_{ik}$ and $s \wedge b_{12} \le f_{ik}$. From $s \wedge a_{21} \le f_{ik}$ we conclude that either $s \le f_{ik}$ or $s = b_{1k} s'$ and $i = 2$. From $s \wedge b_{12} \le f_{jk}$ we conclude that either $s \le f_{ik}$ or $s = a_{i1} s''$ and $k = 2$. Thus either $s \le f_{ik}$ or $s = a_{21}\, b_{12}\, s'''$ and $i = k = 2$. In either case we have $s \le f_{ik}$. We can therefore apply theorem 3 with $t = 1$, $t_1 = a_{21}$ and $t_2 = b_{12}$. This allows us to replace all accesses to z_1 by accesses to z_1' with $res_{\beta',z'} = 1$. Similarly, we can apply theorem 3 to z_3' with $t = a_{11}$, $t_1 = b_{11}$ and $t_2 = b_{12}$. We obtain

We can now start to really prove theorem 1. Let β be an optimal circuit for boolean matrix product, i.e. a circuit of minimal length. We want to show that β is the school method. In the school method we have for every triple (i,j,k) an AND-gate which computes $a_{ij}b_{jk}$ and for every pair (i,k) we have p-1 OR-gates which sum the p products $a_{ij}b_{jk}$, $1 \le j \le p$. We try to locate these gates in circuit β . In order to do so we consider the predicates P on boolean functions which have the property that they hold true for at least one output wire of any circuit for boolean matrix product and that they hold true for no input wire. Thus there must be a gate g in β such that P holds true for (the functions realized at) the output wire of g but does not hold true for any input wire of g. We denote this set of gates by I(P). The gates in I(P) are the gates to be located. Unfortunately, we will not be able to locate all rpq AND-gates in one step. Rather, we will locate only the rq AND-gates which realize the products $a_{i1}b_{1k}$, then eliminate these gates by setting $a_{i1} = 1$ and $b_{1k} = 0$, and finally use induction on p.

The following notation helps to simplify the discussion. If g is a gate then we use $h(h_1,h_2)$ to denote the function realized by the output (left and right input) wire of g.

We will first locate the AND-gates. For $1 \le i \le r$, $1 \le k \le q$ let P_{ik} be the following predicate on boolean functions

$$P_{ik}(h) \Leftrightarrow a_{i1}b_{1k} \le h \text{ and } a_{i1} \not\le h \text{ and } b_{1k} \not\le h,$$

i.e. $a_{i1}b_{1k}$ is prime implicant of h.

Clearly, input variables of β do not satisfy P_{ik} and output f_{ik} satisfies P_{ik}. Hence $I(P_{ik})$ is not empty.

<u>Lemma 1:</u> a) If $g \in I(P_{ik})$ then g is an AND-gate and $a_{i1} \le h_1$ and $b_{1k} \le h_2$ (or vice versa)

b) If $(i_1,k_1) \ne (i_2,k_2)$ then $I(P_{i_1k_1}) \cap I(P_{i_2k_2}) = \emptyset$

Proof: a) Let $g \in I(P_{ik})$. Assume first that g is an OR-gate. Then $h = h_1 \vee h_2$ and $P_{ik}(h)$, $\neg P_{ik}(h_1)$ and $\neg P_{ik}(h_2)$. From $a_{i1}\, b_{1k} \le h$ we conclude that either $a_{i1}\, b_{1k} \le h_1$ or $a_{i1}\, b_{1k} \le h_2$. We may assume $a_{i1}\, b_{1k} \le h_1$ w.l.o.g. . From $\neg P_{ik}(h_1)$ we conclude further that either $a_{i1} \le h_1$ or $b_{1k} \le h_1$ and hence $a_{i1} \le h$ or $b_{1k} \le h$. Thus $\neg P_{ik}(h)$, a contradiction. This shows that all gates $g \in I(P_{ik})$ are AND-gates.

Let $g \in I(P_{ik})$ be an AND-gate. Then $h = h_1 \wedge h_2$ and $\neg P_{ik}(h_1)$and $\neg P_{ik}(h_2)$. From $a_{i1}\, b_{1k} \le h$ we conclude $a_{i1}\, b_{1k} \le h_1$ and $a_{i1}\, b_{1k} \le h_2$ and hence $a_{i1} \le h_1$ or $b_{1k} \le h_1$ and similarly for h_2. If $a_{i1} \le h_1$ and $a_{i1} \le h_2$ then $a_{i1} \le h$, a contradiction. Similarly, if $b_{1k} \le h_1$ and $b_{1k} \le h_2$ then $b_{1k} \le h$, a contradiction. Thus $a_{i1} \le h_1$ and $b_{1k} \le h_2$ or vice versa. This proves part a).

b) Let $(i_1,k_1) \neq (i_2,k_2)$ and $I(P_{i_1k_1}) \cap I(P_{i_2k_2}) \neq \emptyset$, say $g \in I(P_{i_1k_1}) \cap I(P_{i_2k_2})$.
Then one of the following two cases applies.

Case 1: $a_{i_1 1} \le h_1,\ a_{i_2 1} \le h_1$

$b_{1k_1} \le h_2,\ b_{1k_2} \le h_2$

Case 2: $a_{i_1 1} \le h_1,\ b_{1k_2} \le h_1$

$a_{i_2 1} \le h_2,\ b_{1k_1} \le h_2$

In either case we can apply theorem 3. If case 1 applies and $i_1 \neq i_2$ (the case that $k_1 \neq k_2$ is symmetric) then we can apply theorem 3 with $t = 1$, $t_1 = a_{i_1 1}$ and $t_2 = a_{i_2 1}$. We can therefore replace all accesses to h_1 by accesses to $h_1 \vee 1 = 1$. This fixes one input of gate g to a constant and we can therefore eliminate gate g, a contradiciton to the optimality of β. If case 2 applies then we can set both inputs of g to 1 by theorem 3 (cf. the example following theorem 3) and therefore eliminate gate g. Thus we obtained a contradiciton to the minimality of β in either case. This proves part b). □

We turn to counting OR-gates next. Let Q_{ik} be the following predicate on boolean functions.

$$Q_{ik}(h) \Leftrightarrow a_{i1}\, b_{1k} \le h \le A_i \vee b_{1k} \text{ and } h \not\le b_{1k}$$

where $A_i = \bigvee_{j \neq 1} a_{ij}$. We have

<u>Lemma 2:</u> a) $I(Q_{ik}) \neq \emptyset$ if $p \geq 2$

b) If $g \in I(Q_{ik})$ then g is an OR-gate and either $h_1 \leq b_{1k}$ or $h_2 \leq b_{1k}$

c) The sets $I(Q_{ik})$ are pairwise disjoint.

<u>Proof:</u> Similar to the proof of lemma 1. □

What have we achieved at this point? For every pair (i,k) we have located an AND-gate in β which has a_{i1} as prime implicant of one of its input wires; for different pairs we identified different gates. Therefore, if we fix a_{i1} to the constant 1, $1 \leq i \leq r$, then we can eliminate rq AND-gates from β . Similarly, if $p > 1$, then we have located for each pair (i,k) an OR-gate g such that either $h_1 \leq b_{1k}$ or $h_2 \leq b_{1k}$. Also, different gates were located for different pairs. Therefore, if we fix b_{1k} to the constant 0, $1 \leq k \leq q$, then we eliminate rq OR-gates from β. Finally, fixing $a_{i1} = 1$ and $b_{1k} = 0$ for $1 \leq i \leq r$ and $1 \leq k \leq q$ transforms β into a circuit for the functions

$$f_{ik} = \bigvee_{j=2}^{p} a_{ij} b_{jk} ,$$

i.e. into a circuit for the (r,(p-1),q) boolean matrix product. If $p = 1$ then we can still eliminate rq AND-gates. Part a) of theorem 1 follows by a simple induction argument.

It remains to prove part b). Let β be an optimal circuit for the (r,p,r) boolean matrix product. Then β contains exactly rpq AND-gates and r(p-1)q OR-gates. If we apply the elimination process described above to β then we eliminate in each step <u>exactly</u> the gates in $I(P_{ik})$ and and $I(Q_{ik})$, i.e. if $a_{\ell 1}$ is prime implicant of a gate g then g belongs to either $I(P_{ik})$ or $I(Q_{ik})$ for some i and k. In the latter case $a_{\ell 1}$ were also prime implicant of the output of g, a contradiciton to $g \in I(Q_{ik})$. We conclude that $a_{\ell 1}$ is prime implicant of input wires of AND-gates only, $1 \leq \ell \leq r$. Because of the symmetry of boolean matrix product and because we can start the elimination process with any column of A and can also interchange the roles of A and B we conclude that variables are prime implicants of AND-gates only and that the prime implicants of inputs and outputs of OR-gates are monomials of at least two variables. We conclude further, that the inputs to a gate in $I(P_{ik})$ are <u>exactly</u> the variables a_{i1} and b_{1k}. Because of symmetry this is true for every triple (i,j,k), i.e. the rpq AND-gates of β have the input pairs (a_{ij},b_{jk}), $1 \leq i \leq r$, $1 \leq j \leq p$, $1 \leq k \leq q$.

Since the rq output functions are disjunctions of p products $a_{ij}\, b_{jk}$ $(1 \leq j \leq p)$ each, the $r(p-1)\circ q$ OR-gates are needed in order to sum up the outputs of the AND-gates. This proves part b).

□

We want to draw one consequence from theorem 1. Let $(S,\oplus,\odot,0,1)$ be an arbitrary semi-ring. We say that S has characteristic 0 if $1 \oplus 1 \oplus \ldots \oplus 1 \neq 0$ for any number of ones to be added. We have

Theorem 4: Let $(S,\oplus,\odot,0,1)$ be a semi-ring of characteristic 0. Then any straight-line program which computes the (r,p,q) matrix product of matrices over S using operations $\oplus$ and $\odot$ only contains at least rpq multiplications and r(p-1)q additions. Moreover, the school method is the unique optimal program.

Proof: Let β be any straight-line program which computes the (r,p,q) matrix product of matrices over S using operations $\oplus$ and $\odot$ only. In order to prove the theorem it suffices to show that β is transformed into a monotone program β' for boolean matrix product by replacing $\oplus$ by $\vee$ and $\odot$ by $\wedge$.

This can be seen as follows. For $n \in \mathbb{N}$ let $\bar{n} = \underbrace{1 \oplus \ldots \oplus 1}_{n\text{-times}} \in S$.

Then $\bar{n} \neq 0$ for all $n \in \mathbb{N}$ since S has characteristic zero, $\bar{n} + \bar{m} = \overline{n + m}$ by associativity and $\bar{n} \cdot \bar{m} = \overline{n \cdot m}$ by distributivity. Let $S_+ = \{0\} \cup \{\bar{n};\ n \in \mathbb{N}\}$. Then $(S_+,\oplus,\odot,0,1)$ is a semi-ring and the mapping $h: S_+ \to B$ with $h(0) = 0$ and $h(\bar{n}) = 1$ for $n \geq 1$ is a homomorphism into the boolean semi-ring $(B,\vee,\wedge,0,1)$. This shows that β' computes the (r,p,q) boolean matrix product.

□

Theorem 4 applies to a large number of semi-rings, e.g. the reals under addition and multiplication $(\mathbb{R},+,\circ,0,1)$, the extended reals under minimum and addition $(\mathbb{R} \cup \{\infty\}, \min, +, \infty, 0)$, the extended reals under maximum and minimum $(\mathbb{R} \cup \{\infty\}, \max, \min, 0, \infty), \ldots$.

Theorem 4 does not apply to the ring of integers mod p for some integer p. This ring does not have characteristic zero and in fact we can use

Strassen's algorithm in this ring. (Note that $\underbrace{a+\ \dots\ +a}_{(p-1)\text{-times}} = -a \bmod p$ for prime p and hence subtraction reduces to addition).

V. 8. Exercises

1) Show that the following algebraic structures are closed semi-rings.
   a) $(\mathbb{R}_+ \cup \{+\infty\}, \max, \min, 0, \infty)$
   b) $(\mathbb{R}_+ \cup \{+\infty, -\infty\}, \max, +, -\infty, 0)$, where $(-\infty) + (+\infty) = -\infty$.

2) Compute the closure of the elements of the semi-rings of exercise 1.

3) Show:
   a) the null-element 0 of a semi-ring is uniquely defined
   b) $\sum_{i \in \emptyset} a_i = 0$ in a semi-ring

4) Let $G = (V,E)$ be a directed graph and let $c : E \to \mathbb{R}_+$ be a cost function. Define the capacity of a path as the minimum cost of any edge on the path. Show how to compute for every pair (v,w) of points the path of maximal capacity from v to w. Hint: Use one of the semi-rings of exercise 1.

5) Let $G = (V,E)$ be a directed graph and let $c : E \to \mathbb{R}_+$ be a cost function. Show how to solve the all pairs maximum cost path problem.

6) Modify the all pairs least cost path algorithm such that it computes not only the cost of the least cost path but also the paths themselves.

7) Let $G = (V,E)$ be a directed graph and let $c : E \to \mathbb{R}_{\geq 0}$ be a cost function. Compute for each pair (v,w) of vertices the cost of the k cheapest paths from v to w. Find an adequate closed semi-ring.

8) Show that the algebraic structure $(M_n, +, \cdot, 0, I)$ of n x n matrices over a closed semi-ring is a closed semi-ring.

9) Verify formally all identities which were used in proof of theorem 4 of section V.3.

10) Show that M(n), the cost of multiplying two n x n matrices, is non-decreasing.

11) Show that the set of n x n matrices over a ring forms a ring.

12) Let $G = (V,E)$ be an acyclic directed graph and let $c : E \to S$ be a labelling of the edges of G with elements of a semi-ring S. Show how to solve the all-pair path problem using O(ne) semi-ring operations.

13) Let a and b be two n-bit integers. Let $k = \lceil n/2 \rceil$ and write $a = a_1 2^k + a_2$, $b = a_1 2^k + b_2$ where a_1, a_2, b_1 and b_2 are k-bit integers. Then

$$a \cdot b = a_1 b_1 2^{2k} + (a_1 b_2 + a_2 b_1) 2^k + a_2 b_2 .$$

Let $m_1 \leftarrow (a_1 - a_2)(b_1 - b_2)$

$m_2 \leftarrow a_1 b_1$

$m_3 \leftarrow a_2 b_2$

Then $a_1 b_2 + a_2 b_1 = - m_1 + m_2 + m_3$, i.e. we can compute ab using <u>three</u> multiplications of k-bit integers where $k = \lceil n/2 \rceil$.
Show that this observation yields an algorithm which multiplies n-bit integers using $O(n^{\log 3})$ bit operations.

14) Let $x_1, \ldots, x_n$ be integers in the range [0... M-1].
Show how to compute $x_1 + \ldots + x_n$ using O(n log M) bit operations.
Hint: Add the x_i's in the form of a binary tree and observe that the binary representation of a sum of 2^k x_i's has length k + log M.

15) State and prove theorems similar to theorems 1 and 4 of section 7 for transitive closure instead of matrix multiplication.

16) Let T be a binary tree with n leaves. For each node v let w(v) be the number of leaves in the subtree with root v and let bin(w(v)) be the binary representation of w(v). Show that the labelling {bin(w(v)); v a node of T} can be computed with O(n) bit operations. Note that the total length of all labels might be O(n log n) and therefore only an implicite representation of the labelling can be computed. The representation should be such that given v its label bin(w(v)) can be read off in time O(|bin(w(v))|).

V. 9. Bibliographic Notes

The algorithm for solving general path problems goes back to Kleene (56) who found it in the connection with finite automata and regular expressions. The algebraic viewpoint was introduced by Aho/Hopcroft/Ullman (74) and later refined by Fletcher (80). The algorithms for the special cases of section 2 are due to Roy (59), Warshall (62) and Floyd (62). The connection between matrix multiplication and transitive closure was established by Munro (71), Furman (70), and Fischer/Meyer (71). The fast matrix multiplication algorithm of section 4 is due to Strassen (69); an $O(n^{2.5})$ algorithm was recently found by Coppersmith/Winograd (81). The papers by Cohen/Roth (76) and Spieß (76) discuss the problem of implementing the fast matrix multiplication algorithm. Section 5 follows Fischer/Meyer (71), section 6 follows Romani (80), and section 7 discusses work of Paterson (75) and Mehlhorn/Galil (76). The $O(n^{\log 3})$ algorithm for integer multiplication (exercise 13) is due to Karazuba/Offman (62); an O(n logn loglogn) algorithm can be found in Schönhage/Strassen (71).

VI. NP-Completeness

The CLIQUE problem is as follows: Input is an undirected graph $G = (V,E)$ with n nodes and an integer k. The question is to decide whether the complete graph on k nodes is a subgraph of G, i.e. whether there is $V' \subseteq V$, $|V'| = k$ such that $(u,v) \in E$ for all $u,v \in V'$. There is a trivial, but inefficient algorithm to solve the CLIQUE problem. Run through all subsets $V' \subseteq V$ of cardinality k and check whether V' induces a complete graph. There are $\binom{n}{k}$ sets V' with k elements. Thus our simple algorithm checks $\binom{n}{n/2} \geq 2^n/(n+1)$ subsets in the case $k = n/2$. It is simple to check a subset V' for the clique property; time n will certainly suffice, and one time unit is certainly required. We conclude that our naive algorithm has running time at least $2^n/(n+1)$. Before we can state that this is inefficient, we have to define problem size. We assume throughout this chapter, that combinatorial objects, i.e. graphs, integers, sets, ..., are coded over a finite alphabet in some "natural way". More precisely, we assume that graphs are coded by their adjacency matrix, i.e. a graph G with n nodes is coded by a bitstring of length n^2, the entries of the matrix in row major order. Integers are always written in binary and sets are specified by listing their elements in some order. In this way a problem instance of the clique problem is a bistring of length $n^2 + \log(n/2) + 1$, again assuming $k = n/2$ for simplicity. With this convention our naive algorithm accepts the language CLIQUE = $\{w \# v;\ w,v \in \{0,1\}^*,\ |w| = n^2$ for some n and the graph G with adjacency matrix w has a clique of size k, where v is the binary representation of k$\}$ in time $\Omega(2^{\sqrt{m}}/\sqrt{m})$, where m is the length of the input. At the day of this writing there is no algorithm known, which is considerably more efficient than the naive algorithm described above, and we will see in this chapter, that it is very unlikely that there is ever going to be one. We will also see that CLIQUE shares this property with many other combinatorial problems, e.g. the Traveling Salesman Problem and the Satisfiability Problem of propositional logic.

Let us take a closer look at the CLIQUE problem. There are $\binom{n}{k}$ subsets $V' \subseteq V$ of cardinality k, i.e. there are very many candidates for a clique of size k. It is easy to test, whether a subset $V' \subseteq V$ defines a clique, i.e. it is easy to test whether a candidate is indeed a solution. However, the only known way to find a solution is to exhaustively search through all candidates.

This concept is best described by the notion of a <u>nondeterministic algorithm</u>. The instruction set of nondeterministic RAMs contains one more instruction, the nondeterministic choice instruction:

CHOICE Label_1, Label_2

Executing a choice instruction transfers control to either Label_1 or Label_2. There are no probabilities associated with the alternatives as in randomized algorithms, rather the choice is made by a demon. In this way there is a large number of possible computations on any fixed input depending on the sequence of nondeterministic choices made by the demon. A nondeterministic algorithm <u>accepts</u> an input, if there is <u>at least one</u> accepting computation on that input. The time complexity of a nondeterministic algorithm is the length of the shortest accepting computation.

We illustrate the new concept of a nondeterministic algorithm by describing a nondeterministic algorithm for CLIQUE which runs in polynomial time. We use nondeterministic choices to select a candidate set V' and then check deterministically whether it is indeed a solution. More precisely, the algorithm works in three stages. In the first stage the input string w # v is parsed and $n = |w|^{1/2}$ and k, the number represented by bitstring v, are computed. If the input is not of the form w # v or $|w|$ is not a square then the input is rejected. Stage 1 can certainly be done in time $O(n^4)$. In stage 2 we nondeterministically select a subset $V' \subseteq V$ of size k by nondeterministically generating a bitvector A[1.. n] which contains exactly k ones, i.e. A[i] = 1 iff $i \in V'$.

```
for i from 1 to n
do Choice m1, m2;
   m1: A[i] ← 0;
       goto m;
   m2: A[i] ← 1;
       k ← k - 1;
   m:
od
if k ≠ 0 then stop and reject.
```

(Successful) execution of the program above generates one of the $\binom{n}{k}$ subsets $V' \subseteq V$, $|V'| = k$. Stage 2 takes time O(n). In stage 3, V' is checked for the clique property. This can certainly be done in time $O(n^4)$ also. If V' is a clique then the input is accepted, otherwise it is rejected. The algorithm described runs in time $O(n^4) = O(m^2)$ where m is the length of the input. Also, it accepts the language CLIQUE, as we show now. If the graph G = (V,E) does not have a clique of size k, then the subset $V' \subseteq V$ generated in stage 2 does not form a clique and hence there is no accepting compution on input G. Conversely, if G has a clique of size k, say V', then there is a computation which generates that very V' in stage 2. This computation is accepting.

We have thus shown that CLIQUE can be solved in polynomial time by a nondeterministic algorithm. Let NP be the class of problems which can be solved in polynomial time on a nondeterministic machine and let P be the class of problems which can be solved in polynomial time on a deterministic machine. One of the major results of this chapter is:

$$P = NP \quad \text{iff} \quad \text{CLIQUE} \in P$$

Class NP contains a large number of combinatorial problems (cf. setion VI. 5) for which efficient algorithms have been looked for extensively by many researchers, but non has been found so far. If CLIQUE were in P then all these problems would have efficient deterministic algorithms, an unlikely event. Thus CLIQUE $\notin$ P is a safe conjecture.

In the sequel we will have to argue frequently about the class of all algorithms of a certain complexity. In principle we could base the discussion on the RAM model. However, the discussion becomes simpler if we use a simpler machine model: Turing machines (TM). The relation between TMs and real computers is less direct than between RAMs and real computers and therefore complexity bounds derived for TMs are not directly applicable to real computers. However, the loss in efficiency is bounded by a polynomial (Theorem 1 below) and therefore the classes P and NP will be the same for both models.

VI. 1. Turing Machines and Random Access Machines

TMs are a very simple model of universal computers. There are only two parts: a control unit and a storage unit. The storage unit is a single semi-infinite (infinite to the right) tape. The tape is divided into squares which can store a single character of a finite alphabet each. The control unit has a finite number of states, it scans the tape by a single read/write head which is one square in size.

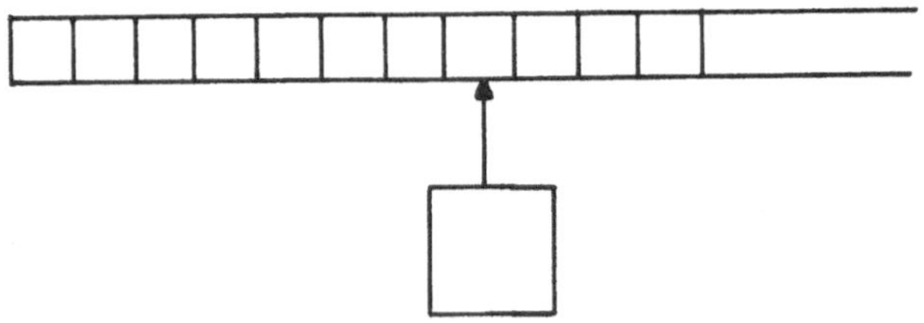

We program TMs by Turing tables. The Turing table specifies for each state of the finite control and each letter of the tape alphabet a set of possible actions (in the case of a nondeterministic machine) or a single action (in the case of deterministic machines). An action consists of three parts: changing the state of the finite control, printing a new symbol on the square under the read/write head and moving the head by at most one square to the left or the right. A TM is started by writing the input string of length n onto the first n squares of the tape, placing the head over the first (leftmost) symbol of the input string and putting the machine into a special state, the initial state. All other squares are initially empty, i.e. contain the symbol $\not b$ of the tape alphabet. The TM then computes as specified by the Turing table until it reaches a pair of state and character scanned by the read/write head for which no action is specified in the Turing table. At this point the machine stops. The output of the computation is the non-empty part of the tape. In this way, we can use TMs to compute functions. Often we use TMs to recognize languages. Two definitions are possible. A TM recognizes a language, if it computes the characteristic function, or we designate a subset of the states as accepting and call a computation accepting if it ends in an accepting state. Both definitions are equivalent; the second one allows for a more natural treatment of nondeterminism.

The details are as follows:

<u>Definition:</u> A nondeterministic TM is a 4-tuple $M = (Z,\Gamma,\delta,F)$. Here $Z = \{Z_1,\ldots,Z_s\}$ is a finite set of states, $\Gamma = \{A_1,\ldots,A_v\}$ is the finite tape alphabet, Z_1 the initial state, $F \subseteq Z$ a set of accepting states

and δ: $Z \times \Gamma \rightarrow 2^{Z \times \Gamma \times \{-1,0,+1\}}$ the transition function. The TM M is deterministic if $|\delta(z,a)| \leq 1$ for every state z and alphabet symbol a. Then δ is equivalent to a partial function δ: $Z \times \Gamma \rightarrow Z \times \Gamma \times \{-1,0,+1\}$ in a natural way. □

We use A_1 to denote the empty tape square and write alternately A_1 or $\not{b}$.

A configuration C is a string in $\Gamma^*(Z \times \Gamma)\Gamma^*$ and describes a snapshot of a computation. If w(z,a)v is a configuration then wav is the tape content, z is the state of the finite control and the head scans symbol a. Let $C_1 = w_1(z_1,a_1)v_1$ and $C_2 = w_2(z_2,a_2)v_2$ be configurations. Then C_2 is a successor configuration of C_1, in symbols $C_1 \vdash C_2$, if:

a) $(z_2,b,-1) \in \delta(z_1,a_1)$ and $w_1 = w_2a_2$ and $v_2 = bv_1$ or

b) $(z_2,a_2,0) \in \delta(z_1,a_1)$ and $w_1 = w_2$ and $v_2 = v_2$

c) $(z_2,b,+1) \in \delta(z_1,a_1)$ and $w_2 = w_1b$ $v_1 = a_2v_2$ or
$v_1 = v_2 = \varepsilon$ and $a_2 = \not{b}$.

$\vdash^*$ denotes the reflexive, transitive closure of relation $\vdash$. A configuration C = w(z,a)v is a halting configuration, if $\delta(z,a) = \emptyset$, it is an accepting configuration, if $z \in F$, and it is initial configuration with respect to string $x = a_1a_2...a_n$, if $z = Z_1$, $w = \varepsilon$, $a = a_1$ and $v = a_2...a_n$.

A computation on input $x \in \Gamma^*$ is a sequence $C_0,C_1,...C_k$ of configuration with $C_i \vdash C_{i+1}$ for $0 \leq i < k$ and C_0 an initial configuration w.r.t. x. A computation is accepting (halting), if C_k is an accepting (halting) configuration. The length of the computation is k.

We are now ready to define the language accepted by a TM and the time complexity of the machine.

<u>Definition:</u> Let M = (Z,Γ,δ,F) be a TM

a) $L(M) = \{x \in \Gamma^*$; there is an accpeting computation of M on input x$\}$ is the language accepted by M

b) Let M be deterministic and total, i.e. there is a halting computation of M on every $x \in \Gamma^*$. Then M computes function $f_M: \Gamma^* \to \Gamma^*$ if for every $x \in \Gamma^*$ the tape content of the halting configuration of the computation of M on input x is $f_M(x)$.

c) (Time complexity T_M of M)

$$T_M(n) = \max_{\substack{x \in L(M) \\ |x|=n}} \min\{k;\ k \text{ is the length of an accepting computation on input } x\}$$

if M is nondeterministic, and

$$T_M(n) = \max_{\substack{x \in \Gamma^* \\ |x|=n}} \{k;\ k \text{ is the length of an halting computation on input } x\}$$

if M is deterministic. Furthermore, $T_M(n) = \infty$ if there is $x \in \Gamma^*$, $|x| = n$, such that M does not halt on input x. □

One word of care is needed at this point. Note that in the definition of running time of nondeterministic machines the maximum is only taken over the strings in the accepted language. For every such string the shortest accepting computation is considered. In the case of deterministic machines the maximum is taken over all inputs of a certain length.

<u>Example:</u> A deterministic TM of time complexity $T(n) = O(n^2)$ which accepts $L = \{w¢w;\ w \in \{0,1\}^*\}$. Let $Z = \{Z_1, Z_2, \ldots, Z_9\}$ be the set of states, $\Gamma = \{0, 1, \bar{0}, \bar{1}, ¢, b̸\}$ be the tape alphabet and $F = \{Z_9\}$ be the set of final states. The transition function δ is defined by

δ	0	1	$\bar{0}$	$\bar{1}$	¢	b̸
Z_1	$Z_2, \bar{0}, 1$	$Z_3, \bar{1}, 1$			$Z_8, ¢, 1$	
Z_2	$Z_2, 0, 1$	$Z_2, 1, 1$			$Z_4, ¢, 1$	
Z_3	$Z_3, 0, 1$	$Z_3, 1, 1$			$Z_5, ¢, 1$	
Z_4	$Z_6, \bar{0}, 0$		$Z_4, \bar{0}, 1$	$Z_4, \bar{1}, 1$		

δ	0	1	$\bar{0}$	$\bar{1}$	¢	b̸
Z_5	$Z_6, \bar{0}, 0$		$Z_5, \bar{0}, 1$	$Z_5, \bar{1}, 1$		
Z_6			$Z_6, \bar{0}, -1$	$Z_6, \bar{0}, -1$	$Z_7, ¢, -1$	
Z_7	$Z_7, 0, -1$	$Z_7, 1, -1$	$Z_1, 0, 1$	$Z_1, 1, 1$		
Z_8						$Z_9, b̸, 1$

The accepting computation on input 01¢01 is as follows:

$(Z_1, 0)1¢01 \vdash \bar{0}(Z_2, 1)¢01 \vdash \bar{0}1(Z_2, ¢)01 \vdash \bar{0}1¢(Z_4, 0)1$

$$\vdash \bar{0}1\not{c}(Z_6,\bar{0})1 \vdash \bar{0}1(Z_7,1)\not{c}\bar{0}1 \vdash (Z_7,\bar{0})1\not{c}\bar{0}1 \vdash \bar{0}(Z_1,1)\not{c}\bar{0}1$$
$$\vdash \bar{0}\bar{1}(Z_3,\not{c})\bar{0}1 \overset{*}{\vdash} \bar{0}\bar{1}\not{c}\bar{0}(Z_8,\bar{1}) \vdash \bar{0}\bar{1}\not{c}\bar{0}\bar{1}(Z_8,\not{b}) \vdash \bar{0}\bar{1}\not{c}\bar{0}\bar{1}(Z_9,\not{b}).$$

The machine defined above compares the words before and after the ¢-sign character by character. It reads a character of the first word in state Z_1, stores the character in the finite control by changing to either state Z_2 or Z_3 and marks the character by baring it. It then moves to the right until it hits the ¢, records that fact in the finite control by changing state to either Z_4 (from Z_2) or Z_5 (from Z_3). It continues moving to the right until if finds an unbarred symbol. At this point the symbol under the reading head is compared with the symbol stored in the finite control. In the case of inequality, i.e. if a 1 is read in state Z_4 or a 0 in state Z_5 the machine halts. In the case of equality, the machine moves the head back to the first unbarred symbol of the first word and enters a new cycle.

We come now to the central definition of the chapter.

<u>Definition</u> (Classes P and NP):

P = {L; $L \subseteq \Gamma^*$ for some finite Γ and there is deterministic TM M and a polynomial p such that L = L(M) and $T_M(n) \le p(n)$ for all n}

NP = {L; $L \subseteq \Gamma^*$ for some finite Γ and there is a nondeterministic TM M and a polynomial p such that L = L(M) and $T_M(n) \le p(n)$ for all n} □

Since every deterministic TM is a nondeterministic TM and since the definition of running time is more strict in the deterministic case, we have the inclusion

$$P \subseteq NP.$$

The famous open problem is: "Is P equal to NP?" The answer to this problem is open; however, there are many reasons to believe that P ≠ NP.

a) There are many problems, e.g. CLIQUE, such that

P = NP iff CLIQUE ∈ P

These problems come from many different areas, e.g. graph theory, operations research, game theory, computer science and number theory. In all these areas a lot of work went into the development of efficient algorithms for these problems. No provably good algorithm was found.

b) Even worse, many algorithms which were suggested for these problems are known to have non-polynomial running time.

We used Turing machines to define classes P and NP. Theorem 1 shows that we might have used logarithmic cost RAMs just as well. We will formally prove this only for languages over the binary alphabet $\{0,1\}$; a generalization to non-binary alphabets is trivial and left to the reader. RAMs were defined in section I.1.; in particular, the I/O-behaviour of RAMs was defined at the end of section I.1.. Let R be a RAM and let $X = a_1 a_2 \ldots a_n \in \{0,1\}^*$, $a_i \in \{0,1\}$. Then the i-th execution of statement $\alpha \leftarrow$ input places $a_i \in \{0,1\} \subseteq \mathbb{N}$ into the accumulator. We say that RAM R accepts $L \subseteq \{0,1\}^*$ iff it computes the characteristic function c_L of L.

<u>Theorem 1</u> (Simulating logarithmic cost RAMs by TMs): Let R be a RAM with logarithmic time complexity $T_R(n)$ and let L be the language accepted by R. Then there is a TM M which accepts L in time $T_M(n) = O(T_R^5(n))$.

<u>Proof:</u> (sketch) We start with a description of the tape of TM M. The tape of M is divided into 8 tracks, i.e. the tape alphabet is Σ^8 for some alphabet Σ. Each single square can contain an element of Σ on each track.

input	$a_1\ a_2\ a_3\ a_4\ \ldots$
memory	address # content # # address # content # # ...
accumulator	
index reg 1	
index reg 2	
index reg 3	
address reg	
scratch reg	

The first track contains the input $a_1 a_2 a_3 \ldots$. Inputs which were read by the RAM are marked. The second track contains the memory of the RAM, more precisely, the second track contains a sequence of pairs (ad_i, $cont_i$), $1 \le i \le m$; ad_i and $cont_i$ are integers written in binary. We maintain the following invariant. Let ad $\in \mathbb{N}$ be an address and let cont be the content of the memory cell of the RAM with address ad. Then there is either no i with ad = ad_i and then cont = 0 or there is an i with ad = ad_i and then cont = $cont_j$ where $j = \max\{i; ad = ad_i\}$. Tracks 3 to 6 are used to store the accumulator and the index registers in binary; finally tracks 7 and 8 are used for intermediate calculations. The RAM-program is stored in the final control of TM M. We sketch the simulation in the case of instruction

$$\alpha \leftarrow \alpha + \rho(3+\gamma_2).$$

1) Add 3 to the content of γ_2 (as stored on track 5) and store the result on track 7, the address-register.
2) Run through the pairs on track 2 and find the largest i with ad_i = ad, the content of track 7. The comparison is done by an algorithm similar to the one described in the example above.
3) If no i is found then place 0 onto the scratch register (track 8), otherwise copy $cont_1$ onto the scratch register. The details are very similar to step 2.
4) Add the content of the scratch register to the accumulator.

All other instructions are simulated in an analogous way. In particular, whenever a store instruction is executed, say cont is stored in cell ad, then a new pair (ad, cont) is added to the list on track 2.

It is easy to program the arithmetic operations in step 1 and 4 on a TM. The running time is proportional to the length of the binary representation of the operands. Since we consider logarithmic cost RAMs this is in turn bounded by the cost of the simulated RAM-instruction.

Steps 2) and 3) are slightly more difficult to deal with. The example above shows that the cost of steps 2 and 3 is bounded by O((length of the inscription of track 2)^2) = O((Number of store instructions executed)$\cdot$(log(maximal content of any cell) + log(maximal address used)))^2).

The number of store instructions is certainly bounded by $T_R(n)$. Also the content of any cell and hence the maximal address is bounded by $2^{T_R(n)}$ since a logarithmic cost RAM is charged one time unit for writing a bit. Hence the cost of steps 2 and 3) is bounded by $O(T_R^4(n))$.

Let us summarize: TM M can simulate a proper RAM-instruction (arithmetic and tests) in time $O(T_R^2(n))$; the square is needed for simulating divisions and multiplications. Furthermore, $O(T_R^4(n))$ steps are needed to simulate a single storage access of the RAM. Thus $O(T_R^5(n))$ steps suffice for the simulation of a $T_R(n)$ time bounded RAM. □

The converse of theorem 1 is much simpler to prove and left to the reader. If L is accepted in time $T_M(n)$ by a TM then L is accepted in time $T_M(n) \log T_M(n)$ by a logarithmic cost RAM. Thus the complexities of a problem on a RAM and a TM are polynomially related. A problem is solvable on a logarithmic cost RAM in polynomial time iff it is solvable on a TM in polynomial time. In other words, the definition of P is fairly robust.

We close by relating deterministic and nondeterministic complexity. A fairly direct simulation yields an exponential loss of efficiency; no more efficient simulation is known.

<u>Definition:</u> A function $T: \mathbb{N} \to \mathbb{N}$ is a <u>step function</u>, if there is a deterministic TM M which stops after exactly T(n) steps on every input of length n. □

Most common functions are step functions, e.g. $T(n) = n$, $T(n) = n\lfloor \log n \rfloor$, $T(n) = n^2$, $T(n) = 2^n$.

<u>Theorem 2</u> (Deterministic Simulation of Nondeterministic Turing Machines): Let T(n) be a step function, let $L \subseteq \Gamma^*$ be a language and let N be a nondeterministic TM which accepts L in time $T_N(n) = O(T(n))$. Then there is a deterministic TM M with $L(M) = L$ and $T_M(n) = O(c^{T(n)})$ for some constant c.

<u>Proof:</u> For every $x \in L$ there is an accepting computation of length $\le T_N(|x|)$. Let $k = \max\{|\delta(z,a)|;\ z$ is a state of N and $a \in \Gamma\}$. Then machine N has the choice between at most k different actions in every

step. Thus there are at most $k^{T_N(|x|)}$ different halting computations of length $\le T_N(|x|)$ on input x. Also $x \in L$ iff one of these computations is accepting. This suggests the following deterministic simulation of N. Let m be such that $T_N(n) \le mT(n)$ for every n. Count form 0 to $k^{mT(n)}$ in base k. Every number ℓ between 0 and $k^{mT(n)}$ represents a possible computation. More precisely, the i-th digit in the k-nary representation of ℓ determines the action in the i-th move of N. It is easy to see that every fixed computation of N may be simulated in time $p(mT(|x|))$ where p is some polynomial. Thus the entire simulation takes time $p(mT(|x|)k^{mT(|x|)} = O(c^{T(|x|)})$ for some constant c. □

VI. 2. Problems, Languages and Optimization Problems

Classes P and NP are sets of languages. However, problems are usually not defined as language recognition problems. Let us for example consider the Traveling Salesman Problem (TSP).

Name: Traveling Salesman Optimization Problem
Input: A distance matrix dist: $[0...n-1]^2 \to \mathbb{N}$
Output: A permutation Π of $[0...n-1]$ which minimizes

$$\sum_{i=0}^{n-1} \text{dist}(\Pi(i), \Pi(i+1 \bmod n))$$

,i.e. a tour through the n cities 0,1,...,n-1 of minimal total length. □

The Traveling Salesman Optimization Problem is definitely not a language. Rather, it requires the computation of a function from n by n matrices dist to permutations of n elements. However, we can associate a recognition problem (language) with the optimization problem in a somewhat artificial way.

Name: Traveling Salesman Recognition Problem (TSP)
Input: A distance matrix dist: $[0...n-1]^2 \to \mathbb{N}$ and integer D
Question: Is there a tour of length at most D, i.e. is there a permutation Π of $[0...n-1]$ such that $\sum_{i=0}^{n-1} \text{dist}(\Pi(i), \Pi((i+1) \bmod n)) \le D$. □

The Traveling Salesman Recognition Problem gives rise to a language in a natural way; namely the language (set) of all problem instances I = (dist,D) of TSP with positive answer, i.e.

$$L_{TSP} = \{(dist,D);\ dist \text{ has a tour of length} \le D\}.$$

Actually, we have to be more precise. A language is a subset of Σ^* for some finite alphabet Σ. Thus instead of talking about problem instances (dist,D) we should rather talk about the endocings of distance matrices dist and integers D over some finite alphabet Σ. There are many possible encodings to choose from. Fortunately, the results of this chapter do not depend on the particular encoding chosen, as long as the encoding is "natural". Nevertheless, we state some general principles.

1) Integers are written in binary.
2) Sequences (sets, matrices) are specified by listing the (encodings of their) elements separated by some special symbol.
3) Graphs are specified by their adjacency matrix; labelled graphs are specified by the matrix of labellings.

What have we achieved now? We associated a language with the Traveling Salesman recognition problem and we can now ask the question whether this language is in P. Even if it were, what would that say about our original problem, the Traveling Salesman optimization problem. We show in this section, that the function which maps distance matrices to optimal solutions would be computable in polynomial time also. So we have not really lost anything when we went from the optimization problem to the recognition problem, at least as far as polynomial time computability is concerned. This observation is not only true for the TSP but also more generally. We start with an alternate characterization of NP.

Theorem 1:

NP = {L; $L \subseteq \Sigma^*$ for some finite Σ and there is a polynomial p and a polynomial time computable predicate $Q \subseteq \Sigma^* \times \Sigma^*$ such that for all $x \in \Sigma^*$:

$$x \in L \quad \text{iff} \quad \exists y \in \Sigma^*: |y| \le p(|x|) \wedge Q(x,y)\}$$

Proof: "$\supseteq$". Let p be a polynomial and let Q be a polynomial time computable predicate, i.e. there is a deterministic TM M which computes $Q(x,y)$ in time $q(|x|, |y|)$ for some polynomial q. The following nondeterministic algorithm accepts L.

(1) On input x, generate a string $y \in \Sigma^*$, $|y| \le p(|x|)$ nondeterministically.

(2) Accept x, if $Q(x,y)$. $Q(x,y)$ is computed using machine M.

The details of step 1 are very similar to the example in the introduction of this chapter and therefore step 1 takes time at most $p(|x|)$ on a RAM. The cost of step 2 is also bounded by a polynomial in $|x|$ and $|y|$, which is in turn bounded by a polynomial in $|x|$. Thus $L \in NP$.

"$\subseteq$". Let $L \in NP$, $L \subseteq \Sigma^*$. Let N be a nondeterministic TM which accepts L in time bounded by polynomial p. As in the proof of theorem 2 let k be the maximal number of actions N can choose from at any step. Then the proof of Theorem VI.1.2. shows that the strings of length $\le p(|x|)$ over a k-ary alphabet encode all possible computations of N on input x. Assume w.l.o.g. that $|\Sigma| \ge k$. Take

$$Q(x,y) = \text{"y encodes an accepting computation of N on input x"}.$$

Then Q is certainly computable in polynomial time and
$L = \{x;\ \exists y\ |y| \le p(|x|) \wedge Q(x,y)\}$ □

The characterization of NP given in theorem 1 is interesting in its own right. There is no explicite mentioning of nondeterminism. Rather, nondeterminism is hidden in the existential quantifier. More mathematically oriented readers may find it helpful to use theorem 1 as the definition of NP.

Definition: A minimization problem is given by a polynomial time computable predicate $Q \subseteq \Sigma^* \times \Sigma^*$ and a polynomial time computable cost function $c: \Sigma^* x \Sigma^* \to \mathbb{N}$. If $Q(x,y)$ then y is a feasible solution for problem instance x with cost $c(x,y)$. If $Q(x,y)$ and $c(x,y) \le c(x,y')$ for all y' with $Q(x,y')$ then y is an optimal ($\hat{=}$ minimal cost) solution for x. The minimization problem is polynomially bounded if there is a polynomial p such that $Q(x,y)$ implies $|y| \le p(|x|)$. □

We only deal with polynomially bounded optimization problems in this book. A similar definition is possible for maximization problem. In the TSP example we have: Q(x,y) if x is the encoding of a distance matrix dist: $[0...n-1]^2 \rightarrow \mathbb{N}$ and y is the encoding of a permutation Π of $[0...n-1]$ and $cost(x,y) = \Sigma\ dist(\Pi(i),\Pi(i+1 \bmod n))$.

Definition: Let (Q,c) be a polynomially bounded minimization problem. We define four versions of that problem.

a) Name: (Q,c)-recognition problem
Input: Instance $x \in \Sigma^*$, integer C
Question: Is there a y with Q(x,y) and $c(x,y) \le C$

b) Name: (Q,c)-optimization problem
Input: Instance $c \in \Sigma^*$
Output: An optimal solution $optsol(x) \in \Sigma^*$ for x

c) Name: (Q,c)-optimal value problem
Input: Instance $x \in \Sigma^*$
Output: Optval(x) = c(x,optsol(x))

d) Name: (Q,c)-witness problem
Input: Instance $x \in \Sigma^*$ and integer C
Output: y = witness(x,C) with Q(x,y) and $c(x,y) \le C$, if any □

We have seen the first two versions in the case of TSP already. The recognition problem asks for the existance of a tour of some length, and the optimization problem requires us to produce an optimal tour. The optimal value problem only asks for the length of the optimal tour and the witness problem asks for a tour of length at most C. We can now start to relate the complexities of the four versions of a problem. It is obvious that the recognition problem is no harder than either the optimal value or the witness problem which in turn are both simpler than the optimization problem. We can capture this fact in the following diagram:

	≤ witness	
recognition		≤ optimization.
	≤ optimal value	

A precise formulation is

Lemma 1: Let (Q,c) be a polynomially bounded optimization problem. Then

a) If function optsol: $\Sigma^* \to \Sigma^*$ is computable in polynomial time, then so are functions optval: $\Sigma^* \to \Sigma^*$ and witness: $\Sigma^* \times \mathbb{N} \to \Sigma^*$.

b) If either function witness or optval is computable in polynomial time then

$L_{(Q,C)} := \{(x,C);\ x \in \Sigma^*,\ C \in \mathbb{N}$ and $\text{optval}(x) \le C\} \in P$.

Proof: Immediate. □

A weak converse of lemma 1 is provided by

Lemma 2: Let (Q,c) be a polynomially bounded optimization problem.

a) If functions witness and optval are computable in polynomial time, then so is optsol.

b) If the recognition problem is in P and $\text{optval}(x) \le 2^{q(|x|)}$ for some polynomial q and all x then optval is computable in polynomial true.

Proof: a) We only have to observe that optsol(x) = witness(x,optval(x)) for all x.

b) We use binary search on the interval $[1 \ldots 2^{q(|x|)}]$ in order to determine the exact value of optval(x).

```
(1) low ← 1; high ← 2^q(|x|);
(2) while high - low ≥ 1
(3) do    middle ← ⌊(high + low)/2⌋
(4)       if x has a solution of cost ≤ middle
(5)       then high ← middle
(6)       else low ← middle + 1
(7) od
(8) optval(x) ← low;
```

It is easy to see that low ≤ optval(x) ≤ high is an invariant of the loop. Hence the program above correctly computes the value of optval(x) in $\log(2^{q(|x|)}) = q(|x|)$ iterations of the loop. In line (4) the polynomial time algorithm for the (Q,c)-recognition problem is used. Thus each iteration of the loop also has polynomial cost. □

It remains to relate the complexity of the (Q,c)-witness problem and the (Q,c)-recognition problem. We treat TSP first and then comment on a general reduction.

<u>Lemma 3:</u> If the Traveling Salesman Recognition Problem is in P then the TSP witness function can be computed in polynomial time.

<u>Proof:</u> The following algorithm computes $\text{witness}_{TSP}(\text{dist},C)$, i.e. computes a tour of length at most C if there is any.

```
(1) define dist': [0...n-1]^2 → ℕ by dist' = dist;
(2) if  dist does not have a tour of length at most C then halt ("there
        is no tour of length ≤ C") fi
(3) for all pairs (i,j), i ≠ j
(4) do  change dist'[i,j] to ∞;
(5)     if dist' still has a tour of length at most C
(6)     then do nothing
(7)     else reverse the change made in line (4) and include edge (i,j)
             into the tour
(8)     fi
(9) od
```

The set of edges selected in line (7) form a tour of length at most C. The polynomial time algorithm for the recognition problem of TSP is used in lines (2) and (5). Note that all problem instances (dist',D) in line (5) are no harder than the original problem (dist,C); in particular, the length of the encoding of these instances is not (much) longer than the encoding of (dist,C). The number of iterations of the loop is clearly bounded by a polynomial in input length, the cost of each iteration is also polynomially bounded. Thus witness_{TSP} can be computed in polynomial time if TSP recognition is in P.

□

The main ingredient in the proof of lemma 3 is <u>selfreduction</u>. In order to find a witness (tour) for an instance of TSP we reduce the problem to a <u>simpler</u> (one less edge with cost $< \infty$) instance of TSP. We decide the simpler problem by the recognition algorithm and thus construct a piece of the witness. A similar approach works for all other problems treated in this book. We illustrate the technique by one more example, the satisfiability problem.

Let $V = \{x_1, x_2, \ldots\}$ be an infinite supply of propositional variables. If x_i is a variable then x_i and $\bar{x}_i$ are literales. We will use $\bar{x}_i$ and $\neg x_i$ interchangable. If $y_1, \ldots, y_k$ are literals then $(y_1 \vee y_2 \vee \ldots \vee y_k)$ is a clause of degree k. Finally if $c_1, \ldots, c_m$ are clauses of degree at most k then $c_1 \wedge c_2 \wedge \ldots \wedge c_m$ is a formula in conjuctive normal form with at most k literals per clause.

A truth assignment is a mapping $\psi: V \to \{0,1\}$. We extend ψ to literals, clauses and formulae by

$$\psi(y) = \begin{cases} \psi(x_i) & \text{if } y = x_i \\ 1 - \psi(x_i) & \text{if } y = \neg x_i \end{cases}$$

$$\psi(y_1 \vee y_2 \vee \ldots \vee y_k) = \max\{\psi(y_i);\ 1 \le i \le k\}$$

$$\psi(c_1 \wedge c_2 \wedge \ldots \wedge c_m) = \min\{\psi(c_j);\ 1 \le j \le m\}$$

A formula α is satisfiable if there is an assignment ψ with $\psi(\alpha) = 1$. The Satisfiability recognition problem is given by:

Name: Satisfiability problem (SAT)
Input: A formula α in conjunctive normal form
Question: Is α satisfiable?

The SAT witness problem is to compute a function witness from formulae to truth assignments, such that $\text{witness}_{SAT}(\alpha)$ satisfies α if α is satisfiable.

Lemma 4: If SAT is in P then witness_{SAT} can be computed in polynomial time.

Proof: The following algorithm computes $\psi = \text{witness}_{SAT}(\alpha)$.

(1) $\alpha' \leftarrow \alpha$;
(2) for all x_i occuring in α
(3) do let α'' be obtained from α' by substituting

the constant 0 for all occurrences of x_i in α'.

(4) <u>if</u> α'' is satisfiable; -- use the algorithm for SAT here

(5) <u>then</u> $\psi(x_i) \leftarrow 0$; $\alpha' \leftarrow \alpha''$

(6) <u>else</u> $\psi(x_i) \leftarrow 1$; $\alpha' \leftarrow$ the formula obtained from
α by substituting 1 for all occurrences of x_i

(7) <u>fi</u>

(8) <u>od</u>

The algorithm is clearly correct and has polynomial running time. □

Again the main ingredient of the proof of lemma 4 is selfreduction. We construct the witness (assignment) piecewise by reducing formula α to a simpler formula (one less variable) and testing the simpler formula for satisfiability.

VI. 3. Reductions and NP-complete Problems

Reductions are a useful tool for classifying problems. We have seen the technique already in the previous section and we will use it extensively throughout the chapter. For example, we showed how to convert an algorithm for TSP recognition into an algorithm for TSP witness, in this way reducing the witness problem to the recognition problem. More generally, reductions allow us to transform solutions for one problem to solutions for other problems.

<u>Definition:</u> a) Let Σ and Γ be finite alphabets. A mapping $f: \Sigma^* \rightarrow \Gamma^*$ is a (polynomial time computable) transformation, if f can be computed in polynomial time on a TM.

b) Let $L_1 \subseteq \Sigma^*$ and $L_2 \subseteq \Gamma^*$ be languages. L_1 is (polynomially, many-one) <u>reducible</u> to L_2, $L_1 \leq L_2$, if there is a transformation f such that

$$x \in L_1 \quad \text{iff} \quad f(x) \in L_2$$

for all $x \in \Sigma^*$.

c) Language L is <u>NP-complete</u>, if

i) $L \in NP$
ii) $L' \leq L$ for all $L' \in NP$. □

Theorem 1 shows the importance of this definition.

Theorem 1: Let L_0 be NP-complete. Then

a) $L_0 \in P$ iff $P = NP$
b) If $L_0 \leq L_1$ and $L_1 \in NP$ then L_1 is NP-complete.

Proof: a) If $P = NP$ then certainly $L_0 \in P$. It remains to prove the converse. Assume that $L_0 \in P$ and let $L \in NP$ be arbitrary. Since $L_0 \in P$ there is a deterministic TM M which accepts L in time bounded by p for some polynomial p. Since L_0 is NP-complete and $L \in NP$ we have $L \leq L_0$. Thus there exists a mapping f with $L = f^{-1}(L_0)$. Let N be a deterministic TM which computes f in time bounded by polynomial q. We construct an acceptor A for L from M and N. A behaves as follows on input x.

(1) Compute f(x) using N in time $q(|x|)$.
(2) Reset the read/write head onto the first symbol of f(x) in time $|f(x)|$.
(3) Decide $f(x) \in L_0$ using M in time $p(|f(x)|)$. If $f(x) \in L_0$ then accept x, otherwise reject x.

The algorithm above clearly accepts L. It has running time $q(|x|) + |f(x)| + p(|f(x)|) \leq r(|x|)$ for some polynomial r. The last inequality follows from the fact that $|f(x)| \leq |x| + q(|x|)$ since a TM can write at most one square in one time unit.

b) We have to show $L \leq L_1$ for every $L \in NP$. Let $L \in NP$ be arbitrary. Since L_0 is NP-complete there is a transformation f such that $L = f^{-1}(L_0)$. Since $L_0 \leq L_1$ there is a transformation g such that $L_0 = g^{-1}(L_1)$. Let $h = g \circ f$. Then $L = f^{-1}(L_0) = f^{-1}(g^{-1}(L_1))$ $= (g \circ f)^{-1}(L_1) = h^{-1}(L_1)$. It remains to show that h is computable in polynomial time. This is easily done by an argument similar to the one used in part a). □

Part a) of theorem 1 states that NP-complete problems are the most difficult problems in NP. If one of them is solvable in polynomial time, then all problems in NP are solvable in polynomial time. Conversely, if

P ≠ NP (and this is believed generally) then no NP-complete problem can be solved in polynomial time.

Part b) introduces a simple, but extremely useful technique for showing NP-completeness. Show first that a particular language L_0 is NP-complete. For language L_0 this must be done the hard way, namely by demonstrating $L \le L_0$ for all $L \in NP$. Once we have extablished NP-completeness for L_0, there is a simpler way of establishing NP-completeness of L_1. Show $L_1 \in NP$ and $L_0 \le L_1$.

The following paragraph assumes some knowledge of recursion theory. In recursion theory many different notions of reducibility were introduced: Turing reducibility, truthtable reducibility, many-one reducibility, one-one reducibility, ... Similar definitions can be made in the context of polynomial time computability. The particular definition chosen here corresponds to many-one reducibility. A comparison of different notions of reducibility is beyond the scope of this book. It can be found in the references.

VI. 4. The Satisfiability Problem is NP-complete

We establish NP-completeness of the Satisfiability problem in this section. SAT was defined in section VI.2..

Name: SAT
Input: A formula α in conjunctive normal form (CNF)
Question: Is α satisfiable?

Theorem 1: SAT is NP-complete.

Proof: We show SAT $\in$ NP first. Let α be a formula in CNF, let V_α be the set of variables occuring in α, and let $|\alpha|$ be the length of the encodind of α. Then certainly $|V_\alpha| = m \le |\alpha|$. We describe a nondeterministic machine N which accepts SAT. On input α, N chooses nondeterministically an assignment ψ: $V_\alpha \to \{0,1\}$ by writing down a bitstring of length m. Then it evaluates α with respect to assignment ψ by one of the well-known methods, e.g. by the stack principle. Machine N accepts α iff $\psi(\alpha) = 1$. N clearly operates in polynomial time and accepts SAT.

Let L $\in$ NP be arbitrary. We have to show L $\leq$ SAT. Since L $\in$ NP there is a nondeterministic TM M which accepts L in time bounded by polynomial p. We will now construct for every input x of M a formula $\alpha(x)$ which describes the behaviour of M on x. In particular, $\alpha(x)$ is satisfiable if M accepts x. The mapping $x \to \alpha(x)$ is the desired transformation.

Machine M has states $Z_1,\ldots Z_s$ and tape alphabet $\Gamma = \{A_1,\ldots A_v\}$. Symbol A_1 denotes the empty tape square, we use A_1 and $\not{b}$ interchangable. Z_1 is the initial state of M and $Z_r, Z_{r+1},\ldots Z_s$ are the final states. We change the transition function δ of M by defining $\delta(z,a) = \delta(z,a,0)$ whenever $\delta(z,a) = \emptyset$. Then M never stops and halting configurations (of the original machine) are repeated forever. Thus: M accepts x iff there is a sequence $C_1, C_2, \ldots, C_{p(n)}$ of configurations such that C_1 is initial configuration for x, $n = |x|$, $C_i \vdash C_{i+1}$ for $0 \leq i < p(n)$, and the state in $C_{p(n)}$ is accepting. Transition function δ of M defines a relation on $Z\times\Gamma\times Z\times\Gamma\times\{-1,0,-1\}$. We number the tuples of this relation in some way; let m be the number of tuples in relation δ.

Let $x \in \Sigma^*$, $|x| = n$ be arbitrary. Formula $\alpha(x)$ is built from the following variables. We also give the intended meaning of each variable.

		intended meaning
$z_{t,k}$	$1 \leq t \leq p(n)$ $1 \leq k \leq s$	$z_{t,k} = 1$, if M is in state Z_k at time t.
$a_{t,i,j}$	$1 \leq t,\ i \leq p(n)$ $1 \leq j \leq v$	$a_{t,i,j} = 1$, if A_j is the content of the j-th tape square at time t.
$s_{t,i}$	$1 \leq t,\ i \leq p(n)$	$s_{t,i} = 1$, if M scans the i-th tape square at time t.
$b_{t,\ell}$	$1 \leq t \leq p(n)$ $1 \leq \ell \leq m$	$b_{t,\ell} = 1$, if line ℓ of δ is used for the transition from time t to time t+1.

Variables $z_{t,k}$ represent the state of the finite control, the $a_{t,i,j}$'s encode the tape content, the $s_{t,i}$'s give the position of the tape head and the $b_{t,\ell}$'s encode the transition behaviour. Since M is p(n) time bounded it can never use more than the first p(n) tape squares. Thus variables $a_{t,i,j}$ and $s_{t,i}$ are only needed for $i \leq p(n)$.

We will next construct formulae which fix the intended meaning of the variables. We have to ensure the

initial condition (M stats in state Z_1, its head is on the first square, and $x\not{b}^{p(n)-n}$ is the tape content), the

boundary condition (at any time unit M is in exactly one state, every tape square contains exactly one symbol, the tape head is at exactly one square, and exactly one line of the Turing table is applied), and the

transition condition (the configurations at subsequent time units are compatible with the Turing table).

Let I be a formula for the initial condition, B be a formula for the boundary condition, and T be a formula for the transition condition. Then

$$\alpha(x) := I \wedge B \wedge T \wedge (z_{p(n),r} \vee z_{p(n),r+1} \vee \dots \vee z_{p(n),s}).$$

It remains to construct I, B and T in CNF. Formula I is easy to construct. Let $x = A_{j1}\, A_{j2} \dots A_{jn}$. Then

$$I = (z_{1,1} \wedge s_{1,1} \wedge a_{1,1,j_1} \wedge a_{1,2,j_2} \wedge a_{1,3,j_3} \wedge \dots \wedge a_{1,n,j_n}$$

$$\wedge\, a_{1,n+1,1} \wedge \dots \wedge a_{1,p(n),1}).$$

I is clearly in CNF; there are $p(n) + 2$ occurrences of variables in I.

Formula 3 is more difficult to construct. In B we want to express facts like: Machine M is in exactly one state at time t. Thus we need a short formula which expresses the fact, that exactly one out of a set of variables is true. Let $x_1,\dots,x_h$ be variables. Then

$$\text{Exactly-One}(x_1,\dots,x_h) = \text{At-least-One}(x_1,\dots,x_h) \wedge \text{At-Most-One}(x_1,\dots,x_h),$$

and

$$\text{At-Least-One}(x_1,\dots,x_h) = (x_1 \vee x_2 \vee \dots \quad x_h)$$

and

$$\text{At-Most-One}(x_1,\ldots x_h) = \neg\text{At-Least-Two}(x_1,\ldots,x_h)$$
$$= \neg \bigvee_{1\le i<j\le h} (x_i \wedge x_j)$$
$$= \bigwedge_{1\le i<j\le h} (\bar{x}_i \vee \bar{x}_j)$$

Formula Exactly-One$(x_1,\ldots,x_h)$ is in CNF; there are exactly $h + 2h(h-1)/2 = h^2$ occurrences of variables in it. A truth assignment ψ of $x_1,\ldots,x_h$ satisfies Exactly-One$(x_1,\ldots,x_h)$ iff $\psi(x_i) = 1$ for exactly one i, $1 \le i \le h$.

We define

$$B = \bigwedge_{1\le i\le p(n)} (B_{\text{state}}(t) \wedge B_{\text{position}}(t) \wedge B_{\text{tape content}}(t) \wedge B_{\text{transition}}(t)).$$

where

$$B_{\text{state}}(t) = \text{Exactly-One}(z_{t,1},\ldots,z_{t,s})$$

$$B_{\text{position}}(t) = \text{Exactly-One}(s_{t,1},\ldots,s_{t,p(n)})$$

$$B_{\text{tape content}}(t) = \bigwedge_{1\le i\le p(n)} \text{Exactly-One}(a_{t,i,1},\ldots,a_{t,i,v})$$

$$B_{\text{transition}}(t) = \text{Exactly-One}(b_{t,1},\ldots,b_{t,m})$$

B is clearly in CNF; there are $p(n)(s^2 + p(n)^2 + p(n)v^2 + m^2)$ occurrences of variables in B. An assignment ψ to the variables of $\alpha(x)$ satisfies B iff for every t there is exactly one j with $\psi(z_{t,j}) = 1$, exactly one h with $\psi(s_{t,h}) = 1,\ldots$.

It remains to define T

$$T = \bigwedge_{1\le t<p(n)} T(i)$$

where T(t) expresses that the transition from time t to t + 1 is compatible with the line of the Turing table selected by variables $b_{t,1},\ldots,b_{t,m}$. Let

Z_{k_ℓ}, A_{j_ℓ}, $Z_{\tilde{k}_\ell}$, $A_{\tilde{j}_\ell}$, R_ℓ, be the ℓ-th line of the Turing table, $1 \le \ell \le m$, i.e. if M is in state Z_{k_ℓ} and reads symbol A_{j_ℓ}, then it <u>can</u> (M is nondeterministic) change state to $Z_{\tilde{k}_\ell}$, print $A_{\tilde{j}_\ell}$ and move the head by $R_\ell \in \{-1,0,1\}$ squares. With this notation we define

$$T(t) = \bigwedge_{1\le i\le p(n)} \Big\{ \bigwedge_{1\le j\le v} (s_{t,i} \vee \bar{a}_{t,i,j} \vee a_{t+1,i,j}) \wedge$$

$$\bigwedge_{1\le \ell\le m} [(\bar{s}_{t,i} \vee \bar{b}_{t,\ell} \vee z_{t,k_\ell}) \wedge (s_{t,i} \vee \bar{b}_{t,\ell} \vee a_{t,i,j_\ell}) \wedge$$

$$(\bar{s}_{t,i} \vee \bar{b}_{t,\ell} \vee z_{t+1,\tilde{k}_\ell}) \wedge (\bar{s}_{t,i} \vee \bar{b}_{t,\ell} \vee a_{t+1,i,\tilde{j}_\ell}) \wedge$$

$$(\bar{s}_{t,i} \vee \bar{b}_{t,\ell} \vee s_{t+1,i+R_\ell})]\Big\}$$

Formula T(t) needs some explanation. When is $(s_{t,i} \vee \bar{a}_{t,i,j} \vee a_{t+1,i,j})$ true? It is true if either $s_{t,i}$ is true, i.e. M scans cell i at time t, or $\bar{a}_{t,i,j}$ is false, i.e. the content of that cell at t is not A_j, or $a_{t+1,i,j}$ is true, i.e. the content of that cell at t + 1 is A_j. In other words, if $s_{t,i}$ is false and $a_{t,i,j}$ is true then $a_{t+1,i,j}$ must be true, i.e. if M does not scan the i-th tape square at time t then the content of that cell does not change. Similarly, when is $(\bar{s}_{t,i} \vee \bar{b}_{t,\ell} \vee a_{t,i,j_\ell})$ true? Well, if $s_{t,i}$ is true and $b_{t,\ell}$ is true then a_{t,i,j_ℓ} must be true also, i.e. if M scans cell i at time t and we want to apply the ℓ-th transition, then cell i better contains A_{j_ℓ}. Formula T is clearly CNF, there are p(n)(3v + 15m) occurrences of variables in T. This finishes the construction of formula $\alpha(x)$.

<u>Fact 1:</u> Formula $\alpha(x)$ can be constructed in polynomial time given x, i.e. the mapping $x \to \alpha(x)$ is a transformation.

<u>Proof:</u> Formula (x) is clearly in CNF. There are $p(n) + 2 + p(n)(s^2 + p(n)^2 + p(n)v^2 + m^2) + p(n)^2(3v + 15m) + s = O(p(n)^3)$ occurrences of variables in $\alpha(x)$. If we write indices of variables in binary, i.e. a single variable requires space O(log p(n)), then the natural encoding of $\alpha(x)$ over the alphabet $\{(,),\wedge,\vee,\neg,s,z,a,b,0,1\}$ has

length $O(p(n)^3 \log p(n))$. The structure of formula $\alpha(x)$ is very simple; expression I depends on x in a very simple way, the other parts B and T only depend on $n = |x|$. Thus $\alpha(x)$ can be constructed in polynomial time by a TM. □

Next we have to formally relate $x \in L$ and the satisfiability of $\alpha(x)$.

Fact 2: If $x \in L$ then $\alpha(x)$ is satisfiable.

Proof: If $x \in L$ then there is a sequence $C_1, C_2, \ldots, C_{p(n)}$ of configurations such that C_1 is initial configuration of M for x, $C_i \vdash C_{i+1}$ for $1 \le i < p(n)$, and the state in $C_{p(n)}$ is accepting. Define truth assignment ψ by

$$\psi(z_{t,k}) = \begin{cases} 1 & \text{if } z_k \text{ is the state in } C_t \\ 0 & \text{o.w.} \end{cases}$$

$$\psi(a_{t,i,j}) = \begin{cases} 1 & \text{if } A_j \text{ is the symbol on the i-th tape square of } C_t \\ 0 & \text{o.w.} \end{cases}$$

$$\psi(s_{t,i}) = \begin{cases} 1 & \text{if the i-th square is scanned in } C_t \\ 0 & \text{o.w.} \end{cases}$$

and

$$\psi(b_{t,\ell}) = \begin{cases} 1 & \text{if the } \ell\text{-th line of the Turing table of M is used in the transition from } C_t \text{ to } C_{t+1} \\ 0 & \text{o.w.} \end{cases}$$

It is a simple exercise to check that ψ indeed satisfies α. □

Fact 3: If $\alpha(x)$ is satisfiable then $x \in L$.

Proof: Let ψ be a truth assignment which satisfies $\alpha(x)$. Then $\psi(B) = 1$, also, and hence for example $\psi(B_{state}(t)) = \psi(\text{Exactly-One}(z_{t,1}, \ldots, z_{t,s}))$ $= 1$ for all t. Thus for every t there is exactly one k, say k(t), such that $\psi(z_{t,k}) = 1$. Similarly, for every t there is exactly one i, say i(t) such that $\psi(s_{t,i})$ and one ℓ, say $\ell(t)$, such that $(b_{t,\ell}) = 1$. Finally, for every t and i there is exactly one j, say j(t,i), such that $\psi(a_{t,i,j}) = 1$. We conclude that the true variables define a configuration C_t for every t: $z_{k(t)}$ is the state, $A_{j(t,1)} A_{j(t,2)} \cdots A_{j(t,p(n))}$ is the tape content, and i(t) is the position of the read/write head. Assignment ψ also satisfies subformula I. Hence $k(1) = 1$, if $i(1) = 1$,

$j(t,1) = j_1, \ldots$ where $x = A_{j_1} A_{j_2} \ldots$. Thus C_1 is initial configuration of M on input x. Next observe that $\psi(z_{p(n),r} \vee \ldots \vee z_{p(n),s}) = 1$ and hence $r \le k(p(n)) \le s$. Thus the state in $C_{p(n)}$ is accepting. It remains to show $C_t \vdash C_{t+1}$ for $1 \le t < p(n)$.

We also have $\psi(T(t)) = 1$. Thus $\psi(s_{t,i} \vee \bar{a}_{t,i,j} \vee a_{t+1,i,j}) = 1$ for all i and j. In particular for $i \neq i(t)$ and hence $\psi(s_{t,i}) = 0$ and $j = j(i,t)$ and hence $\psi(a_{t,i,j}) = 1$, we infer $\psi(a_{t+1,i,j}) = 1$. Thus the content of the i-th tape square is the same in C_t and C_{t+1} for $i \neq i(t)$, i.e. C_t and C_{t+1} differ at most in the vicinity of the tape head. We also have for all i and ℓ

$$\psi((\bar{s}_{t,i} \vee \bar{b}_{t,\ell} \vee z_{t,k_\ell}) \wedge (\bar{s}_{t,i} \vee \ldots) \vee \ldots \vee (\ldots \vee s_{t+1,i+R_\ell})) = 1$$

Thus $k(t) = k_\ell$, $j(t,i(t)) = j_\ell$, $k(t+1) = \tilde{k}_\ell$, $j(t+1, i(t+1)) = j_\ell$, and $i(t+1) = i(t) + R_\ell$. In other words: line $\ell(t)$ of M's Turing table is applicable to C_t and yields C_{t+1} when applied to C_t. Thus C_{t+1} is successor configuration of C_t.

In summary, we have shown that there is an accepting computation of M on input x, i.e. $x \in L$. □

Facts 1, 2 and 3 establish that $L \le SAT$. Since L was arbitrary, we conclude $L \le SAT$ for every $L \in NP$. □

SAT is our first NP-complete problem. We will use it to show NP-completeness of many other problems in the next section. Before doing so, we show that SAT remains NP-complete if we restrict ourselves to formulae with at most three literals per clause.

Name: SAT(3)
Input: A formula α in CNF with at most three literals per clause.
Question: Is α satisfiable?

Theorem 2: SAT(3) is NP-complete

Proof: We only have to show $SAT \le SAT(3)$; $SAT(3) \in NP$ is trivial. In order to reduce SAT to SAT(3) we have to replace clauses of arbitrary degree by clauses with degree 3. Let $x_1 \vee x_2 \vee \ldots \vee x_n$ be a clause.

Let $y_1,\dots,y_n$ be new variables. Consider

$$\alpha = (x_1 \vee \bar{y}_1) \wedge (y_1 \vee x_2 \vee \bar{y}_2) \wedge \dots \wedge (y_{n-1} \vee x_n \vee \bar{y}_n) \vee y_n$$

<u>Claim:</u> Let ψ: $\{x_1,\dots,x_n\} \to \{0,1\}$ be a truth assignment. There is an extension φ: $X \cup Y \to \{0,1\}$ with $\varphi(\alpha) = 1$ iff $\psi(x_1 \vee \dots \vee x_n) = 1$.

<u>Proof:</u> "$\Leftarrow$": Assume $\psi(x_1 \vee \dots \vee x_n) = 1$. Let i_0 be the least i such that $\psi(x_i) = 1$. Define

$$\varphi(z) = \begin{cases} \psi(x_j) & \text{if } z = x_j \text{ for some } j \\ 0 & \text{if } z = y_j \text{ for some } j < i_0 \\ 1 & \text{otherwise} \end{cases}$$

Then $\varphi(\alpha) = 1$ as the reader can check easily.
"$\Rightarrow$" Let $\varphi : X \cup Y \to \{0,1\}$ be a truth assignment with $\varphi(\alpha) = 1$. We have to show $\varphi(x_1 \vee x_2 \vee \dots \vee x_n) = 1$.

Assume otherwise. Then $\varphi(x_i) = 0$ for all i. We show $\varphi(y_i) = 0$ for all i by induction on i. Since $\varphi(x_1 \vee \bar{y}_1) = 1$ we must have $\varphi(y_1) = 0$. Next, we infer from $\varphi(y_1 \vee x_2 \vee \bar{y}_2) = 1$ that $\varphi(y_1) = 0$. Similarly, we conclude $\varphi(y_3) = \dots \varphi(y_n) = 0$ and hence $\varphi(\alpha) = 0$, a contradiction. □

The reduction from SAT to SAT(3) is easy now. Replace any clause with more than three literals by a set of clauses as described above. □

How about SAT(2)? Is it still NP-complete? No, SAT(2) is in P (exercise 6).

<u>VI. 5. More NP-complete Problems</u>

We extend our list of NP-complete problems and show NP-completeness of clique, vertex cover, hamiltonian cycle, traveling salesman, integer programming, 3-dimensional matching, knapsack, scheduling independent tasks and precedence contrained scheduling.

Name: CLIQUE
Input: Undirected graph $G = (V,E)$ and integer k
Question: Is there a clique of size k in G, i.e. is there $V' \subseteq V$ with $|V'| = k$ and $(v,w) \in E$ for all $v,w \in V'$

<u>Theorem 1:</u> CLIQUE is NP-complete.

<u>Proof:</u> CLIQUE $\in$ NP was shown in the introduction. We finish the proof by showing SAT(3) $\le$ CLIQUE. Let $x = c_1 \wedge \ldots \wedge c_k$ be a formula in CNF with at most three literals per clause. Let $c_i = x_{i1}^{\beta i1} \vee x_{i2}^{\beta i2} \vee x_{i3}^{\beta i3}$ where $\beta_{ih} \in \{0,1\}$ and x^1 denotes x and x^0 denotes $\bar{x}$. We construct undirected graph $G = (V,E)$ with

$$V = \{v_{ih}, \ 1 \le i \le k, \ 1 \le h \le 3\}$$

and $(v_{ih}, v_{jm}) \in E$ iff $i \neq j$ and $(x_{ih} \neq x_{jm}$ or $\beta_{ih} = \beta_{jm})$, i.e. if v_{ih} and v_{jm} are not complements of each other.

<u>Claim:</u> α is satisfiable iff G has a clique of size k.

<u>Proof:</u> "$\Rightarrow$": Let ψ be a truth assignment with $\psi(\alpha) = 1$ and hence $\psi(c_i) = 1$ for all i, $1 \le i \le k$. For every i there must be h, say h(i), such that $\psi(x_{ih(i)}^{\beta ih(i)}) = 1$. Let $V' = \{V_{i,h(i)}; \ 1 \le i \le k\}$. Then V' is a clique of size k.

"$\Leftarrow$". Let $V' \subseteq V$ be a clique of size k. Since $(v_{ih}, v_{jm}) \in E$ implies $i \neq j$ we conclude that $V' = \{v_{i,h(i)}; \ 1 \le i \le k\}$ for some function h. Define truth assignment ψ by

$$\psi(x) = \begin{cases} 1 & \text{if } x = x_{i,h(i)} \text{ for some } i \text{ and } \beta_{i,h(i)} = 1 \\ 0 & \text{if } x = x_{i,h(i)} \text{ for some } i \text{ and } \beta_{i,h(i)} = 0 \\ \text{arbitrary} & \text{otherwise} \end{cases}$$

ψ is well-defined. If $\psi(x)$ were not well-defined then there must be i and j, $i \neq j$, such that $x = x_{ih(i)} = x_{jh(j)}$ and $\beta_{ih(i)} \neq \beta_{jh(j)}$. However, this implies $(v_{ih(i)}, v_{jh(j)}) \notin E$, a contradiction. Thus ψ is well defined. Also $\psi(x_{ih(i)}^{\beta ih(i)}) = 1$ for all i and hence $\psi(\alpha) = 1$. □

G can clearly be constructed from α in polynomial time. Thus Sat(3) $\le$ CLIQUE □

Name: (0,1) - Integer Programming (IP)

Input: Integer matrix C and integer vector d
Question: Is there (0,1)-vector c such that $Cc \geq d$?

Theorem 2: (0,1)-Integer Programming is NP-complete.

Proof: IP ∈ NP is obvious; guess vector c nondeterministically and check $Cc \geq d$. We show SAT ≤ IP. Let $\alpha = z_1 \wedge \dots \wedge z_k$ be a formula in CNF and let $x_1, \dots, x_n$ be the variables occuring in α. Define C and d as follows: $C = (C_{ij})_{1 \leq i \leq k,\ 1 \leq j \leq n}$ and $d = (d_i)_{1 \leq i \leq k}$

where

$$C_{rj} = \begin{cases} 1 & \text{if } x_j \text{ occurs in } z_i \\ -1 & \text{if } \bar{x}_j \text{ occurs in } z_i \\ 0 & \text{otherwise} \end{cases}$$

$$d_i = 1 - \#\text{ of variables } x_j \text{ with } \bar{x}_j \text{ occurs in } z_i$$

Claim: α is satisfiable iff there is (0,1)-vector c such that $Cc \geq d$.

Proof: "⇒" Let ψ be an assignment with $\psi(\alpha) = 1$. Define $c_j = \psi(x_j)$ for all j. Then

$$(Cc)_i = \sum_{j=1}^{n} C_{ij}\, c_j = \sum_{x_j \in z_i} \psi(x_j) - \sum_{\bar{x}_j \in z_i} \psi(x_j)$$

$$\geq 1 - \sum_{x_j \in z_i} 1 = d_i$$

since there is either $x_j \in z_i$ with $\psi(x_j) = 1$ or $\bar{x}_j \in z_i$ with $\psi(x_j) = 0$.

"⇐". Let c be a (0,1)-vector with $Cc \geq d$. Define truth assignment ψ by $\psi(x_j) = c_j$. We claim $\psi(\alpha) = 1$. Assume otherwise. Then there must be an i such that $\psi(z_i) = 0$; in particular $\psi(x_j) = c_j = 0$ if $x_j \in z_i$ and $\psi(x_j) = c_j = 1$ if $\bar{x}_j \in z_i$. Hence

$$d_i \leq (Cc)_i = \sum_{x_j \in z_i} c_j - \sum_{\bar{x}_j \in z_i} c_j = - \sum_{\bar{x}_j \in z_i} 1 < d_i$$

a contradition. Thus $\psi(\alpha) = 1$. □□

Name: Vertex Cover (VC)

Input: Undirected graph $G = (V,E)$ and integer k

Question: Is there $V' \subseteq V$, $|V'| = k$ such that for every edge $(v,w) \in E$ either $v \in V'$ or $w \in V'$.

Theorem 3: Vertex Cover is NP-complete.

Proof: VC $\in$ NP is obvious. We show CLIQUE $\le$ VC. Let $G = (V,E)$ be an undirected graph and let k be an integer. Let $\hat{G} = (V, V \times V - E)$ be the complement of V and let $\hat{k} = |V| - k$. Then V' is a clique in G iff $V - V'$ is a vertex cover of $\hat{G}$. Thus G has a clique of size k iff $\hat{G}$ has a vertex cover of size $\hat{k}$. The mapping $G \to \hat{G}$ is clearly computably in polynomial time. □

Name: Directed Hamiltonian Cycle (DHC)

Input: Directed graph $G = (V,E)$

Question: Is there a simple cycle in G which goes through all vertices, i.e. is there a sequence $v_0,\ldots v_{n-1}$ with $v_i \neq v_j$ for $i \neq j$ and $(v_i, v_{(i+1) \bmod n}) \in E$ for $0 \le i < n$, $n = |V|$.

Theorem 4: Directed Hamiltonian Cycle is NP-complete.

Proof: DHC $\in$ NP is obvious. We show VC $\le$ GHC. Let $G = (V,E)$ be an undirected graph and k be an integer. For every node v_i let $e_{i1}, e_{i2}, \ldots, e_{ih_i}$ be the edges incident to v_i.

We construct directed graph $G' = (V',E')$ by

$$V' = \{a_1,\ldots,a_k\} \cup \{(i,j,\alpha);\ 1 \le i \le n,\ 1 \le j \le h_i,\ \alpha \in \{0,1\}\}$$

and

$$\begin{aligned} E' = {} & \{(a_r,(i,1,0));\ 1 \le r \le k,\ 1 \le i \le n\} \cup \\ & \{((i,j,0),(i,j,1));\ 1 \le i \le n,\ 1 \le j \le h_j\} \cup \\ & \{((i,j,1),(i,j+1,0));\ 1 \le i \le n,\ 1 \le j \le h_i\} \cup \\ & \{((i,h_i,1),a_r);\ 1 \le i \le n,\ 1 \le r \le k\} \cup \\ & \{((i,j,0),(i',j',0));\ e_{ij} = (v_i,v_{i'}) \text{ and } e_{i'j'} = (v_{i'},v_i)\} \cup \\ & \{((i',j',1),(i,j,1));\ e_{ij} = (v_i,v_{i'}) \text{ and } e_{i'j'} = (v_{i'},v_i)\}. \end{aligned}$$

The following diagram illustrates the construction for $V = \{v_1,v_2,v_3,v_4\}$, $E = \{(v_1,v_2),(v_2,v_2),(v_3,v_4)\}$ and $k = 2$. We have $e_{21} = (v_2,v_1), e_{22} = (v_2,v_3), e_{31} = (v_3,v_2)$ and $e_{32} = (v_3,v_4)$. Nodes a_1 and a_2 are not drawn.

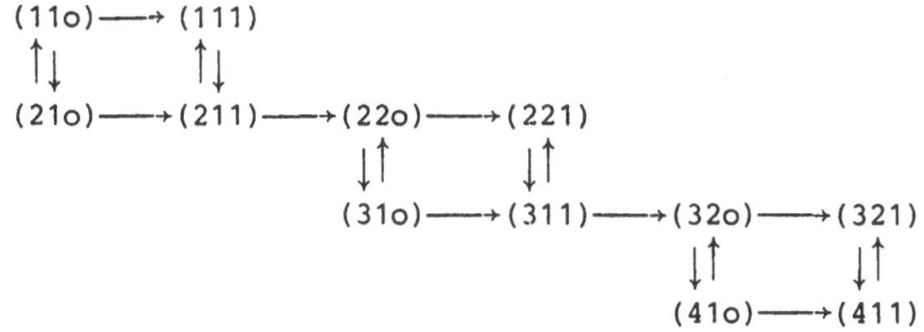

Node cover $\{v_1,v_3\}$ of G corresponds to Hamiltonian path a_1,(11o),(21o),(211),(111),a_2,(31o),(22o),(221),(311),(32o),(41o),(411),321),a_1 in G'.

<u>Claim:</u> G has a node cover $\tilde{V} \subseteq V$ of size k iff G' has a Hamiltonian cycle.

<u>Proof:</u> "$\Rightarrow$": Let $\tilde{V} = \{v_{i_1}, v_{i_2}, \ldots, v_{i_k}\}$ be a node cover of G of size k. We construct a Hamiltonian cycle in G' inductively. We start in node a_1 and go to $(i_1,1,0)$ first. Suppose now, that we reached node $(i_1,j,0)$.

<u>Case 1:</u> $e_{i_1,j} = (v_{i_1}, v_{i'})$ and $v_{i'} \notin \tilde{V}$. Then we proceed $(i_1,j,0) \to (i',j',0) \to (i',j',1) \to (i_1,j,1)$. Here $e_{i'j'} = e_{i_1 j}$.

<u>Case 2:</u> $e_{i_1,j} = (v_{i_1}, v_{i'})$ and $v_{i'} \in V$. Then we proceed directly to $(i_1,j,1)$.

We have reached node $(i_1,j,1)$ by now. If $j + 1 < h_{i_1}$ then we proceed to $(i_1,j+1,0)$, otherwise we reached a_2. From a_2 we go to $(i_2,1,0), \ldots$. In this way we construct a Hamiltonian cycle in G'.

"$\Leftarrow$". Suppose that G' has a Hamiltonian cycle C. We note some properties of C first. Consider one of the squares

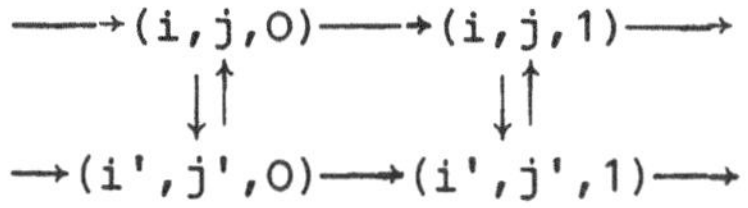

and assume that C enters the square through the left upper corner, i.e. through node (i,j,O). Then it leaves the square through one the right corners. If C leaves the square through the right lower corner, node (i',j',1), then either (i,j,1) or (i',j',O) is not on C, a contradiction. Hence C leaves the square through node (i,j,1). Thus the four corners of the square are traversed in one of the two following ways.

either 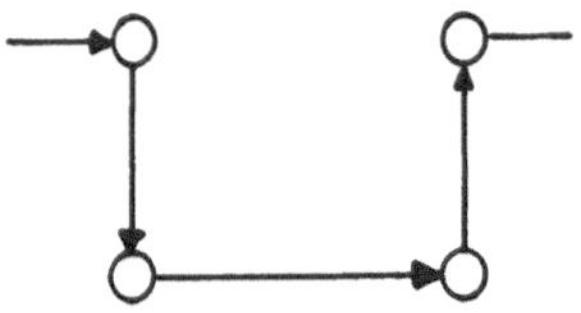 or 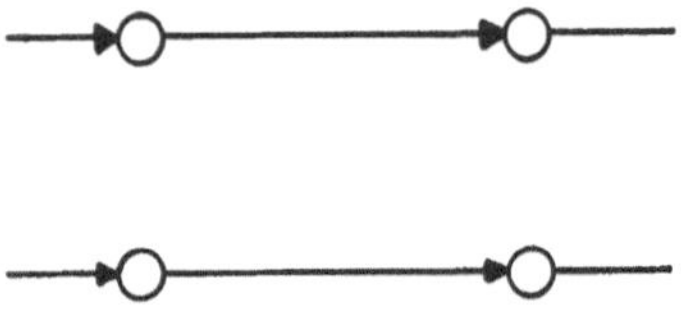

C goes through nodes $a_1,\dots,a_k$. The edges emanating from a_r, $1 \le r \le k$, end in nodes (i,1,0), $1 \le i \le n$. Let $(i_r,1,0)$ be the node following a_r in cycle C. We show that $\tilde{V} = \{v_{i_r} ; 1 \le r \le k\}$ is a vertex cover.

C goes from a_r to $(i_r,1,0)$. The argument above shows that the subsequent nodes on C are essentially the nodes $(i_r,j,0),(i_r,j,1)$, $1 \le j \le h_{i_r}$. However, between $(i_r,j,0)$ and $(i_r,j,1)$ there is possibly a detour to nodes (i',j',0) and (i',j',1) for some i',j'.

It is now easy to show to V is a vertex cover. Let $e \in E$ be arbitrary, say $e = (v_i,v_{i'})$. Consider the square corresponding to e. It is traversed in one of the two possible ways described above. In the first case node v_i is in $\tilde{V}$, in the second case v_i and $v_{i'}$ are in $\tilde{V}$. □□

Name: Undirected Hamiltonian Cycle (UHC)
Input: Undirected graph G = (V,E)
Question: Is there a simple cycle which goes through every node, i.e. is there a sequence $v_0,\dots,v_{n-1}$ such that $v_i \neq v_j$ for $i \neq j$ and $(v_i,v_{(i+1)\bmod n}) \in E$ for $0 \le i \le n$, $n = |V|$.

<u>Theorem 5:</u> UHC is NP-complete.

<u>Proof:</u> We show DHC ≤ UHC. Let G = (V,E) be a directed graph. Construct undirected graph G' from G by replacing every node v

by

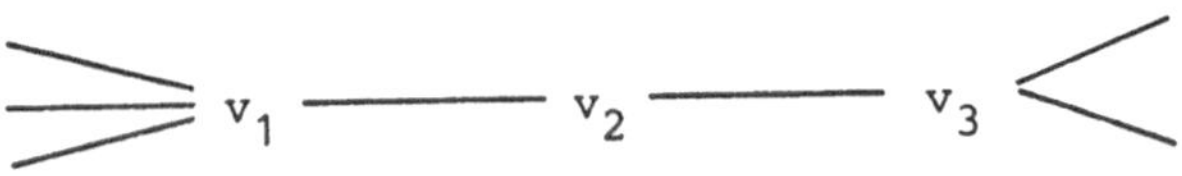

There is a one-to-one correspondence between Hamiltonian cycles of G and G' because in G' a cycle must enter through v_1 (or v_3) then go to v_2 and then continue to v_3 (or v_1). □

Name: Symmetric Traveling Salesman Problem with Triangle Inequality (ΔTSP).

Input: A matrix dist: $[0...n-1]^2 \to \mathbb{N}$ and integer k. Matrix dist is symmetric and satisfies the triangle inequality, i.e. dist(i,j) + dist(j,k) ≥ dist(i,k) for all i,j and k.

Question: Is there a tour of length at most k, i.e. a permutation Π of [0...n-1] such that

$$\sum_{i=0}^{n-1} \text{dist}(\Pi(i),\Pi((i+1) \bmod n)) \leq k?$$ □

Theorem 6: ΔTSP is NP-complete.

Proof: We show UHC ≤ ΔTSP. Let G = (V,E) be an undirected graph with V = [0...n-1]. We define

$$\text{dist}(i,j) = \begin{cases} 1 & \text{if } (i,j) \in E \\ 2 & \text{otherwise.} \end{cases}$$

and k = n. Then G has a Hamiltonian cycle iff dist has a tour which uses only edges of length 1 iff dist has a tour of length at most n.

□

Name: 3-Dimensonal Matching (3DM)
Input: Sets X,Y,Z of equal cardinality and a relation $U \subseteq X \times Y \times Z$
Question: Is there $U' \subseteq U$, $|U'| = X$, which covers all elements of $X \cup Y \cup Z$, i.e. $\forall w \in X \cup Y \cup Z \ \exists u \in U'$ such that $u = (w, \ , \ )$ or $u = (\ ,w, \ )$ or $u = (\ , \ ,w)$. □

One can think of X as boys, Y as girls, Z as houses and U the compatibility relation between boys, girls and houses. The question is to find a complete matching. The corresponding 2-dimensional problem is equivalent to finding complete matchings in bipartite graphs. It can be solved in polynomial time (chapter IV).

Theorem 7: 3DM is NP-complete.

Proof: 3DM is obviously in NP. We show SAT(3) $\le$ 3DM to prove completeness of 3DM. Let $\alpha = C_1 \wedge C_2 \wedge \ldots \wedge C_{k-1}$ be an instance of SAT(3) in variables $x_1,\ldots,x_n$. We will construct an instance I of 3DM such that α is satisfiable iff I has a solution. We specify the triples in U in three groups. The tiles in the first group are used to select a truth assignment, the tiles in the second group are used to check for satisfaction and the tiles in the third group perform garbage collection.

Group 1: Selecting a truth assignment. For every variable x_i, $1 \le i < n$, we have 2k triples

$$G_{i1} = \{(a_{ij},x_{ij},b_{ij}),\ (b_{ij},\bar{x}_{ij},a_{i,(j+1)\bmod k});\ 0 \le j < k\}$$

There will be no other triples containing points a_{ij} and b_{ij}, $1 \le i \le n$, $0 \le j < k$. The triples in group one can be visualized as follows (the case k = 3 is shown):

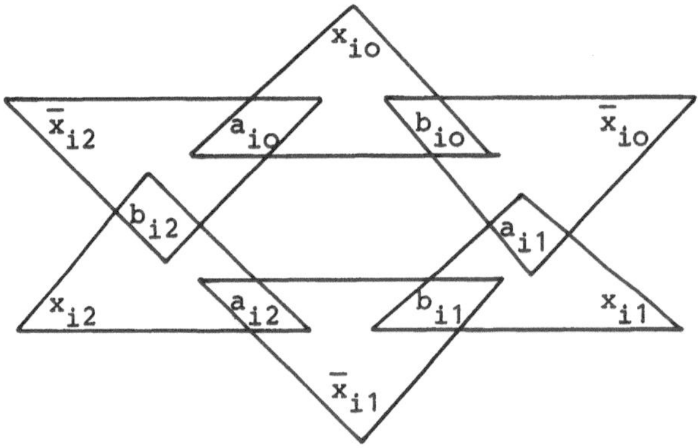

There are exactly two ways of covering points a_{ij}, b_{ij}, $0 \le j < k$, using the triples in G_{i1}. One leaves all points $x_{i,j}$ exposed and covers all points $\bar{x}_{i,j}$, $0 \le j < k$ [x_i is assigned true], and the other one leaves all points $\bar{x}_{i,j}$ exposed and covers all points $x_{i,j}$, $0 \le j < k$ [x_i is assigned false]. In this manner, the triples in G_{i1} fix a truth assignment.

Group 2: Checking for Satisfaction. For every clause C_j, $0 \le j < k$, we have triples (C_j^1, ℓ, C_j^2) for every literal ℓ appearing in clause C_j; i.e. we have either one, two or three triples for clause C_j. There are no other triples containing points C_j^1 and C_j^2. Suppose now that the tiles in group 1 are placed already. Then points C_j^1 and C_j^2 can be covered iff there is some i such that $x_{i,j}$ (or $\overline{x}_{i,j}$) appears in C_j and is left exposed by the tiles in group 1. Thus points C_j^1, C_j^2, $0 \le j < k$, can be covered iff the truth assignment specified by the triples in group 1 satisfy α.

Group 3: Gargabe Collection. At this point we constructed an instance I of 3DM from α with the following property. If α is unsatisfiable then there can be no complete matching in I. If α is satisfiable then there is a way to select the triples in group 1 and 2 such that points a_{ij}, b_{ij}, $\underline{C}_j^1$ and C_j^2 are all covered and exactly $nk - k = (n-1)k$ of the points x_{ij}, $\overline{x}_{ij}$ are uncovered. Thus in group 3 we add triples

$$\{(h_r, x_{ij}, g_r);\ 1 \le r \le (n-1)k,\ 1 \le i \le n,\ 0 \le j \le k\}$$

which allow us to complete the covering.

It is now easy to see that the instance $I(\alpha)$ of 3DM defined above can be indeed constructed in polynomial time given α and that α is satisfiable iff $I(\alpha)$ allows for a complete matching. This shows SAT(3) $\le$ 3DM.

□

Name: KNAPSACK
Input: A set $a_1, \ldots, a_n$, b of integers
Output: Is there a $J \subseteq [1,\ldots,n]$ such that $\sum_{j \in J} a_j = b$

Theorem 8: KNAPSACK is NP-complete.

Proof: KNAPSACK is apparently in NP. We show 3DM $\le$ KNAPSACK to prove completeness. Let $X = \{x_1, \ldots, x_q\}$, $Y = \{y_1, \ldots, y_q\}$, $Z = \{z_1, \ldots, z_q\}$ and $U \subseteq X \times Y \times Z$, $|U| = m$, be an instance of 3DM. We construct an instance of KNAPSACK from it.

For every triple $u_\ell = (x_i, y_j, z_k) \in U$ define integer a_ℓ by

$$a_\ell := 2^{s(2q+i-1)} + 2^{s(q+j-1)} + 2^{s(k-1)}$$

where $s := \lceil 1 + \log m \rceil$, i.e. the binary representation of a_ℓ consists of 3q blocks, the first q blocks representing points in X, the second q blocks representing points in Y and the last q blocks representing points in Z. A block is $s := 1 + \lceil \log m \rceil$ bits long and either contains (the binary representation of) integer 0 or 1 depending on whether the corresponding points belongs to the triple or not. Finally let

$$b := \sum_{j=1}^{3q} 2^{s(j-1)}$$

, i.e. every block of b contains integer 1. Next note that if $U' \subseteq U$ is a solution of 3DM then $b = \sum_{u_\ell \in U'} a$. However, if $U' \subseteq U$ is not a solution of 3DM then $b \neq \sum_{u_\ell \in U'} a$. This follows from the fact that $|U'| \le |U| = m$ and hence the one's in any block can add up to at most m. Thus there can be no overflow from one block to the next. □

It is worthwhile to take a closer look at the problem instances of KNAPSACK constructed in the proof of theorem 14. We showed NP-completeness of KNAPSACK by a two step reduction:

$$\text{SAT}(3) \le \text{3DM} \le \text{KNAPSACK}$$

Suppose that we start out with a formula with k clauses in n variables. From this we construct instances of 3DM with $q = |X| = |Y| = |Z| = 2nk$ and $m = |U| = 2nk + 3k + (nk)^2 \le q^2$. The reduction from 3DM to KNAPSACK then yields $m + 1 = O(q^2)$ numbers of length at most $3q(1+\lceil \log m \rceil) = O(q \log q)$. Thus a problem instance obtained in this way has length $L = O(q^3 \log q)$. However, $b = (2^{s3q-1})/(2^s-1) = \Omega(2^{q \log q}) = \Omega(2L^{1/3})$, i.e. the numerical value of b is exponential in the size of the problem instance. The very large value of b is intrinsic to NP-completeness as we will see in the next section on dynamic programming. We will show there that KNAPSACK can be solved in time O(nb).

Name: Scheduling Independent Tasks (SIT).

Input: A sequence $(t_1,\ldots,t_n)$ of time requirements for n jobs, $t_i \in \mathbb{N}$, a number $m \in \mathbb{N}$ of machines and a deadline T.

Output: Is there a schedule $S: [1\ldots n] \to [1\ldots m]$ such that for every $j \in [1\ldots m]$ $\sum_{i \in S^{-1}(j)} t_i \le T$, i.e. is it possible to distribute the jobs onto the machines such that all jobs are finished before time T?

Theorem 9: Scheduling Independent Tasks (SIT) is NP-complete.

Proof: SIT $\in$ NP is obvious. We show KNAPSACK $\le$ SIT. Let $a_1,\ldots,a_n,b$ be an instance of KNAPSACK and let $c = a_1 + a_2 + \ldots + a_n$. We may assume w.l.o.g. that $c \ge 2b$. Consider the following instance of SIT: $a_1,a_2,\ldots,a_n$, $c - 2b$ are the time requirements of $n + 1$ jobs, $m = 2$ and $T = c - b$. If the instance of KNAPSACK has solution J then assigning the jobs in J and the job with cost $c - 2b$ to machine 1 and all other jobs to machine 2 is a solution to the instance of SIT. Conversely, let $S: [1..\, n+1] \to \{1,2\}$ be a solution of SIT. Assume w.l.o.g. that $S(n+1) = 1$. Let $J = S^{-1}(1) \cap [1\ldots n]$. Then $c - b = T = c - 2b + \sum_{i\in J} a_i$ and hence J solves the instance of KNAPSACK. □

The proof of Theorem 9 actually shows a stronger result than claimed. Scheduling Independent Tasks remains NP-complete for any fixed number $m \ge 2$ of machines.

Name: Precedence Constrained Scheduling (PCS)

Input: A number $n \in \mathbb{N}$ of unit-cost jobs, a number $m \in \mathbb{N}$ of machines, a deadline $T \in \mathbb{N}$ and a precedence relation R on the jobs, i.e. $([1\ldots n],R)$ is an acyclic graph.

Question: Is there a schedule $S: [1\ldots n] \to [1\ldots T]$ such that $|S^{-1}(t)| \le m$ for all t and $(i,j) \in R \Rightarrow S(i) < S(j)$ for all i,j. □

Theorem 1o: Precedence Constrained Scheduling (PCS) is NP-complete.

Proof: PCS $\in$ NP is obvious. We show CLIQUE $\le$ PCS. Let $G = (V,E)$ be an undirected graph without isolated vertices and $k \in \mathbb{N}$ be an instance of CLIQUE. We construct an instance I of PCS from it with deadline $T = 3$ such that there is a feasible schedule iff G has a clique of size k. The jobs in I consist of 5 groups: the vertices V of G, the edges E of G, and three non-empty sets of fill-in jobs F_1,F_2,F_3, i.e. $n = |V| + |E| + |F_1| + |F_2| + |F_3|$. Furthermore $R = F_1 \times F_2 \cup F_2 \times F_3 \cup V \times F_3 \cup \{(v,e);\ v \in V,\ e \in E$ and v is incident to e}. In a feasible schedule all jobs in F_i are executed at time i, $1 \le i \le 3$. Also only vertices and no edges are executed at time one and all vertices must be executed before time three. We complete the construction by chosing $|F_i|$, $1 \le i \le 3$, and m appropriately.

$$|F_1| \geq 1 \quad |F_2| \geq 1 \quad |F_3| \geq 1,$$

$$k + |F_1| = n-k + k(k-1)/2 + |F_2| = e-k(k-1)/2 + |F_3|$$

$$m = k + |F_1|$$

It is easy to see that $|F_1|$, $|F_2|$ and $|F_3|$ exist. It remains to relate the existance of a clique of size k in G with the existance of a schedule of length 3. Note first that there are exactly 3m jobs, i.e. in a schedule of length three all machines must be busy at all times. Next note that a feasible schedule has to schedule exactly k vertices, say $V' \subseteq V$, at time one and the remaining n-k at time two. Hence a schedule of length three exists iff exactly $k(k-1)/2$ edges can be scheduled at time two. However, only edges between nodes of V' can be scheduled at time two and there are at most $|V'|(|V'|-1)/2 = k(k-1)/2$ of them. Equality holds iff V' is a clique of size k. □

Again, the proof of theorem 1o actually shows a somewhat stronger result. PCS remains NP-complete if only instances with deadline T = 3 are considered.

VI. 6. Solving NP-complete Problems

We have seen that NP-complete problems are probably very hard to solve. Nevertheless, they occur frequently and have to be solved in practice. What can we do? There are several useful approaches.

a) Special cases: Reexamine the problem at hand. Do you really want to solve the NP-complete problem in its full generality, or is it good enough to solve a special case? The special case might have a polynomial time solution. Precedence Constrained Scheduling is a good example. At least the following special cases of PCS are in P: The case of only two processors and the case of the precedence relation being a forest.

b) Dynamic Programming and Branch-and-Bound are two problem solving techniques which can be applied to most NP-complete problems. We treat these techniques in detail in this section. Both techniques are essentially clever variants of exhaustive search. Dynamic Programming yields surprisingly efficient algorithms for some problems, e.g. KNAPSACK, Branch-and-Bound uses lower bounds on the cost of optimal solutions to guide the search.

c) Probabilistic analysis can sometimes show that the hard instances of an NP-complete problem are quite rare. It is therefore possible to design algorithms algorithms with good expected running time. Of course, there is always the problem of justifying the probability distribution postulated on the problem instances.

d) Approximation algorithms can sometimes yield very good solutions in little time. Section VI.7. is devoted to approximation algorithms.

e) Heuristics: Finally there is still room for heuristics, i.e. for algorithms which seem to work well in practice but for a reason nobody understands.

VI. 6.1 Dynamic Programming

Dynamic Programming is a clever form of exhaustive search. We illustrate the method on two examples: TSP and KNAPSACK.

Consider an instance dist: $[0...n-1]^2 \to \mathbb{N}$ of TSP. Naive exhaustive search has to test n! possibilities. Dynamic programming allows us to cut down on that number considerably, although it is still neccessary to test an exponential number of candidates. We construct iteratively optimal tours through k cities, k = 1,2,3,... . Since every tour has to go through city 0 we start our tours w.l.o.g. in city 0. For $S \subseteq [1...n-1]$ and $i \in S$ let C(S,i) be the minimal length of any tour which starts in city 0 goes through all cities in S and ends in city i. Then

$$C(\{i\},i) = dist(0,i) \text{ for } 1 \le i \le n-1$$

and

$$C(S,i) = \min_{k \in S-\{i\}} [C(S-\{i\},k) + dist(k,i)]$$

for $|S| \ge 2$. The length of the optimal tour is given by $\min\{C([1...n-1],i) + dist(i,0),\ 1 \le i \le n-1$. The optimal tour itself is also easily constructed. One only has to store along with C(S,i) the value of k which defines C(S,i). Then the optimal tour can be constructed in a second pass over the matrix of C(S,i)'s. The total cost of this algorithm is

$$O(n-1 + \sum_{\ell=2}^{n-1} \underbrace{\binom{n-1}{\ell}\cdot \ell}_{\substack{\text{number of } C(S,i)\\ \text{with } |S| = \ell}} \cdot \underbrace{(\ell-1)}_{\text{number of } k\text{'s}})$$

$= O((n-1)(n-2)2^{n-3} + (n-1))$. Thus dynamic programming reduces the number of candidates to be tested from N! to $n^2 2^n$, a drastic improvement.

KNAPSACK is another illustrative example. Let $a_1,\dots,a_n,b$ be an instance of KNAPSACK. Define bitvector $B[0..\,b]$ by:

$$B[s] = \begin{cases} 1 & \text{if } s = \sum_{i=1}^{b} a_i x_i \text{ for some } (x_1,\dots,x_n) \in \{0,1\}^n \\ 0 & \text{otherwise.} \end{cases}$$

Vector B can be computed in time O(nb) by the following algorithm.

```
B[0] ← true; B[s] ← false for 1 ≤ s ≤ b;
for i ∈ [1...n]
do  - - B[s] = 1 iff s = Σ_{j=1}^{i-1} a_j x_j for some (x_1,...,x_{i-1}) ∈ {0,1}^{i-1};
for s from b step - 1 to x_i
do if B[s-x_i] then B[s] ← true od;
od
```

__Theorem 1:__ KNAPSACK can be solved in time O(nb).

__Proof:__ The algorithm given above solves KNAPSACK in time O(nb). □

What happened? The simple algorithm above solves KNAPSACK in polynomial time and hence establishes P = NP. Is the entire chapter a fraud? No! Running time is polynomial in the value of b but not in the length of the binary representation of b. The reader should go back to the remark following theorem VI.5.6. at this point. We argued there that the reduction of 3DM to KNAPSACK generates problem instances of KNAPSACK where b is exponential in the size of the instance. Hence the dynamic programming algorithm for KNAPSACK has running time exponential in the size of the input. Nevertheless, theorem 1 is interesting from a practical point of view, because it seems to be the case that in "realistic" instances of KNAPSACK the a_i's and b are bounded by a polynomial in n. The special case of such instances can be solved in polynomial time by dynamic programming. This phenomenon is interesting enough to deserve its own name.

Definition: Let I be an instance of some algorithmic problem, typically I is a set of graphs, integers, sets, ... Then number(I) is the largest integer occuring in I.

Definition: An algorithm for a combinatorial problem is pseudo-polynomial if its running time on instance I is polynomial in size(I) and number(I).

We can now rephrase theorem 1. KNAPSACK has a pseudo-polynomial algorithm. So do Weighted KNAPSACK and Scheduling Independent Tasks for every fixed number of machines (exercises 15 and 16). A pseudo-polynomial algorithm is a good thing to have. Whenever the problem instances contain only small numbers, i.e. number(I) $\le$ p(size(I)) for some polynomial p, then a pseudo-polynomial algorithm is indeed an algorithm with polynomial running time. Does every NP-complete problem has a pseudo-polynomial algorithm? The answer is no provided that P $\neq$ NP.

Definition: An NP-complete problem is strongly NP-complete iff it stays NP-complete when integers are coded in unary. □

When we introduced NP-complete problems we were not very specific about endocings. However we put forth one principle: integers are coded in binary (or decimal) notation, i.e. the representation of integer n has length log n. If we code integer n in unary, i.e. as a sequence of n ones, then the representation of n has length n. A strongly NP-complete problem is NP-complete even when we use this very redundant encoding of integers. Most of the problems in section VI.5. are strongly NP-complete because these problems do not involve numbers at all or only in an inessential way. Examples are SAT, 3DM, CLIQUE (note that we may assume k $\le$ |V| w.l.o.g), VC, DHC, UHK, PCS and Δ TSP (note that all edges have length one or two in the problem instances constructed in the NP-completeness of Δ TSP Strongly NP-complete problems do not have pseudo-polynomial algorithms provided that $P \neq NP$.

Theorem 2: If a strongly NP-complete problems has a pseudo-polynomial algorithm then $P = NP$.

Proof: If integers are coded in unary then number(I) $\leq$ size(I) for all instances I. Hence a pseudo-polynomial algorithm is a polynomial algorithm is the usual sense. □

SAT, 3DM and CLIQUE are not very interesting strongly NP-complete problems because numbers do not play a crucial role in these problems. A more interesting example is provided by:

Name: 3-Partition.

Input: Integers $c_1,\ldots,c_{3n}$ such that $B/4 < c_i < B/2$ for all i, where $B = (c_1 + \ldots + c_{3n})/n$.

Question: Is there a partition $T_1,\ldots,T_n$ of $\{1,\ldots,3n\}$ such that $\sum_{j \in T_i} c_j = B$ for all i. □

Theorem 3: 3-Partition is strongly NP-complete.

Proof: The proof is by a lengthy reduction from 3DM and can be found in M.R. Garey/D.S. Johnson: Complexity Results for Multiprocessor Scheduling under Resource Constraints, SICOMP 4 (1975), 397-341. □

Note that in any solution for the 3-Partition problem all sets T_i must have cardinality exactly three. Hence asking a solution to Scheduling Independent Tasks with 3n jobs of time requirements $c_1,\ldots,c_{3n}$, deadline $T = 3$ and $m = n$ machines is equivalent to 3-Partition. Thus SIT is strongly NP-complete.

VI. 6.2 Branch and Bound

Branch and Bound is another variant of exhaustive search. The branch step corresponds to exhaustive search. However, the feasible solutions generated in the branch step are not searched in an arbitrary order. Rather, easily computable bounds on the cost of an optimal solution are used to direct the search for an optimal solution. More concretely, let I_o be an instance of a minimization problem. In a branch step we generate from I_o simpler instances $I_1,\ldots,I_k$ of the same problem such that:

1) Every feasible solution L of I_i, $1 \le i \le k$, corresponds to a feasible solution $g_i(L)$ of I_o and $\{g_i(L);\ 1 \le i \le k$ and L is feasible solution of $I_i\}$ is the set of all feasible solutions of I_o. The g_i's are very often the identity function. The branch step splits problem I_o into subproblems $I_1,\ldots I_k$.

2) For every I_i, $1 \le i \le k$, one computes a lower bound C_i on the cost of solutions $g_i(L)$ of I_o where L is a feasible solution of I_i (bound). Then the cost of an optimal solution of I_o is at least $\max\{C_i;\ 1 \le i \le k\}$. The next branch step is applied to the node with the least C-value.

Branch and Bound steps are iterated until an instance I is obtained such that the feasible solutions for I can be computed directly in little time and such that I has a feasible solution L for which the cost of g(L) is no larger than the C-values of all unexpanded subproblems. Then L is an optimal solution. Branch and Bound has a strong similarity to finding least cost paths in directed graphs. This relation is worked out in exercise 17.

For a concrete example we take the Traveling Salesman problem. We need a lower bound on the cost of an optimal tour first. Since every city has to entered and left on an optimal tour

$$\sum_{i=0}^{n-1} \left(\min_{j \ne i} dist(i,j) + \min_{j \ne i} dist(j,i)\right)/2$$

is a lower bound on the cost of an optimal tour. Consider the following instance on four cities A,B,C,D. Function dist is given by matrix

I_o =

	A	B	C	D
A	∞	3	2	7
B	4	∞	3	6
C	1	1	∞	3
D	1	6	6	∞

City A has to left somehow. It is either left on the road to C (the city closest to A) or it is not left on the road to C. We can thus generate the following subproblems I_1 and I_2 from I_0. In I_1 we make sure that road AC is taken by setting AB $\leftarrow$ AD $\leftarrow \infty$. Since C cannot be entered twice on an optimal tour we can also change BC and BD to infinity. In I_2 we make sure that road AC is not taken by changing its length to ∞. We obtain

$$I_1 = \begin{matrix} \infty & \infty & 2 & \infty \\ 4 & \infty & \infty & 6 \\ \infty & 1 & \infty & 3 \\ 1 & 6 & \infty & \infty \end{matrix} \qquad\qquad I_2 = \begin{matrix} \infty & 3 & \infty & 7 \\ 4 & \infty & 3 & 6 \\ 1 & 1 & \infty & 3 \\ 1 & 6 & 6 & \infty \end{matrix}$$

bound = (2+4+1+1+1+1+2+3)/2 = 7.5 bound = (3+3+1+1+1+1+3+3) = 8

Subproblem I_1 has the smaller bound. Thus I_1 is branched in the next step. We can continue from city C to either B or to another city. This generates subproblem I_3 where we make sure that CB is taken (and hence CD, AB and DB cannot be taken) and I_4 where we make sure that CB is not taken.

$$I_3 = \begin{matrix} \infty & \infty & 2 & \infty \\ \infty & \infty & \infty & 6 \\ \infty & 1 & \infty & \infty \\ 1 & \infty & \infty & \infty \end{matrix} \qquad\qquad I_3 = \begin{matrix} \infty & \infty & 2 & \infty \\ 4 & \infty & 3 & 6 \\ \infty & \infty & \infty & 3 \\ 1 & 6 & 6 & \infty \end{matrix}$$

bound = (2+6+1+1+1+12+6)/2 = 10 bound = (2+3+3+1+1+6+2+3)/2 = 10.5

At this point we know that all solutions of I_3 (I_4) have length at least 10(10.5) and hence all solutions of I_1 have length at least 10. Thus I_2 is branched in the next step. Continuing in this way we generate the following tree of subproblems. The edge labels in this tree indicate the edge which was either chosen or excluded and the node labels indicate the bound (cf. figure on next page).

Subproblems I_7 and I_3 allow only one tour each, namely A→C→B→D→A and A→B→C→D→A of cost 10 each. All feasible solution of the other subproblem have cost larger than 10. Thus the two tours given above are the only optimal tours.

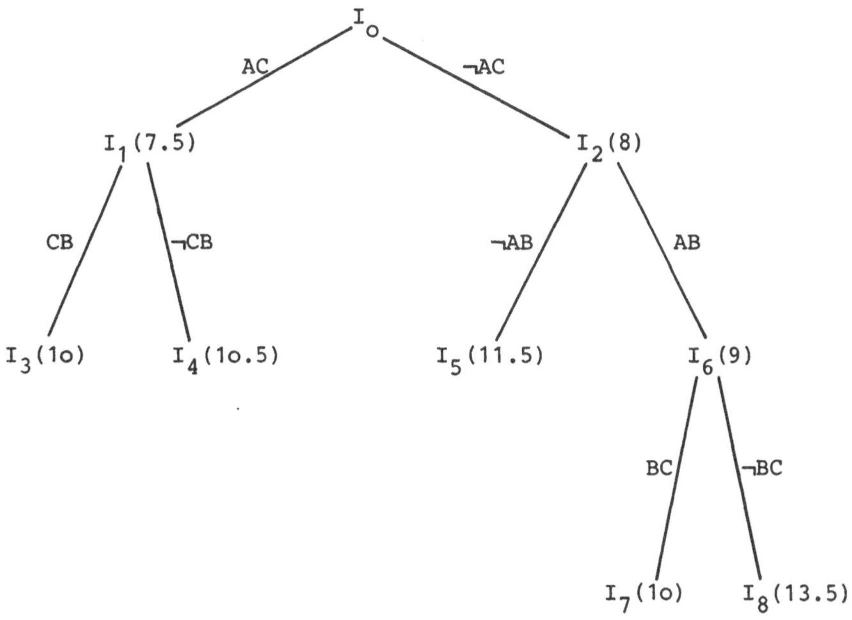

Our simple branch and bound algorithm can be improved in at least two ways.

a) Better lower bounds focus the direction of the search more directly towards optimal solutions. We only used the fact so far, that every city has to entered and left at least once. The additional requirement that every city is entered and left exactly once improves the lower bound considerably in many cases. A solution to that problem (called weighted matching) can be found in polynomial time (cf. VI.7.3.); it consists of a set of cycles in the graph.

b) Improving the branch step. So far we included or excluded an arbitrary edge in the branch step. The improved lower bound suggests an improved strategy. Take a cycle of minimum length in the solution to the matching problem and generate subproblems by excluding one of the edges of the cycle.

Branch and bound techniques are very often a dramatic improvement over pure exhaustive search. Nevertheless, it is easy to show than our simple approach still has exponential running time (exercise 18).

Even branching by itself can sometimes yield reasonable algorithms.

Theorem 4: Let G = (V,E) be an undirected graph and let sopt be the size of an optimal vertex cover. Then a vertex cover of size sopt can be found in time $O(2^{sopt}\ |E|)$.

Proof: Note first that at least one of the two endpoints of any edge is in any optimal cover. This suggest the following simple algorithm. Take any edge (v,w) of G and generate two subproblems. In the first subproblem node v is added to the cover and all edges incident to v are deleted from the graph; in the second subproblem node w is added to the cover and all edges incident to w are deleted from the graph. Generate the tree of subproblems bradth-first. Then a tree of depth sopt with 2^{sopt} nodes is generated. In every node we spend time at most $O(|E|)$.

□

Theorem 4 describes an algorithm whose running time is polynomial in problem size and exponential only in the size of the solution. Hence such an algorithm is very useful if we know in advance that the problem instance at hand has a small solution. A similar phenomenon holds true for cycle cover (exercise 19).

VI. 7. Approximation Algorithms

Many NP-complete problems are naturally formulated as optimization problems. In fact, the Traveling Salesman problem had to be artificially formulated as a language recognition problem. Similarly, Scheduling Independent Tasks can be formulated as an optimization problem in even two ways. Given a set $t_1,\ldots,t_n$ of time requirements of n jobs we can either fix the number m of machines and ask for the minimal deadline or we can fix the deadline and ask for the minimal number of machines. The latter problem is usually called bin packing. In the preceding section we studied dynamic programming and branch-and-bound algorithms for finding optimal solutions. Although these algorithms were more efficient than pure exhaustive search their running time is still exponential. It is then natural to ask for approximation algorithms which yield nearly optimal solutions in little time. In section III.4. we described linear time algorithms for finding nearly optimal binary search trees; in contrast, the best known algorithm for optimum trees had quadratic running time. The savings are even more substantial in the case of NP-complete problems.

We describe approximation algorithms for various NP-complete problems. A first example is the Traveling Salesman problem with triangle inequality (Δ TSP). A very simple algorithm always produces a tour of length at most twice the length of the optimum tour. It has running time $O(n^2)$. An improved algorithm with running time $O(n^4)$ always finds a tour of length at most 3/2 the length of the optimum tour. No better approximation algorithm for Δ TSP is known. It is useful to introduce some additional terminology at this point.

Definition: Let (Q,C) be a polynomially bounded minimization problem, in particular $Q \subseteq \Sigma^* \times \Sigma^*$ and $c: \Sigma^* \times \Sigma^* \to \mathbb{N}$ (cf. VI.2.). An algorithm A, which computes a mapping $f_A: \Sigma^* \to \Sigma^*$ from problem instances to feasible solutions, is a g-approximate algorithm if

$$\frac{c(I,f_A(I))-c(I,f_{opt}(I))}{c(I,f_{opt}(I))} \le g(c(I,f_{opt}(I)))$$

for every problem instance I. Here $f_{opt}: \Sigma^* \to \Sigma^*$ maps instances to optimal solutions and $g: \mathbb{N} \to \mathbb{R}$ is some function. □

In this terminology, we described an $g(x) = 2/x$ approximate algorithm for optimum search trees in section III.4. and will describe an $g(x) = 0.5$ approximate algorithm for Δ TSP in VI.7.1..

The situation is even better for Scheduling Independent Tasks when we ask to minimize the deadline. We describe an 1/3-approximate algorithm with running time $O(n \log n)$ first and then improve it to an ε-approximate algorithm for any $\varepsilon > 0$. The running time of the ε-approximate algorithm is $O(n \log n + m^{(m-1)/\varepsilon})$, a polynomial in n for any fixed ε. □

Definition: A polynomial time approximation scheme for a minimization problem (Q,c) takes problem instances I and performance guarantees $\varepsilon > 0$ and returns ε-approximate solutions. For any fixed $\varepsilon > 0$ the running time is bounded by a polynomial in instance size. □

The algorithm referred to above is a polynomial time approximation scheme for SIT(m), Scheduling Independent Tasks on m machines. Unfortunately, the complexity of the algorithm is not so good as a function of

$1/\varepsilon$. In 7.3. we describe an algorithm for the weighted KNAPSACK problem whose running time is polynomial in instance size and $1/\varepsilon$, a full polynomial approximation scheme.

Definition: A polynomial time approximation scheme is full if its running time is bounded by $p(n,1/\varepsilon)$, a polynomial in input size n and performance guarantee ε. □

VI. 7.1 Approximation Algorithms for the Travelling Salesman Problem

We start with a simple and efficient 1-approximate algorithm for the Travelling Salesman problem with triangle inequality, the once-around-a-least-cost-spanning-tree algorithm.

Let dist: $[0\ldots n-1]^2 \to \mathbb{R}$ be an instance of ΔTSP, i.e. dist(i,j) = dist(j,i) and dist(i,j) + dist(j,k) $\geq$ dist(i,k) for all i,j and k. We use C_{opt} to denote the length of an optimal Travelling Salesman tour. We can define a network N = (V,E,c) from dist in a natural way: V = {0...n-1}, E = V x V and c(i,j) = dist(i,j) for all i,j. Let (V,T) be a least cost spanning tree of N; it can be found by the methods of section IV.8.. Tree (V,T) gives rise to a tour (not necessarily a

Example: Network N below has an optimal Travelling Salesman tour of cost C_{opt} = 6. It is shown wiggled. A minimum cost spanning tree has cost 4.

N =

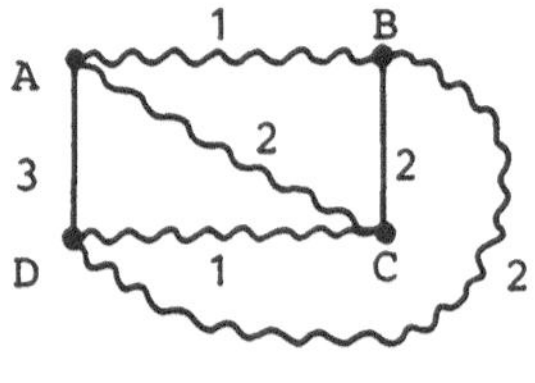

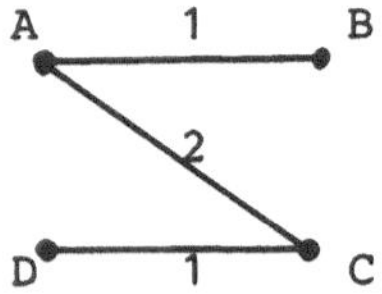

It gives rise to a tour (once around the tree) A,B,A,C,D,C,A of length 8

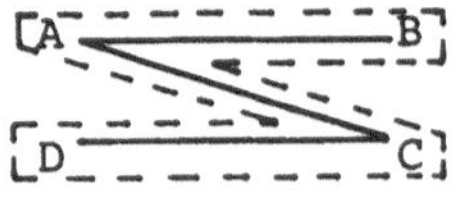

which can be shortened to a Travelling Salesman Tour A,B,C,D,A of length 7.

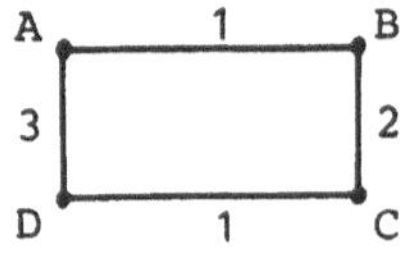

□

Travelling Salesman tour) which uses every edge of T twice. We only have to run around the tree once. This tour can be shortened to a Travelling Salesman Tour by introducing shortcuts. The shortcuts do not increase cost because of the triangle inequality. The details are as follows.

Lemma 1: Let dist be an instance of Δ TSP, let $N = (V,E,c)$ be the associated network, and let (V,T) be a least cost spanning tree of N. Then

$$C(T) = \sum_{e \in T} c(e) \le C_{opt}$$

where C_{opt} is the length of an optimal Travelling Salesman Tour.

Proof: An optimal Travelling Salesman tour minus any edge is a spanning tree and has therefore cost at least $C(T)$. □

A sequence $S = v_0, v_1, \ldots, v_{m-1}, v_0$ is a tour of N if $(v_i, v_{i+1}) \in E$ for all i and $V = \{v_0, v_1, \ldots, v_{m-1}\}$, i.e. every node is visited. Its cost is $C(S) = \sum_{i=0}^{m} c(v_i, v_{(i+1) \bmod m})$. It is a Travelling Salesman tour if $m = |V|$.

Let (V,T) be a spanning tree of N. The once-around-the-tree-tour S is defined as follows. Let $r \in V$ be arbitrary. If $V = \{r\}$ then S consists of node r only. If $|V| > 1$ then let $r_1, \ldots, r_k$ be the neighbours of r in (V,T) and let S_i be the once-around-the-tree-tours of the subtrees rooted at r_i. Then $S = r\ S_1\ r\ S_2\ r \ldots r\ S_k\ r$. It is easy to see that S can be constructed in time $O(n)$ from (V,T) by depth first search.

Lemma 2: Let (V,T) be a least cost spanning tree of N and let S be the once-around-the-tree-tour of T. Then $C(S) \le 2\, C_{opt}$.

Proof: $C(S) \le 2\, C(T)$ since every edge of T is used twice in S; $C(T) \le C_{opt}$ by lemma 1. □

Lemma 3: Let S be a tour of N. Then there is a Travelling Salesman Tour of N of cost at most $C(S)$.

Proof: Let $S = v_0, v_1, \ldots, v_{m-1}, v_0$. If $m = |V|$ then there is nothing to show. Otherwise there must be a least j, say j_0, such that there is an $i < j$ with $v_i = v_j$. Consider $S' = v_0, v_1, \ldots, v_{j-1}, v_{j+1}, \ldots, v_{m-1}, v_0$.

We have

$$C(S') = C(S) - c(v_{j-1},v_j) - c(v_j,v_{j+1}) + c(v_{j-1},v_{j+1}) \le C(S)$$

since dist and hence c satisfies the triangle inequality. Thus S' has cost at most C(S) and one less node than S. Iterating the construction produces a Travelling Salesman tour. □

We summarize:

Theorem 1: There is a 1-approximate $O(n^2)$ algorithm for Δ TSP; here n is the number of cities.

Proof: A least cost spanning tree can be found in time $O(n^2)$ by the results of section IV.8.. The remainder of the construction takes time O(n). □

In the Euclidian case we can do even better. The Euclidian Travelling Salesman problem is as follows. Given are n cities in the plane (in $\mathbb{R}^2$). The distance between two cities is the Euclidian distance. We will see in chapter VII that Euclidian least cost spanning trees can be found in time O(n log n).

Theorem 2: There is an 1-approximate O(n log n) algorithm for the Euclidian TSP.

Proof: Immediate from the discussion above. □

Can we improve upon theorem 1. Lemma 2 is at the heart of the construction above. It also suggests an improvement. There is another way of visualizing the once-around-the-tree-tour. Let (V,T) be a least cost spanning tree. If one draws every edge of T twice then we obtain a Eulerian graph, i.e. a graph where every node has even degree. Such a graph has a Eulerian tour, i.e. a tour which uses every edge (of the expanded graph) exactly once; cf. exercise 14. Eulerian tours in Eulerian graphs can be constructed in linear time. We turned (V,T) into a Eulerian graph by doubling every edge and thus doubling the cost. Hence we will obtain a better approximation algorithm for Δ TSP if we find a cheaper way of turning (V,T) into a Eulerian graph. Let V_{odd} be the set of nodes of odd degree in (V,T). A solution is to give exactly the nodes in V_{odd} an additional edge. This is always possible, since the cardinality of V_{odd} is even. Therefore a least cost matching of V_{odd} will turn (V,T) into a Eulerian graph.

Example: In our previous example, V_{odd} = {B,D}. Adding edge (B,D) turns the spanning tree into a Eulerian graph. It gives rise to a tour A,B, D,C,A of cost 6, the optimum. □

Definition: Let N = (V,E,c) be an undirected network. A complete matching is a set $M \subseteq E$ of edges such that $|M| = |V|/2$ and no two edges in M share a common endpoint. The cost of M is $C(M) = \sum_{e \in M} c(e)$. □

Lemma 4: Let dist be an instance of Δ TSP and let N = (V,E,c) be the associated network. Let (V,T) be a least cost spanning tree of N and let V_{odd} be the set of nodes of odd degree in (V,T).

a) $|N_{odd}|$ is even

b) The subnetwork of N induced by V_{odd} has a complete matching M of cost $C_{opt}/2$.

Proof: a) Let $deg_T(v)$ be the degree of v in (V,T). Then

$$2|T| = \sum_{v \in V} deg_T(v) = \sum_{v \in V_{odd}} deg_T(v) + \sum_{v \in V - V_{odd}} deg_T(v)$$

Thus $\Sigma\ \{deg_T(v);\ v \in V_{odd}\}$ is even and hence $|V_{odd}|$ must be even

b) Let $v_0, v_1, \ldots, v_{n-1}, v_0$ be a Travelling Salesman Tour of cost C_{opt}. Let $v_{i_1}, v_{i_2}, \ldots, v_{i_{2k}}$ be the nodes in V_{odd}; $|V_{odd}| = 2k$ and $i_1 < i_2 < \ldots < i_{2k}$. Then $M_1 = \{(i_{2j-1}, i_{2j});\ 1 \le j \le k\}$ and $M_2 = \{(i_{2j}, i_{2j+1});\ 1 \le j < k\} \cup \{(i_{2k}, i_1)\}$ are two complete matchings of V_{odd}. Also

$$C(M_1) + C(M_2) = \sum_{j=1}^{2k-1} c(v_{i_j}, v_{i_{j+1}}) + c(v_{i_{2k}}, v_{i_1})$$

$$\le \sum_{\ell=1}^{n-1} c(v_\ell, v_{(\ell+1) \bmod n}) = C_{opt}.$$

The inequality follows from the triangle inequality. Note that

$c(v_{i_j}, v_{i_{j+1}}) \le c(v_{i_j}, v_{i_j+1}) + \ldots + c(v_{i_{j+1}-1}, v_{i_{j+1}})$ by the triangle inequality. Hence $\min(C(M_1), C(M_2)) \le C_{opt}/2$. □

Theorem 2: There is an 0.5-approximate $O(n^3)$ algorithm for Δ TSP; n is the number of cities.

Proof: A least cost spanning tree (V,T) can be found in time $O(n^2)$. Clearly V_{odd} can then be extracted time O(n). A least cost matching M of V_{odd} can be found in time $O(n^3)$ (cf. E. Lawler: Combinatorial Optimization: Networks and Matroids). Then $(V, T \cup M)$ is a Eulerian graph with $C(T) + C(M) \le 3\, C_{opt}/2$. Next we construct a Eulerian tour of $(V, T \cup M)$ and shorten it to a Travelling Salesman tour as described in lemma 3. Altogether, we obtained a tour of length at most $3\, C_{opt}/2$. □

The performance bounds given for the once-around-the-tree-algorithm and the 0.5-approximate algorithm are best possible in the following sense. One can find a class of problem instances (exercise 21) where the approximation algorithm produce tours with length almost $(1+\varepsilon)C_{opt}$; here $\varepsilon = 1$ or $\varepsilon = 0.5$ respectively.

Can we find an ε-approximate algorithm (with polynomial running time and some $\varepsilon > 0$) for every NP-complete problem or are there NP-complete problems which resist even approximate solutions provided that P ≠ NP. Unfortunately, the second alternative is true and TSP without triangle inequality provides us with an example.

Theorem 3: Let $\varepsilon > 0$ be arbitrary. If there is an algorithm A with the following properties

a) A's running time is polynomially bounded,

b) for every symmetric distance matrix dist: $[0 \ldots n-1]^2 \to \mathbb{N}$, A constructs a Travelling Salesman tour of length at most $(1+\varepsilon)C_{opt}$, where C_{opt} is the length of the optimal Travelling Salesman tour,

then P = NP.

Proof: Assume that A exists. Let p be a polynomial which bounds the running time of A. We will show that UHC (undirected Hamiltonian cycle) is in P. Since UHC is NP-complete this implies P = NP.

Let $G = (V,E)$ be an instance of UHC with $V = \{v_0,\ldots,v_{n-1}\}$. Define dist: $[0\ldots n-1]^2 \to \mathbb{N}$ by

$$\text{dist}(i,j) = \begin{cases} 1 & \text{if } (v_i,v_j) \in E \\ \lceil \varepsilon \cdot n \rceil + 2 & \text{otherwise} \end{cases}$$

Matrix dist is clearly symmetric. Furthermore, if G has a Hamiltonian cycle then dist has a Travelling Salesman tour of length n and if G does not have a Hamiltonian cycle then every Travelling Salesman tour has length at least $(n-1) + \lceil \varepsilon n \rceil + 2 > (1+\varepsilon)n$ with respect to dist. What does algorithm A do on instance dist? It constructs a tour of length C. We distinguish two cases.

Case 1: $C > (1+\varepsilon)n$. Since $C \le (1+\varepsilon)C_{opt}$ by assumption b) on A, we conclude $C_{opt} > n$. Thus G does not have a Hamiltonian cycle.

Case 2: $C \le (1+\varepsilon)n$. Then $C = n$ by the discussion above. Thus G has a Hamiltonian cycle.

This shows that we can use algorithm A to solve UHC. Matrix dist requires $O(n^2 \log(\ n+2)) = O(n^2 \log n)$ bits to write down. Since A's running time is bounded by polynomial p, we conclude that UHC can be solved in time $O(p(n^2 \log n))$. Hence UHC $\in$ P and therefore P = NP. □

Theorem 3 shows that NP-complete problems can behave dramatically different with respect to approximation. We will see more of this in sections to come. It is not known whether Δ TSP has an ε-approximate algorithm for some $\varepsilon < 1/2$. It is also not known whether the existence of such an algorithm is excluded by the assumption P $\neq$ NP.

VI. 7.2 Approximation Schemes

The situation is better with respect to the Scheduling Independent Tasks (SIT) optimization problem. We are given the time requirements $t_1,\ldots,t_n$ of a set of n jobs and a number m of machines and are asked to find a schedule $S: [1\ldots n] \to [1\ldots m]$ which minimizes the finishing time $T = \max_j \Sigma \{t_i, S(i) = j\}$. Throughout this section we use T_{opt} to denote the finishing time of an optimal schedule. We describe an 1/3 approximate algorithm first and then improve it to an approximation scheme for SIT(m). In SIT(m) the number of machines is not an input to the algorithm but fixed in advance.

The 1/3-approximate algorithm is based on a very simple idea: Schedule long jobs first and always schedule a job on a machine which was used least so far. The details are as follows.

Assume w.l.o.g. that $t_1 \geq t_2 \geq \ldots \geq t_n$. In fact, reordering the jobs takes time $O(n \log n)$ and is the most time consuming part of the algorithm Construct $S: [1\ldots n] \rightarrow [1\ldots m]$ by

```
(T1,...,Tm) ← (0,...,0);       -- Tj time units are used up
                               -- on machine j so far
for i from 1 to n
do  let j be such that Tj = min(T1,...,Tm);
    S[i] ← j;
    Tj ← Tj + ti
od
```

We refer to the schedule constructed by this algorithm as the longest processing time (LPT) schedule S_{LPT}. Its finishing time is denoted by T_{LPT}. If the T_i's are kept in a heap then one iteration of the loop takes time $O(\log m)$, for a total running time of $O(n \log m)$.

<u>Theorem 4:</u> The LPT algorithm is an $1/3-1/3m$ approximate algorithm for Scheduling Independent Tasks.

<u>Proof:</u> (Indirect) Assume otherwise. Let I be an instance of SIT with a minimal number of jobs such that $(T_{LPT}(I)-T_{opt}(I))/T_{opt}(I) > 1/3-1/(3m)$. Here $T_{opt}(I)$ is the finishing time of an optimal schedule S_{opt}: $[1\ldots n] \rightarrow [1\ldots m]$ and $T_{LPT}(I)$ is the finishing time of the LPT schedule S_{LPT}.

<u>Lemma 1:</u> If $S_{LPT}(n) = j$ then $\Sigma\, \{t_i;\ S_{LPT}(i) = j\} = T_{LPT}(I)$, i.e. job n finishes at time $T_{LPT}(I)$.

<u>Proof:</u> Assume otherwise. Then the LPT algorithm also constructs a schedule of length $T_{LPT}(I)$ for jobs $t_1,\ldots,t_{n-1}$. Denote the problem instance with time requirements $t_1,\ldots,t_{n-1}$ by I'. Then $T_{LPT}(I') = T_{LPT}(I)$. Also $T_{opt}(I') \leq T_{opt}(I)$ since I' is a "subinstance" of I. Hence

$$T_{LPT}(I') - T_{opt}(I') \geq T_{LPT}(I) - T_{opt}(I)$$

$$> [1/3 - 1/(3m)]\ T_{opt}(I)$$

$$\geq [1/3 - 1/(3m)]\ T_{opt}(I')$$

Thus I' is a counterexample with one fewer job than I, a contradiction to the choice of I. □

We will next show that the LPT algorithm constructs a bad schedule only if $T_{opt}(I)$ is small.

Lemma 2: $T_{opt}(I) < 3\ t_n$.
Consider the state $(T_1,\ldots,T_m)$ of the LPT algorithm just prior to scheduling job t_n. Let $T_k = \min(T_1,\ldots,T_m)$. Then t_n is scheduled on machine k and $T_k + t_n = T_{LPT}(I)$ by lemma 1. Hence $t_1 + \ldots + t_{n-1} \geq m(T_{LPT}(I) - t_n)$ or

$$t_1 + \ldots + t_n \geq m\ T_{LPT}(I) - (m-1)\ t_n.$$

Next note that $T_{opt}(I) \geq (t_1 + \ldots + t_n)/m$, since every job has to executed on some machine and hence

$$((m-1)/m)\ t_n \geq T_{LPT}(I) - T_{opt}(I) > [1/3 - 1/(3m)]\ T_{opt}(I).$$

The last inequality follows from the fact that I is a counterexample. Thus $3t_n > T_{opt}(I)$. □

In lemma 3 we finish off the contradiction and show that the LPT algorithm indeed constructs optimal schedules if $T_{opt}(I)$ is small.

Lemma 3: If $T_{opt}(I) < 3t_n$ then $T_{LPT}(I) = T_{opt}(I)$.

Proof: If $S_{opt} = S_{LPT}$ then there is nothing to show. Assume otherwise. Since $t_1 \geq t_2 \geq \ldots \geq t_n$ there can be no more than two jobs scheduled on any machine. Hence $n \leq 2m$. We may assume $n = 2m$ by adding jobs $n+1,\ldots,2m$ with time requirements $t_{n+1} = \ldots = t_{2m} = 0$. The LPT algorithm schedules jobs j and $2m+1-j$ on machine j, $1 \leq j \leq m$. Let j be maximal such that $T_{LPT}(I) = t_j + t_{2m+1-j}$. Construct a graph G with nodes $V = [1...n]$ as follows. Draw a red edge (i,k) if $S_{opt}(i) = S_{opt}(k)$ and draw a green edge (i,k) if $S_{LPT}(i) = S_{LPT}(k)$, i.e. if $i + k = 2m + 1$. Since every node has degree exactly two in graph G (recall that exactly two jobs are scheduled on any machine by S_{opt} and S_{LPT}), the connected components of G are simple cycles. Consider the component containing node j. It contains nodes $j_1,...,j_\ell$, $2m+1-j_1,...,2m+1-j_\ell$ for some $j_1,...,j_\ell \in [1...m]$. Since the red edges also form a matching on these nodes there must be a red edge (i,k) such that $i \le j$ and $k \le 2m+1-j$. Hence $T_{opt}(I) \ge t_i + t_k \ge t_j + t_{2m+1-j} = L_{LPT}(I)$. □

Lemmas 1, 2 and 3 imply that I does not exist. □

In exercise 25 it is shown that the worst case performance of the LPT algorithm is indeed $1/3-1/(3m)$. The LPT algorithm processes long jobs first. This principle works quite well for a number of problems; cf. exercise 22 on bin packing and exercise 26 on the KNAPSACK problem. This suggests that we can do even better if we are very careful with the longest jobs, say if we schedule the longest k jobs optimally. This leads to the LPT(k)-algorithm: Schedule the k longest jobs optimally (in time m^k by branch and bound), then continue with LPT.

<u>Theorem 5:</u> The LPT(k) algorithm always produces an $(m-1)/(k+1)$-approximate schedule.

<u>Proof:</u> Let $t_1 \ge t_2 \ge ... \ge t_n$ be the time requirements of a set of n jobs and let $T_{LPT(k)}$ (T_{opt}) be the finishing time of the LPT(k) (optimal) schedule. We have to show that

$$T_{LPT(k)} - T_{opt} \le ((m-1)/(k+1))\ T_{opt}.$$

Let t be the length of an optimal schedule for jobs $1,...,k$. If $T_{LPT(k)} = t$ then the claim is obviously true. So assume otherwise. Let $j > k$ be a job with finishing time $T_{LPT(k)}$. Then all processors are busy up to time $T_{LPT(k)} - t_j$ and hence $(t_1 + ... + t_{j-1})/m \ge T_{LPT(k)} - t_j$. Also $T_{opt} \ge (t_1 + ... + t_j)/m$ and hence

$$T_{LPT(k)} - T_{opt} \le ((m-1)/m)\ t_j \le ((m-1)/m)\ t_{k+1}$$

$$\le (1-1/m)(m/(k+1))\ T_{opt} \le ((m-1)/(k+1)\ T_{opt}$$

The next to last inequality follows from $T_{opt} \geq (t_1 + \ldots + t_{k+1})/m \geq (k+1)t_{k+1}/m$. □

At this point we almost arrived at an approximation scheme for SIT(m), Scheduling Independent Tasks on m machines. Let $\varepsilon > 0$ be arbitrary. Choose k such that $(m-1)/(k+1) \leq \varepsilon$; $k = \lfloor (m-1)/\varepsilon \rfloor$ will certainly do. Then use the LPT(k) algorithm to construct an ε-approximate schedule. The running time of LPT(k) is $O(m^k)$ for finding an optimal schedule for the k longest jobs plus $O(n \log n)$ for sorting and scheduling the n-k remaining jobs. Thus total running time is $O(n \log n + m^k) = O(n \log n + m^{m/\varepsilon})$. This is polynomial in n for every fixed ε.

Theorem 6: There is a polynomial approximation scheme for SIT(m) which constructs ε-approximate solutions in time $O(n \log n + m^{m/\varepsilon})$ for any $\varepsilon > 0$.

Proof: By preceding discussion. □

Can we always turn an ε-approximate algorithm for some ε into a polynomial approximation scheme as we did for SIT(m)? Note that Δ TSP is not a counterexample; there we just do not know how to do better that 0.5 approximate solutions. There is no reason to believe that 0.5 is a boundary which stands up forever. However, our second NP-complete scheduling problem is an example.

Theorem 7: a) There is a 1-approximate linear time algorithm for Precedence Constrained Scheduling (PCS).

b) If there is an 1/4-approximate polynomial time algorithm for PCS then P = NP.

Proof: a) Consider any instance of PCS. Let n be the number of jobs, m the number of machines and R be the precedence relation on jobs. Let T_{opt} be the finishing time of an optimal schedule. For any job $i \in [1 \ldots n]$ define its depth by $\mathrm{depth}(i) = 1 + \max\{\mathrm{depth}(j);\ (j,i) \in R\}$. As always, the maximum of the empty set is defined to be zero. Then $T_{opt} \geq LB := \max(\lceil n/m \rceil, \mathrm{maxdepth})$ where $\mathrm{maxdepth} = \max\{\mathrm{depth}(i); 1 \leq i \leq n\}$. It remains to be shown that we can always schedule all jobs in $2 \cdot LB$ time units. For d, $1 \leq d \leq \mathrm{maxdepth}$ let $L_d = \{i;\ \mathrm{depth}(i) = d\}$ be the jobs of depth d. We schedule the jobs in L_d for time units

$\sum_{j<d} \lceil |L_j|/m \rceil + 1, \ldots, \sum_{j\le d} \lceil |L_j|/m \rceil$. Then the maximal time unit used is

$$\sum_{j\le \text{maxdepth}} \lceil |L_j|/m \rceil \le \sum_j (|L_j|/m+1) = n/m + \text{maxdepth} \le 2\ LB$$

b) Recall the NP-completeness proof of PCS (theorem VI.5.7.). The instances of PCS constructed in the reduction CLIQUE ≤ PCS had either finishing time three or four. More precisely, they had finishing time three iff we start with a graph which does have a clique and finishing time four otherwise. Suppose now that we have an 1/4-approximate algorithm for PCS. Then we can use it to solve CLIQUE because the approximation algorithm must be an exact algorithm on the instances constructed by the reduction. □

VI. 7.3 Full Approximation Schemes

We will now turn to the ultimate in approximation algorithms: full approximation schemes. We will also get to know a very important technique for approximation algorithms: scaling. Scaling is applicable to many problems; it is particularly appropriate when we have a pseudo-polynomial algorithm around.

In section VI.6.1. we described a pseudo-polynomial algorithm for the KNAPSACK problem. This was extended to the weighted KNAPSACK problem in exercise 15. Let $c_1, \ldots, c_n, w_1, \ldots, w_n, K$ be an instance I of the weighted KNAPSACK problem. Exercise 15 shows how to compute $C_{opt}(I) = \max\{\sum_i c_i x_i;\ x_i \in \{0,1\},\ \sum x_i w_i \le K\}$ in time $O(n\, C_{opt}) = O(n^2 \max c_i)$.

Let S be any integer. We scale the costs by S and obtain a scaled instance $I_S = (\lfloor c_1/S \rfloor, \ldots, \lfloor c_n/S \rfloor, w_1, \ldots, w_n, K)$. What does scaling do for us? First of all, the scaled instance can be solved by our pseudo-polynomial algorithm in time $O(n\, C_{opt}(I_S)) = O(n\, C_{opt}(I)/S)$, which can be made arbitrarily small by choosing S large enough. Secondly the optimal solution for the scaled instance is a very good solution of the original problem. More precisely, let $(x_1, \ldots, x_n) \in \{0,1\}^n$ be such that $C_{opt}(I_S) = \sum_i x_i \lfloor c_i/S \rfloor$ and $\sum_i x_i w_i \le K$ and let $(y_1, \ldots, y_n) \in \{0,1\}^n$ be such that $C_{opt}(I) = \sum y_i c_i$ and $\sum y_i w_i \le K$. Then

$$\begin{aligned} C_{opt}(I) &= \sum y_i c_i \\ &\ge \sum x_i c_i \qquad \text{, since } (y_1, \ldots, y_n) \text{ is optimal for I} \end{aligned}$$

$$= S\ \Sigma\ x_i c_i/S$$
$$\geq S\ \Sigma\ x_i \lfloor c_i/S \rfloor$$
$$\geq S\ \Sigma\ y_i \lfloor c_i/S \rfloor \qquad \text{,since } (x_1,\ldots,x_n) \text{ is optimal for } I_S$$
$$\geq S\ \Sigma\ y_i (c_i/S-1)$$
$$\geq C_{opt}(I) - nS$$

Thus $(C_{opt}(I) - \Sigma\ x_i c_i)/C_{opt}(I) \leq nS/C_{opt}(I)$. We summarize in

Lemma 1: Let S be any integer. Then in time $O(n\ C_{opt}(I)/S)$ we can compute an $nS/C_{opt}(I)$-approximate solution, namely $\Sigma\ x_i c_i$ where $(x_1,\ldots,x_n)$ is the optimal solution vector for the scaled problem.

It remains to choose S appropriately. Let $\varepsilon > 0$ be arbitrary. Setting $S = \varepsilon\ C_{opt}(I)/n$ gives us an ε-approximate algorithm with running time $O(n^2/\varepsilon)$. There is a catch, however; we do not know $C_{opt}(I)$. After all the purpose of the algorithm is to approximate $C_{opt}(I)$. The way out is to use a reasonable approximation for $C_{opt}(I)$ in the definition of S.

A first attempt is to use $S = \lfloor \varepsilon \max c_i/n \rfloor \leq \varepsilon\ C_{opt}(I)/n$. Then we obtain an ε-approximate algorithm with running time $O(n\ C_{opt}(I)/S) = O(n^2(\max c_i)/S) = O(n^3/\varepsilon)$ which is much worse than what we would get with the optimal choice of S. The reason is of course that we used only very weak bounds on $C_{opt}(I)$, namely $\max c_i \leq C_{opt}(I) \leq n \max c_i$. A much better bound is provided by exercise 26. There it is shown that C with $C_{opt}(I) \geq C \geq C_{opt}(I)/2$ can be computed in time $O(n \log n)$. Setting $S = \lfloor \varepsilon\ C/n \rfloor$ we obtain an ε-approximate algorithm with running time $O(n\ C_{opt}/S) = O(n^2/\varepsilon)$.

Theorem 8: The weighted KNAPSACK problem has a full polynomial approximation scheme; more precisely, an ε-approximate solution can be computed in time $O(n^2/\varepsilon)$ for any $\varepsilon > 0$.

Proof: By the discussion above. □

The technique described above is not only applicable to the weighted KNAPSACK problem. We can rather state quite generally: Scaling + Pseudo-polynomial algorithm ➡ good approximation algorithm (cf. exercises 27 and 28). In fact, the connection between pseudo-polynomial algorithms and full approximation schemes is even stronger. The existence of a full approximation scheme implies the existence of a pseudo-polynomial algorithm.

Theorem 9: Let (Q,C) be a polynomially bounded minimization problem. For instance x let optval(x) be the cost of an optimal solution for x. If (Q,c) has a full polynomial approximation scheme and optval(x) is polynomially bounded in the size(x) of x and the largest integer number(x) appearing in x then (Q,c) has a pseudo-polynomial algorithm.

Proof: Let A be a full approximation scheme for (Q,c). Choose $\varepsilon = 1/(p(\text{size}(x), \text{number}(x)) + 1)$ where polynomial p is such that $\text{optval}(x) \le p(\text{size}(x), \text{number}(x))$ for all instances x. Let y be the solution produced by A on inputs x and ε. Then

$$\begin{aligned} 0 &\le c(x,y) - \text{optval}(x) && \text{,by definition of optval}(x) \\ &\le \varepsilon \cdot \text{optval}(x) && \text{,since A is an approximation scheme} \\ &< 1 && \text{,by definition of } \varepsilon. \end{aligned}$$

Thus c(x,y) = optval(x), y is an optimal solution for x. Furthermore, the running time of A on inputs x and ε is bounded by a polynomial in size(x) and $1/\varepsilon$ which in turn is a polynomial in size(x) and number(x). So (Q,c) has a pseudo-polynomial algorithm. □

Theorem 9 has strong implications for strongly NP-complete problems. They cannot have a full polynomial approximation scheme.

Theorem 10: SIT does not have a full polynomial approximation scheme (provided that $P \neq NP$).

Proof: SIT satisfies the assumption of theorem 9. Note that the total time requirement of all jobs is certainly an upper bound for the finishing time. Also SIT is strongly NP-complete (theorem VI.6.3.) and therefore does not have a pseudo-polynomial algorithm (provided that $P \neq NP$, theorem IV.6.2.). □

VI.8. The Landscape of Complexity Classes

The main concern of this chapter were NP-complete problems and how to cope with them. In this section we go beyond NP-completeness and relate the complexity classes P and NP to various other classes. Moreover, we list a number of problems and give their status with respect to these classes.

The following diagram shows a relevant part of the landscape of complexity classes.

$$
\begin{array}{ccccccccc}
 & & RP & \subseteq & NP = \Sigma_1 \subseteq \Sigma_2 \subseteq \Sigma_3 \subseteq \Sigma_4 \subseteq & \ldots & & & \\
 & \nearrow & & \searrow & & \searrow & & \nearrow & \\
P \subseteq LVP = & RP \cap co-RP & & & BPP & & & & PSPACE \\
 & \searrow & & \nearrow & & \nearrow & & \searrow & \\
 & & co-RP & \subseteq & co-NP = \Pi_1 \subseteq \Pi_2 \subseteq \Pi_3 \subseteq \Pi_4 \subseteq & \ldots & & &
\end{array}
$$

The classes P and NP were defined above. The class PSPACE is the set of languages which can be recognized by polynomially space bounded Turing machines. For class PSPACE it is irrelevant whether deterministic or nondeterministic machines are considered (Savitch (70)).
The classes $\Sigma_1, \Sigma_2, \Sigma_3, \ldots$ and $\Pi_1, \Pi_2, \Pi_3, \ldots$ form the polynomial hierarchy (Stockmeyer/Meyer (73)). These classes are defined as follows:

$\Sigma_i = \{L;\ L \subseteq \Gamma^*$ for some finite alphabet Γ and there is some polynomial time computable predicate $p(x,y_1,\ldots,y_i)$ and a polynomial q such that for all $x \in \Gamma^*$:
$x \in L$ iff $\exists y_1\ \forall y_2\ \exists y_3 \ldots (|y_1| \le q(|x|)$ and
$\ldots\ |y_i| \le q(|x|)$ and $p(x,y_1,\ldots,y_i))\}$

$\Pi_i = co - \Sigma_i$

where $co - C = \{\Gamma^* - L;\ L \in C$ and Γ a finite alphabet$\}$ for any class C of languages. The languages in Σ_i are defined by formulae with i alternations of quantifiers starting with an existential quantifier. The quantifiers range over all strings whose length is polynomially bounded in the length of x. Similarly, the languages in Π_i are defined by formulae with i alternations of quantifiers starting with an universal quantifier. In theorem 1 of section 2 we proved $NP = \Sigma_1$.

The inclusions $\Sigma_i \subseteq \Sigma_{i+1}$, $\Sigma_i \subseteq \Pi_{i+1}$, $\Pi_i \subseteq \Sigma_{i+1}$, and $\Sigma_i \subseteq$ PSPACE for for all i are obvious. It is not known whether the polynomial hierarchy is infinite or collapses at some finite level.

The remaining classes are defined by probabilistic machines (cf. section I.2).
We have

BPP = $\{L;\ L \subseteq \Gamma^*$ for some finite alphabet Γ and there is a polynomial computable predicate $p(x,y)$ and a polynomial q such that
$x \in L \Rightarrow |\{y;\ |y| = q(|x|) \text{ and } p(x,y)\}| \geq 3/4\ |\Gamma|^{q(|x|)}$
$x \notin L \Rightarrow |\{y;\ |y| = q(|x|) \text{ and } \neg p(x,y)\}| \geq 3/4\ |\Gamma|^{q(|x|)}\}$

Thus a language is in BPP (bounded probability of error) if it can be recognized by a probabilistic machine whose worst-case running time is polynomially bounded and whose answers are reliable with probability 3/4. Algorithms in this class are also referred to as polynomially bounded Monte Carlo algorithms. In the definition of RP (random P) we allow only one-sided error.

RP = $\{L;\ L \subseteq \Gamma^*$ for some finite alphabete Γ and there is a polynomial time computable predicate $p(x,y)$ and a polynomial q such that
$x \in L \Rightarrow |\{y;\ |y| = q(|x|) \text{ and } p(x,y)\}| \geq 3/4\ |\Gamma|^{q(|x|)}$
$x \notin L \Rightarrow |\{y;\ |y| = q(|x|) \text{ and } \neg p(x,y)\}| = |\Gamma|^{q(|x|)}\}$

Thus a language L is in RP if a string $x \in L$ is accepted with probability at least 3/4 and a string outside L is never accepted. In other words, there is a probabilistic algorithm whose worst-case running time is bounded by a polynomial. Moreover, its "yes-answers" are completely reliable but its "no-answers" are not, i.e. there is a possibility that $x \in L$ and the algorithm outputs no. However, the probability that an element $x \in L$ is declared to be outside L is at most 1/4. The inclusions RP $\subseteq$ BPP, co - RP $\subseteq$ BPP, RP $\subseteq$ NP and co - RP $\subseteq$ co - NP are obvious. Again it is not known whether any of these inclusions is proper. We remark in passing that the quantitiy 3/4 in the definition of RP and BPP is not sacred. Any real a with $1/2 < a < 1$ could be taken instead of 3/4. This follows immediately from the results of section I.2. Also, we might require that only the expected running time is bounded by a polynomial without any change in the language classes.

Finally, in the definition of class LVP (Las Vegas P) we allow no probability of error and require only that the expected running time is polynomially bounded.

LVP = {L; $L \subseteq \Gamma^*$ for some finite alphabet Γ and the characteristic function of L is computed by a Las Vegas algorithm (cf. section I.2) whose running time is bounded by a polynomial}

The following theorem states the two non-trivial inclusions in the diagram above.

Theorem 1: a) LVP = RP $\cap$ co - RP

b) BPP $\subseteq \Sigma_2$

Proof: a) We show LVP $\subseteq$ RP, LVP $\subseteq$ co - RP and RP $\cap$ co - RP $\subseteq$ LVP. Consider LVP $\subseteq$ RP first. If L $\subseteq$ LVP then we can recognize L by an algorithm A whose expected running time is bounded by a polynomial, say q, and whose outputs are completely reliable. Consider the following algorithm A': On input x it runs algorithm A for at most $10q(|x|)$ steps. If A has terminated before that time (and this occurs with probability exceeding 9/10) then A' outputs whatever A outputs. If A has not terminated within $10q(|x|)$ steps then A' outputs no. In this way the yes-answers of A' are completely reliable but the no-answers are not. However, the probability of a no - answer for $x \in L$ is at most 1/10. Thus $L \in$ RP and hence LVP $\subseteq$ RP.

A similar argument shows LVP $\subseteq$ co - RP. (A' outputs yes if the clock is exhausted).

We turn to the inclusion RP $\cap$ co - RP $\subseteq$ LVP next. Let $L \in$ RP $\cap$ co - RP. Then we have probabilistic algorithms A_1 and A_2 such that

1) the worst-case running time of A_1 and A_2 is bounded by a polynomial, say q,

2) the yes-answers of A_1 and the no-answers of A_2 are reliable,

3) the probability that A_1 gives a wrong answer is at most 1/4 and the probability that A_2 gives a wrong answer is at most 1/4.

We show how to recognize L with zero probability of error and polynomial average running time. Let x be arbitrary. Consider the following experiment.

Choose a random y with $|y| = q(|x|)$ and compute $A_1(x,y)$ and $A_2(x,y)$. This takes time $O(q(|x|)$. If $A_1(x,y)$ = yes then x belongs to L and if $A_2(x,y)$ = no then x does not belong to L (note that $A_1(x,y)$ = yes and $A_2(x,y)$ = no simultaneously is impossible). In either case we have decided the membership of x with respect to L correctly. The final case to consider is $A_1(x,y)$ = no and $A_2(x,y)$ = yes. Then $x \in L$ and $x \notin L$ are both conceivable. If $x \in L$ then the answer $A_1(x,y)$ = no is wrong and this event has probability at most 1/4 and if $x \notin L$ then the answer $A_2(x,y)$ = yes is wrong and this event has probability at most 1/4. In either case, we see that the probability that we cannot decide the membership of x in L is at most 1/4. Hence the probability that i experiments are needed to decide membership is at most $1/4^{i-1}$ and hence the expected number of experiments needed is $\sum_{i \geq 0} i/4^{i-1} = O(1)$. This proves $L \in LVP$.

b) A proof can be found in Sipser (83) or Lautemann (84) □

None of the inclusions in the diagram above are known to be proper. However, the inclusions are not independent. For example, it is known that RP = NP implies $\Sigma_2 = \Sigma_3 = \Sigma_4 = \ldots$ (Karp/Lipton (80)). We will now turn to problems and give a list of problems and their status with respect to these classes.

Name: Quantified Boolean Formulae (QBF)

Input: A quantified boolean formula of the form $Q_1x_1\ Q_2x_2 \ldots Q_mx_m$ $E(x_1,\ldots,x_m,y_1,\ldots,y_n)$ where E is a boolean expression over operators and, or, not, $x_1,\ldots,x_m,y_1,\ldots,y_n$ are boolean variables, and $Q_i \in \{\exists,\forall\}$ is a quantifier.

Output: Yes, if the formula is satisfiable, and no, otherwise.

Theorem 2 (Stockmeyer/Meyer (73): QBF is PSPACE-complete.

There are no complete problems known for the classes of the polynomial hierarchy, except for classes Σ_1 (NP-complete) and Σ_2.

Name: Uniquely optimal Traveling Salesman Tour (UOTS)
Input: An instance of the traveling salesman problem
Output: Yes, if there is a unique optimal tour, and no, otherwise

Theorem 3 (Papadimitriou (82)): UOTS is Σ_2-complete.

Another example of a Σ_2-complete problem is given in Huynh (82): the inequivalence problem for context-free grammars with one letter terminal alphabet.

For the probabilistic classes LVP, RP, co - RP, BPP there are no known complete problems. In fact, Adleman (78) gives strong reasons that these classes cannot contain complete problems.

Name: PRIMES
Input: an integer n in binary notation.
Output: yes, if n is a prime, and no, otherwise.

Theorem 4 a) PRIMES $\in$ co - NP
b) PRIMES $\in$ NP
c) PRIMES $\in$ co - RP

Proof: a) is trivial, b) can be found in Pratt (75) and c) can be found in Solovay/Strassen (77). We give a very brief sketch of part c). For integers p and q which are relatively prime the Legendre symbol (q/p) is defined by

$$(q/p) = \begin{cases} 1 & \text{if } q \text{ is a quadratic residue mod } p\text{, i.e. } q = x^2 \bmod p \text{ for some } x \\ -1 & \text{otherwise.} \end{cases}$$

An efficient algorithm for computing the Legendre symbol is well-known; it is based on the law of reciprocity, namely $(q/p) = -(p/q)$ if $p = q = 3 \bmod 4$ and $(q/p) = (p/q)$ otherwise. Furthermore, when $q > p$ and hence $q = mp + r$ for some $r < p$ then $(q/p) = (r/p)$. These three relations immediately suggest a polynomial time algorithm for computing the Legendre symbol which is similar to the Euclidian algorithm for greatest common divisors.

The important observation is now that if p is prime then

$(a/p) = a^{(p-1)/2}$ mod p for all a, $1 \leq a \leq p - 1$. However, if p is not prime then the above relation holds for at most half the a's which are relatively prime to p. This follows from the fact that the set of a's for which the above relation holds is a proper subgroup of the multiplicative group of integers which are relatively prime to p.

This suggests the following algorithm. In order to check primality of p select a random integer a, $1 \leq a < p$. If a and p are not relatively prime (a gcd calculation) then p is composite. Otherwise we check the relation $(a/p) = a^{(p-1)/2}$ mod p; note that $a^{(p-1)/2}$ mod p can be computed by repeated squaring (cf. section I.1). If the inequality does not hold then p is composite. If the equality holds then p may be prime or composite. However, if p is composite then the equality holds with probability at most 1/2. Repeating the experiment for several a's reduces the probability of error below 1/4. Hence COMPOSITE $\in$ RP or PRIMES $\in$ co - RP. □

Another interesting example of a problem in co - RP is given by

Name: Checking Polynomial Identities (CPI)
Input: an identity of the form $Q \equiv P$ where Q and P are expressions formed from real variables $x_1, x_2, \ldots$ using the operators +, -, and $\cdot$.
Output: yes, if the identity is true, and no otherwise.

Theorem 5 (Schwartz (80)): CPI $\in$ co - RP

We close this section with some problems which were recently shown to be in P.

Name: Linear Programming (LP)
Input: an integer matrix A and an integer vector b
Output: yes, if there is a real vector x with $Ax \leq b$.

Theorem 6 (Khachiyan (79)): LP $\in$ P

If we require the solution vector to be integer then we arrive at the integer programming problem. It is NP-complete as was shown in section 5. However, for every fixed dimension there is a polynomial algorithm.

Name: Integer Programming in d-dimensional space (IPd)
Input: An n by d integer matrix A and an integer vector b.
Output: yes, if there is a d-dimensional integer vector x with
$Ax \le b$, and no, otherwise.

Theorem 7 (Lenstra (84)): IPd $\in$ P for every fixed d.

An improved algorithm for IPd can be found in Kannan (83). Finally, we want to mention the graph isomorphism problem.

Name: Graph Isomorphism (GI)
Input: Undirected Graphs $G_1 = (V_1,E_1)$ and $G_2 = (V_2,E_2)$.
Output: yes, if G_1 and G_2 are isomorphic, and no, otherwise. G_1 and G_2 are isomorphic if there is a bijection $a: V_1 \to V_2$ with $(v,w) \in E_1$ iff $(a(v),a(w)) \in E_2$.

Clearly, GI $\in$ NP. It is not known whether GI is NP-complete. Various special cases of GI have been shown to be in P, e.g. graphs of bounded valence (Luks (80)), and k-contractible graphs (Miller (83)).

VI. 9. Exercises

1) Let $L = \{w ¢ v;\ w,v \in \{0,1\}^* \text{ and } w \neq v\}$. Describe deterministic and nondeterministic TMs which accept L. Run time?

2) Show that $T(n) = n$, $T(n) = n^2$, $T(n) = n\lfloor\log n\rfloor$, $T(n) = 2^n$ are step functions.

3) Consider RAMs where the only arithmetic operations are addition and subtraction. Show that theorem VI.1.1. is true for unit-cost RAMs.

4) The CLIQUE optimization problem is to find a largest clique in an undirected graph. Prove lemmas 2 and 3 of VI.2. for CLIQUE.

5) Same as exercise 4) but for the KNAPSACK problem.

6) Show that SAT(2) is in P. (Hint: Let α be a formula with at most 2 literals per clause. Let $x_1,\dots,x_n$ be the variables occuring in α. Construct a directed graph with nodes $x_1,\dots,x_n$, $\overline{x}_1,\dots,\overline{x}_n$ as follows. If $y_1 \vee y_2$ is a clause of α then add directed edges $\overline{y}_1 \rightarrow y_2$ (interpretation: if $\overline{y}_1$ is true then y_2 must be true) and $\overline{y}_2 \rightarrow y_1$. Then α is satisfiable iff there is no cycle of the form $x_i \rightarrow \dots \rightarrow \overline{x}_i \rightarrow \dots \rightarrow x_i$. Cycles of this form can be detected by determining the strongly connected components of the graph.

7) Show that the weighted Knapsack problem is NP-complete.

Name: Weighted Knapsack

Input: Integers $w_1,\dots,w_n$ (the weights), $c_1,\dots,c_n$ (the costs), K,C

Question: Are there $x_i \in \{0,1\}$, $1 \le i \le n$, such that $\Sigma\, w_i x_i \le K$ and $\Sigma\, c_i x_i \ge C$?

8) Show that partition is NP-complete

Name: Partition

Input: Integers $a_1,\dots,a_n$

Question: Is there $I \subseteq [1\dots n]$ such that $\sum_{i\in I} a_i = \sum_{i\notin I} a_i$?

9) Show that Chromatic Number is NP-complete

Name: Chromatic Number

Input: Undirected graph $G = (V,E)$, integer k

Question: Is there a node coloring with at most k colors, i.e. is there a mapping $c: V \rightarrow [1\dots k]$ such that $c(v) \neq c(w)$ for all $(v,w) \in E$?

(Hint: Show SAT(3) $\le$ Chromatic Number)

1o) Show that Planar 3-SAT is NP-complete

Name: Planar 3-SAT

Input: A formula α in CNF such that the following bipartite graph (V,E) is planar. V is the set of variables and clauses of α and $(v,c) \in E$ for variable v and clause c if either v or $\overline{v}$ occurs in c.

Question: Is α satisfiable?

11) Show that Bandwidth is NP-complete

Name: Bandwidth

Input: Undirected graph $G = (V,E)$, integer K

Question: Is there a bijection $f: V \to [1...|V|]$ such that $|f(u) - f(v)| \le K$ for all $(u,v) \in E$.

12) Show that Cycle Cover is NP-complete

Name: Cycle Cover

Input: Undirected graph $G = (V,E)$, integer K

Question: Is there a set $V' \subseteq V$, $|V'| = k$, such that every cycle in G contains at least one node in V'.

13) Show that SIT(2) (Scheduling on <u>two</u> machines) is in P.
(Hint: Schedule by depth in the graph $G = (V,E)$).

14) Eulerian Cycle is in P

Name: Eulerian Cycle

Input: Undirected graph $G = (V,E)$

Question: Is there a cycle which uses every edge exactly once, i.e. is it possible to order $E = \{e_1,...,e_m\}$ such that e_i and e_{i+1} have a common endpoint, $1 \le i < m$.

(Hint: Show that a Eulerian Cycle exists iff every node has even degree). Derive a linear time algorithm to construct a Eulerian Cycle.

15) Design a pseudo-polynomial time algorithm for the weighted Knapsack optimization problem, i.e. given $w_1,...,w_n$, $c_1,...,c_n$, K compute C_{opt} = $\max\{\sum_{i=1}^{n} c_i x_i;\ x_i \in \{0,1\}$ and $\sum w_i x_i \le K\}$. (Hint: For $0 \le c < \infty$ and $0 \le j \le n$ let $F(c,j) = \min(\{\infty\} \cup \{w;$ there is $(x_1,...,x_j) \in \{0,1\}^j$ such that $\sum_{i=1}^{j} c_i x_i = c$ and $\sum_{i=1}^{j} w_i x_i = w\})$. Then $F(0,0) = 0$ and $F(c,0) = \infty$ for $c > 0$ and $F(c,j+1) = \min\{F(c,j),\ F(c-c_{j+1}) + w_{j+1}\}$. Show that the relevant part of table F, i.e. $F(c,j) \le K$, can be computed in time $O(n\ C_{opt}) = O(n^2 \max c_i)$. Also, vector $(x_1,...,x_n)$ can be found in that time bound).

16) Design a pseudo-polynomial time algorithm for Scheduling Independent Tasks for fixed number m of machines. (Hint: Let $t_1,\ldots,t_n$ be the time requirements of n jobs and let T be the deadline. For $i \in [0\ldots n]$ let $f(i) = \{(T_1,\ldots,T_m);\ T_j \le T$ and there is a partial schedule $PS: [1\ldots i] \to [1\ldots m]$ such that $T_j = \Sigma\ \{t_k;\ k \le i$ and $PS(k) = j\}$ for $1 \le j \le m\}$. Then $f(0) = (0,0,\ldots,0)$ and $f(i+1) = \{(T_1',\ldots,T_m');$ there is $(T_1,\ldots,T_m) \in f(i)$ and $k \in [1\ldots m]$ such that $T_k' = T_k + t_{i+1}$ and $T_j' = T_j$ for $j \neq k\}$. Derive an $O(nm(T+1)^m)$ algorithm for these observations).

17) Let $G = (V,E)$ be a directed graph, let s and t be distinguished nodes and let $c: E \to \mathbb{R}_+$ be a non negative cost function on the edges. For a node $v \in V$ let $\mu(s,v)$ be the cost of the least cost path from s to v. A function $g: V \to \mathbb{R}_{\ge 0}$ is called an estimator if $g(v) \le \{\min c(p);$ p is a path from v to t$\}$. In section IV.7.2 we treated algorithms for comting $\mu(s,t)$ using an estimator g.

a) Formulate Branch and Bound in the terminology of finding least cost paths. What is c and g in the case of the branch and bound algorithm for the traveling salesman problem discussed in section 6.2.

b) Are the estimators which arise from the branch and bound algorithms consistent in the sense of section IV.7.2, i.e. $g(v) + c(v,w) \ge g(w)$ for all edges $(v,w) \in E$?

18) Use the branch and Bound algorithm of section VI.5. to solve the following problem with n + 6 cities $v_0,v_1,v_2,w_0,w_1,w_2,x_0,\ldots,x_{n-1}$.

$\text{dist}(v_i,v_{i+1 \bmod 3}) = 2$		$i = 0,1,2$
$\text{dist}(v_i,w_i) = 1$		$i = 0,1$
$\text{dist}(v_2,w_2) = 0$		
$\text{dist}(w_i,v_i) = 2$		$i = 0,1,2$
$\text{dist}(w_i,w_{i+1 \bmod 3}) = 1$		$i = 0,1,2$

$$\begin{array}{ll} dist(w_i, x_j) = 1 & \text{for } i = 0,1,2 \\ dist(x_j, w_i) = 1 & j = 0,1,\ldots n-1 \\ dist(x_j, w_j) = 1 & j = 0,1,\ldots n-1 \\ dist(x_j, x_k) = 0 & \text{for } j,k = 0,\ldots,n-1 \end{array}$$

The remaining distances are infinite. Run the algorithm with starting points v_1 and v_3 respectively and always proceed to the city with smallest distance.

19) Design an $O((\log sopt)^{sopt} |E|)$ algorithm for finding an optimal cycle cover of an undirected graph (cf. exercise 12). (Hint: Use the following graph-theoretic lemma: If G is a graph of minimum degree three and if G has p pairwise disjoint cycles then G has a cycle of length $O(\log p)$. Also a shortest cycle containing a fixed node v can be found in time $O(|E|)$ by breadth-first search).

20) Repeat the Branch-and-Bound algorithm for TSP using the weighted matching problem as a lower bound on cost.

21) Design a class of examples where the once-around-the-tree algorithm for ΔTSP actually constructs a tour which has almost twice the length of the optimum. Similarly for the 0,5 approximate algorithm.

22) Bin Packing

Input: Integers $\ell_1,\ldots,\ell_n$ and bound L
Output: Minimal m such that there is a mapping $S: [1\ldots n] \to [1\ldots m]$ with $\Sigma \{\ell_i;\ S(i) = j\} \le L$ for all j, $1 \le j \le m$

a) Show that the recognition version (m is additional input) is NP-complete.

b) Design approximation algorithms for bin packing. (Hint: the following strategies are good: Start with empty bins 1,2,3,... . Add objects one by one. When a new object is added place it into the least numbered (first fit) or the fullest (best fit) bin which can still take the object. These two rules can either be applied to the objects in any order or to the objects in order of decreasing length. First fit and best fit use at most $(17/10)\ m_{opt} + 2$ bins and first fit and best fit decreasing use at most $(11/9)\ m_{opt} + 2$ bins.

23) Design a 1-approximate algorithm for vertex cover (Hint: start with graph $G = (V,E)$; take any edge and remove both endpoints and all edges adjacent to them from the graph. Repeat).

24) Design a $g(x) = O((\log x)^2)$ - approximate algorithm for cycle cover (exercise 12 and 19). (Hint: start with graph $G = (V,E)$; search for shortest cycle and remove all nodes of the cycle. Repeat).

25) (Worst case performance of LPT algorithm). Let $n = 2m + 1$ and $t_i = 2m - \lfloor (i+1)/2 \rfloor$, $1 \le i \le 2m$, $t_{2m+1} = m$. Construct optimal and LPT schedule.

26) Let $w_1,\dots,w_n,c_1,\dots,c_n$, K be an instance of the weighted Knapsack problem (cf. exercises 7 and 15). Assume w.l.o.g. that $c_1/w_1 \ge c_2/w_2 \ge \dots \ge c_n/w_n$ and $w_i \le K$. Consider the following algorithm.

```
c ← 0; W ← 0
for i from 1 to n
do    if W + w_i ≤ K
      then x_i ← 1; C ← C + c_i
      else x_i ← 0
      fi
od
C ← max  ({C} ∪ {c_i ; 1 ≤ i ≤ n})
```

Let C_{alg} be the value of C after termination and let $C_{opt} = \max\{\sum_i c_i y_i;\ y_i \in \{0,1\}$ and $\sum w_i y_i \le K\}$. Show $C_{opt} \ge C_{alg} \ge C_{opt}/2$, i.e. the algorithm above is 0,5-approximate. (Hint: Let $(y_1,\dots,y_n)$ be an optimal solution, and let i be minimal such that $x_{i+1} = 0$. Then $i \ge 1$, $w_1 + \dots + w_i \le K < w_1 + \dots + w_i + w_{i+1}$, and $C_{alg} \ge c_1 + \dots + c_i$. Also $C_{opt} = \sum c_j y_j = \sum_{j \le i} c_j + \sum_{j \le i} (c_j/w_j) w_j (y_j - 1) + \sum_{j>i} (c_j/w_j) w_j y_j \le \sum_{j \le i} c_j + (c_{i+1}/w_{i+1}) (\sum_{j \le i} w_j (y_j - 1) + \sum_{j \ge i} w_j y_j) \le C_{alg} + (c_{i+1}/w_{i+1}) (\sum_j w_j y_j - \sum_{j \le i} w_j) \le C_{alg} + (c_{i+1}/w_{i+1}) (K - \sum_{j \le i} w_j) \le C_{alg} + (c_{i+1}/w_{i+1}) w_{i+1} \le C_{alg} + c_{i+1} \le 2C_{alg}$). □

27) Describe a full approximation scheme for the Knapsack problem (Hint: Use scaling and the pseudo-polynomial algorithm for Knapsack).

28) Describe a full approximation scheme for SIT(m). (Hint: Use scaling, the pseudo-polynomial algorithm from exercise 16 and the LPT algorithm to get a good initial value of T_{opt}).

VI. 10. Bibliographic Notes

A detailed treatment of Turing machines can be found in the books by Hopcroft/Ullman (69) and Paul (78). The connection between recognition and optimization problems, in particular the concept of self-reducibility, is treated by Schnorr (76). Ladner/Lynch/Selman (74), Ladner (75) and Mehlhorn (76) investigate the properties of polynomial transformations. Theorem 5 (NP-completeness of SAT) is by St. Cook (71). Most NP-complete problems of section 5 are taken from the paper of R. Karp (72). NP-complete scheduling problems can be found in J. Ullmann (75), Planar 3-SAT is from D., Lichtenstein (1982) and Bandwith is from Papadimitriou (76). The concept of strong NP-completeness was introduced by Garey/Johnson (78). Their book is also an extensive treatment of NP-completeness. Held/Karp describe the dynamic programming approach to TSP, a more detailed treatment of branch-and-bound methods for TSP is contained in Christofides' book. Christofides is also the author of the 0,5-approximate algorithm for ΔTSP. Theorem 4 of section 6 and exercises 19 and 24 are from B. Monien (82), exercise 17 is from N. Nillson (71), and exercise 22 is from Johnson et. al. (74). De la Vargee/Lueker (81) describe a full approximation scheme for bin packing, the approximate algorithms for SIT are taken from Graham (69), and the full approximation scheme for Knapsack is by Ibarra/Kim (75) and Lawler (77).

IX. Algorithmic Paradigms

There are basically two ways for structuring a book on data structures and algorithms: problem or paradigm orientéd. We have mostly followed the first alternative because it allows for a more concise treatment. However, at certain occassions (e.g. section VIII.4 on the sweep paradigm in computational geometry) we have also followed the second approach. In this last chapter of the book we attempt to review the entire book from the paradigm oriented point of view.

Solving an algorithmic problem means to search for a solution to the problem within a set of possible candidates (= search space, state space).

Exhaustive search, i. e. a complete scan of the state space, is the most obvious searching method. Pure exhaustive search is rarely efficient and should only be used for small state spaces. We found several ways of improving upon exhaustive search, most notably branch and bound, tabulation, and dynamic programming. In the branch and bound approach (VI.6.2) to optimization problems one explores the state space in the order of decreasing promise, i. e. one has the means of estimating the quality of partial solutions and always works on the partial solution with maximal promise. The precision of the search depends on the quality of the estimates. It is usually quite difficult (or even impossible) to analyse the complexity of branch and bound algorithms in a satisfying way.

In more structured state spaces one can use dynamic programming and tabulation (III.4.1, IV.7.3, and VI.6.1). Dynamic programming is particularly useful when the problem space ist structured by size in a natural way and when solutions to larger problems are easily obtained from solutions to (all, sufficiently many) smaller problems. In this situation it is natural to solve all conceivable subproblems in order of increasing size in a systematic way. The efficiency of dynamic programming is directly related to the size of the state space. We encountered a large state space in the application to the travelling salesman problem (VI.6.1) and a fairly small state space in the application to optimum search trees (III.4.1) and least cost paths (IV.7.3). In some occassions, e. g. III.4.1, the search could be restricted to a suitably chosen subset of the state space.

Tabulation (III.4.1) is a general method of obtaining dynamic programming algorithms from top-down exhaustive search algorithms. The idea is to store the solutions to all solved subproblems in a table for latter look-up. We have used this idea for converting a backtracking algorithm for optimum search trees into the dynamic programming algorithm and for simulating 2-way deterministic pushdown automata in linear time on a RAM. The latter simulation led to the linear time pattern matching algorithm.

The divide - and - conquer paradigm is also applied to problem spaces which are structured by size. A problem instance is solved by generating several subproblems (divide), solving the subproblems (conquer), and combining the answer to the subproblems to an answer for the original problem instance (merge). The efficiency of the method is determined by the cost of generating the subproblems, the number and the size of the subproblems, and the cost of merging the answers. Divide - and - conquer algorithms lead to recursive programs and their analysis leads to recursion equations. We discussed recursion equations in sections II.1.3 and VII.2.2. The paradigm of divide - and - conquer was used very frequently in this book: in sorting and selection algorithms (II.1.2, II.1.3, and II.4), in all data-structures based upon trees (III.3 to III.7, VII.2.1 and VII.2.2, and VIII.5.1), in the planar separator theorem and its applications (IV.10), in the matrix multiplication algorithms (V.4), and in the divide - and conquer algorithms for computational geometry (VIII.5.2). Finally, the treatment of decomposable searching problems and dynamization (VII.1) has a very close relationship to the divide - and - conquer paradigm. In most applications of the paradigm a natural structure of the problem instances was used for the division step. For example, if the problem instance is a tuple then we can split the tuple into its first and its second half (merge sort, binary search, matrix multiplication,...) and if the problem instance is a set of objects from an ordered set then we can split the set into its lower and its upper half (the linear time selection algorithm, applications in geometry,...). The situation was slightly different in multidimensional divide - and - conquer (VII.2.2). There we frequently solved an instance of size n in d-dimensional space by generating two d-dimensional subproblems of size about n/2 and one (d-1)-dimensional subproblem of size n. Another interesting application of the paradigm is to planar graphs. We have seen two strategies. The first strategy is given by the planar separator theorem of section IV.10.2. It allows us to split a planar graph of n nodes into two subgraphs of about half the size by the removal of only $O(\sqrt{n})$ nodes. Moreover, the separating set can be determined in linear time. We used the planar separator theorem in several efficient algorithms on planar graphs, e. g. least cost path, chromatic number, ... The second strategy is given by the fact that a planar graph always contains a large set of independent nodes of small degree. We used this fact in searching planar subdivisions (VIII.3.2.1) and in the hierarchical representation of convex polyhedra (VIII, exercise 2).

Trees are a prime example for the divide - and - conquer paradigm. In trees one either organizes the universe (section III.1 on TRIES) or one organizes the set to be stored in the tree. The latter approach was used in sections III.3 to III.7 and leads to balanced trees. In these trees one chooses an element of the set for the root which balances the subproblems. In balanced trees for unweighted data balancing is done either according to the cardinality of the subproblems (weight - balanced trees) or according to the height of the subtrees (height - balanced trees). In trees for weighted data balancing is done according to the probability of the subproblems. We have also seen on two occassions (III.6.1 on weighted dynamic trees for multidimensional searching and VIII.5.1.3 on segment trees) that search structures for unweighted complex data can sometimes be constructed from trees for simpler but weighted data. The former approach, i. e. organizing the universe, was used in section III.1 on TRIES and in the static version of interval, priority search, and segment trees (VIII.5.1). The organization of the universe gives rise to particularly simple tree structures.

Closely related to trees which organize the universe are key transformation (=hashing) and direct access(II.2, III.2 and III.8). In these methods one uses the key or a transformed key in order to directly access data. This immediately implies small running times. Another application of the very same idea is presorting, i. e. transforming a problem on an arbitrary set into a problem on a sorted set by sorting. It is then often possible to identify the objects with an initial segment of the integers which opens up all methods of direct access. We used presorting in sections VII.2.2 on multi-dimensional divide - and - conquer and in section VIII.5 on orthogonal objects in computational geometry.

In graphs we studied two methods for their systematic exploration: breadth - first and depth - first search. Breadth - first search is particularly useful for distance type problems and was therefore used intensively in least cost path computations (IV.7). Depth - first search has the important property that components are explored one by one and is therefore the natural method of exploration in connectivity problems. We used DFS to determine biconnected and strongly connected components and to test planarity.

Frequently, solutions to problem instances can be found iteratively or in a step by step fashion. Examples are the construction of optimal merging patterns (II.1.4), network flow and matching problems (IV.9), the construction of least cost spanning trees (IV.8), and the construction of convex hulls (VIII.2). In some of these examples (e. g. least cost spanning trees or optimal merging patterns) each step performs an action which is locally optimal. This variant of iteration is sometimes called the greedy approach. In other applications of this paradigm (e. g. network flow) a solution is improved iteratively. Frequently, the concept of augmentation applies to these situations.

In the chapter on algorithmic geometry we discussed the sweep paradigm at length (VIII.4, VIII,5.1). Its power stems from the fact that it reduces the dimension of geometric problems for the cost of turning static into dynamic problems. In particular, two-dimensional static problems can often be reduced to one-dimensional dynamic problems which can then be solved using some sort of balanced tree.

The method of reduction also played a major role in other parts of the book. The entire chapter on NP - completeness is centered around the notion of reduction or transformation. We used reductions to structure the world of problems, to define and explore classes of equivalent problems (VI.1 to VI.5), to transfer algorithms (from network flow to matching in IV.9, from matrix product over the integers to matrix product over the set of booleans in V.5, from iso - oriented objects to general objects in VIII.5.2, and from straight-line to circular objects in VIII.6), and to transfer lower bounds (from sorting to element uniqueness in II.6, from decision trees to RAMs in II.3 and from boolean matrix product to matrix product over semi-rings of characteristic zero in V.7).

Balancing is also an important concept. In least cost path computations (IV.7) we balanced the cost of various priority queue operations by a careful choice of the data structure, in multi - dimensional trees (VII.2.1) we balanced the power of the coordinates by using them in the split fields in cyclic order, and in divide - and - conquer algorithms we always tried to balance the size of the subproblems. It is important to observe that perfect balancing is usually not required in order to obtain efficient solutions; approximate balancing will also do. In fact, approximate balancing is called for in order to cope with dynamic behavior. A typical example are balanced trees. In BB[α]-trees (VIII.5.1) we do not require each node to have root balance in the range [1/3,2/3] although such a tree always exists but leave more leeway and in height-balanced trees (VIII.5.2) we allow nodes to have between a and b sons. Introducing an amount of freedom beyond the necessary amount often has dramatic effects on the (amortized) behavior of these schemes. Again, balanced trees are typical examples but so are the dynamization methods of VII.1. For example, BB[α]-trees work for $\alpha \leq 1-\sqrt{2}/2$, but $\alpha < 1-\sqrt{2}/2$ improves the amortized rebalancing cost dramatically. Similary (a,b)-trees work for $b \geq 2a-1$ but choosing $b \geq 2a$ improves the behavior considerably (III.5.2 and III.5.3).

Another way of interpreting approximate rebalancing is redundancy, i.e. to allow additional freedom in representation. The concept of redundancy can also be applied to storage space. We saw at several occassions, most notably range trees (VII.2.2) and dd-trees (VII.2.1), that storing objects several times can reduce search time considerably. In dd-trees multi-dimensional objects are stored without redundancy; they provide us with rootic search time and it was shown in VII.2.3.1. that this is optimal. Range trees store data in a hightly redundant fashion: they use non-linear storage space and provide us with polylogarithmic search time. In fact, the slack parameter of range trees allows us to trade between time and space.

Redundant structures frequently show good amortized behavior because rebalancing a node of a redundant structure moves the node away from the critical situations. Amortized analysis was used in the sections on dynamization and weighting (VII.1), range trees (VII.2.2), (dynamic) interval (VIII.5.1.1) and segment trees (VIII.5.1.3), BB[α]-trees (III.5.1), (a,b)-trees (III.5.3) and the union-find problem (III.8). A general discussion of the bank account paradigm for amortized analysis can be found in section III.6.1.

Worst case analysis (and amortized analysis which is the worst case analysis of sequences of operations) is the dominant method of analysis used throughout this book. Expected case analysis was done in only a few places; e. g. quicksort (II.3), selection (II.4), TRIES (III.1.1), hashing (III.2), interpolation search (III.3.2), weighted trees (III.4), self-organizing linear search (III.6.1.1),and transitive closure (IV.3). Expected case analysis rests upon an a-priori probability distribution on problem instances and therefore its predictions should be interpreted with care. In particular, it should always be checked whether reality conforms with the probability assumptions. Note however, that the expected running of many algorithms is fairly robust with respect to changes in the distribution. For example, a near-optimal search tree for distribution ß ist also a near-optimal search tree for distribution ß' provided that ß and ß' do not differ too much. Furthermore, a careful analysis of algorithms with small expected running time sometimes leads to fast algorithms with small wort case running time (e.g. selection) or to fast probabilistic algorithms (e.g. quicksort and hashing).

Self-organization is another important principle. In self-organizing data structures the items compete for the good places in the structure and high-frequency elements are more likely to be there. This results in good expected and sometimes also amortized behavior.

Generalization was the central theme of chapter V and also section VII.1. In chapter V we dealt with path problems over closed semi-rings, a generalization of least cost paths, transitive closure, maximal cost paths, and many other path problems. In section VII.1 we derived general methods for dynamizing static data structures for decomposable and order decomposable searching problems. Numerous applications of these general methods can be found in chapters VII and VIII.

The last two principles which we are going to discuss are approximation algorithms and probabilistic algorithms. These paradigms suggest to either change the problem to be solved (solve a simpler problem) or to change our notion of computation (use a more powerful computing machine). We observed at several places that a "slight" change in the formulation of a problem can have a drastic effect on its complexity: The satisfiability problem with three literals per clause is NP-complete but with two literals per clause it becomes fairly simple, the precedence constrained scheduling problem is NP-complete but if the precedence relation is a tree or there are only two machines then the problem is in P. Similarly, the computation of the convex hull of a point set takes time $\theta(n \log n)$ but if the points are sorted by x-coordinate then time $O(n)$ suffices. For optimization problems there is a standard method for simplifying the problem; instead of asking for an optimal solution we are content with a nearly optimal solution. This approach is particularly important when the optimization problem is NP-complete and therefore we devoted the entire section V.7 to approximation algorithms for NP-complete problems. We saw that some NP-complete problems resist even approximate solution but many others have good or even very good approximation algorithms. Even inside P approximation algorithms are important. A good example are the weighted trees of section III.4. The best algorithm for constructing optimum weighted trees has running time $\theta(n^2)$ and there is an $O(n)$ algorithm which constructs nearly optimal trees. Already for moderate size n, say $n = 10^4$, the difference between n^2 and n is substantial.

Probabilistic algorithms are based on a more flexible notion of computation, i. e. it is postulated that a perfect coin is available to the machine. (Less than perfect coins will also do for fast probabilistic algorithms as we saw in section I.2). We encountered probabilistic algorithms in many different contexts, e. g. the construction of perfect hash functions (III.2.3), universal hashing (III.2.4), probabilistic quicksort (II.1.3), graph connectivity (IV.9.2) and primality testing (VI.8). These applications may be grouped into two classes. In the first class coin tosses are used to randomize inputs (probabilistic quicksort, universal hashing). Typically, a random transformation is applied to the input and then a standard deterministic algorithm with small expected running time is used. The expected running time of the probabilistic algorithm on a fixed input then matches the expected running of the deterministic algorithm. The important difference is that the randomized algorithm controls the dices but a deterministic algorithm does not; the latter is at the mercy of its user who generates the problem instances. In the second class (construction of perfect hash functions, graph connectivity, primality testing) coin tosses are used to randomize the search for an element of some set with a desirable property. Typically, the property is easily checked and the elements having the property are abundant. However, no intimate knowledge about their location is available.

The design of an efficient algorithm is particularly satisfying if its performance matches a lower bound and hence the algorithm is optimal. Unfortunately, only a few algorithms have been shown to be optimal. We saw three approaches to proving lower bounds in this book. The first approach is the information-theoretic one and the typical argument goes as follows: In order to distinguish between N possibilities any algorithm requires log N steps. Of course in order to make this argument sound one has to define and study the primitive operations, the set of possible outcomes, and how the primitives operate on the set of possible outcomes. We used the information-theoretic approach in sections II.1.6 and II.3 on lower bounds for sorting and related problems, in section III.4 on searching in weighted sets, and in a modified form also in section VII.3.1 on lower bounds for partial match retrieval in minimum space. The second approach is by simplification which we used to prove the lower bound on the complexity of matrix multiplication (V.7). In this approach one designs transformation rules which allow to simplify an optimal program without increasing cost. The final product of the simplification process is then amenable to direct attack. The third approach uses combinatorial methods and was used in the sections on dynamization (VII.1.1) and the spanning bound (VII.3.2). In this approach one relates the complexity of an algorithm to a combinatorial quantity (the spanning complexity of a family of sets in VII.3.2 and various path lengths of binary trees in VII.1.1) and then analyses the combinatorial quantity.

Bibliography

We use the following abbreviations for journals and proceedings:

ACTA	Acta Informatica
CACM	Communications of the ACM
EIK	Elektronische Informationsverarbeitung und Kybernetik
FCT	Foundations of Computing Theory
FOCS	IEEE Symposium on Foundations of Computer Science
ICALP	International Colloquium on Automata, Languages and Programming
Inf & Control	Information and Control
IPL	Information Processing Letters
JACM	Journal of the ACM
JCSS	Journal fo Computer and System Sciences
LNCS	Springer Lecture Notes in Computer Science
MFCS	Mathematical Foundations of Computer Science
SICOMP	SIAM Journal of Computing
STOC	ACM Symposium on Theory of Computing
TCS	Theoretical Computer Science

Aho, A.V., Hopcroft, J.E., Ullman, J.D. (1974): The Design and Analysis of Computer Algorithms, Addison Wesley

Becker, M., Degenhardt, W., Doenhardt, J., Hertel, S., Kaninke, G., Keber, W., Mehlhorn, K., Näher, S., Rohnert, H., Winter, T., (1982): A Probabilistic Algorithm for Vertex Connectivity of Graphs, IPL 15, 1982, 135-136

Bellman, R.E. (1958): On a Routing Problem, Quart. Appl. Math. 16, 87-90

Bloniarz, P. (1980): A shortest-path algorithm with expected time $O(n^2 \log n \log^* n)$, 12th STOC, 378-384

Busacker, R.G., Gowen, P.J. (1961): A Procedure for Determining a Family of Minimal-Cost Network Flow Patterns, O.R.O. Technical Paper 15

Cheriton, D., Tarjan, R.E. (1976): Finding Minimum Spanning Trees, SICOMP 5, 724-742

Christofides, N. (1975): Graph Theory: An Algorithmic Approach, Academic Press

Christofides, N. (1976): Worst-Case Analysis of a New Heuristic for the Traveling Salesman Problem, Technical report, GSIA, Carnegie-Mellon University

Cohen, J., Roth, M. (1976): On the Implementation of Strassen's Fast Multiplication Algorithm, ACTA INFORMATICA 6, 341-356

Cook, S.A. (1971): The Complexity of Theorem Proving Procedures, 3rd STOC, 151-158

Coppersmith, D., Winograd, S. (1981): On the Asymptotic Complexity of Matrix Multiplication, 22nd FOCS, 82-100

de la Vega, W.F., Lueker, G.S. (1981): Bin packing can be solved within $1+\varepsilon$ in linear time, Combinatorica 1, 349-356

Dijkstra, E.W. (1959): A note on two problems in connexion with graphs Num. Math. 1, 269-271

Dinic, E.A. (1970): Algorithm for Solution of a Problem of Maximum Flow in a Network with Power Estimation, Soviet Math. Dokl. 11, 1277-1280

Edmonds, I., Karp, R.M. (1972): Theoretical Improvements in Algorithmic Efficiency of Network Flow Problems, JACM 19, 248-264

Even, S., Tarjan, R.E. (1975): Network Flow and Testing Graph Connectivity, SICOMP 4, 307-518

Fischer, M.J., Meyer, A.R. (1971): Boolean Matrix Multiplication and transitive closure, 12th FOCS, 129-131

Fletcher, J. (1980): A More General Algorithm for Computing Closed Semiring Costs Between Vertices of a Directed Graph, CACM 23, 350-351

Floyd, F.W. (1962): Algorithm 97: shortest path, CACM 5, 345

Ford jr., L.R., Fulkerson, D.R. (1962): Flows in Networks, Princeton University Press

Furman, M.E. (1970): Application of a method of fast multiplication of matrices to the problem of finding the transitive closure of a graph, Soviet Math. Dokl. 11, 1252

Galil, Z. (1976): On Enumeration Procedures for Theorem Proving and for Integer Programming, 3rd ICALP, 355-381

Galil, Z., Naamad, A. (1979): Network Flow and Generalized Path Compression, 11th STOC, 13-26

Garey, M.R., Johnson, D.S. (1978): Strong NP-completeness Results: Motivation, Examples and Implications, JACM 25, 499-508

Garey, M.R., Johnson, D.S. (1979): Computers and Intractability, a guide to the theory of NP-completeness, W.H. Freeman and Company

Gondran, J. (1975): Algèbre linéaire et cheminement dans un graph, R.A.I.R.O. 9

Goralcikova, A., Koubek, V. (1979): A reduct and closure algorithm for graphs, MFCS 79, LNCS 74, 301-307

Graham, R.L. (1969): Bounds on Multi-processor Timing Anomalies, SIAM J. Applied Math. 17, 416-429

Hart, P., Nilsson, N., Raphael, B. (1968): A Formal Basis for the Heuristic Determination of Minimum Cost Paths, IEEE Trans. Sys. Sci. Cybernetics, SSC 4, 100-107

Held, M., Karp, R.M. (1962): A Dynamic Programming Approach to Sequencing Problems, J. SIAM 10, 196-210

Hopcroft, J.E., Karp, R.M. (1975): An $O(n^{2.5})$-Algorithm for Matching in Bipartite Graphs, SICOMP 4, 225-231

Hopcroft, J.E., Tarjan, R.E. (1974): Efficient Planarity Testing, JACM 21, 549-568

Hopcroft, J.E., Ullman, J.D. (1969): Formal langugages and their relation to automata, Addison Wesley Publishing Company

Huynh, T.D. (1982): Deciding the Inequivalence of Context-Free Grammars with 1-Letter Terminal Alphabet is Σ_2^p-complete, 23rd FOCS, 21-31

Ibarra, O.H., Kim, C.E. (1975): Fast Approximation Algorithms for the Knapsack and Sum of Subset Problems, JACM 22, 463-468

Itai, A., Shiloach, Y. (1979): Maximum Flow in Planar Graphs, SICOMP 8, 135-150

Johnson, D. (1977): Efficient Algorithms for Shortest Paths in Sparse Networks, JACM 24, 1-13

Johnson, D., Dewers, A., Ullman, J., Garey, M., Graham, R. (1974): Worst Case Performance Bounds for Simple One-Dimensional Packing Algorithms, SICOMP 3, 299-325

Kahn, A.B. (1962): Topological Sorting of Large Networks, CACM 5, 558-562

Kannan, R. (1983): Improved algorithms for integer programming and related lattice problems, 15th STOC, 193-206

Karazuba, A., Ofman, Y. (1962): Multiplication of Multidigit Numbers on Automata, Doklady Akademija Nauk SSSR 145, 293-294

Karp, R.M. (1972): Reducibility among combinatorial problems, in Miller and Thatcher: Complexity of Computer Computations, Plenum Press

Karp, R.M., Lipton, R.J. (1980): Some connections between non-uniform and uniform complexity classes, 12th STOC, 302-309

Karzanov, A.V. (1974): Determining the Maximal Flow in a Network by the Method of Preflows, Soviet Math. Dokl. 15, 434-437

Khachiyan, L.G. (1979): Linear Programming in Polynomial Time, Doklady Akademija Nauk SSSR 244, 1093-1096

Kleene, S.C. (1956): Representation of events in nerve nets and finite automata, Automata Studies, Princeton University Press

Kruskal jr., J.B. (1956): On the shortest spanning subtree of a graph and the traveling salesman problem, Proc. Amer. Math. Society 7, 48-50

Lautemann, C. (1984): BPP and the Polynomial Hierarchy, IPL, to appear

Lawler, E.L. (1977): Fast Approximation Algorithms for Knapsack Problems, 18th FOCS, 206-213

Lenstra jr., H.W. (1983): Integer Programming with a fixed number of variables, Mathematics of Operations Research, to appear

Lichtenstein, D. (1982): Planar Satisfiability and its Uses, SICOMP 11, 329-343

Lipton, R., Tarjan, R.E. (1977): A separator theorem for planar graphs, Conference on Theoretical Computer Science, Waterloo, 1-10

Lipton, R., Tarjan, R.E. (1977): Applications of a Planar Separator Theorem, 18th FOCS, 162-170

Luks, E. (1980): Isomorphism of Graphs of Bounded Valence can be Tested in Polynomial Time, 21st FOCS, 42-49

Malhotra, V.M., Pramodh Kumar, M., Maheshwari, S.N. (1978): An $O(n^3)$ Algorithm for Finding Maximum Flows in Networks, IPL 7, 277-278

Mehlhorn, K. (1976): Polynomial and Abstract Subrecursive Classes, JCSS 12, 147-178

Mehlhorn, K., Galil, Z. (1976): On the Complexity of Monotone Realization of Matrix Multiplication, Computing 16, 99-111

Mehlhorn, K., Schmidt, B.H. (1983): A single source shortest path algorithm for graphs with separators, FCT 83, LNCS 158, 302-309

Miller, G.L. (1983): Isomorphism of k-Contractible Graphs: A Generalization of Bounded Valence and Bounded Genus, Inf. & Control 56, 1-20

Monien, B. (1982): Personal communication

Munro, I. (1971): Efficient determination of the transitive closure of a directed graph, IPL 1, 56-58

Newell, W.S. (1958): Optimal Flow through Networks, Technical Report, MIT

Nilsson, N. (1971): Problem Solving Methods in Artificial Intelligence, McGraw-Hill

Papadimitriou, C.H. (1976): The NP-completeness of the Bandwidth Minimization Problem, Computing 16, 263-270

Papadimitriou, C.H. (1982): On the Complexity of Unique Solutions, 23rd FOCS, 14-20

Paterson, M.S. (1975): Complexity of Monotone Network for Boolean Matrix Product, TCS, 1, 13-20

Paul, W. (1978): Komplexitätstheorie, Teubner-Studienbücher Informatik, Teubner Verlag, Stuttgart

Pratt, V.R. (1975): Every prime has a succint certificate, SICOMP 4, 214-220

Prim, R.C. (1957): Shortest Connection Networks and some Generalizations, Bell Systems Tech. J. 36, 1389-1401

Rivest, R.L., Vuillemin, J. (1975): A generalization and proof of the Anderaa-Rosenberg conjecture, 7th STOC, 6-11

Romani, F. (1980): Shortest-Path Problem is not harder than Matrix Multiplication, IPL 11, 134-136

Sahni, S. (1975): Approximate Solutions for the 0-1 knapsack problem, JACM 22, 114-125

Savitch, W.J. (1974): Relationship between nondeterministic and deterministic tape complexities, JCSS, 177-192

Schnorr, C.P. (1976): Optimal Algorithms for Self-Reducible Problems, 3rd ICALP, 322-337

Schnorr, C.P. (1978): An Algorithm for Transitive Closure with Linear Expected Time, SICOMP 7, 127-133

Schönhage, A., Strassen, V. (1971): Schnelle Multiplikation großer Zahlen, Computing 7, 281-292

Schwarz, J.T. (1980): Fast probabilistic algorithms for verification of polynomial identities, JACM 27, 701-717

Simon, K. (1983): Ein neuer Algorithmus für die transitive Hülle von gerichteten Graphen, Dipl.-Arb., FB 10, Univ. des Saarlandes

Sipser, M. (1983): A Complexity Theoretic Approach to Randomness, 15th STOC, 330-335

Sleator, D.D. (1980): an O(nm logn) Algorithm for Maximum Network Flow, Ph.D. thesis, Standford

Soloway, R., Strassen, V. (1977,1978): A fast Monte-Carlo test for Primality, SICOMP 6, 84-85 and SICOMP 7, 118

Spieß, J. (1974): Untersuchung zur Implementierung der Algorithmen von S. Winograd und V. Strassen zur Matrizenmultiplikation, GWDG-Bericht Nr. 10, Aug. 74

Stockmeyer, L.J., Meyer, A.R. (1973): Word problems requiring exponential time, 5th STOC, 1-9

Strassen, V., (1969): Gaussian Elimination is not optimal, Num. Math. 13, 354-356

Tarjan, R.E. (1972): Depth first search and linear graph algorithms, SICOMP 1, 146-160

Tarjan, R.E. (1981): A unified approach to path problems, JACM 28, 577-593

Ullman, J.D. (1975): NP-complete Scheduling Problems, JCSS 10, 384-395

Yao, A.C. (1975): An O(|E|loglog|V|) algorithm for finding minimum spanning trees, IPL 4, 21-23

Subject Index

W. M. Waite, G. Goos

Compiler Construction

1984. 196 figures. XIV, 446 pages
(Texts and Monographs in Computer Science)
ISBN 3-540-90821-8

Contents: Introduction and Overview. - Properties of Programming Languages. - Properties of Real and Abstract Machines. - Abstract Program Representations. - Elements of Formal Systems. - Lexical Analysis. - Parsing. - Attribute Grammars. - Semantic Analysis. - Code Generation. - Assembly. - Error Handling. - Optimization. - Implementing the Compiler. - Appendix A: Sample Programming Language LAX. - Appendix B: Useful Algorithms for Directed Graph. - Bibliography. - Index.

This text, written by two leaders in the field of compiler construction, explains to the reader how compilers for programming languages are built. Describing the necessary tools (and how to create and use them), the authors break the task into modules, placing equal emphasis on the action and data aspects of compilation. Attribute grammars are used extensively to provide a uniform treatment of semantic analysis, competent code generation and assembly. The authors also show how intermediate representations can be chosen automatically on the basis of attribute dependence. Thus semantic analysis, code generation and assembly no longer appear idiosyncratic, but are discussed in terms of a uniform model subject to automation. This will improve the reader's understanding of the compilation process and of the decisions that must be made when designing a compiler.

Springer-Verlag
Berlin
Heidelberg
New York
Tokyo